Introduction to Microcomputing with Applications

Introduction to Microcomputing with Applications

Alan C. Elliott
Academic Computing Services
University of Texas Southwestern Medical Center
Dallas, Texas

West Publishing Company
St. Paul • New York • Los Angeles • San Francisco

Copyeditor: Martha Knutson
Composition: Rolin Graphics
Artwork: Rolin Graphics
Cover art: Artform Communications, Inc.
Interior design: Lois Stanfield

50 W. Kellogg Boulevard
P.O. Box 64526
St. Paul, MN 55164-1003

Printed in the United States of America

96 95 94 93 92 91 90 89 8 7 6 5 4 3 2 1 0

LIBRARY OF CONGRESS
Library of Congress Cataloging-in-Publication Data

Elliott, Alan C., 1952–
Introduction to microcomputing with applications/Alan C. Elliott.
p. cm.
Includes index.
ISBN 0-314-47014-X
1. Microcomputers. 2. Electronic data processing. I. Title.
QA76.5.E5485 1989
004.16—dc19 88-23828
CIP

Trademark Acknowledgments

Apple, Apple II, Apple LaserWriter, and Macintosh are registered trademarks of Apple Computer, Inc.

dBASE III Plus is a registered trademark of Ashton-Tate.

IBM is a registered trademark of International Business Machines Corporation.

Lotus and Lotus 1-2-3 are registered trademarks of Lotus Development Corporation.

MicroPro and WordStar are registered trademarks of MicroPro International Corporation.

Microsoft is a registered trademark of Microsoft Corporation.

Norton Integrator is the trademark of Peter Norton Computing, Incorporated.

PageMaker is a trademark of Aldus Corporation.

PC-File is a registered trademark of ButtonWare, Inc. and Jim Button.

ProComm is a registered trademark of Datastorm Technologies, Inc.

Ventura Publisher is a registered trademark of Ventura Software, Inc.

WordPerfect is a registered trademark of WordPerfect Corporation.

Dedication

To Annette

CONTENTS IN BRIEF

PREFACE		xxi
CHAPTER 1	Microcomputers: Taking a Peek "Under the Hood"	1
CHAPTER 2	Getting to Know the IBM PC	27
CHAPTER 3	Introduction to DOS, Part I	49
CHAPTER 4	Introduction to DOS, Part II	75
GUEST ESSAY	Microcomputers in a Medical Office	101
CHAPTER 5	Introduction to Word Processing	103
CHAPTER 6	Word Processing, Part II	147
CHAPTER 7	Introduction to Spreadsheets	175
CHAPTER 8	Advanced Spreadsheet Topics	215
CHAPTER 9	Introduction to Database Management Systems	239
CHAPTER 10	Database Management Systems, Part II	277
CHAPTER 11	Tips on Selecting Hardware and Software	317
GUEST ESSAY	An Introduction to Desktop Publishing	341
CHAPTER 12	Special Topics	343
INDEX		377
QUICK REFERENCE CARD		391

CONTENTS

CHAPTER 1 **Microcomputers: Taking a Peek "Under the Hood"** 1

THE COMPUTER AS AN APPLIANCE 2

Computers are a Part of the Real World 2

Choosing a Computer is Like Choosing a Car 2

EARLY ATTEMPTS AT COMPUTING 2

Computing as a Challenge of Science 3

Cogs as Calculators 4

The Invention of the Computer Card 6

ONES AND ZEROS 8

THE ASCII STANDARD 9

Extended ASCII 10

WAR SPEEDS UP COMPUTER DEVELOPMENT 10

The First American Computers 10

The First European Computers 11

Von Neumann Defines the Digital Computer 11

Transistors Replace Vacuum Tubes 12

The Computer's Brain—ON/OFF Switches 12

Smaller, Smaller, Smaller 12

Computers on a Chip 13

THE MICROCOMPUTER MARKET ARRIVES 13

Silicon Valley and the Homebrew Computer Club 14

EMERGENCE AS A BUSINESS TOOL 14

IBM Enters the Microcomputer Market 14

The IBM PC Standard Emerges 16

Successors to the Original PC 16

Compatibles and Clones 16

COMPUTER LANGUAGES 17

Application Software 18

THE MEMORY OF THE COMPUTER 19

RAM and ROM 20

PERIPHERAL STORAGE OF INFORMATION ON THE COMPUTER 20

Hard Disks 20

Other Means of Memory Storage 20

How Much Data can be Stored on Disk? 21

ENTERING INFORMATION INTO THE COMPUTER 21

The Mouse 21

The Joystick 23

Other Input Devices 23

GETTING INFORMATION OUT OF THE COMPUTER 23

Computer Printers 23

VERSATILE MACHINE 24
SUMMARY 24
KEY TERMS 24
QUESTIONS 25
LABORATORY EXERCISES 25

CHAPTER 2 **Getting to Know the IBM PC** **27**
THE PARTS OF THE PC 28
THE KEYBOARD 28
The Typewriter Keys 28
Function Keys 33
Numeric and Cursor Keypad 33
Repeating Keys 33
THE COMPUTER MONITOR 36
The Monochrome Monitor 36
The Single-Color Graphics Monitor 38
Color Monitors 38
INSIDE THE COMPUTER CABINET 38
The Computer's Memory 38
The Expansion Slots 39
The Power Supply 39
Other Things Inside the Computer Cabinet 40
THE DISK DRIVES 40
The Names of the Disk Drives 41
Kinds of Disk Drives 41
THE MASTER DISKETTE—DOS 42
How to Hold a Diskette 43
Proper Care for Floppy Diskettes 43
Caring for 3.5-inch Diskettes 44
TURNING ON THE COMPUTER 44
Something Went Wrong? 45
Entering the Date and Time 45
Types of Prompts 46
THIS IS ONLY THE BEGINNING 46
SUMMARY 46
KEY TERMS 47
QUESTIONS 47
LABORATORY EXERCISES 47

CHAPTER 3 **Introduction to DOS, Part I** **49**
MANAGING RESOURCES 50
MANAGING RESOURCES ON A COMPUTER 50
DOS Changes Over Time 51
SPECIFIC USES OF DOS 52
Booting 52
FILES ON DISK 52
File Types 54
Global File Characters 56

DOS AS A COMMAND LANGUAGE 57
DOS Prompts 57
DOS Commands and Syntax 57
THE FIVE MOST COMMONLY USED DOS COMMANDS 58
The DIR Command 58
The ERASE Command (or DEL) 62
The RENAME Command 63
The COPY Command 64
The FORMAT Command 66
INTERNAL AND EXTERNAL DOS COMMANDS 70
CHANGING THE DEFAULT DRIVE 71
SUMMARY 71
KEY TERMS 71
QUESTIONS 72
LABORATORY EXERCISES 72

CHAPTER 4 **Introduction to DOS, PART II** **75**
COMMONLY USED DOS COMMANDS 76
The CHKDSK (Check Disk) Command 76
The CLS (Clear the Screen) Command 76
The DISKCOPY Command: Copying one disk to another 77
The PRINT Command: Printing a file to the line printer 78
The TYPE Command: Typing a file to the monitor 79
COMMANDS RELATING TO USING THE HARD DISK 80
If you are Using a Floppy-Based System 81
Many More Files 81
Directory Structure 81
The Root Directory and Beyond 82
MANAGING THE DIRECTORIES 82
Directory Names 83
How to Create and Use a New Directory 84
Changing from Directory to Directory 84
Removing an Empty Directory 85
Using Directories 86
A Directory of the Directories 87
The PATH Command 87
The PROMPT Command 89
BATCH FILES 90
Creating a Batch File 91
The AUTOEXEC.BAT File: Automating Commands at Boot Time 92
THE CONFIG.SYS FILE 92
THE WARM BOOT 93
SAFETY FIRST. . . . DEVELOP AND FOLLOW A BACKUP PROCEDURE 93
The BACKUP Command 94
The RESTORE Command 95
A Disaster Plan 95
Keep Disks Free of Unneeded Files 96
Alternatives to the DOS Backup Command 96
Backup vs. Copying 96

SUMMARY 96
KEY TERMS 97
QUESTIONS 97
LABORATORY EXERCISES 98
GUEST ESSAY: Microcomputers in a Medical Office 101

CHAPTER 5 **Introduction to Word Processing** **103**

PRELIMINARIES ABOUT THE SOFTWARE 104
CASE STUDY: WordPerfect, WordStar and Your Word Processor 104
THE TYPEWRITER GETS A SLOW START 104
The Processing of Words 105
THE ADVENT OF MICROCOMPUTER WORD PROCESSING 105
The Modern Word Processing System 105
BEFORE YOU USE A WORD PROCESSOR 107
THE LANGUAGE OF THE WORD PROCESSOR 107
CASE STUDY: WordPerfect—The Command Keys 109
CASE STUDY: WordStar Professional—The Command Structure 109
CASE STUDY: Your Word Processor—Commands 109
WORD PROCESSING VOCABULARY 112
SELF-PACED TUTORIALS 113
BEGINNING THE WORD PROCESSING PROGRAM 113
CASE STUDY: WordPerfect—Beginning the Program 113
CASE STUDY: WordStar—Beginning the Program 113
CASE STUDY: Your Word Processor—Beginning the Program 115
SETTING UP THE WORD PROCESSOR FOR YOUR DOCUMENT 115
Creating a New Document 116
CASE STUDIES: WordPerfect, WordStar, and Your Word Processor—Entering Text 116
IMPORTANT KEYSTROKES 118
CASE STUDY: WordPerfect Cursor Control 118
Summary of WordPerfect Cursor Control Commands 118
CASE STUDY: WordStar Cursor Control 120
Summary of WordStar Cursor Control Commands 120
CASE STUDY: Your Word Processor—Cursor Movement 121
THE SAMPLE LETTER 121
Make This Simple Correction 123
SAVING AND PRINTING THE DOCUMENT 124
CASE STUDY: WordPerfect—Saving and Printing 124
CASE STUDY: WordStar—Saving and Printing 124
CASE STUDY: Your Word Processor—Saving and Printing 125
ENDING THE PROGRAM 125
CASE STUDY: WordPerfect—Ending the Program 125
CASE STUDY: WordStar—Ending the Program 127
CASE STUDY: Your Word Processor—Ending the Program 127
MAKING CHANGES TO THE DOCUMENT 127
CASE STUDY: WordPerfect—Editing an Existing Document 128
CASE STUDY: WordStar—Editing an Existing Document 130
CASE STUDY: Your Word Processor—Editing an Existing Document 131

WORKING WITH BLOCKS AND SECTIONS OF TEXT 133
CASE STUDY: WordPerfect—Block Functions 133
CASE STUDY: WordStar—Block Functions 134
CASE STUDY: Your Word Processor—Block Functions 135
DOCUMENT FORMATTING 136
CASE STUDY: WordPerfect—Formatting and Margins 136
CASE STUDY: WordStar—Formatting and Margins 138
CASE STUDY: Your Word Processor—Formatting and Margins 139
SUMMARY 140
KEY TERMS 140
QUESTIONS 140
LAB EXERCISES 141

CHAPTER 6 **Word Processing, Part II** 147
TEXT EXAMPLES DISK 148
THE SEARCH AND REPLACE COMMANDS 148
CASE STUDY: WordPerfect—Search and Replace 149
CASE STUDY: WordStar—Search and Replace 149
CASE STUDY: Your Word Processor—Search and Replace 150
PITCHES, FONTS, AND LINE SPACING 151
You Try It 152
CASE STUDY: WordPerfect—Changing Pitch and Line Spacing 153
CASE STUDY: WordStar—Changing Pitch and Line Spacing 153
CASE STUDY: Your Word Processor—Choosing Pitch and Line Spacing 154
CASE STUDY: WordPerfect—Bold, Underline and Italics 155
CASE STUDY: WordStar—Bold, Underline and Italics 155
CASE STUDY: Your Word Processor—Boldface, Underlining and Italics 156
WORKING WITH LONG DOCUMENTS 156
Widows and Orphans 156
Conditional Paging 156
Page Numbering 157
Sample Multipage Document 157
CASE STUDY: WordPerfect—Page Numbers and Paging 157
CASE STUDY: WordStar—Page Numbers and Paging 159
CASE STUDY: Your Word Processor—Page Numbers and Paging 160
HEADERS AND FOOTERS 161
CASE STUDY: WordPerfect—Headers and Footers 161
CASE STUDY: WordStar—Headers and Footers 161
CASE STUDY: Your Word Processor—Headers and Footers 162
USING A SPELLING CHECKER 163
CASE STUDY: WordPerfect—Spelling Checker 163
CASE STUDY: WordStar—Spelling Checker 163
USING AN ON-LINE THESAURUS 165
CASE STUDY: WordPerfect—On-Line Thesaurus 165
CASE STUDY: WordStar—On-Line Thesaurus 165

CASE STUDY: Your Word Processor—On-Line Spelling Checker and Thesaurus 167
ADDITIONAL NOTES ABOUT WORD PROCESSORS 167
OTHER WordPerfect Features 167
OTHER WordStar Features 168
SUMMARY 168
KEY TERMS 168
QUESTIONS 169
LABORATORY EXERCISES 170

CHAPTER 7 **Introduction to Spreadsheets** **175**
CASE STUDY: Lotus 1-2-3 and Your Spreadsheet Programs 176
PENCILS AND ERASERS 176
The Software That Sells Computers 176
SPREADSHEET PROGRAMS 178
What a Spreadsheet Program Can Do 178
Description of the Spreadsheet 178
The Structure of the Spreadsheet 180
COMMANDS IN A SPREADSHEET PROGRAM 180
CASE STUDY: How Lotus Commands Are Given 180
COMMANDS ON THE LOTUS 1-2-3 WORKSHEET MENU 182
CASE STUDY: Your Spreadsheet Program—How Commands Are Given 183
BASIC SPREADSHEET OPERATIONS 184
CASE STUDY: The Basics of Lotus 1-2-3 184
Moving Around in 1-2-3 184
Entering Information into 1-2-3 186
The Ready Indicator in 1-2-3 186
Correcting Entries in 1-2-3 187
CASE STUDY: The Basics of Your Spreadsheet Program 187
THE CONTENTS OF CELLS 188
CASE STUDY: Text and Values in Lotus 1-2-3 188
CASE STUDY: Text and Values in Your Spreadsheet Program 189
ARITHMETIC OPERATORS 190
CASE STUDY: Arithmetic Operators in Lotus 1-2-3 190
CASE STUDY: Arithmetic Operators in Your Spreadsheet Program 190
FORMATTING NUMBERS IN CELLS 191
CASE STUDY: Formatting Numbers in Lotus 1-2-3 191
CASE STUDY: Formatting Numbers in Your Spreadsheet Program 192
COLUMN WIDTHS 192
CASE STUDY: Changing Column Widths in Lotus 1-2-3 193
CASE STUDY: Changing Column Widths in Your Spreadsheet Program 193
ORDER OF CALCULATION 194
CASE STUDY: Calculation Order for Lotus 1-2-3 194
CASE STUDY: Calculation Order for Your Spreadsheet Program 194

PRINTING SPREADSHEET RESULTS 195
CASE STUDY: Output to a Printer or to a File in Lotus 1-2-3 195
CASE STUDY: Printing to a Printer or File in Your Spreadsheet Program 196
USE OF FUNCTIONS 198
CASE STUDY: Use of Functions in Lotus 1-2-3 198
CASE STUDY: Use of Functions in Your Spreadsheet Program 199
CREATING A SPREADSHEET EXAMPLE 200
Changing Values 201
Editing an Entry 201
MORTGAGE EXAMPLE 202
Enter Your Favorite Loan 203
Enter This Table Yourself 203
Saving the Table 204
The Formulas in the Mortgage Table 204
BUDGET EXAMPLE 205
SUMMARY 207
KEY TERMS 207
QUESTIONS 208
LABORATORY EXERCISES 209

CHAPTER 8 **Advanced Spreadsheet Topics** **215**
ADVANCED SPREADSHEET TOPICS 216
MANIPULATING BLOCKS OF CELLS: MOVE, COPY, AND ERASE 216
Absolute and Relative Cell Reference 217
CASE STUDY: Move, Copy, and Erase in Lotus 1-2-3 218
An Example Using the Move and Copy Commands 218
Erasing Portions of the Table 219
An Example: Erasing Cells 219
CASE STUDY: How to Move, Copy, and Erase in Your Spreadsheet Program 220
INSERTING AND DELETING ROWS AND COLUMNS 220
CASE STUDY: Insertions and Deletions in Lotus 1-2-3 221
CASE STUDY: Insertions and Deletions in Your Spreadsheet Program 221
ASSIGNING NAMES TO CELLS 222
CASE STUDY: Range Names in Lotus 1-2-3 223
CASE STUDY: Range Names in Your Spreadsheet Program 223
LOCKING AND UNLOCKING CELLS 223
CASE STUDY: Protecting Cells in Lotus 1-2-3 223
An Example Using Cell Protection 224
CASE STUDY: Protecting Cells in Your Spreadsheet Program 224
GRAPHIC CAPABILITIES 224
Pie Chart Example 225
CASE STUDY: Creating a Graph in Lotus 1-2-3 227
Printing Graphs in Lotus 1-2-3 228
CASE STUDY: Creating a Graph in Your Spreadsheet Program 228

OTHER FEATURES OF LOTUS 1-2-3 229
- Windows 229
- Macros 230
- Database 230
- New Versions 230

SUMMARY 230
- Lotus 1-2-3 Commands 230

QUESTIONS 232
LABORATORY EXERCISES 235

CHAPTER 9 **Introduction to Database Management Systems** **239**
- CASE STUDY: dBase III Plus and Your Database Program 240

COLLECTING INFORMATION 240
- The Computer to the Rescue 241
- Computers Can Do It Well 242

DEFINING A DATABASE 242
USER INTERFACES TO DATABASE PROGRAMS 242
- Menu-Driven Database Systems 242
- Program-Driven Database Systems 243
- Command-Driven Database Systems 243
- Multiple-Interface Database Systems 243
- CASE STUDY: dBASE III Plus 244
- CASE STUDY: Your Database Program 244

PUTTING THE DATABASE TOGETHER 245
FIELDS, RECORDS AND FILES 246
- A Structure for the Glider Club Database 248
- CASE STUDY: Defining a Structure in dBase III Plus 249

CREATION OF THE DATABASE ON THE COMPUTER 250
- CASE STUDY: Defining a Structure in Your Database Program 252
- CASE STUDY: Creating a Database in dBase III Plus 252
- If you Do Not Get The Dot Prompt 252
- Stopping dBase III Plus 253
- If you Are Using a Floppy-Based System 253
- Creating a Database 253
- Entering Each Field Description 254
- Ending the Creation Process 255
- CASE STUDY: Creating a Database in Your Database Program 256

ENTERING INFORMATION INTO THE DATABASE 256
- Validity Checking Schemes 256
- Entry Techniques 257
- Ending The Entry Process 257
- CASE STUDY: Data Entry in dBase III Plus 257
- CASE STUDY: Data Entry in Your Database Program 258

ONCE INFORMATION IS IN THE DATABASE 258
- Queries: Asking the Database a Question 259
- Reports: Summary Information From The Database 260
- Data Extraction 260
- CASE STUDY: Examining the database in dBase III Plus 260
- The Difference Between Display and List 261
- Searching a Database 262
- Ending dBase III Plus 263

CASE STUDY: Examining the Database in Your Database Program 264
ON-LINE HELP 264
CASE STUDY: The dBase III Plus Help Facility 264
CASE STUDY: The Help Facility in Your Database Program 265
ADDING, EDITING AND DELETING RECORDS 266
CASE STUDY: Adding, Editing, and Deleting Records in dBase III Plus 266
Adding Records to a Database 266
Editing a Record 266
Deleting Records 267
CASE STUDY: Adding, Editing, and Deleting Records in Your Database Program 269
SUMMARY 270
KEY TERMS 271
QUESTIONS 271
LABORATORY EXERCISES 272

CHAPTER 10 **Database Management Systems, Part II** **277**
MAKING USE OF THE DATABASE 278
CASE STUDY: The USE command in dBase III Plus 278
CASE STUDY: Using a Database in Your Database Program 279
SETTING UP THE DATABASE ENVIRONMENT 279
CASE STUDY: The SET command in dBASE III Plus 279
Help Menus 279
"DISPLAY STATUS" Set Commands and Function Key Settings 280
CASE STUDY: Setting up the Environment in Your Database Program 283
QUERIES: SELECTING OUTPUT WITH CONDITIONAL SEARCHES 283
Selecting Output by Expression List 283
Selecting Output by Scope 284
Selecting Output by Condition 284
Relational and Logical Operators 285
Logical Operators 285
FOR and WHILE 286
CASE STUDY: Conditional Searches in dBASE III Plus 287
CASE STUDY: Conditional Searches in Your Database Program 288
PUTTING YOUR RECORDS IN ORDER: SORTING AND INDEXING 288
Sorting 289
Indexing 289
CASE STUDY: Sorting and Indexing in dBase III Plus 290
Using Indexes 291
CASE STUDY: Sorting and Indexing in Your Database Program 292
MANIPULATING DATABASE INFORMATION 293
Functions 293
CASE STUDY: Functions in dBase III Plus 293
Date Functions 293
String (Character) Functions 295
Mathematical Functions 297

CASE STUDY: Functions in Your Database Program 299
MAKING MAJOR CHANGES TO THE DATABASE STRUCTURE 300
CASE STUDY: Modifying Structure in dBase III Plus 300
The Replace Command 302
CASE STUDY: Modifying the Database Structure in Your Database Program 302
WRITING DATABASE REPORTS 303
CASE STUDY: Reports in dBase III Plus 303
Summary Reports 304
Creating a Customized Report 304
Printing the Report 307
The Assist Program 307
CASE STUDY: Reports in Your Database Program 309
SUMMARY 310
Command Summary 210
QUESTIONS 311
LABORATORY EXERCISES 312

CHAPTER 11 **Tips on Selecting Hardware and Software** **317**
DECIDING ON YOUR NEEDS 318
What Will Your Computer Do? 318
Software Before the Hardware 318
Compatibility 318
SELECTING SOFTWARE 319
Popular Word Processing Programs 319
Popular Spreadsheet Programs 321
Popular Database Programs 322
Specialty Software 323
CHOOSING MICROCOMPUTER HARDWARE 324
Major Families of Computers 324
The Microprocessor 324
Expansion Slots 325
THE IBM PERSONAL COMPUTER FAMILY 326
CHOOSING A CLONE COMPUTER 327
OPERATING SYSTEMS FOR THE IBM PC 327
THE APPLE FAMILY OF COMPUTERS 328
COMPATIBILITY BOARDS BRIDGE GAPS BETWEEN COMPUTERS 329
HOW MUCH COMPUTER YOU NEED 330
ADD-ONS FOR YOUR COMPUTER 330
Monitor and Display Adapters 331
Monitor compatibility 332
PRINTERS 333
MODEMS 333
OTHER ADD-ONS TO CONSIDER 335
WHERE AND HOW TO BUY A PERSONAL COMPUTER 336
Clone Computers and Upgraded Major Brands 336
SHAREWARE SOFTWARE 338
SUMMARY 339
QUESTIONS 339
LABORATORY EXERCISES 340
GUEST ESSAY: An Introduction to Desktop Publishing 341

CHAPTER 12 Special Topics 345

SECTION 1: IBM UTILITY PROGRAMS 344
CASE STUDY: The Norton Utilities 344
The Norton Integrator 344
ALTERNATE BACKUP-TO-DISK PROGRAMS 348
CASE STUDY: Fastback 348
SECTION 2: THE OS/2 OPERATING SYSTEM 349
Multitasking 349
New OS/2 Versions of Programs 349
OS/2 Real and Protected Modes 349
The Look of OS/2 350
The Program Selector 350
SECTION 3: WINDOWS 351
Using a Mouse 352
To Use a Mouse or Not? 353
Selecting Programs to Run 354
Not Quite Multitasking 354
The Control Menu 355
Icons 356
Pull-Down Menus 356
Windows—The Wave of the Future? 357
SECTION 4: COMMUNICATIONS 357
CASE STUDY: ProComm 358
ProComm Setup 358
Dialing Directory 359
ProComm Plus Commands 360
Exchanging Files 361
Hayes Modem Compatibility 361
Ending The ProComm Program 362
SECTION 5: DESKTOP PUBLISHING SOFTWARE 362
The Laser Printer 362
The Postscript Printer Definition Language 362
Desktop Publishing Software 362
The Program Environment 365
CASE STUDY: Main Screen Controls for Pagemaker 365
CASE STUDY: Creating a Document with Pagemaker 368
Page Setup 368
The Toolbox 368
Typing in the Headline 368
Selecting the Font for the Headline 371
Drawing a Line Under the Headline 371
Entering a Graphic From Another Source 371
Entering and Manipulating Text 373
Finishing up Details 373
Printing and Saving the Document 375
Concluding Remarks About Desktop Publishing 375
INDEX 377
QUICK REFERENCE CARD 391

PREFACE

Institutions of higher education are increasing their use of microcomputers in the curriculum. Accreditation committees for colleges and universities are expecting institutions to address computer literacy. Employers in the business and professional job market often expect graduates to have computer skills.

The two major components in providing students with the skills to use computers in the college and business environment are the use of the operating system, and the use of application programs. Three application programs that are of particular interest are word processing, database and spreadsheets. Other topics that need to be addressed in preparing a student for intelligent microcomputer usage are a knowledge of the components of the computer, an introduction to communications, utility software, desktop publishing, and future directions of computing. The wider the student's understanding of how a computer works, and how a user interacts with the computer, the easier it is for the student to acclimate to new computing situations.

Few books cover all of these components. Instructors have often had to supplement courses with outside reading or texts. This text solves this problem by giving the instructor access to all of these computing topics in one book.

TEXTBOOK OBJECTIVE

This text attempts to provide students with computing tools for college while at the same time preparing them for the job market. Businesses usually want their new employees to have knowledge of commonly used software. They want employees to feel comfortable with computing; to be able to think through new computing situations; to adapt to new software; and often to assist in choosing the correct computer configurations to meet the needs of specific tasks.

This text introduces the student in a simple way to how computers "think," often taking away the mystery that causes computer phobia. This includes information about the computer's components as well as an introduction to its operating system, DOS. Major application packages, including Wordstar, WordPerfect, dBASE III Plus and Lotus 1-2-3 are taught in a tutorial fashion with case studies. Students can follow this text while performing realistic tasks with the software. In addition, case studies for generic software are provided so students using different application programs can still use the text, and compare their software with that which is most commonly used in the business world. The text is designed so the instructor may choose to cover one software package in each applications area (e.g., WordPerfect *or* WordStar *or* the instructor's personal choice of a word processor).

Other specialty software are introduced briefly. These include Fastback, Norton Utilities, Procomm Communication Software, Aldus Pagemaker and the OS/2 Operating System.

Upon completing this book, the student will have specific skills in using the most common application software, and will have a broad knowledge of other important uses of computing.

SOFTWARE USED IN THIS TEXT

The software packages used in this textbook have been carefully chosen to represent the most commonly used packages available on the IBM PC compatible family of computers. Information about the operating system is valid for all versions of PC-DOS and MS-DOS. Application software packages in the areas of word processing, database and spreadsheet are all well known. In addition, each chapter has case study questions specifically designed for students to use in the event they happen to be using a different software package for one of the applications. The word processing packages described include WordStar Professional (version 4.0) and WordPerfect (versions 4.2). The database program described is dBASE III Plus and the spreadsheet program used is Lotus 1-2-3 (version 2.0). Other versions of these programs may also be used, and there are some compatible software packages such as the VP-Planner or Twin spreadsheet programs that can be used in lieu of the more famous package.

A diskette is available which contains sources files to be used by students in performing end of chapter exercises. Professors may contact their local West sales representative for further information regarding the diskette.

SOFTWARE AVAILABILITY

The software mentioned in this text is readily available "off the shelf." In addition, the companies that produce this software have on-going educational programs that allow educational institutions to purchase copies at reduced prices. In some instances, demo copies suitable for using in a classroom are available for free or at a very low cost. Since these programs change with time, please contact the educational representative from these companies to determine your best method of acquiring these products.

(WORDSTAR)	MicroPro International 33 San Pablo Avenue San Rafael, CA 94903
(WORDPERFECT)	WordPerfect Corp. 1555 N. Technology Way Orem, UT 84057
(DBASE III)	Ashton-Tate 20101 Hamilton Avenue Torrance, CA 90502
(LOTUS 1-2-3)	Lotus Development Corp. 55 Cambridge Parkway Cambridge, MA 02142

HARDWARE

The most commonly used microcomputer today in the business world is the IBM PC compatible family of computers. This computer introduced microcomputing to the business world, and will remain the major kind of small business computer for many years. Although the text makes certain comparisons to other popular computers, all of the tutorial lessons and exercises assume the use of software on an IBM PC compatible microcomputer.

HOW TO USE THE TEXT

Many parts of the text are written in a tutorial fashion. Usually, a subject will be introduced and explained in general terms. Then, specific examples of what has been explained will be given, often with pictures of what the reader would see on the computer screen. In fact, the student can perform each example on the computer as he or she is reading the text.

Information about how to use software is given in small portions that build up to the completion of a task. For example, word processing uses the creation of a letter and the creation of a multipage document to explain various abilities of word processing. A database is conceived, created, manipulated and used for reports to teach the use of a database program. Several spreadsheets of increasing complexity are created to illustrate the uses of a spreadsheet program.

The exercises at the end of each chapter build on the examples in the text, often taking the student further in process.

The text assumes that the software package is already configured and installed on a computer for the student's use. Since each student lab situation is different, the instructor may need to cover details of how the use of your school's computers differ in any way from what is described in the text.

The text is set up in a logical order, introducing computing and DOS, then introducing the most common application packages and finally introducing other computing topics. The application packages may be presented in any order, and most topics in the book may be skipped without affecting the understanding of subsequent chapters. For example, if students have already had an introduction to DOS, chapters 3 and 4 may be skipped or skimmed.

EXAMPLES DISK

An examples disk is available to use with this book. This disk contains files that are referred to in end-of-the-chapter exercises, particularly for the applications chapters. There are often two or more versions of similar files. For example, a word processing document will be on disk three times, with extensions .WP, .WS and .TXT, which are a WordPerfect version, a WordStar version and a Text (ASCII) version.

QUICK REFERENCE CARD

Also included with the text is a quick reference card. This card may be removed from the text and used by the student as a quick reminder of the commands and procedures learned in the text. The Quick Reference card contains information about DOS, WordStar, WordPerfect, dBASE III and Lotus 1-2-3.

ACKNOWLEDGEMENTS

Writing a textbook is a multi-year process, and many people become involved. This text grew out of a course within Academic Computing Services at the University of Texas Southwestern Medical Center. Several people in the department contributed to suggestions, discussions and criticisms that helped in the process. Thanks go to department directors Bill Sholar and Joan Reisch and to fellow instructor Wanda Dunn.

Richard Jones was very helpful in the development of the contents of the book. Thanks also goes to Stacy Lenzen and Susanne Spellacy of West Publishing in their help during the text's production stages.

I was also very fortunate in having several educators review the manuscript and provide valuable comments. These include:

Herbert F. Rebhun, University of Houston–Downtown
Terri Hanson, Lee College
Woody Martin, Chaffey College
Kip Irvine, Miami-Dade Community College
L. Wayne Horn, Pensacola Junior College
Steven A. Scott, Northeastern Oklahoma A&M College
Richard L. Smith, Austin Community College
Pat Ormond, Utah Technical College
Gary Gleason, Pensacola Junior College
Laura Saret, Oakton Community College
Russell Anderson, Weber State
C. David Rolfe, Central New England College
Linda Gammill, Weber State
Dick Bernardin, Cape Cod Community College
Kathy Wreden, University of Arizona
Leroy Robbins, Bee County College

Introduction to Microcomputing with Applications

CHAPTER 1

Microcomputers: Taking A Peek "Under the Hood"

CHAPTER OVERVIEW. This chapter introduces essential computing concepts. It briefly relates the history of computing, specifically focusing on how microcomputers came into being. It describes how a computer "thinks" and what the essential components of a modern computer are, and introduces the student to the meaning of today's most common computer terms.

CHAPTER OBJECTIVES

Upon completion of this chapter, you will be able to:

- Describe how computers evolved into the microcomputers we are using today.
- Describe some of the major differences among the IBM family of microcomputers on the market since 1981.
- Describe the most common types of software used on microcomputers.
- Describe how information is stored internally in the machine as well as how it is stored externally.
- Describe common input and output devices for the computer.

THE COMPUTER AS AN APPLIANCE

The computer has been called "*the* appliance for the last half of the twentieth century". This description gives us an image of how common computers are becoming at work and at home. Some bright-eyed futurists envision computers "taking over" major parts of our lives—replacing teachers, making our decisions, and even replacing our body parts. None of this will ever happen. Computers will *assist* us in teaching—did the slide projector replace any teachers you know about? Computers can *help* make decisions—but who do you think will be held responsible for a bad decision in business, the computer or the person in charge? The computer will even help us when our body parts become worn or damaged—but they will never be a substitute for the real thing.

Computers are a Part of the Real World

So much for fantasy. Computers are a real part of our world. You and I will be dealing with them, and we need to know something about how they work. As we will begin to see, computers are basically dumb. They can do a few small things very well, and they can do those things very fast. They cannot "think"; they can only mimic. They will only do what we tell them to do, or what some programmer before us told them to do. In this chapter, we "look under the hood" of the computer to discover a little about how it works. This will take away some of the mystery and aura surrounding the silicon miracle.

Choosing a Computer is Like Choosing a Car

Why do you need to know anything about what is inside the computer? The same question could be asked by someone beginning to learn how to drive a car. If you know some of the basic information about what the computer is doing, and how it is doing it, you will likely be able to learn faster how to "drive" the thing. Also, you will probably be in a position to buy, or participate in the decision to buy, a computer in the next months or years. Buying a computer is much like buying a car. You could get stuck with one that would not meet your needs unless you know the difference between automatic transmissions and stickshifts, or between four cylinders and V-8's.

This chapter will look briefly at major events that led to the invention of the computer, and will introduce some common computer jargon. Basic information about the machine (hardware) and the programs that run the machine (software) will also be covered.

EARLY ATTEMPTS AT COMPUTING

Ig had 99 sheep to count. As he herded them and his family around the Mesopotamian river valley in search of food and water, he wanted to make sure all his animals were in the fold. For each animal, he kept a stone in a leather bag. At the end of the day, his son, Og, would run the sheep into a makeshift pen. Ig would have all of the stones in his hand. As an animal passed, he would place one stone in the bag. If all the stones were accounted for, he had nothing to worry about. If there were not enough sheep for his stones, he had better start a search. As more sheep were born, Ig added new stones. If he sold, slaughtered, or lost an animal, he would remove a stone. It was a crude but efficient way of keeping track of his inventory.

Ig had a simple computing task. However, as civilization grew, so did the need for more complex calculations. Numbering systems appeared almost four thousand years ago, some based on the decimal system of 10, which we use today, and some based on systems of 12 or even 60. Once number systems were defined, mathematicians began to learn how to manipulate numbers—adding, subtracting, multiplying, and dividing. About fifteen hundred years ago, the first successful mechanical calculating machine, the abacus, was invented (see figure 1.1). The abacus is an arrangement of rods containing beads that are moved back and forth to form numerical patterns. The abacus is still used in some oriental cultures today.

Computing as a Challenge of Science

In the seventeenth century, methods of improving the speed and accuracy of calculating became the pet projects of several famous scientists. In 1614, John Napier of Scotland discovered logarithms. A logarithm is an exponent of a base number, indicating to what power the base must be raised to get a desired number. For example, the number required to raise the base number 10 to the number 100 is 2.

$$10^2 = 100$$

which implies

$$\text{LOG}(100) = 2 \text{ (base 10)}$$

FIGURE 1.1.
An abacus

The advantage of logarithms is that to multiply two numbers which are expressed in logarithms of the same base number, you can simply add the exponents. Multiplication is replaced by an easier process, addition. Napier's logarithm tables were soon combined into the slide rule by William Oughtred in the 1620s. The slide rule was one of the primary calculating devices for scientists for over four-hundred years, until the advent of the electronic calculator in the 1970s.

Cogs as Calculators

The slide rule and logarithms were tremendous advances in speeding up individual calculations, but there was another serious problem that they did not solve. This was the repetitive calculation of numbers such as in census taking, taxation, inventory, and other business transactions. Blaise Pascal was the son of a French tax official. Inspired by his father's tedious work, Pascal invented an adding machine in 1642, when he was nineteen years old. It consisted of a series of dialing wheels, which when turned added numbers together to form a sum (see figure 1.2). You probably have a similar type of machine in your car today—the odometer, which counts the number of miles traveled. This basic design was perfected in 1672 by a German, Gottfried Leibniz, who added the capabilities of speeding repetitive calculations and automating multiplying and dividing.

In 1822 Charles Babbage, an English mathematician, devised the theory for a machine that could compute and print lengthy scientific tables. He called the invention the Difference Engine (see figure 1.3). A tremendous amount of public funds went into the building of the Difference Engine, but

FIGURE 1.2.
Pascal's calculator

after ten years, it still did not work. Babbage did not give up. He theorized a new machine, named the Analytic Engine, that could analyze algebraic equations (see figure 1.4). This machine also proved too complicated to build. The theories of Babbage were on target, but too far ahead of technology to work. The early computers of the twentieth century were based in part on the works of these early inventors.

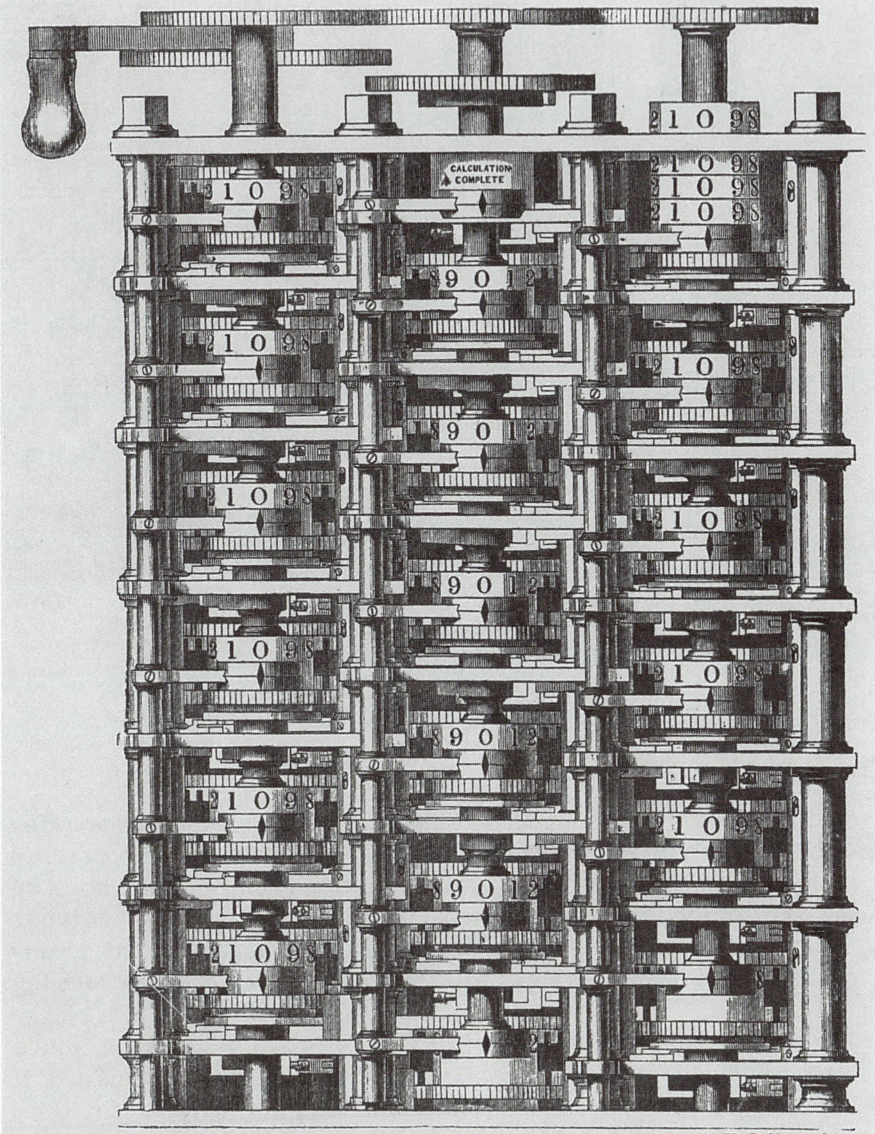

B. H. Babbage, del.

Impression from a woodcut ot a small portion of Mr. Babbage's Difference Engine No. 1, the property of Government, at present deposited in the Museum at South Kensington.

It was commenced 1823.
This portion put together 1833.
The construction abandoned 1842.
This plate was printed June, 1853.
This portion was in the Exhibition 1862.

FIGURE 1.3.
Babbage's difference engine

FIGURE 1.4.
Babages analytical engine

The Invention of the Computer Card

Another invention that influenced computing was the automated weaving loom built by Joseph Jacquard in 1804. This machine was based on a series of cards. Each having a particular pattern of holes. Each pattern of holes on the card corresponded to a pattern to be woven. By placing these cards one after another, the weaver could quickly design a woven pattern. This greatly automated the industry, cutting down labor costs and weaving time (see figure 1.5).

Almost 75 years later John Shaw Billings, a census official in the United States, was trying to develop a way to speed up the analysis of census data. It had taken as long as seven and a half years to count previous returns. Billings thought the tabulations could be performed using punched cards. No one knows if this idea came from Jacquard's loom, but the similarity is striking. Billings' son-in-law, Herman Hollerith, took the idea and developed the first "computer" cards.

The cards were the size of a dollar bill, and had 12 rows of 20 holes to be punched. Thus, 240 "Yes/No" items could be recorded on each card by

FIGURE 1.5. Jacquard's loom

punching a hole in the proper slot. A hole punched in a particular spot on the card was a "yes", and no hole meant "no". Once the cards were created, they were run through a counting machine (see figure 1.6). The machine pressed 240 pins onto the card. If there was a hole in one of the spots, the pin completed an electrical circuit, and a count was made for that item. Hollerith's device shortened the census counting by over one-third. The company which got its start from this machine has remained a key player in the development of computing. After several name changes, in 1924 the company was named International Business Machines (IBM).

Holleriths Co.

FIGURE 1.6.
Hollerith tabulating machine

ONES AND ZEROS

Although some of the early attempts at creating a computing machine used the decimal system of numbers from 0 to 9, the system that seemed to make the most sense in computing was the binary system, which consists of only two numbers, 0 and 1. Machines like Hollerith's tabulator could more easily understand a binary situation, such as having a hole in the card or not. In fact an entire mathematical system had been devised that fit well into the computing framework. George Boole, a nineteenth-century mathematician, had devised an algebraic system based on binary numbers. This system used 0's and 1's and a collection of symbols and rules to represent logical reasoning. The number 1 came to represent a statement which was true, while 0 meant a false statement. for example, a census card for a city dweller might report a 1 for the question "Do you live in town?", while a farmer's card would have a 0 for that question. To manipulate and combine statements, Boole's algebra used the terms "AND", "OR", and "NOT." Thus, in Boole's system, the logical statement "1and 1" is true and it's "answer" is 1.That is, if the first item is true and the second item is true, then the combination is true. True/False tables can be devised so that all combinations of statements can be evaluated. The term NOT simply changes the statement from True to False or vice versa. (See figure 1.7.)

These operations are all that are needed to add, subtract, multiply and divide, as well as to evaluate any logical statements. As it turns out, 1's and 0's are easily implemented in the electronic world. If there is voltage, it is a "1". If there is absence of voltage, it is a "0". By placing together numerous circuits, patterns of 0's and 1's can be manipulated. The binary system can also be used to represent numbers in the decimal system. See figure 1.8 for some examples.

THE ASCII STANDARD

In time, some standards emerged for using the binary system. The ASCII (American Standard Code for Information Interchange, pronounced "ASK-KEY" system of representing letters, numbers and other characters was developed. In this system, a pattern of eight "bits", which are the 0's and 1's, define a particular ASCII character, or "byte". Four bits define a "nibble". Thus, in the same way that the patterns on Jacquard's cards instructed the loom to create a design, the patterns of 1's and 0's can be used to instruct an electric circuit to perform a certain task. Figure 1.9 is a table of ASCII codes, and figure 1.10 illustrates the difference between a bit, a byte, and a nibble.

Logical AND's

Statement	Result
1 AND 1	1
1 AND 0	0
0 AND 1	0
0 AND 0	0

Logical OR's

Statement	Result
1 OR 1	1
1 OR 0	1
0 OR 1	1
0 OR 0	0

FIGURE 1.7.
Truth Tables

Decimal	Binary
1	1
2	10
3	11
4	100
5	101

FIGURE 1.8.
Examples of decimal and binary numbers

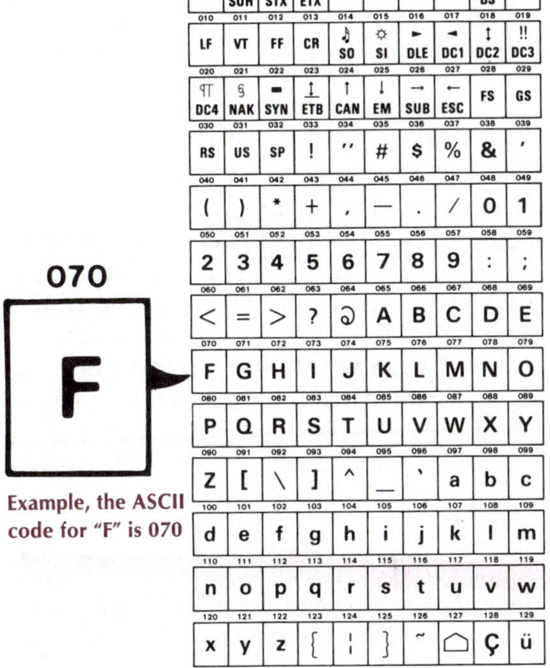

000 NUL	001 ☺ SOH	002 ● STX	003 ♥ ETX	004 ♦	005 ♣	006 ♠	007 BEL	008 ◘ BS	009 HT
010 LF	011 VT	012 FF	013 CR	014 ♪ SO	015 ☼ SI	016 ► DLE	017 ◄ DC1	018 ↕ DC2	019 !! DC3
020 ¶ DC4	021 § NAK	022 ▬ SYN	023 ↨ ETB	024 ↑ CAN	025 ↓ EM	026 → SUB	027 ← ESC	028 FS	029 GS
030 RS	031 US	032 SP	033 !	034 ''	035 #	036 $	037 %	038 &	039 '
040 (	041)	042 *	043 +	044 ,	045 —	046 .	047 /	048 0	049 1
050 2	051 3	052 4	053 5	054 6	055 7	056 8	057 9	058 :	059 ;
060 <	061 =	062 >	063 ?	064 @	065 A	066 B	067 C	068 D	069 E
070 F	071 G	072 H	073 I	074 J	075 K	076 L	077 M	078 N	079 O
080 P	081 Q	082 R	083 S	084 T	085 U	086 V	087 W	088 X	089 Y
090 Z	091 [	092 \	093]	094 ^	095 _	096 `	097 a	098 b	099 c
100 d	101 e	102 f	103 g	104 h	105 i	106 j	107 k	108 l	109 m
110 n	111 o	112 p	113 q	114 r	115 s	116 t	117 u	118 v	119 w
120 x	121 y	122 z	123 {	124 ¦	125 }	126 ~	127 ⌂	128 Ç	129 ü

Example, the ASCII code for "F" is 070

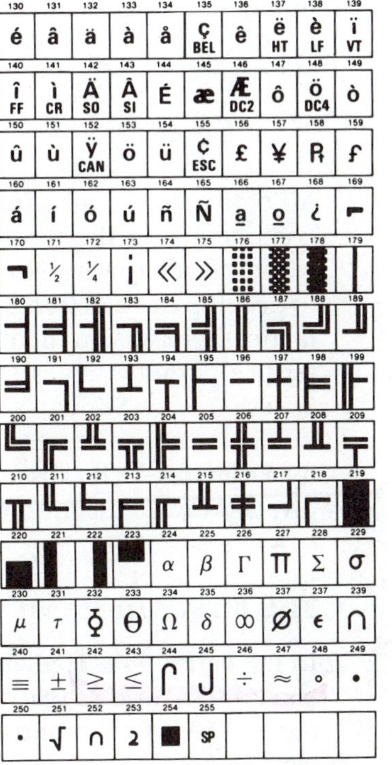

130 é	131 â	132 ä	133 à	134 å	135 ç BEL	136 ê	137 ë HT	138 è LF	139 ï VT
140 î FF	141 ì CR	142 Ä SO	143 Å SI	144 É	145 æ	146 Æ DC2	147 ô	148 ö DC4	149 ò
150 û	151 ù	152 ÿ CAN	153 Ö	154 Ü	155 ¢ ESC	156 £	157 ¥	158 ₧	159 ƒ
160 á	161 í	162 ó	163 ú	164 ñ	165 Ñ	166 ª	167 º	168 ¿	169 ⌐
170 ¬	171 ½	172 ¼	173 ¡	174 «	175 »	176 ░	177 ▒	178 ▓	179 │
180 ┤	181 ╡	182 ╢	183 ╖	184 ╕	185 ╣	186 ║	187 ╗	188 ╝	189 ╜
190 ╛	191 ┐	192 └	193 ┴	194 ┬	195 ├	196 ─	197 ┼	198 ╞	199 ╟
200 ╚	201 ╔	202 ╩	203 ╦	204 ╠	205 ═	206 ╬	207 ╧	208 ╨	209 ╤
210 ╥	211 ╙	212 ╘	213 ╒	214 ╓	215 ╫	216 ╪	217 ┘	218 ┌	219 █
220 ▄	221 ▌	222 ▐	223 ▀	224 α	225 β	226 Γ	227 π	228 Σ	229 σ
230 µ	231 τ	232 Φ	233 Θ	234 Ω	235 δ	236 ∞	237 ø	237 ∈	239 ∩
240 ≡	241 ±	242 ≥	243 ≤	244 ⌠	245 ⌡	246 ÷	247 ≈	248 °	249 •
250 ·	251 √	252 ⁿ	253 ²	254 ■	255 SP				

FIGURE 1.9.
ASCII table

FIGURE 1.10.

Bits, Nibbles, and Bytes

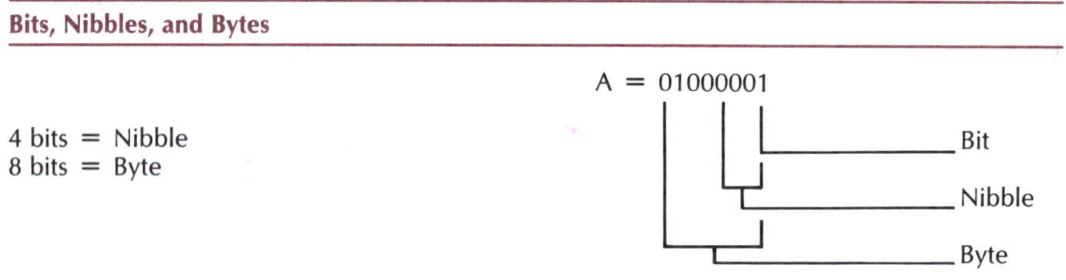

Notice that the letter "A" is coded as character 65 (or 01000001 in binary), and "a" is coded as character 92. All of the lowercase numbers are numbered 32 higher than their uppercase forms. Also notice that the first 31 ASCII characters are special characters that are usually not printed characters. For example, ASCII character 10 is a line feed (LF), character 12 is a form feed (FF), and character 27 is the "escape" character. The keyboard characters begin with the space as character 32, and on through the tilde "˜" as character number 126.

Extended ASCII

The remaining characters in the table are called "extended" characters. These characters may not be the same from computer to computer. The ones shown here are those used on IBM PC-type computers. Since these characters are not on the keyboard, they must be requested in a special way. For example, to make the Greek letter beta "β" appear on the screen (character number 225), hold the ALT key down while at the same time entering the number 225 on the numeric keypad. Lift up the ALT key and the beta should appear. Some PC software and printers do not support these IBM extended characters.

WAR SPEEDS UP COMPUTER DEVELOPMENT

All of the inventions and theories mentioned up to this point are important components in the development of the computer we know today. As the world moved toward World War II, scientists in America and Europe began to develop the electronic computer independently. On both sides of the Atlantic, there was an increasing need for the calculation of complex and extensive numeric tables to use in solving ballistic problems. In the United States, George Stibitz, working for Bell Labs in 1937, developed electronic Boolean gates to represent the AND, OR, and NOT concepts using electricity. From this, Bell Labs developed a machine that could add, subtract, multiply, and divide electronically.

The First American Computers

In the early 1940s IBM and Howard Aiken of Harvard built a huge machine named the MARK I that was fifty-one feet long and eight feet high. It contained 750,000 parts and 500 miles of wire and could add numbers up to 23 digits in a then-dizzying three-tenths of a second (see figure 1.11). In 1942, separate from the IBM machine, John Mauchly and Presper Ekert began the development of a vacuum tube computer at Moore School of Engineering. It was dubbed the ENIAC. However, this computer was not available for use until 1945, when the war had ended. Once tested, it ran a thousand times faster than MARK I.

The First European Computers

Across the ocean in Germany, a young man named Konrad Zuse designed a simple computer on his kitchen table, which he called the Z1. During the early stages of the war, the machine progressed to the Z2, Z3, and Z4. In 1941, once Zuse realized that a computer using vacuum tubes rather than electromagnetic switches would run a thousand times faster than the current machine, he applied for government support. He was turned down, since the Germans felt that the war would soon be won. In a project code-named Ultra, the British were developing an electro-mechanical device which was used to break some of Germany's wartime codes. In 1943, the British created a vacuum tube model of their computer, and named it the Colossus.

Von Neumann Defines the Digital Computer

As the war was ending, a brilliant scientist named John von Neumann began to work with Mauchly and Eckert on a new version of the ENIAC, named EDVAC. Von Neumann's description of the function and layout of the digital computer defined concisely the theory of computing. Today, many scientists refer to digital computers as "von Neumann machines". Mauchly and Ekert were outraged that von Neumann gained so much notority on "their" invention. Meanwhile, IBM and Aiken disagreed over the MARK I, and court cases involving these early computer pioneers have continued into the 1980s. Mauchly and Eckert left Moore and founded the UNIVAC computer company, which eventually was bought by Remington Rand. Aiken parted from

FIGURE 1.11.
The Mark I computer at Harvard

IBM and created several more MARK computers. IBM went full speed into computer development and is now the world's largest computer marketer. John von Neumann continued to work on computers for the military and helped design a machine used to solve problems associated with the development of the hydrogen bomb. This machine was called the Mathematical Analyzer, Numerator, Integrator and Computer—or MANIAC for short.

Transistors Replace Vacuum Tubes

The thousands of vacuum tubes in the early computers caused problems. Machine rooms often heated up to over 100 degrees, even with air conditioning. Furthermore, the vacuum tubes needed a tremendous amount of electricity and were prone to failure. These problems with the vacuum tubes could easily have limited the reasonable size of computers, and could have relegated computers to gigantic tools of big government. The development of the transistor, just at the right time, began a process of miniaturization that continues today.

The Computer's Brain—On/Off Switches

Computers need a series of on/off switches to simulate the 0's and 1's of Boolean logic. The Mark I, and Z1 computers used electromechanical switches, which could be switched from "off" to "on" and vice versa by applying a voltage to a magnet that opened or closed the circuit. The vacuum tube simulated this mechanical switch, and was faster. In the late forties and early fifties, the team of John Bardeen, William Shockley, and Walter Brattain of Bell Labs perfected the transistor. The transistor also simulated the early electromechanical switches, but had neither the power needs nor the heat problems of the vacuum tubes.

The transistor greatly reduced the size of the computer. At the same time, it allowed more complex computers to be built. The only drawback was that in the early 1950s, a transistor cost about eight dollars and a vacuum tube cost only seventy-five cents. Part of the problem was the cost of the main ingredient in the device, germanium, which was more expensive than gold. This problem did not last long. Gordon Teal of Texas Instruments soon devised a way of creating a transistor out of less-expensive silicon—the main ingredient in ordinary sand. Figure 1.12 depicts several of these devices.

Smaller, Smaller, Smaller

Once it was known how to make a transistor "switch" from inexpensive materials, the electronics industry concentrated on making them smaller. Jack Kirby of Texas Instruments and Robert Noyce of Fairchild devised ways of creating many transistors all at once on one piece of silicon, and thus introduced the integrated circuit. Now hundreds, and soon thousands, of transistors could be etched into a small silicon "chip."

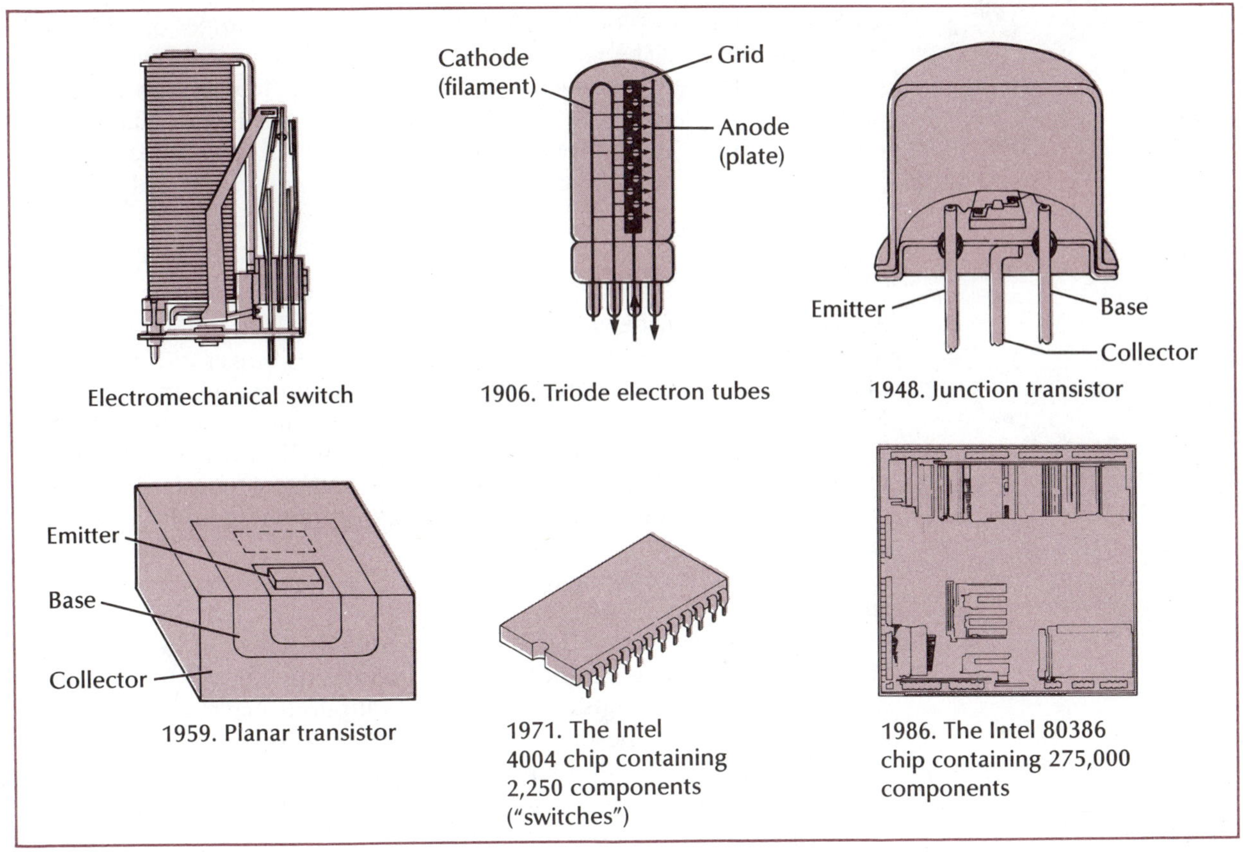

FIGURE 1.12.
From switch to transistor

Computers on a Chip

In 1971, Ted Huff of Intel introduced a fingernail-size chip that contained 2,250 transistors, call the "4004". The remarkable feature of this chip was that it contained all of the basic elements of a complete computer. It could add two 4-bit numbers in 100 millionths of a second. However, it was very limited in its capabilities, and was used only for specialized purposes. The Intel 8080 chip, introduced in 1974, was the first microprocessor for general purpose use. It could add two 8-bit numbers in 2.5 millionths of a second, and was the chip used in many of the early microcomputers.

THE MICRO-COMPUTER MARKET ARRIVES

After the introduction of the 8080 chip, several small companies began offering computer hobby kits. The company generally accepted as producing the first mass-marketed microcomputer was MITS (Micro Instrumentation and Telemetry Systems) which produced the Altair 8800. This computer, which sold for $397 as a kit, and $498 assembled, was popular with electronic buffs.

Orders for more than 4,000 flooded the Albuquerque offices of MITS in the first three months. The machine had no keyboard or monitor, and was programmed with a series of switches. The results appeared as a series of lights on the control panel. Even with its crude user controls, the Altair sparked clubs all over the United States, and soon other small companies were making "add-ons" to the basic computer to make it more usable.

Silicon Valley and the Homebrew Computer Club

A place in California between San Francisco and San Jose named "Silicon Valley" soon became the center of the microcomputer universe. Here, a group of bearded, blue-jeaned computer hackers began an organization called the Homebrew Computer Club. Members included some of the engineers from Silicon Valley's top electronics corporations as well as young computer enthusiasts. The meetings were marked with the sharing of state-of-the-art secrets, new ideas and theories. It was a caldron of a new industry about to emerge.

Members of this club included Stephen Wozniak and Stephen Jobs, who later founded Apple Computers. Stephen Leininger, who developed the Radio Shack Model I, also traces his roots to Homebrew. In 1977 the Apple II computer, the Radio Shack Model I, and the Commodore Pet computers were introduced (see figure 1.13). These computers made a break with the hobby computers of the previous several years. They came with a built-in keyboard, access to a video screen, and had some basic software programs available. This new look for the computer made it more acceptable to the general public. They were a success. Radio Shack was backlogged for more than a year on orders of its computer. Apple's sales the first year soared to $2.7 million. The Commodore Pet became especially popular in Europe.

EMERGENCE AS A BUSINESS TOOL

Even with these early successes of the microcomputer, the small computer was not readily accepted as a business tool. Although it could add and subtract, it required a programmer to do any real work. The marketplace provided the answer with the emergence of a number of software companies writing programs for these computers. One of these software companies was Software Arts. In 1979, it introduced the first really successful business software, VisiCalc. This spreadsheet program mimicked the function of an accountant's worksheet, and made budgeting, forecasting, and monetary analysis easy. Most observers agree that VisiCalc was the primary tool that first introduced the microcomputer to the business world.

IBM Enters the Microcomputer Market

In 1981, IBM entered the microcomputer market with its IBM PC. This computer was based on Intel's next generation of microprocessor chips, named the 8088, which could manipulate 16 bits of information at once, an improvement over the 8080's capability of manipulating only 8 bits of information.

a. 1975 Altair 8800
b. 1981 IBM PC
c. 1977 Apple II
d. 1977 Radio Shack Model I
e. 1977 Commodore Pet

FIGURE 1.13.
The first microcomputers

Not only was the IBM PC a remarkable improvement in microcomputers, it had the name that business trusted—IBM. Over the next several years, the microcomputer industry saw two primary "families" of computers emerge. One family, following the IBM PC standard, is based on the Intel 8088 chip and its successors, the Intel 80286 and 80386 chips. The other major group is the Apple family, based on the MOS 6502 chip (Apple II) and Motorola 68000 chip (Macintosh).

The IBM PC Standard Emerges

The IBM Personal Computer had an immediate impact on the microcomputer industry. Suddenly, the micro was a legitimate business machine. The computer stores that had been full of hackers in blue jeans were now attracting corporate buyers in business suits. Most of the other computer makers recognized the significance of the emerging IBM standard and began to produce "IBM PC compatible" computers. These included Radio Shack (Tandy), Texas Instruments, Wang, AT&T, and many others.

The basis for the IBM PC standard came not only from the Intel microprocessor chip, but also from a software program that manages the resources of the computer. This program, written by Microsoft, was named PC-DOS by IBM, and is known as MS-DOS on other computers. "DOS", which rhymes with "Ross", stands for Disk Operating System.

Successors to the Original PC

IBM has introduced a series of computers since the introduction of the IBM PC in 1981. Riding on IBM's coattails, a gigantic new industry has emerged as companies have developed both software and hardware support for the computers. As an advance over the IBM PC, which used floppy disk drives for data storage, IBM introduced the IBM PC/XT. The XT computer introduced the hard (or fixed) disk storage device. The Portable PC provided a way to easily move a PC from location to location. IBM stopped producing this machine as a result of competition from the Compaq computer company, which made a superior product. IBM attempted to produce an affordable home computer with the IBM PCjr. The "Junior" also failed to survive the competition, mainly from Tandy, Commodore and Apple II computers. IBM's introduction of the AT computer, based on Intel's new 80286 chip, has been a success. In 1986, IBM introduced the PC Convertible, a lap-top computer. This computer contains the power of the IBM PC in a twelve-pound package smaller than a briefcase (see figure 1.14).

Compatibles and Clones

By the mid-1980s most components of the IBM PC were readily available off the shelf. The main component that "patents" the IBM PC is a small chip called the BIOS, which stands for BASIC INPUT/OUTPUT SYSTEM. This chip contains the basic "brains" of the computer. This component has been

FIGURE 1.14.
Major Variations of IBM PC's

Date	Chip	Name	Added Features
1981	8088	IBM PC	
1983	8088	IBM PC/XT	Hard disk
1983	8088	Portable PC	Portability
1984	8088	IBM PCjr	Low cost
1985	80286	IBM PC/AT	Faster, more memory
1986	80C88	Convertible	Small, 3.5-inch disk
1986	80286	New PC/XT	Faster
1987	8088 80286 80386	IBM PS/2 series	Smaller, faster computer. Also new Micro Channel bus

"cloned" (duplicated) by several electronics firms. With this cloned BIOS, computer manufacturers have been able to produce microcomputers that are virtually identical to the original IBM PC. This allows them to take advantage of the thousands of software and add-on hardware products already existing in the marketplace.

COMPUTER LANGUAGES

The language that a computer understands is a string of 0's and 1's—"on" and "off" switches. This, of course, is not how the average user communicates with the computer. Beginning with the MARK I computer at Harvard, programmers have searched for ways to communicate with the machine in a language other than the raw machine language. Since patterns of 0's and 1's had particular meanings for a computer, the first language was created to substitute small words or mnemonics for particular computer operations. For example, suppose the pattern "00010001" tells the computer to add two numbers together. Using the new language, the programmer enters the word ADD on a typewriter terminal. A series of commands create a program, containing other commands such as SUB, MUL, DIV, JMP, MOV, etc. When the programmer is finished writing a program, the computer translates the ADD and the other commands back to something it can understand (i.e., "00010001"). This process was called *assembling the code,* and the early computer language was dubbed *assembly* language.

Assembly language is known as a "low-level" language since it is so close to the machine's real language. Higher-level languages were soon developed that enabled programmers to communicate with the computer in more English-like phrases. When the programmer had finished writing a program in one of these new languages, another program called a *compiler* or *interpreter* converted the code into the 0's and 1's of machine language. There have been a number of computer languages developed in the past forty years. Most of them aim to help the programmer solve a particular kind of problem. Some programming languages are listed in figure 1.15, and some sample code from a high level language (BASIC) is illustrated in figure 1.16.

FIGURE 1.15.
Some popular programming languages

Name	Purpose
Assembly	System Programming
C	System and Application Programming
COBOL	Business, Accounting
BASIC	All-purpose, Beginner's Language
Pascal	Teaching Language
FORTRAN	Scientific Programming
MUMPS	Medical Applications
LISP	Artificial Intelligence

FIGURE 1.16.
A sample high level language program in BASIC

```
0  PRINT ''THIS IS A VERY FINE DAY''
10 INPUT ''ENTER YOUR AGE'';AGE
20 PRINT ''NEXT YEAR YOU WILL BE''; AGE + 1 ;'' YEARS OLD.''
30 END
```

Application Software

Most people who now use computers do not need to communicate using languages. Instead, programs called "application packages" are used. These application packages were originally written in a programming language, and then translated (converted, or compiled) into the language of the computer. Some common types of application programs include word processors, spreadsheet programs, database programs, and the like. See figure 1.17 for a listing of some of the more popular application programs.

A *word processor* is a software program that allows the computer to store textual information (such as letters, reports, and novels). The computer functions somewhat like a typewriter. However, instead of the text appearing on paper (at least initially), it appears as characters on the computer screen. The word processor's user can write and correct words on the screen, and experiment with margins, formats, and wording before actually printing the results out on a printer.

A *spreadsheet* program is a software program that emulates a bookkeeper's columnar worksheet. In a spreadsheet, you can "write down" columns of numbers, add those numbers together, and perform other mathematical functions. Spreadsheets are often used to keep budgets, financial records, and other data. One important aspect of a spreadsheet that makes it particularly useful is its ability to be programmed. For example, a proposed budget can be entered into a spreadsheet. Monthly and yearly sums may be defined. Then, if a single number in the spreadsheet is changed, the computer can automatically recalculate the table and adjust all of the sums, totals, and other calculations to fit the change. This has become known as the power to ask "what if" questions on the computer.

A *database* is a software program that stores and manipulates information. For a doctor's office, this information might be the names, addresses, and

WORD PROCESSORS	SPREADSHEETS	INTEGRATED
Wordperfect	Lotus 1-2-3	Lotus 1-2-3
Multimate	Lotus Symphony	Lotus Symphony
WordStar	Supercalc	Framework
pfs:write	Multiplan	Ability
PC-Write	Excel	Microsoft Works
Microsoft Word	Framework	
Sammna	pfs:First Choice	

DATABASES	OTHERS
dBASE III, IV	BPI Accounting
R:Base 5000	Sidekick
Reflex	Norton Utilities
Knowledgeman	Flight Simulator
PC-File	Procomm (communications)

FIGURE 1.17.
Some of the most common application programs

amount of money owed for all patients with charge accounts. It could also contain counts of inventory items, or personnel information. Financial information is often kept in a database, where it can then be used to produce reports daily, monthly, or yearly. A database is the type of software that is used to store information that can then be searched, listed, or used in summary reports.

Application programs allow people with limited knowledge about how a computer works to use a microcomputer. The user does not have to know about the 0's and 1's being moved around in the computer's memory. Thus, when the computer is operating under the control of a word processor, the user interacts with that program, and the program itself interacts with the internal workings of the computer. There is an almost limitless number of applications that a computer can perform. This is made evident by the thousands of commercial software packages on the market today.

THE MEMORY OF THE COMPUTER

As we have seen, the memory of the computer contains a series of 0's and 1's. These 0's and 1's are stored in tiny memory elements etched onto a silicon chip. They are like thousands of on/off switches. The computer can turn them on and off individually, and thus manipulate its own memory. Memory is generally measured in "bytes". Recall that a byte is 8 bits (8 on/off switches). A byte is sometimes called a "character", since characters like "A", "B", and "C" are also represented with a byte.

Microcomputer memory is usually created in banks of 1024 bytes. This is often called 1K, where K is often rounded off to 1000 bytes. When a computer is said to be a 64K machine, it means that it has about 64,000 bytes of memory. When a computer's memory gets to be larger than 1000K, it is generally measured in "megabytes" or millions of bytes. Thus, 2MB (megabytes) of memory is 2000K or 2 million bytes.

RAM and ROM

There are two basic kinds of memory in the computer, RAM and ROM. RAM stands for Random Access Memory, and ROM stands for Read-Only Memory. ROM is permanent memory placed in the computer at the factory. It contains the necessary information for the computer to know how to start up (or begin to "boot"). The ROM BIOS in an IBM PC is that bit of machine code that makes the computer know how to work. Other software interacts through the BIOS to instruct the inner workings of the machine. RAM, on the other hand, is accessible to the user. It has nothing stored in it while the computer is off. When the computer is turned on, RAM, is available to store letters, programs, graphics, and any other thing the computer wishes to "think" about. The memory size of a computer measures its RAM. If a machine is said to have 256K of memory, it means there are about 256,000 bytes of accessible memory (RAM). The original PC is limited in access to about 640K of RAM memory.

PERIPHERAL STORAGE OF INFORMATION ON THE COMPUTER

The computer's memory exists in an electronic world that relies on a constant current. When that current is off, the computer's memory vanishes (except for the ROM). If you write a letter on the computer using your favorite word processor, and then switch the computer off, the contents of that letter vanish forever. How, then, can the computer be used to store information permanently? The answer for most microcomputers is the floppy (or flexible) disk.

The "floppy" used on most IBM PC's is a 5.25 inch sheet of magnetically coated Mylar housed in an envelope. Beginning with the PS/2 series, 3.5-inch diskettes also began to be used. When the diskette is placed in the disk drive, the magnetic disk spins, and information is written to or read from it through a small read/write head that moves along the surface of the disk.

The surface of the diskette is similar to the surface of a tape in a tape recording cassette or a VCR tape. A certain magnetic condition of the surface is read (or written) by the read/write head in the disk drive as a "0" or a "1"—mimicking the computer's memory.

Hard Disks

An improvement on the floppy disk is the hard (or fixed) disk. A hard disk works exactly like a floppy disk, but it is housed in a dust-free environment. Since dust is absent, the disk can spin faster, and read and write onto smaller areas of the disk. This allows one hard disk to hold as much information as thirty to sixty floppy diskettes, and to access that information much faster.

Other Means of Memory Storage

Any device that can be made to store and retrieve on/off type signals can be a computer's memory. Many home computers use cassette recorders. A recorder can read and write one type of signal as a "0" and another as a "1", and thus store computer memory. Punched cards and punched tape were used for many years to store computer data. The most recent innovation in computer storage is the laser disk. These platters, similar in nature to the compact disks CD's that are used by record manufacturers, can be made to hold gigabytes (billions of bytes) of information. Entire encyclopedias and other large volumes of information can be stored on these disks.

How Much Data Can be Stored on Disk?

The volume of data that can be stored on a diskette is usually measured in bytes, or characters. Thus, 360K is roughly 360,000 characters of information. a double-spaced typed sheet of paper contains about 1500 characters, so 360K will hold about 240 pages of information. Figure 1.18 compares certain types of disks, and how much data they will hold (using the IBM PC as the guide). Recall that *K* means thousands of bytes and *MB* (megabytes) means millions of bytes. The following terms are used in the table: *SS* means single-sided, *DS* means double-sided, *DD* means double-density, and *HD* means high density (quad density).

ENTERING INFORMATION INTO THE COMPUTER

The primary way humans communicate with the computer is through the keyboard. This keyboard is similar to the one on a typewriter, but there are some important differences.

Figure 1.19 is a diagram of a typical computer keyboard (from the IBM PC). Specific features of the keyboard will be discussed in chapter 2.

The Mouse

Another way to talk to the computer is with a device called a *mouse*. A mouse is a small box big enough to fit in the palm of your hand. It usually contains one or more buttons. By moving the mouse around on a flat surface, you can control where the cursor (or when using a mouse, an arrow) is pointing on the computer screen. Thus, you can point to options on a menu, and select your options by pressing a button on the mouse. In many applications, the mouse is a faster way to make choices than the keyboard (see Figure 1.20).

Type of diskette	Bytes	"Pages"
SS/DD (5.25")	160K	120
DS/DD (5.25")	360K	240
DS/HD (5.25")	1.2MB	900
3.5" diskette	720K	480
3.5" diskette	1.44MB	960
Hard disk	10MB	7,500
Hard disk	20MB	15,000
Hard disk	30MB	22,500

FIGURE 1.18.
Relative capacities of diskettes

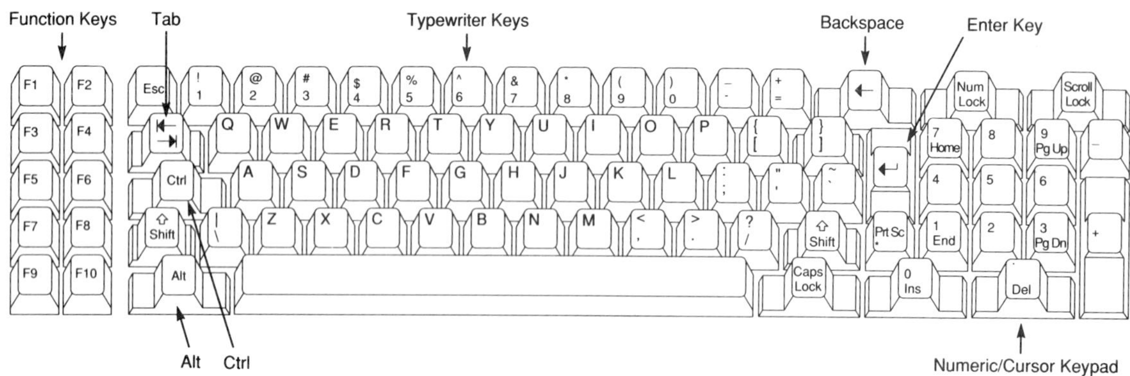

FIGURE 1.19.
The IBM PC keyboard

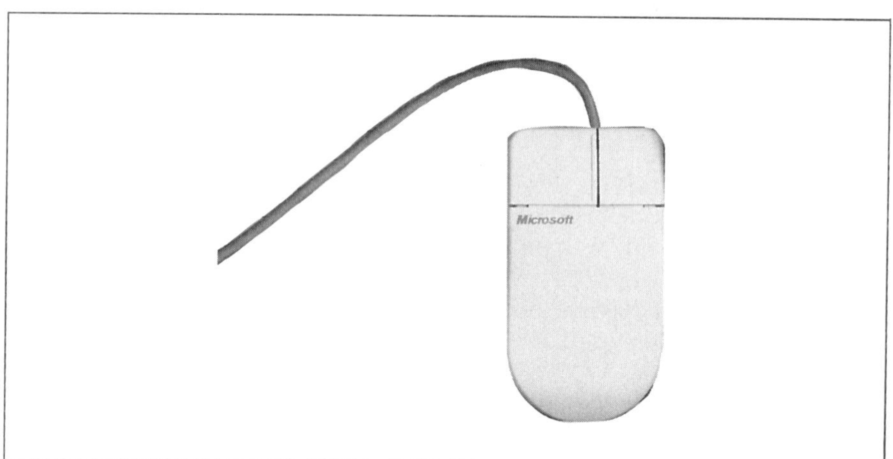

FIGURE 1.20.
Input devices

The Joystick

The joystick is a small device containing a movable handle that can be used to control the cursor or other "action" on the computer monitor. Joysticks are often used in games, although they are sometimes used in application programs also. A joystick may have one or more buttons, like a mouse, that can be used to select options from a menu (see figure 1.20).

Other Input Devices

Other devices that are used to talk to the computer include light pens, digital tablets, touch screens, and voice decoders. A light pen is a device that looks like a pen. It is pointed at the screen, and is used to select options from a menu, or to "draw" on the screen. A digital tablet is a flat "drawing board". You can draw pictures, such as maps, on the board, and the image will be transferred to the computer screen. A "touch screen" allows the user to select menu options by pointing to them on (and touching) the screen. A voice decoder allows the user to actually talk to the computer. The decoder must first be trained to the user's voice and can be taught to recognize hundreds of words.

GETTING INFORMATION OUT OF THE COMPUTER

Devices that are used by the computer to communicate to us include the monitor (screen), the printer, plotters, and speakers. The monitor is the TV-type device that displays words and pictures. Monitors come in a variety of capabilities (and prices), which range from the ability to display only textual material in one color to monitors that can display text and pictures in hundreds of colors.

Computer Printers

Printers allow you to create a permanent record of information from the computer. There are several kinds of printers. The most common type is the dot matrix printer. This printer forms characters by printing an arrangement of dots in a matrix. The most common size is an 9-pin dot matrix, although some of the newer dot matrix printers use a grid of 24 dots. Some dot matrix printers can also print graphic images. Another type of printer, the daisy wheel printer produces letters in the same way as a standard typewriter. It creates letters on the page by pressing a key against a ribbon. Daisy wheel printers create most of what is called "letter-quality" printing, although many dot matrix printers can now create characters that are almost as nice. Laser printers create images in much the same way as a photocopying machine. They can create almost typeset quality printing, and their introduction enabled the "desktop publishing" revolution to get under way.

Other methods of output include plotters, speakers, and communication devices. Plotters are devices that allow the computer to draw pictures. Speakers are used to give users auditory feedback (bells, for instance) to play music, or even to talk to the user. Communication devices allow the computer to send and receive messages across telephone lines.

A VERSATILE MACHINE

After being hundreds, even thousands of years in the making, the computer industry is finally in its infancy. We are just beginning to understand the potential of the machine. It cannot "think", but what it can do, it does very fast. It can obey our instructions and perform repetitious tasks without tiring. It can store vast amounts of data, and search for information from millions of possibilities in just seconds. We are beginning to understand how to communicate with the computer in simpler ways. Soon, the computer will be able to clearly understand speech. Also, the computer is being "taught" to talk in voices that sound remarkably clear and unaccented.

Today, there are computers in our cars, our ovens, and our phones. There are many millions of computers in use today, and most people don't even know where they are. As the computer gets "smarter", and as we discover more uses for the device, it will continue to go "underground", and blend into more parts of our everyday life.

SUMMARY

Computers were invented because of our needs for record keeping and mathematical calculation. The crude mechanical devices developed hundreds of years ago provided the groundwork for the modern electronic computers of today. The development of the transistor and its subsequent miniaturization resulted in the creation of the microcomputer. Once a small, affordable computer became available for business use, the industry exploded with software and peripheral devices to support the computer.

KEY TERMS

Define the following terms in your own words:

Hardware

Software

Logarithm

Computer card

Binary

Boolean logic

ASCII

Extended ASCII

Von Neumann machine

Transistor

Silicon

Integrated circuit

Microprocessor

Computer chip

Floppy disk

Hard disk

BIOS

Computer language

Application software

Word processor

Database program

Spreadsheet program

Megabyte

Mouse

Joystick

QUESTIONS

Write a short answer in your own words for each of the following questions.

1. Name some everyday devices that are not computers, but contain computers.
2. Why is it that the world of electronics fits in so well with the 0/1 way of performing calculations? What were Jacquard's and Hollerith's contributions to laying the groundwork for computing?
3. What does a transistor do (at least in computer memory)? How did the transistor improve early electronic computers?
4. What is the ASCII standard?
5. What do ROM and RAM mean, and how are they different?
6. What is a bit? What is a byte?
7. What is the most common device for storing permanent information from the microcomputer in magnetic form?
8. List several ways in which computers affect the way you work or go to school (for example, record keeping, tools, measuring devices, etc.).
9. If computers continue to get smaller and smaller, what are some potential uses for them in the future? For example, how could they improve automobiles, medicine, telephones, stereos, vacuum cleaners, etc?
10. If you were going to write a book 400 pages long, about how many bytes of storage would that require on a hard disk?

LABORATORY EXERCISES

Lab Exercise 1. Survey at least 10 different experienced microcomputer users, and ask them what word processor, database, and spreadsheet program they use. Also ask them what brand of computer they use, and what kind of printer (dot matrix, laser, other). What seem to be the most popular programs in each category? What are the most popular computer brand and printer type? Summarize your results with the rest of the class.

Lab Exercise 2. Survey 10 different ads in one or more computer magazines specializing in IBM PC type computers (e.g. PC, PC World, PC Week, etc.). Select retail ads that contain a variety of software and/or computer equipment. From these ads, attempt to determine the most popular brands of

a. Word processors
b. Database programs
c. Spreadsheet programs
d. Printers

CHAPTER 2

Getting to Know the IBM PC

CHAPTER OVERVIEW. This chapter introduces the main components of the IBM Personal Computer. Of particular interest are the keyboard, the types of monitors, the disk drives, and the inside of the computer cabinet.

CHAPTER OBJECTIVES

Upon completion of this chapter, you will be able to:

- Describe the various components of the IBM PC keyboard and their functions.
- Describe the most common monitor options available for the IBM PC type of computer.
- Describe the kinds of disk drives commonly used on the IBM PC type of computer.
- Describe some of the major components inside the IBM PC computer cabinet.
- Describe how to start up the computer.

THE PARTS OF THE PC

The IBM Personal Computer in its several configurations consists of three major parts. These are the computer cabinet, the monitor, and the keyboard. In the case of the Portable PC, the monitor is connected to the computer cabinet. Figures 2.1, 2.2, and 2.3 illustrate these major components on the IBM PC, the Convertible, and the PS2/Model 50. However, just like televisions and AM/FM radios, these parts come in different styles and with different features. It is important for the computer user to know what kinds of features are available on the various components. For example, some monitors are best for word processing, some are best for graphics, and some are just inexpensive. What best serves your computer needs? Similarly, there are different keyboards and different versions of computers with various features. In your use of computers, it is helpful to know some of these differences.

THE KEYBOARD

The keyboard is the primary input device to the computer. In the IBM PC family, there are at least four major versions of the keyboard: the original-style PC keyboard, the original-style AT keyboard, the Convertible keyboard and the Enhanced Personal Computer keyboard. All of these keyboards have four important areas: the function keys, the numeric keypad, the cursor pad(s), and the typewriter keys. Figure 2.4 illustrates the location of these parts on several versions of the keyboard.

The Typewriter Keys

The most familiar part of each version of the keyboard is the typewriter keys. These are the keys which are laid out like a typewriter keyboard. The long key on the bottom of the keyboard is called the space bar, and is used to type

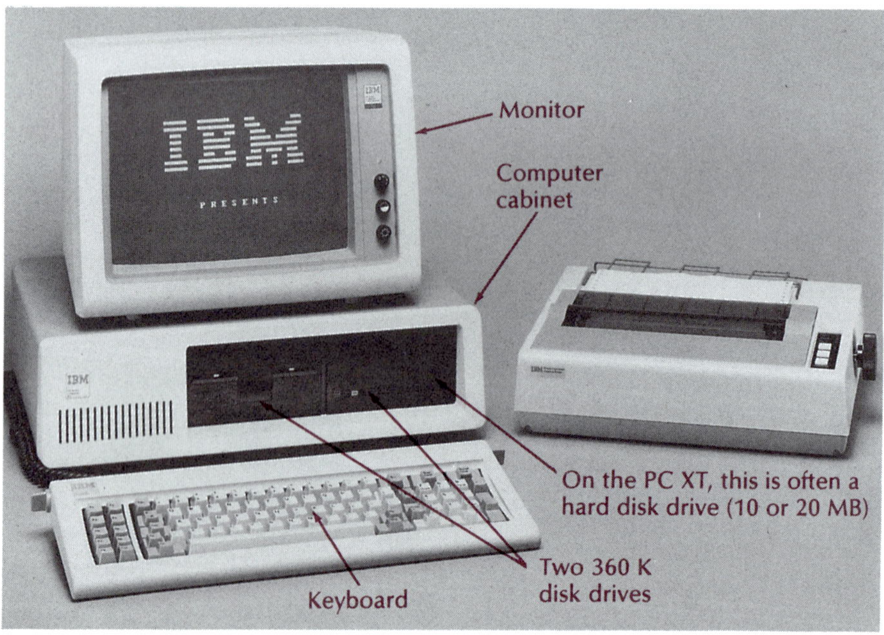

FIGURE 2.1. The IBM PC

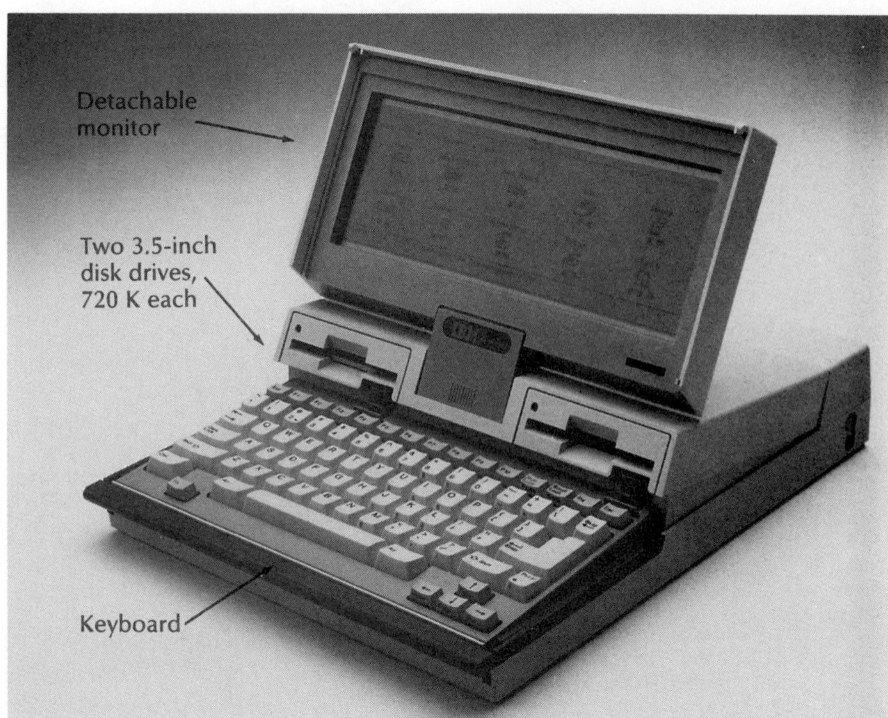

FIGURE 2.2.
The IBM PC convertible

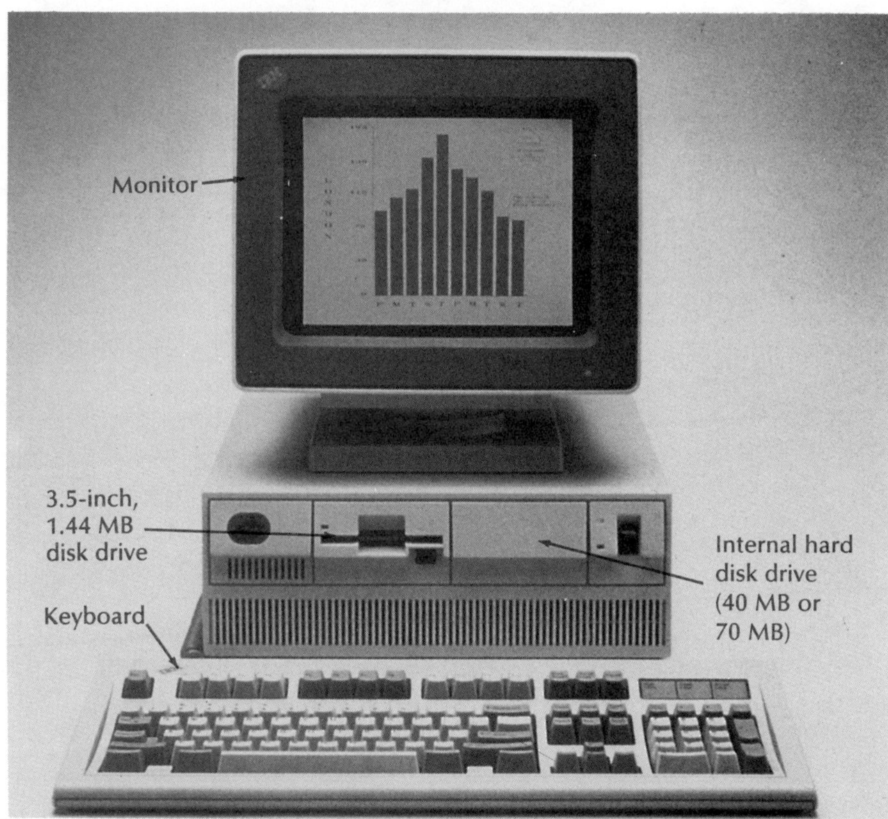

FIGURE 2.3.
The IBM PS/2 Model 50

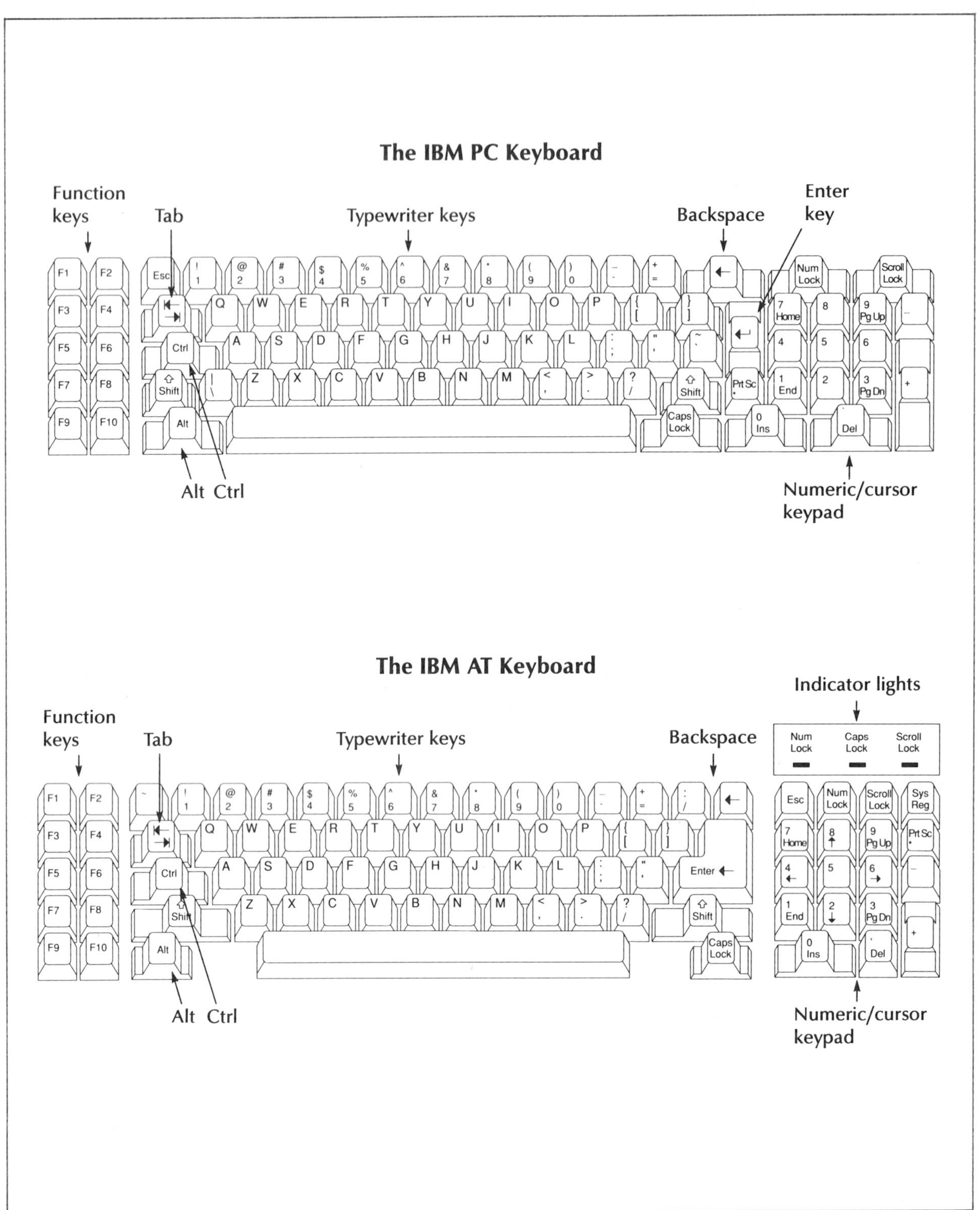

FIGURE 2.4.
IBM keyboards

The Enhanced XT/AT Keyboard

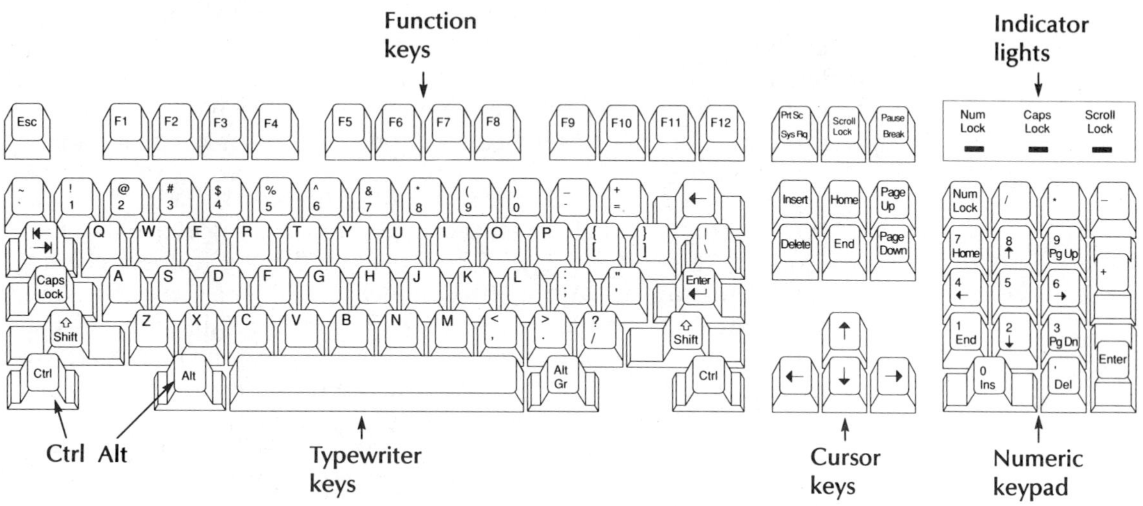

The PC Convertible Keyboard

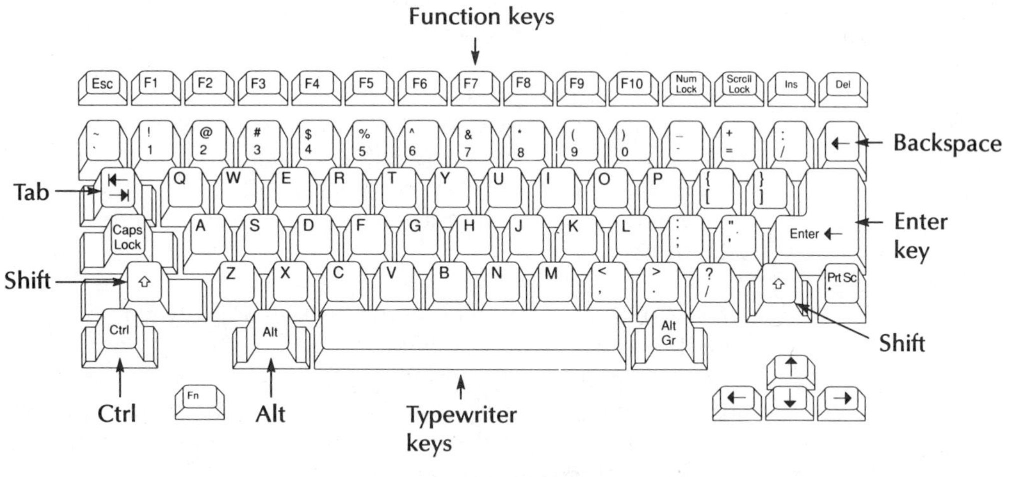

a space or blank. Above the space bar are the alphabet keys. The top row of keys are the number keys. Most keys have double meanings. For example, the alphabet keys can type upper or lowercase letters, such as "A" or "a".

The Shift Keys. On each side of the alphabet keys is a key with an arrow pointing up, as in figure 2.5. These are the Shift keys. They can change the meaning of some of the other keys on the keyboard. When the "A" key is pressed, the result is usually the lowercase letter "a". However, if the Shift key is depressed while the "A" key is pressed, the result will be the uppercase letter "A". The number keys at the top of the screen show their alternate meanings above each number. There are also several other keys which have two characters, such as the colon/semicolon key or less than/comma key.

The Caps Lock Key. To the right of the space bar is a key labeled "CAPS LOCK". This is a toggle key that changes the meaning of the Shift key. When CAPS LOCK is off, the SHIFT behaves as indicated in the preceding paragraph. Pressing the CAPS LOCK key once turns on the CAPS LOCK mode. On the AT or Enhanced keyboard, a green indicator light indicates that CAPS LOCK is on. On the other styles of keyboards, you don't know until you press another key. When CAPS LOCK is on, the meaning of the SHIFT key is reversed. Now if a letter key is pressed (without a SHIFT), an uppercase letter appears on the screen. With CAPS LOCK on and the SHIFT depressed, the "A" will result in the lowercase letter "a". The CAPS LOCK setting only affects the letter keys—number keys are not affected.

The Enter Key. The large key to the right of the typewriter keys is called the ENTER key. It is illustrated in figure 2.5 and is signified by the left-pointing arrow with a tail. This key is sometimes called the RETURN key or carriage return key. In most applications, the computer does not respond to what you type until you press this key.

The Backspace Key. Just above the ENTER key is a key with a left-pointing arrow, illustrated in figure 2.5. This is known as the backspace key, or correction key. During the typing of information, you may notice a mistake. Pressing this key backs the cursor up one space, erasing the last character typed. Repeated pressing will erase more characters, back to the beginning of the line if necessary.

The Tab Key. To the left of the "Q" key is a key with arrows pointing right and left, as illustrated in figure 2.5. This is the TAB key. It is usually but not always implemented in software to move the cursor over to the right to a certain preset column position. If this key is implemented in this way, pressing the TAB key will tab the position of the cursor to the right, and SHIFT-TAB will move the cursor to the left.

The CTRL and ALT Keys. The CTRL key (called the "Control" key) and the ALT key are special keys which are used like a SHIFT key. They are illustrated in figure 2.5. They change the meanings of certain keys. For example, a program may have a command called Control-P (also denoted as CTRL-P or

^P). To employ this command you would depress the CTRL key with one finger, and *while the CTRL is depressed,* you would press the "P" key once (do not hold it down more than a second). An ALT-P would be typed by holding the ALT key down, and pressing the "P" key. Control and ALT commands are common in many programs.

The Function Keys

On the standard PC and AT keyboards, there are ten keys to the left of the typewriter keys. These keys are labeled F1 to F10, and are known as the function keys. On the Enhanced keyboard, there are 12 function keys, located above the typewriter keys (see figure 2.4). These keys are used by application software to mean different things. For example, the F1 key may be implemented as the HELP key. In some applications you, the user, can program these keys to have meanings that will help you reduce the number of keystrokes you would normally take to give your program some command. In computer manuals, these function keys will be denoted by specifications such as "F1" or "Fn1". When you see this, it *does not* mean to press the F key, and then the 1 key—it means to press the function key labeled "F1".

The Numeric and Cursor Keypads

The bank of keys to the right of the typewriter keys doubles as both a numeric and a cursor keypad (see figure 2.4). A key located above this pad, labeled "NUM LOCK", controls the identity of these keys. When NUM LOCK is off, these keys are in cursor mode, and when the NUM LOCK key is on, the keys produce numbers. On the Enhanced keyboard, a green light indicates when the NUM LOCK is on; that is, when the keypad is in numeric mode. On the Enhanced and Convertible keyboards, separate cursor keys are also supported, in an inverted "T" configuration. They are always in cursor mode.

In cursor mode, the arrows on the keypad are used to move the cursor on the computer screen. This may be implemented in different ways in different software applications. In numeric mode, the keypad produces numbers, just like the number keys on the top row of the typewriter keys.

The keypad also contains other specialized keys. These keys have different meanings according to the software application program in use. Note that on the PC/AT keyboard, the ESC or Escape key is a part of this keypad, whereas on the PC keyboard, the Escape key is located to the far left of the typewriter keys, and on the Enhanced keyboard, the Escape key is to the far left, standing alone at the top of the keyboard.

Repeating Keys

The character keys on the keyboard are designed to repeat when depressed for more than an instant. Thus, if you press and hold the "A" key down, you will soon have a string of A's on the screen: AAAAAAAAAA. This is not true of the SHIFT, CTRL, ALT, CAPS LOCK, NUM LOCK, or SCROLL LOCK keys.

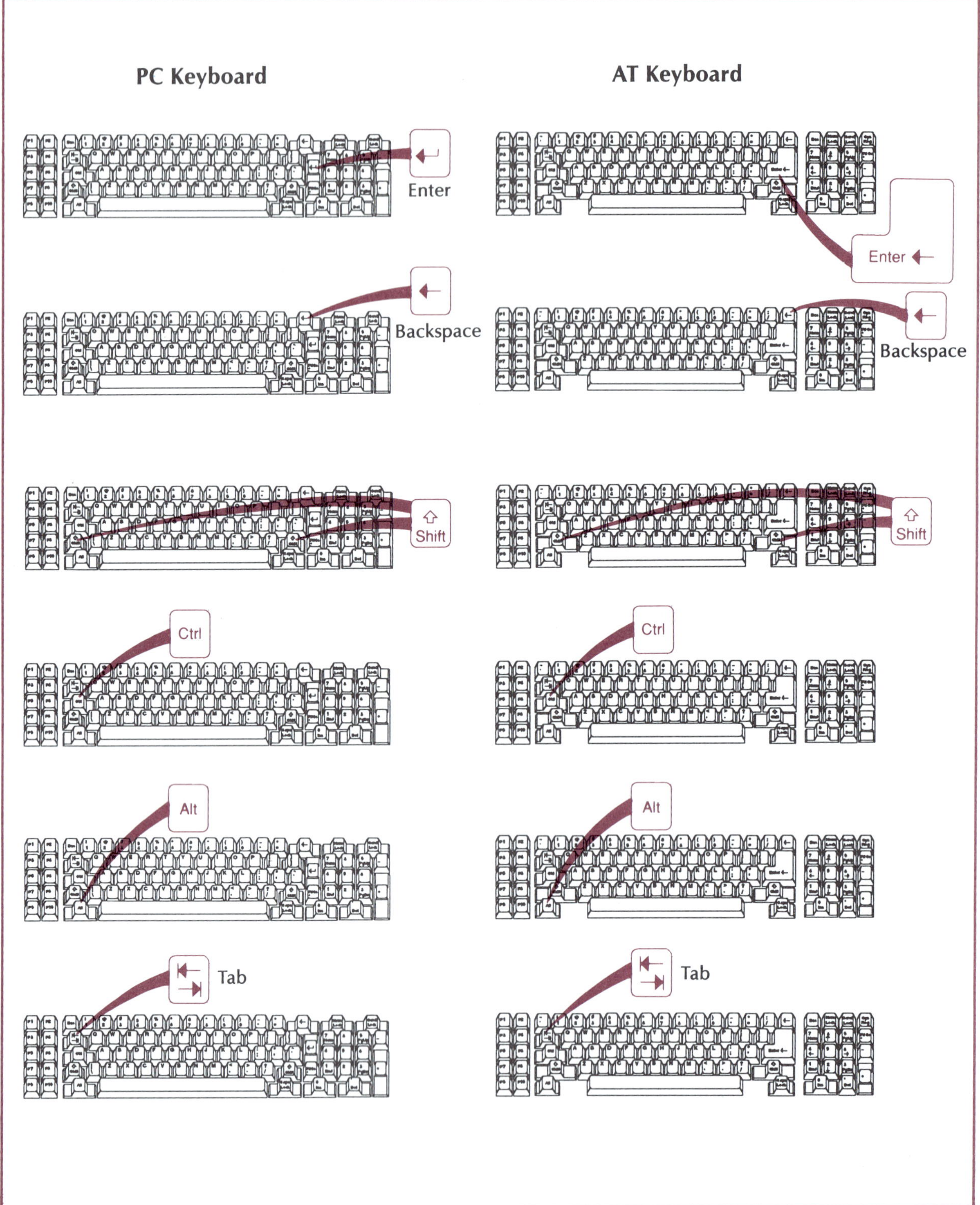

FIGURE 2.5.
Locations of special keys on four major types of IBM PC family keyboards

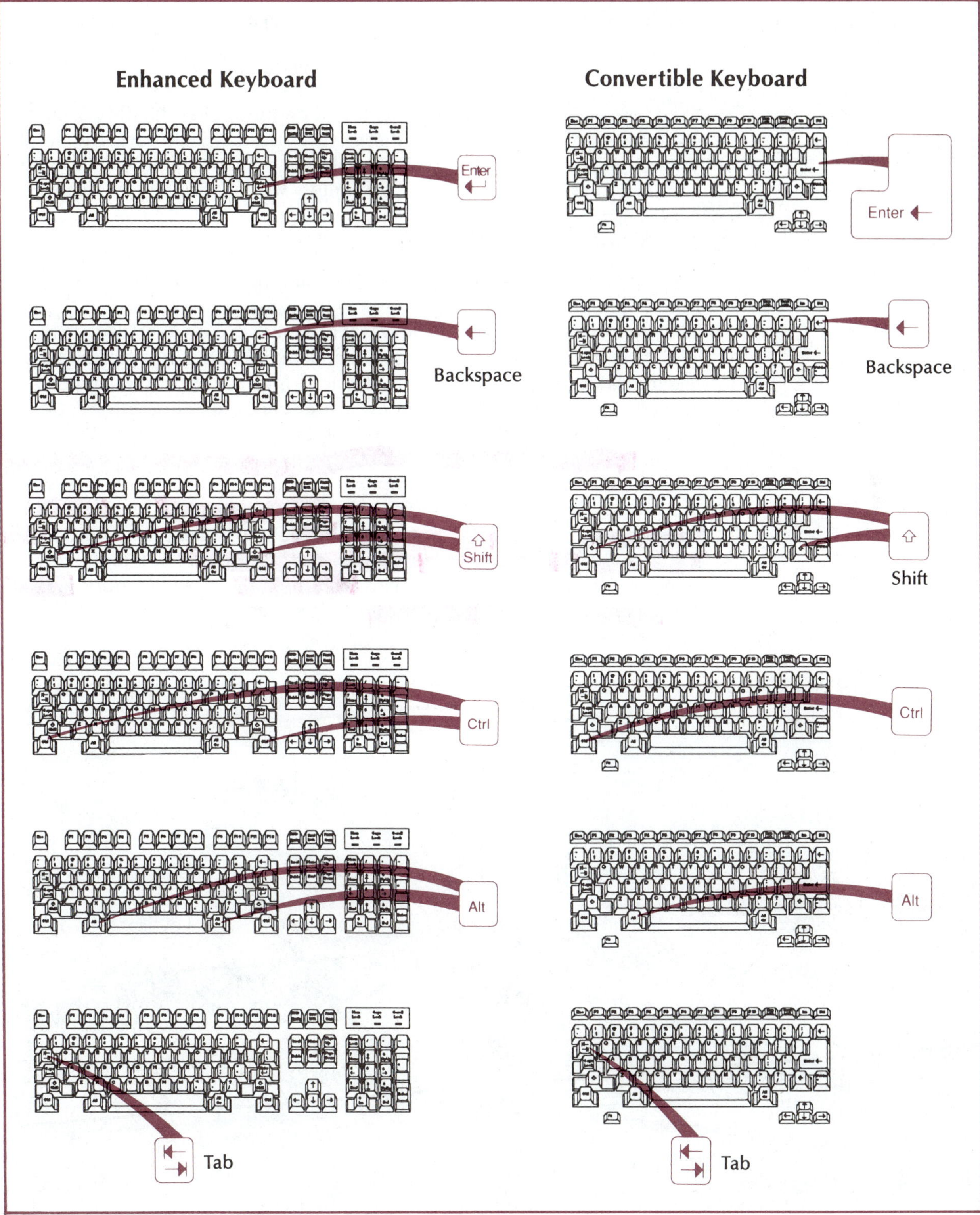
Enhanced Keyboard
Convertible Keyboard
Enter
Enter
Backspace
Backspace
Shift
Shift
Ctrl
Ctrl
Alt
Alt
Tab
Tab

Some people have a tendency to press and hold a key, as they can on a standard typewriter. If you do this, you may get too many keystrokes of that key.

THE COMPUTER MONITOR

There are several kinds of monitors found on the IBM PC family of computers, generally categorized into three types: the monochrome, the single-color graphics, and the multicolor graphics monitors (see figure 2.6). More information about the selection of monitors will be covered in chapter 11.

The Monochrome Monitor

The monochrome monitor, as its name implies, can only produce one color—green (or sometimes amber). However, another feature of the IBM-type monochrome monitor is the way it produces text on the screen. Character images, such as the letter A, are formed on the screen as a matrix of dots. The more dots used in forming the character image, the clearer it appears on the screen. The monochrome monitor used more dots in the formation of characters than did other early PC monitors.

The monochrome monitor is usually plugged in directly to the computer case, and comes on when the computer is turned on. It has no on/off switch of its own. This kind of monitor is the choice for those users doing text-oriented tasks such as word processing. With a special adapter called a "Hercules" board, it is possible to produce graphic images on a monochrome monitor. Characters are formed with higher clarity on this monitor than on the composite or RGB monitors, to be described in the following paragraphs.

FIGURE 2.6. Types of monitors

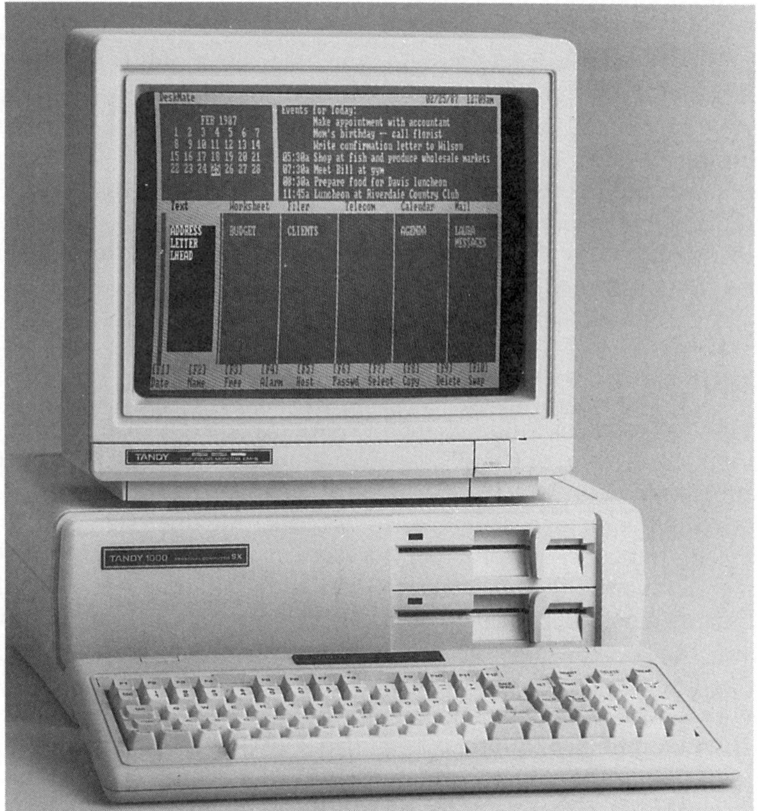

RGB Color Monitor

EGA Color Monitor

VGA Color Monitor

The Single-Color Graphics Monitor

The single-color graphics monitor, or composite monitor, typically produces one color, either green or amber. It is able to produce graphic images such as pie charts and pictures, which are not possible on the standard monochrome monitor. These are often called "pixel" graphics. A pixel is a single dot on the computer screen. Thus, a graphics monitor can control each dot on the screen separately, producing complex images. However, the text on this monitor is very poor. It would not be the choice for doing any textually-oriented computer work.

Color Monitors

Color monitors continue to increase their capabilities. The original color monitor available for IBM PC-type computers is called an RGB (Red, Green, Blue) monitor or CGA (Color Graphics Adapter). It is capable of producing both three-color graphic images (plus black) and up to sixteen colors of text. In terms of pixels, the CGA monitor has a maximum resolution of 600 by 200 pixels. However, the text on an CGA monitor still does not match the clarity of the original monochrome monitor. The text on a CGA monitor is formed with a matrix of 8 by 8 pixels per character. The next step up in color monitors is the Enhanced Graphics Monitor (EGA), which was introduced in 1984. An EGA monitor has a maximum resolution of 600 by 350 pixels. Characters on a EGA monitor are formed with a matrix of 8 by 14 pixels, and it gives the readability of the original monochrome monitor.

Beginning with the PS/2 series of IBM computers, a new variety of monitor was introduced, called Vector Graphics Adapter, (VGA). On this monitor, 256 colors can be displayed at one time from a selection of 262,144 possible colors. A VGA monitor has a maximum resolution of 640 by 480 pixels in graphics mode. It can produce spectacular color images, and the text is very nice.

INSIDE THE COMPUTER CABINET

The computer cabinet houses the "brains" of the computer. The actual heart of the IBM PC is a small microprocessor about the size of a pack of gum. From this chip, all other components of the computer are told what to do and when. In the IBM PC and Convertible, this is an Intel 8088 or 80C88 chip. In the IBM AT and the new version of the XT, it is an Intel 80286 chip. The microprocessor is located on a circuit board which lies horizontally near the bottom of the computer cabinet. It is called the "system board". Many other chips are connected to this board, each having some function in the running of the computer. Figure 2.7 illustrates the typical setup inside an IBM PC.

The Computer's Memory

In addition to the microprocessor chip, the system board contains computer memory. This is where information is stored, which tells the computer how to perform tasks. There are two basic kinds of memory, as mentioned earlier, called ROM (Read-Only Memory) and RAM (Random Access Memory). ROM

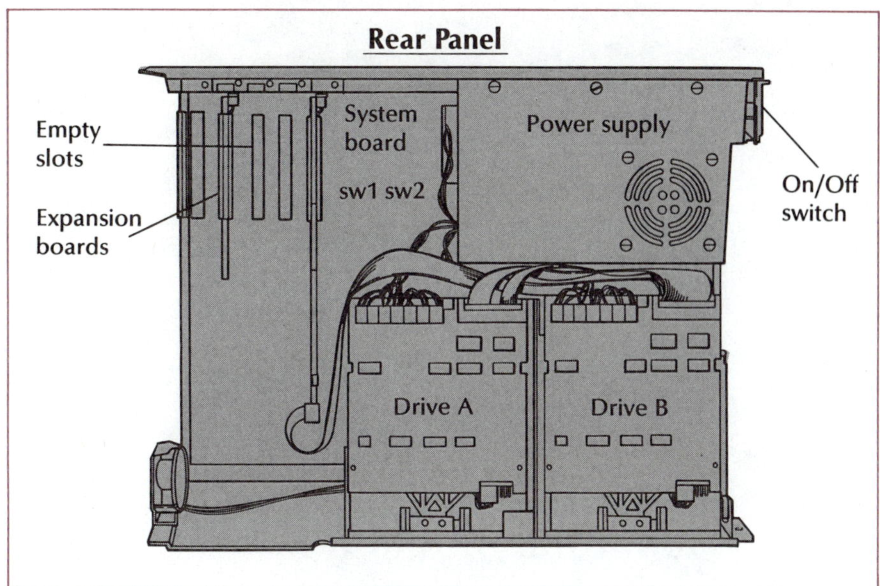

FIGURE 2.7.
Diagram of the inside of an IBM PC

is used to store instructions that are never changed, and must always be available to the computer. When the computer is turned on and "booted" it gets its first bits of information from ROM memory. RAM memory, on the other hand, is *volatile*; that is, when the computer is turned off, any information in RAM is lost. RAM is used to store information such as programs and data, which the computer is currently using. This information may be stored to disk or other devices before the computer is turned off.

The Expansion Slots

On the system board are several slots, or plugs, where other circuit boards can be connected to the system board. These boards may add extra memory, provide connection to a printer, provide access to a disk drive, or other functions. One of the factors making the IBM PC as successful as it has been is the ease with which a user may purchase and plug in peripheral boards to expand the functions of the computer. Figure 2.8 illustrates a typical expansion board. It is generally very easy to add a new feature to a PC by installing a new board. The new board is simply plugged in to an empty slot. Instructions for the board may also require that you set some switches that are located on the board, to match the kind of computer configuration you are using.

The Power Supply

The large rectangular box located at the back of the computer is the power supply. This box provides power to the various components of the computer, such as the system board and disk drives. Because most components of the PC operate on 6 to 12 volts, the power supply is necessary to "step down" the 110 volts from the wall to the range of volts needed for the computer. The

FIGURE 2.8.
Example of an expansion card

power supply is one of the most common items to need replacement in a PC. If you are handy with a screw driver, it takes only a few minutes to replace a power supply.

Other Things Inside the Computer Cabinet

Inside the computer cabinet is where all of the computing action takes place. With all of these things happening, it may get warm in there. You may notice a number of vent slots in the cabinet, and a fan in the back of the cabinet. These items are there to insure adequate ventilation. An enemy of the computer is dust. If these vents get full of dust, the computer may heat up, and components may fail. Therefore, it is important to vacuum the slots on occasion, and to keep the computer out of a dusty or warm environment.

There are several other items in the cabinet that you may be called upon to deal with. In the system board, there are often open chip slots that can be filled with extra memory or processors. In particular, if you are using software that does lots of mathematical calculations, you may want to plug in a chip called a math coprocessor to the system board. If your computer does not contain its full share of memory, you may want to add memory chips to the system board. Although you do need to be careful when adding or changing components in the computer cabinet, the IBM PC computer was built to allow you easily to access and change its components.

THE DISK DRIVES

A typical PC contains one or more disk drives. These may be floppy disk drives or hard (fixed) disks. These disk drives get power from the power supply, and are connected to the computer by a ribbon cable to a controller card, which is plugged into one of the expansion slots provided on the system board. Since disk drives usually require a large amount of wattage from the power supply, the addition of more than two to a computer may require that you also add a higher-wattage power supply to the computer to provide adequate power.

The most common method of data storage on microcomputers today is the 5.25-inch floppy diskette. Even those computers with hard disks often use floppy diskettes for backup or data transfer. In the future, the 3.5-inch disk may become the standard.

The Names of the Disk Drives

Disk drives are given single-letter names, followed by a colon, such as A:, B:, C:, etc. On a two-disk-drive PC, the left drive is A: and the right drive is B:. On a standard XT with a hard disk, the left drive functions as both A: and B:, while the hard disk is drive C:. On an AT two floppy drives are located to the right, with the top drive being A: and the bottom B:. The internal hard disk is named C:. On a PCjr, the sole drive operates as both A: and B:. These names can be different, depending on how your machine is configured. Standard disk drive names are illustrated in figure 2.9.

Kinds of Disk Drives

There are at least three basic designs for diskette drives. The first two types use floppy diskettes. The full-height drive, which is about three inches tall,

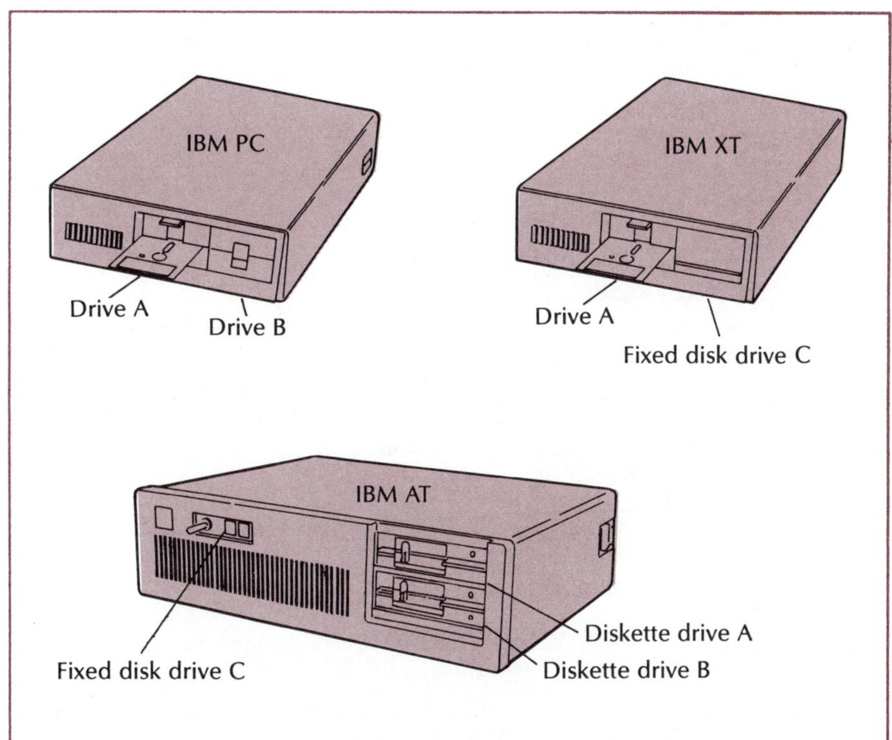

FIGURE 2.9.
Disk drive names

has a small door or flap that must be opened in order to insert or remove a diskette. A half-height drive has a knob which must be turned to allow the insertion of a diskette. Usually these drives use double-sided double-density (DS/DD) diskettes, which store about 360K of information. The IBM PC/AT also supports floppy diskette drives which use 1.2MB (megabyte) diskettes. With the introduction of DOS 3.2, IBM began supporting the 3.5-inch diskette. This diskette, although smaller than the 5.25-inch standard diskette, holds 720K or 1.44MB of memory. These types of disk drives are illustrated in figure 2.10.

THE MASTER DISKETTE—DOS

The computer is basically dumb. It only has enough knowledge stored in ROM to understand how to begin "coming to life". The real information that tells the computer how to operate is stored on disk. This can be either on a diskette or on a hard disk. The information is referred to as DOS, or Disk Operating System. In the IBM PC family of computers, this is called PC-DOS. On most clone computers, the operating system is called MS-DOS. They are virtually identical. The information contained in DOS tells the computer how to operate. The procedure of turning on a computer and loading DOS is called *booting* the computer.

FIGURE 2.10.
Three Kinds of Disk Drives

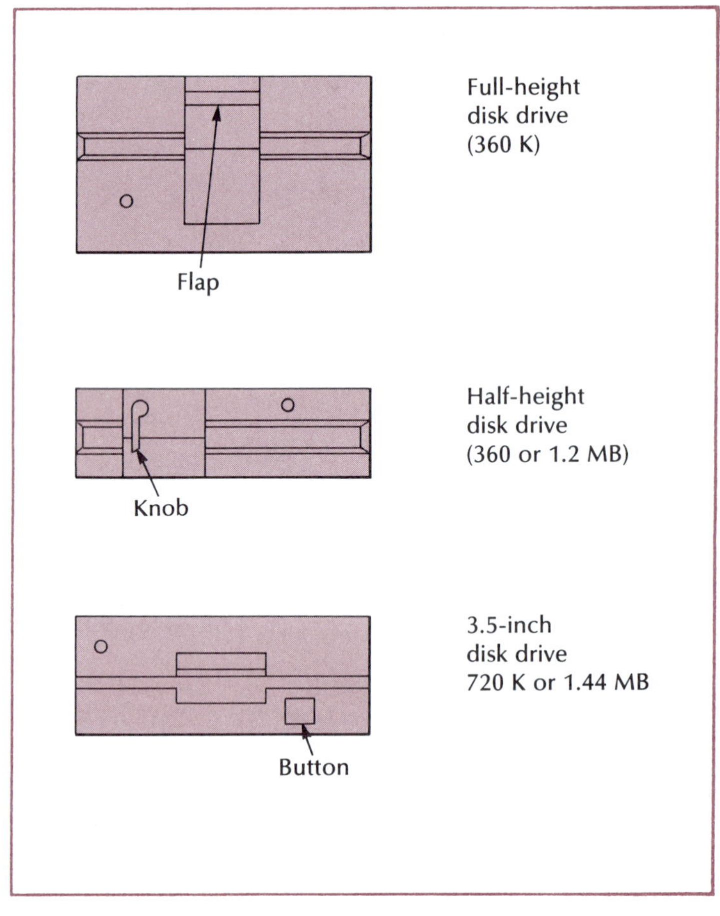

If you are using a floppy-based system, you need to insert a DOS diskette in the A: drive each time you turn the computer on. The DOS diskette comes with your system. In fact, you will usually have two DOS disks, one labeled "Supplemental Programs". *Do not boot* with that diskette. Use the other one. You will probably boot the system with copies of the original diskette rather than the original diskette.

If you are using a hard-disk system, the DOS system must be on the hard disk for the computer to boot without a diskette. Chances are DOS has already been placed on your disk, and you simply need to turn the computer on for it to boot itself and come to life.

How to Hold a Diskette

Hold the DOS disk, or any disk for that matter, by the label with the label facing up, as in figure 2.11. Make sure the drive door or knob on the A: drive is open, and carefully slide the diskette into place. When it is almost in, it requires an additional push to seat it properly into place. Once the diskette is in place, close the drive door or knob. *Do not* force the drive closed. If you have trouble closing the door, wiggle the diskette in place, and try again.

Proper Care for Floppy Diskettes

Have you ever seen what happens to a record when it is left out on the dashboard of a car on a 100-degree August day? It is not a pretty sight. Diskettes, like records, require some special care. Diskettes are made of a thin sheet of plastic covered with a magnetic coating. A small head in the disk drive reads

FIGURE 2.11.
How to hold a diskette

and writes magnetic signals. This process is very sensitive to foreign particles such as hair, dust, and smoke. When working with diskettes, there are some standard precautions you should take:

1. Never touch the magnetic surface of the diskette with your fingers. Always keep it in its sleeve when not in use. The 3.5-inch diskettes do not require sleeves.
2. Never expose a diskette to a magnetic field (this can erase your data). This includes a speaker, a radio, anything with a motor, etc.
3. Do not bend the diskette.
4. Keep the diskette in its jacket to keep it away from foreign particles.
5. Never let the diskette get too hot or cold. An acceptable range is 50 to 120 degrees Fahrenheit.
6. Be careful not to subject the disk to moisture.

Caring for 3.5-inch Diskettes

Care for the 3.5-inch diskette is somewhat simpler than for the 5.25-inch floppy diskette. This diskette has a spring-loaded flap covering the magnetic portion of the disk, so that it is not exposed when out of the disk drive. This makes it less vulnerable to dust, fingerprints, and other foreign materials. Nevertheless, you must be careful not to expose it to extremes of temperature, moisture (e.g., coffee spills), or magnets.

TURNING ON THE COMPUTER

Once the DOS disk is in place, you can turn on the power to the computer. On the PC, XT, and AT the on/off switch is on the right panel of the computer cabinet, toward the back of the cabinet. On some versions of the computer, you must also turn on the monitor (and printer, etc).

At first, nothing seems to happen when the computer is turned on. It is going through a self-test procedure called POST (Power-On Self-Test). This self-test is directed by the information stored in ROM memory. Soon, a blinking underline appears at the top left of the screen. On some versions of the computer, you may see the computer count its memory, with numbers appearing at the upper left corner of the screen. It takes as long as a minute for the self-test to finish.

After a while, the computer produces a single "beep". The red light on the floppy diskette (or hard disk) comes on. This indicates that the computer is reading the DOS information from the disk into its memory (RAM). Finally, copyright information appears on the screen, and you are ready to compute! A typical opening screen for an IBM PC is illustrated in figure 2.12. If the computer does not have a built-in clock, it may require that you enter the date and time, which will be discussed later.

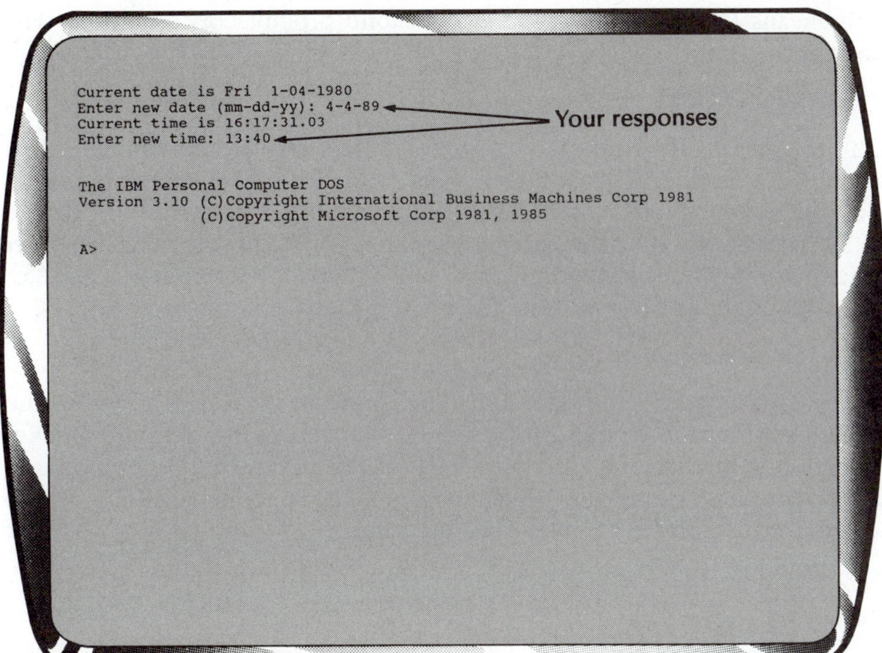

Current date is Fri 1-04-1980
Enter new date (mm-dd-yy): 4-4-89
Current time is 16:17:31.03
Enter new time: 13:40
Your responses
The IBM Personal Computer DOS
Version 3.10 (C)Copyright International Business Machines Corp 1981
(C)Copyright Microsoft Corp 1981, 1985
A>

FIGURE 2.12.
Typical boot screen

Something Went Wrong?

If the scenario described above does not take place, or an error message appears on the screen, something is wrong! Don't panic. Check to make sure that the proper diskette is in the computer, and that it is properly in place, with the disk drive closed. Check to see if all plugs are properly plugged in tightly. Turn the computer off. Carefully try again.

If you turn on the computer without a DOS diskette in place, the computer will be in the BASIC language. The copyright for BASIC will appear, along with an "Ok". If this happens, make sure your DOS diskette is properly in place, and try again.

Entering the Date and Time

Some computers have a clock which automatically sets the date and time. If this is the case with your computer, you may skip this explanation.

The computer will ask for information concerning the date and time (see figure 2.12). Its first prompt is:

```
Enter new date (mm-dd-yy):
```

The proper way to enter a date is Month-Date-Year, using numbers to signify each component. For example:

```
Enter new date (mm-dd-yy):10-23-90
```

This means October 23rd, 1990. The second prompt concerns time. The prompt is:

```
Enter new time:
```

On the IBM PC, time is measured in the military way. Hours from midnight to noon are numbered from 0 to 12, and hours from one o'clock to eleven o'clock are numbered 13 to 23. Thus, if the time is 3:30 p.m., military time is 15:30. That is, add 12 to the 3 to get 15. The minutes stay the same. To enter time, place a colon between the hour and minute. Do not put an "a.m." or "p.m." designation. To enter the time 3:30 p.m. type:

```
Enter new time:15:30
```

It is possible to skip the date and time question by simply pressing the ENTER key for each prompt. However, the system uses this date and time information to mark files created or accessed. For backup and reference purposes, date and time are vital. If your computer does not have a clock, always take the extra moment to enter date and time.

Types of Prompts

Once you have answered the date and time questions, the computer should respond with a *DOS prompt*. This will be

```
A>
```

on a diskette-booted system, or

```
C>
```

on a hard-disk-booted system. The "A > " or "C > " tells you which disk drive you are "logged into". This can be changed, as you will discover later.

Your computer may not display these prompts. Instead, it may present a menu of options. The PC can be configured to display a picture menu, allowing you to select your choice of tasks from this menu. One of the prompts will be "DOS". If you choose this option, you will exit the menu program, and get a DOS prompt like the ones described previously.

THIS IS ONLY THE BEGINNING

Now that you have successfully booted the computer, it is at your command. However, you must know what commands the computer will understand. The next chapter will discuss more capabilities of the Disk Operating System.

SUMMARY

The microcomputer is made up of a number of components. There are a variety of monitors, disk drives, and keyboards that may be used with the computer. The central piece of software required to operate the computer is DOS, the disk operating system. DOS is required to boot the computer.

KEY TERMS

Define the following terms in your own words:

Computer cabinet

Monitor

Keyboard

Control command

System board

Expansion slot

Power supply

Math co-processor

DOS

POST

Military time

QUESTIONS

Write a short answer in your own words for each of the following questions.

1. What governs the meanings of the keys on the numeric pad to the right of the typewriter keys?
2. If CAPS LOCK is on, what do you get when you press the "T" key? the ";" key? the "3" key on the top row? With CAPS LOCK on, what do you get if you press a SHIFT-T?
3. Why is DOS needed when the computer is turned on?
4. What are some precautions to take when working with a diskette?
5. If the time is 5:45 p.m., what would the time be according to the computer's clock (military time)? What about 12:30 in the morning? Why is it important to make sure the date and time are correct?
6. What happens if you hold a keyboard key down for several seconds?
7. What is the purpose of the function keys? Why do they change meanings?
8. As described in the text, what kind of monitor can produce the most colors? What kind of adapter do you need to be able to produce graphic images on a monochrome monitor? Of the computer monitors discussed, which ones are capable of producing the best text?
9. What is the POST? When does it occur? Where does the computer get instructions for how to do the POST?
10. What are expansion slots used for? Give some examples.
11. Explain how the information on a diskette can be lost.
12. What happens if an IBM PC is turned on, and the DOS diskette is not available?

LABORATORY EXERCISES

Lab Exercise 1. Inventory the following items on the personal computer to which you have access:

a. What kind of monitor does it have?
b. What kind of floppies does it use? How much storage capacity do the disks have?
c. What are the names of the floppy drives and/or hard-disk drives?
d. If there is a printer attached, what kind is it? (Dot matrix (9-pin or 24-pin?), laser, key-impact, etc.)
e. What other peripherals are attached to the computer?

CHAPTER 3

Introduction to DOS, Part I

CHAPTER OVERVIEW. This is the first of two chapters that discuss the Disk Operating System: PC-DOS, or MS-DOS. This chapter will introduce the concept of the operating system, and will discuss the syntax of DOS commands. The most commonly used DOS commands will also be introduced.

CHAPTER OBJECTIVES

Upon completion of this chapter, you will be able to:

- Describe the purpose of PC-DOS/MS-DOS, and list some of its specific uses.
- Describe a disk file and know how to use correct file names.
- Describe the use of global file characters.
- Describe the two basic rules of DOS command syntax.
- Describe the use of the DOS commands DIR, ERASE, FORMAT, COPY, and RENAME.
- Describe how to change default disk drives.
- Describe the difference between internal and external DOS commands.

MANAGING RESOURCES

Computer resources must be managed just like any other resource. For example, consider these everyday occurrences:

1. Mary drove up to the drive-in window at the First National Bank of Silicon Valley. She had the day's earnings from her bakery. She made out the deposit ticket, and gave the ticket and cash to the teller. She felt sure that when the time came she could go back to the bank, and they would return her money.
2. At the swimming pool, Harry checks in people's shoes and other things, and puts them in a metal basket for safekeeping while they are swimming in the pool. When someone checks in their personal items, Harry gives the swimmer a little tag with a number on it. When the swimmer returns the tag to him, he knows where to look for their basket of things.
3. Terry is the office manager. When something needs to be filed, it is given to Terry, who places it in the proper place in the file cabinets. When someone wants something back, they ask Terry for the file, Terry looks through the cabinet and returns the file to whoever wanted it. Terry also copies files, and gets rid of old files when asked.

Mary, Harry, and Terry were all involved in similar tasks—storing something and getting it back. The same kind of thing goes on all around us every day. Information is just one more thing that needs to be stored somewhere so that it can later be retrieved. Since the computer mainly deals with information, it makes sense that it has a "manager" that puts information somewhere, and retrieves it again when needed. On the IBM Personal Computer, the manager is called the Disk Operating System, or DOS (pronounced "doss") for short. PC-DOS manages the resources of the IBM Personal Computer. Some computers use a virtually equivalent DOS called MS-DOS, which stands for Microsoft DOS. Microsoft is the company that designed DOS for the IBM family of personal computers.

MANAGING RESOURCES ON A COMPUTER

On a personal computer, information is usually stored on disk in the form of computer files. Somehow the computer needs to keep track of the names and locations of the files on disk. Also, there needs to be some facility for making copies of files, erasing files, and performing other managerial functions concerning the resources of the computer. DOS manages these resources under the direction of you, the computer operator.

You must direct the "manager's" activities. What needs to be filed? What needs to be erased? What needs to be copied? The manager will not make those decisions—you make the decisions. You are the computer operator. That means that you have a powerful array of things you can do with the computer, but it also means that you are responsible for making sure that all the necessary tasks on the computer are performed, like putting the right diskette in the right disk drive, backing up the information, and loading software. You will be responsible for knowing what commands to use to tell DOS what to do. Although there are dozens of possible commands, it usually takes an understanding of only a handful of commands to make the computer accomplish the tasks you have in mind.

This chapter will concentrate on those few commands that are most necessary in the everyday use of DOS.

DOS Changes Over Time

When the IBM PC was first introduced in October of 1981, it operated under the PC-DOS operating system, version 1.0. Since that time, there have been several changes in PC-DOS, and newer versions have been released. Because you will likely find several versions in use in any business or university, it is helpful to know some of the differences that exist between the various versions. Some earlier versions of PC-DOS are not fully compatible with the newer versions.

Why do they keep changing it? The primary reason for changing DOS is so that it will support new devices that are introduced on new versions of the PC. Usually, this has to do with advancements in disk storage. For example, when the PC was first introduced, it supported only single-sided diskettes—diskettes that stored information only on one side. When two-sided disks were introduced, it required a new version of DOS, and DOS version 1.1 was released. Along with supporting new disk devices, new versions of DOS have also improved and changed some other features, such as support for new kinds of monitors and other peripherals.

The various changes in PC-DOS are outlined in figure 3.1. Usually, changes in DOS are considered "upwardly compatible." That is, new versions of DOS are able to read information from disks created with old versions of DOS. However, the opposite may or may not be true. For example, a major change was made in DOS 2.0 in the way information is stored on disk. This means that a diskette prepared with DOS 2.0 cannot be read on a machine using DOS 1.1 or DOS 1.0. Another drastic change in operating systems is the introduction of the OS/2 operating system. It is not really a new

FIGURE 3.1.
The Versions of PC-DOS

Version	Primary Feature
1.0	Supports single-sided diskettes (160K)
1.1	Supports 2-sided diskettes (320K)
2.0	Supports hard disks and a sub-directory file structure (2-sided disks now 360K)
2.1	Supports the half-height diskettes on the IBM PCjr.
3.0	Supports the 1.2 megabyte (MB) floppy and other new functions of the IBM PC AT.
3.1	Supports networking.
3.2	Supports 760K 3.5-inch disks, laptop computer.
3.3	Supports 1.44MB 3.5-inch floppy, and the PS/2 series of computers.
4.0	Supports pull-down menus and hard disk drive use past the previous 32MB limit.
OS/2	A new operating system to support multi-tasking and more memory.

version of DOS, but it is a close and more sophisticated relative. This operating system was introduced with the IBM PS/2 series of computers. The OS/2 operating system allows access to more memory on the PS/2 computers (and older PC AT's), and the operation of more than one program at once (multitasking). An overview of the OS/2 operating system is given in chapter 12.

SPECIFIC USES OF DOS

The computer hardware by itself does not "know" how to do many tasks. What it can do is match patterns of 0's and 1's, and those patterns can be made to cause the computer to follow commands that programmers have stored in its memory. It is able to follow those commands very fast. Since the computer knows so little, there has to be a way to "teach" it quickly what to do. That is what happens when the computer is "booted". We discussed booting briefly in chapter 2, and now we will describe it in more detail.

Booting

Within the PC, there is a small amount of information always present in its ROM (Read-Only Memory). This memory includes BIOS (Basic Input Output System), and some other diagnostic and language programs. This memory does *not* contain DOS. How then can the computer operate? If we were to turn the computer on, it would know how to do very little, because it would only have the most primitive instructions. That is the reason that DOS must be loaded into memory every time the computer is turned on. In computer jargon, loading DOS into the memory is called "booting" the machine, which comes from the old saying "pulling yourself up by your own bootstraps." The computer knows enough to look for DOS on a disk in the disk drive, and to begin to read it. It "pulls itself" to life by reading its instructions from the DOS program on disk. The booting process occurs when the computer is turned on, or when special keystrokes are given to tell it to re-boot after it has already been turned on.

Figure 3.2 illustrates what happens to memory when the computer is booted. Before the computer is turned on, its RAM (Random Access Memory) contains nothing. When the computer reads DOS from disk, it stores part of that information in RAM. This part of RAM is now reserved for DOS, and as long as the computer is on, it cannot be used for any other program. The remainder of RAM is reserved for other programs to use. This means that if a computer has 640K of RAM, and DOS takes up 30K of RAM, then only 610K is left for the actual running of application programs.

Once DOS is loaded into memory from your diskette, the computer can perform many management functions. Most of these functions are ways of accessing and manipulating information on disk. Before discussing what specific tasks DOS can do, you must first understand the concept of computer files.

FILES ON DISK

A *file* is a fundamental concept in understanding how a computer operates. You can compare a computer file with files that are used in the workplace. Almost everyone is familiar with files in a file cabinet. Those little manila folders with the tabs on top have been used in offices for over a hundred years

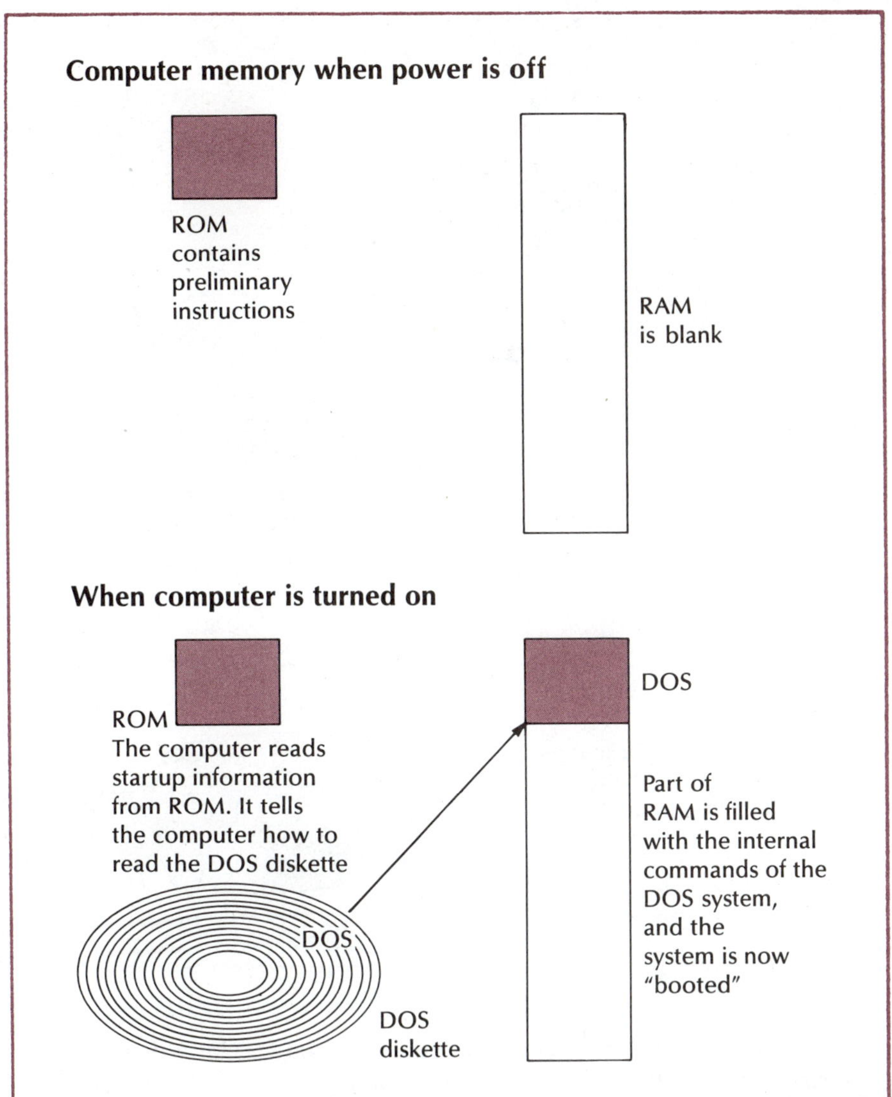
Computer memory when power is off
ROM
contains
preliminary
instructions
RAM
is blank
When computer is turned on
ROM
The computer reads
startup information
from ROM. It tells
the computer how to
read the DOS diskette
DOS
DOS
diskette
DOS
Part of
RAM is filled
with the internal
commands of the
DOS system,
and the
system is now
"booted"

FIGURE 3.2.
Booting DOS into the computer

(see figure 3.3). The folders contain information about some person, item, contract, etc. Some identifying name is written on the folder's tab. If the folder contains the budget for May of 1989, the tab may read "BUDGET MAY 89". If the folder contains a copy of the annual report it may read "ANNUAL REPORT". The name on the tab gives a short description of the contents of the file. Files are not usually placed in the file drawers at random. All of the budget files may be in one drawer, while all of the report files are in another drawer. In fact, one whole file cabinet may be reserved for reports, while another contains only financial information.

Using the illustration of the manila folder, it is easy to understand the concept of a computer file. Like a physical file, a computer file contains information. It may be your resumé, your monthly budget, an economics report, or a software program. Instead of having physical pieces of paper, the file consists of the electronically stored information on the disk. Just like the

FIGURE 3.3.
Office files and computer files

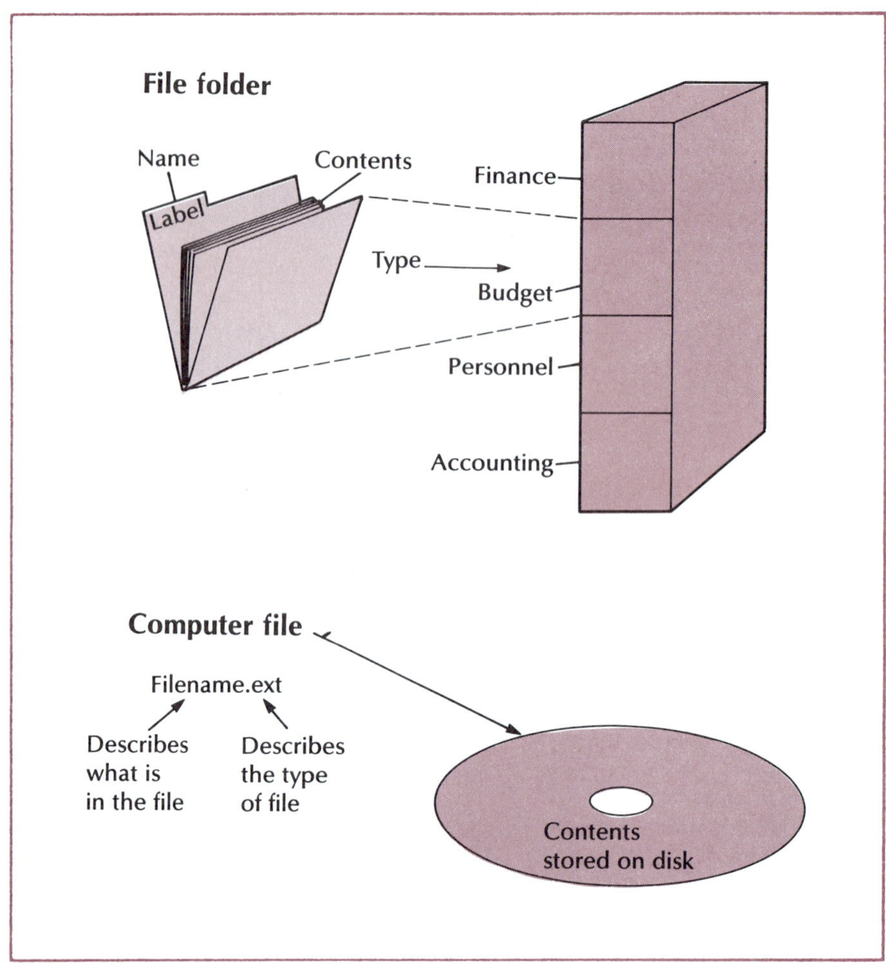

folder tabs, each file has a name, called a "filename". The filename usually describes briefly what is in the file (in 8 characters or less). Your resumé may be named "RESUME", while the May 1989 budget may be named "BUDMAY89".

File Types

What kind of file is it? How do you tell letters from budgets? In the case of computer files, there is a second part to the name, called the *extension*, that can be used to specify the type of information in the file (although that is not the only use of the extension). The extension has up to three characters and is separated from the filename with a period. Thus the RESUME file may be specified as "RESUME.JOB". This extended name is called the *file specification*, or filespec for short. File extensions tell you and/or the computer what kind of information is in the computer file. There are some conventions, or common standards, of how extensions are used. For example, files on disk that contain DOS commands usually end with the extension ".COM", meaning command. BASIC language programs end with the extension ".BAS". Files that contain textual material may use the extension ".TXT", and so on. Figure 3.4 lists some of the common extensions in use. Notice that many file extensions are not required. They can be whatever you decide is appropriate, or you can choose not to have an extension at all. You may want to call data files ".DAT" or ".DTA". It usually makes little difference. However, there are some kinds of files that DOS expects with a certain extension. You will need to be aware of the extensions that DOS has specified for a particular use, so you can choose your own extensions without causing conflicts with these predefined extensions.

File Specifications. **File specifications consist of one to eight characters, (the filename), plus an optional extension of up to three characters. The filename and the extension are separated by a period. Examples are:**
MYFILE.DOC
COMMAND.COM
SIMPLE
REQUEST.LET
080989.DAT

Permitted characters for file names include all letters and numbers (UPPERCASE and lowercase are considered the same), plus any other characters on the keyboard *except*

```
.''/\[]:|<>+=; and ,
```

A space in a filename is sometimes allowed by programs, but it is not universally allowed, so it should be avoided. Some of these restricted characters, like the dot ".", are used at specific points in a file specification. The dot is used to separate a filename from the extension. The uses of other special characters will be discussed later.

Common Extensions Expected by DOS:	
filename.COM	A command program (i.e., DOS commands)
filename.EXE	An executable program (software)
filename.BAS	A BASIC language program
filename.BAT	A BATCH command file (a type of DOS file)
OTHER CONVENTIONS YOU OR YOUR SOFTWARE DECIDE UPON:	
filename.TXT	A "text" file (standard ASCII)
filename.DBF	A dBASE database file
filename.WKS	A Lotus 1-2-3 spreadsheet file
filename.PRN	A Lotus print-to-disk file

FIGURE 3.4.
Extensions for computer file names

File names should be selected which describe the contents of the file, and extensions (if used) should tell what kind of file it is. When using related files, it is also desirable to select names that are similar. For example, if you were writing a three-part paper, you might want to name the files

PART1.TXT		PART.1
PART2.TXT	or	PART.2
PART3.TXT		PART.3

If you were collecting monthly data, you might want to call the files containing the information

MAY89.DAT		MAY.89
JUNE89.DAT	or	JUNE.89
JULY89.DAT		JULY.89

Global File Characters

One major reason for selecting such similar names is the ability to manipulate groups of files at one time. If the files are named with similar names, DOS will allow the user to specify more than one file at a time using *wild cards* or *global file characters*. These global file characters are the asterisk "*" and the question mark"?". Like a wild card in a poker game, or the blank file in the game of Scrabble, the "*" and "?" can mean any character. The asterisk "*" can substitute for any number of characters, and the question mark "?" can substitute for one character. Perhaps this is best explained with an example. If you wanted to copy all of your data files from one disk to another, you would have to tell DOS by name which files to copy. Suppose your files were named

JAN, FEB, MAR, ... , DEC

Then to copy all twelve files would take twelve commands, each command specifying one file to copy. However, if the files were named

JAN.DAT, FEB.DAT, MAR.DAT, ... , DEC.DAT

all of the files could be copied using the one file specification "*.DAT". The specification "*.DAT" means all files, no matter what the filename, as long as the extension is ".DAT". In the same way, if the files were named

DAT.JAN, DAT.FEB, ... , DAT.DEC

then the specification "DAT.*" would address all of the files with filename "DAT", and with any extension. The other wild card, "?", replaces only one character. Thus the specification, "???.DAT" would substitute for up to three characters in a filename. It would select J.DAT, JA.DAT, and JAN.DAT, but not "JANU.DAT" or "JANUARY.DAT", since they have more than three characters in the filenames.

The wild card specification "*.*" selects all files of all filenames and extensions. Specific uses of wild cards will be given as DOS commands are introduced.

DOS AS A COMMAND LANGUAGE

So far we have seen that PC-DOS acts as a "manager", keeping track of files in the computer. However, it cannot act until it is instructed to do so—and you, the user, are the one, who will usually give DOS those instructions.

Like a programming language, PC-DOS has *commands* to specify tasks for the computer. What is a command? A DOS command is usually a word (often a verb) that tells DOS what you want it to do. Sometimes the command is followed by one or more other words that clarify what task the command is to perform. For example, the command, CHKDSK (Check Disk) tells DOS to check the files on disk, and that command can stand alone without any other information. On the other hand, the command COPY requires that you also specify what to copy, so the command must be followed by some additional words.

DOS Prompts

Before you can enter a command, you must be sure the computer is ready to accept your instructions. When the *DOS prompt* is visible on the computer screen, it means that DOS is waiting for you to type in a DOS command (or a program command). The DOS prompt is usually a letter (A,B,C etc) followed by the " > " symbol. Thus, the prompt:

```
A>
```

means that DOS is waiting for instructions. The "A" tells you that the A disk drive is the "logged in" drive or the "default" drive. That means that if DOS needs to look on disk for some information, it will automatically look on the A: drive, unless you direct it to look somewhere else. If you are using a hard-disk system, the default disk drive is usually C:, and the prompt will be:

```
C>
```

specifying that you are currently logged in to the C: drive.

DOS Commands and Syntax

Once a prompt has appeared, you can type a DOS command on the keyboard. It will appear on the screen just after the prompt. For example, the command to get a directory of the names of the files on disk is "DIR". Therefore, to tell DOS to display the directory of the disk, enter the command

```
C>DIR
```

and press the ENTER key. DOS will then display the names of the files on the disk in drive C: on the screen. The ENTER key must be pressed at the end of each command.

It is very important to type DOS commands correctly—to use correct *syntax*. DOS is very restrictive about its syntax, and it will not understand your command unless you follow its rules carefully. The first rule of DOS syntax concerns the names of disk drives. For example, you can add more information to the DIR command to ask DOS to display a directory of a disk other than the default disk. To get a directory of the files on the diskette in the A: drive, the command would be:

```
C>DIR A:
```

Notice that the name of the drive is not just "A", it is "A:". This is a very important point. Whenever the name of a disk drive appears in a command it *must* be a single letter followed by a colon ":". One of the most common mistakes for new DOS users is to specify a drive name with "A" or ":A" rather than the correct "A:". Remember this point.

Another important requirement of DOS syntax is placing a space after the main command and before (and between) any qualifiers. For example, the command "DIRA:" will not work, because there is not a blank space between "DIR" and "A".

Remember these two basic DOS syntax rules:

1. Whenever referring to a disk drive name in a DOS command, always follow the drive name letter with a colon. Examples are "A:", "B:", and "C:".
2. Always place a blank space between the DOS command and any qualifier. For example, the command to display a directory of the B: drive would be "DIR B:". Notice the required space between the "DIR" and the "B:".

THE FIVE MOST COMMONLY USED DOS COMMANDS

Although there are dozens of DOS commands, there are only a few that are the most commonly used. They are the commands DIR, ERASE, RENAME, COPY, and FORMAT. Learn these commands first. Other commands will use a similar syntax, and will be easy to use once you know these core commands.

The DIR Command

The DIR command has already been used in an example. Here we will describe its capabilities more completely. Two important points that will be presented in this text for each command are the *purpose* of the command, and the *format*.

The DIR Command.

PURPOSE: Displays the names of files on disk. May also list the size of the files and the date and time of creation.

FORMAT: DIR [d:] [filespec] [/P] [/W]

This description may look a bit confusing at first, but it can be broken down into small understandable pieces. The first thing in the DIR command is the command itself, "DIR". The brackets"[ ]" in the format description contain *optional* pieces of the command. Since everything else is in brackets, the minimum version of the command is:

```
C>DIR
```

(your prompt will probably be "C > " if you are using a machine with a hard disk, or "A > " if you are using a machine with a floppy disk.)

Assuming you are logged into the A: drive, DOS will list files on the A: disk, as in figure 3.5.

The first column in this list contains filenames. The second column lists extensions. Notice that the file named "BUDGET has no extension. The next column contains the size of the file in bytes, which is roughly equivalent to the number of characters in the file. The fourth column contains the last date the file was changed, and the final column gives the time of the last change. As you may recall, when file specifications are used a dot "." is placed between the filename and the extension. An example usually is "COMMAND.COM". Unfortunately, the directory list does not put the dot between the filename and extension, but it is to be understood that the dot is there. Following the directory listing of the files is a message explaining that there were 8 files in the list. The "264832 bytes free" means that there are 264, 832 bytes still remaining on the disk that can be used. It is helpful to pay attention to this number, so you do not run out of space on the disk.

The next section of the DIR command is "[d:]". The "d:" stands for any disk drive name such as "A:" or "B:". (Remember that there must be a colon fol-

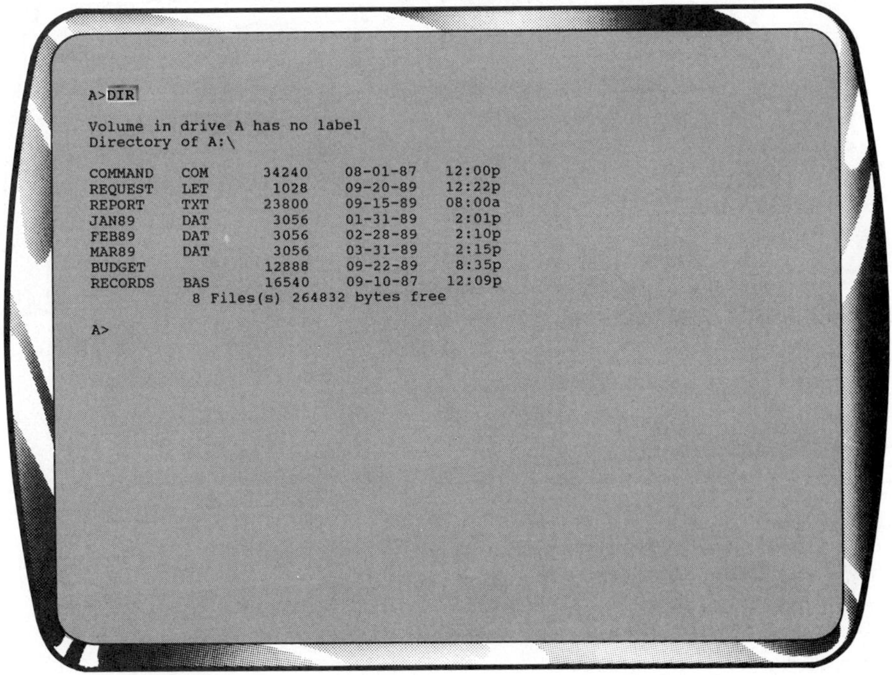

A>DIR
Volume in drive A has no label
Directory of A:\
COMMAND COM 34240 08-01-87 12:00p
REQUEST LET 1028 09-20-89 12:22p
REPORT TXT 23800 09-15-89 08:00a
JAN89 DAT 3056 01-31-89 2:01p
FEB89 DAT 3056 02-28-89 2:10p
MAR89 DAT 3056 03-31-89 2:15p
BUDGET 12888 09-22-89 8:35p
RECORDS BAS 16540 09-10-87 12:09p
8 Files(s) 264832 bytes free
A>

FIGURE 3.5.
A typical directory

lowing the drive letter.) If a drive name is not specified, the DIR command lists the names of the files in the default drive, in this case A:. To obtain a listing of files on the B: drive, the command would be:

```
A>DIR B:
```

Notice the required space between the command and the optional drive name. Following the [d:] option is the option specified as "[filespec]". This is simply a file specification, such as we described earlier, which consists of a filename and optional extension. Using the global file character "*", a directory can be requested for a group of files. To get a directory of only the files with the extension ".DAT", the command would be:

```
A>DIR *.DAT
```

which would produce the directory illustrated in figure 3.6.

The command to get a directory of all files beginning with the letter "R" would be:

```
A>DIR R*.*
```

which would result in the listing illustrated in figure 3.7.

This can be handy when you are looking for a particular file on a disk that contains dozens of files. In fact, a hard-disk directory can contain hundreds of files. If you remember a little about the name, you can usually limit the DIR listing, without having to look through a hundred files to find the one you want.

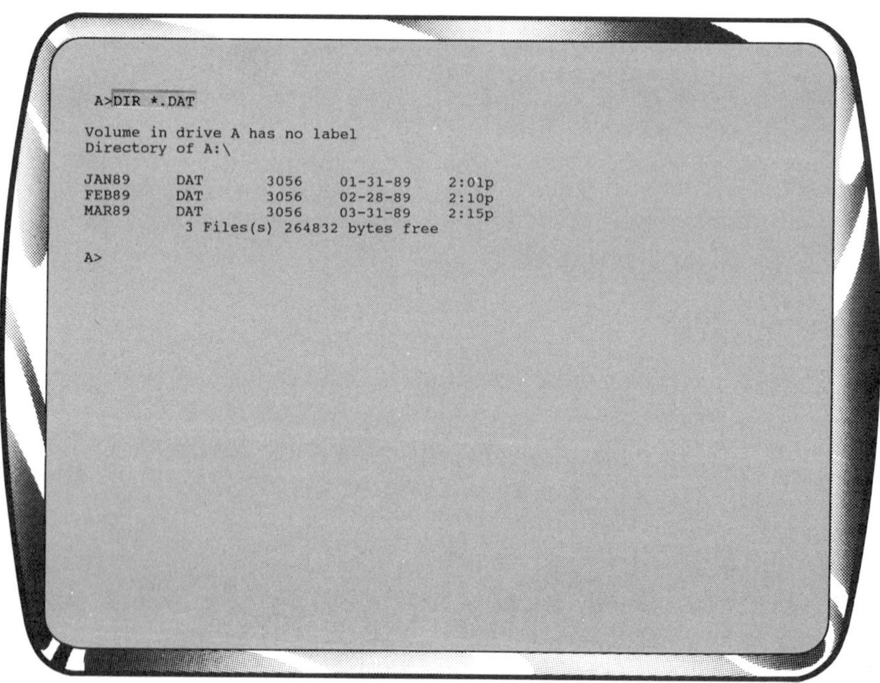
A>DIR *.DAT
Volume in drive A has no label
Directory of A:\
JAN89 DAT 3056 01-31-89 2:01p
FEB89 DAT 3056 02-28-89 2:10p
MAR89 DAT 3056 03-31-89 2:15p
3 Files(s) 264832 bytes free
A>

FIGURE 3.6.
A directory of files with extension ".DAT"

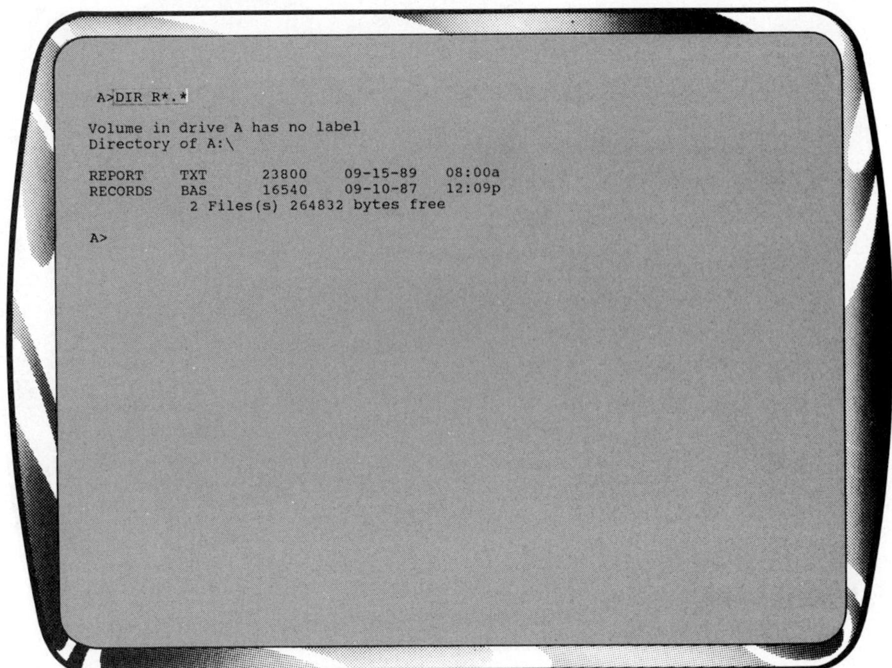
A>DIR R*.*
Volume in drive A has no label
Directory of A:\
REPORT TXT 23800 09-15-89 08:00a
RECORDS BAS 16540 09-10-87 12:09p
2 Files(s) 264832 bytes free
A>

FIGURE 3.7.
A directory of files beginning with "R"

The final options in the DIR command are [/P] and [/W]. These options are sometimes called 'switches'. The /P option instructs DOS to pause when a screenful of files is listed. If there are over 22 files in the directory, they will normally scroll off the screen during a listing of the directory. With the "/P" pause option, the first 23 files will be listed, and the message

```
Strike a key when ready. . .
```

will appear at the bottom of the screen. When you press a key, the next 23 files are listed, and so on until they have all been listed.

The "/W" option stands for "wide" listing. In this version of the listing, only the file specifications are given, with several files listed on each line. This allows more files to appear on one the screen. For example, the command

```
A)DIR /W
```

would produce the listing illustrated in figure 3.8.

Several of these options can be combined to get the type of directory listing desired. For example, the command:

```
A)DIR B:*.DAT/W
```

would list all of the files on the "B:" disk that had a ".DAT" extension, and the listing would be in wide format. Notice in this command that there is no space between the "B:" and the filename "*.DAT". A space between ".DAT" and "/W" is optional. The disk drive name is an integral part of the file specification, and there is never a space between it and the file name.

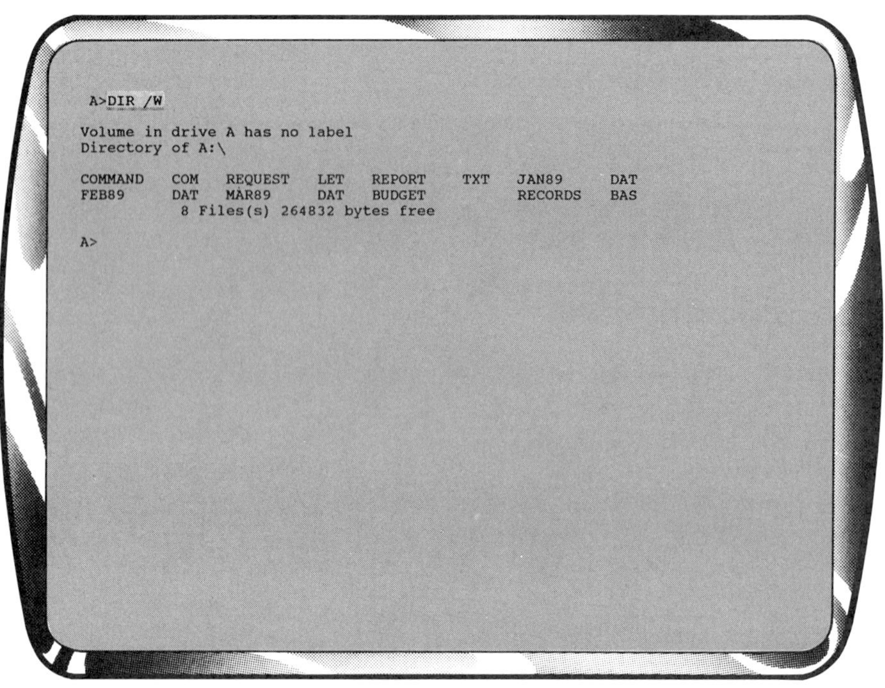

A>DIR /W
Volume in drive A has no label
Directory of A:\
COMMAND COM REQUEST LET REPORT TXT JAN89 DAT
FEB89 DAT MAR89 DAT BUDGET RECORDS BAS
8 Files(s) 264832 bytes free
A>

FIGURE 3.8.
A directory using the "wide" option

The ERASE Command (or DEL)

The ERASE and DEL commands are identical. This discussion will use ERASE. It is essential that you (the computer operator) pay attention to what is on your disks, and how much space has been used. A common problem in using a computer is running out of space on a diskette. The ERASE command is available to remove unneeded files from disk, and to free that space for use by other files.

The ERASE Command.

PURPOSE: To remove from the disk directory the specified files.

FORMAT: ERASE [d:] [filespec]

The ERASE command, like most DOS commands, can be used on a single file, or (using the global file characters) multiple files. The command to ERASE the single file named "REQUEST. LET" would be:

```
A>ERASE REQUEST.LET
```

or equivalently:

```
A>DEL REQUEST.LET
```

To erase a whole group of files using the global file character "*", the command to erase all files with the extension ".DAT" would be:

```
A>ERASE *.DAT
```

The command to erase all files is on the default disk (A:)

```
A>ERASE *.*
```

Naturally, this command must be used with caution. When this command is entered, DOS will prompt you with the question

```
Are you sure (Y/N)?
```

DOS is offering you a chance to change your mind before erasing everything on your disk.

One common use of the ERASE command is to get rid of unwanted backup files often labeled with the extension ".BAK". Some programs create duplicate versions of files. That is, when an original file, say REQUEST.LET, is altered, the new altered file is named REQUEST.LET, but the old version of the file is automatically saved as "REQUEST.BAK", or some other similar name. This is a precaution, so that if the new file is somehow lost or garbled, you can return to the previous version of the file. However if many backup files are created, it can fill up the disk quickly. Essentially, you will have two copies of every file. It is a good idea to get rid of the backup files occasionally. The command is:

```
A>ERASE *.BAK
```

Pay attention to the amount of available disk space. As was illustrated earlier, the amount is given when you enter a DIR command.

The RENAME Command

At times, you may need to change the name of a file. Suppose you were using a word processor and wanted to save a file named REPORT, but you misspelled it "REPOTR". Once you are back to DOS, the easiest way to correct the problem is with the RENAME command.

The RENAME Command.

PURPOSE: Changes the name of a file on disk from the first name listed in the command to the second name.

FORMAT: REN[AME] [d:] filespec1 filespec2

Notice that the command RENAME can be abbreviated "REN". Basically, the RENAME command has the form "RENAME oldname newname", where "oldname' is the current name of a file and "newname" is the name you want the file to have. There is a space between the oldname and newname specifications. For example, the command to rename the file REQUEST.LET to REQUEST.TXT is:

```
A>RENAME REQUEST.LET REQUEST.TXT
```

Global file characters may be used to rename a group of related files. For example, the command to rename the files on the disk in the A: drive JAN.DAT, FEB.DAT, . . . , DEC.DAT to the new names JAN.OLD, FEB.OLD, . . . , DEC.OLD would be:

```
A>RENAME *.DAT *.OLD
```

A file cannot be renamed to have a filename that already exists. For example, if the file REQUEST.TXT already is on disk, the command "RENAME REQUEST.LET REQUEST.TXT" will fail. Also, note that RENAME is not a copy command, which means that you cannot try to rename a file from one disk to another. For example, the command

```
A>RENAME A:REQUEST.LET B:REQUEST.LET
```

is incorrect, and will not work. A file cannot be renamed across disks.

The COPY Command

The COPY command is one of the most powerful and frequently used DOS commands. It allows you to make identical copies of files from one disk to another, or to make a duplicate copy of a file on the same disk under a different name.

The COPY Command.

PURPOSE: Copies one or more files to another disk, or to the same disk under a new name.

FORMAT: COPY [d:] filespec [d:] [filespec]

Perhaps more easily remembered, the COPY command has the form "COPY source destination". Unlike the RENAME command that simply changes the name of a file on disk, the COPY command makes a new copy of an existing file. You can compare it to making a photocopy of a piece of paper. The copy looks exactly like the original.

The copy command can be used to copy files from one disk to another disk. For example, the command to copy the file named REPORT.TXT from the current default disk A: to disk C: would be

```
A>COPY REPORT.TXT C:REPORT.TXT
```

The "source" in this command is the file REPORT.TXT, and the destination is the disk drive C:.

DOS allows you to leave off the name of the destination file if it will be the same as the original file. Thus, the command

```
A>COPY REPORT.TXT C:
```

does the same copy as the previous command. On the other hand, suppose you wanted to do the same copy from drive A: to drive C:, but you were currently logged into drive C:. The full command for this copy would be:

```
C>COPY A:REPORT.TXT  C:REPORT.TXT
```

but it could be abbreviated to:

```
C>COPY A:REPORT.TXT
```

THE "source" is 'A:REPORT.TXT", but no destination is given. In this case, DOS assumes the destination to be the current default drive, which is C:. Study the last few examples until you understand why they do the same copy.

The COPY command can be used to copy files that are not even on the default disk drive. Suppose you are logged into the C: drive, and you wish to copy the file "REPORT.TXT" from the A: disk to the B: disk. The command would be:

```
C>COPY A:REPORT.TXT B:
```

The source is "A:REPORT.TXT" and the destination is "B:".

It is also possible to change the name of a file during a COPY. For example, in the previous example, suppose you wanted the file on the B: disk to be named RPT.TXT instead of REPORT.TXT, as it is called on the A: disk. The command would be:

```
C>COPY A:REPORT.TXT B:RPT.TXT
```

This time, the destination contains a file name, and the source file will be renamed as it is copied. The COPY command can also be used to copy a file on the same disk to a different file name. For example, to make a duplicate copy of the file REPORT.TXT, calling the duplicate copy REPORT.DUP, you could use the command

```
C>COPY REPORT.TXT REPORT.DUP
```

Notice that since both the source and destination files are on the default disk, it was not necessary to put a C: in the file specifications.

Attempting to copy a file to itself will result in an error. For example, the command "COPY REPORT.TXT REPORT.TXT" is not allowed, and the following error message will result:

```
File cannot be copied onto itself
0 file(s) copied
```

The COPY command can also be used with multiple files, using the global file characters. For example, the command to copy all of your ".DAT" files from disk C: to disk A: would be:

```
C>COPY *.DAT A:
```

If you happen to be logged into the A: disk at the time, the command would be

```
A>COPY C:*.DAT
```

Notice in this COPY command that the source is on disk C:, and there is no destination given. DOS assumes that the destination is the default disk drive, A:. Therefore, this command copies all ".DAT" files from the C: drive to the A: drive.

The FORMAT Command

The FORMAT command is used to prepare diskettes (and hard disks) for use. When diskettes are purchased, they cannot simply be put into the disk drive and used. They must first be formatted. Formatting specifies how information is to be stored on disk. The way PC-DOS stores information has changed over time. The way Apple, Commodore, and other computers store information on disk is different from the way the IBM PC stores it. This could have meant that diskettes would have to be made for every different brand of computer and every version within a brand. Fortunately, that is not the case. Diskettes fresh out of the box can be used on any number of machines. But once they are formatted for a particular machine, they must be used only on that type of machine (i.e., the IBM family of compatible computers, or Apple, or Commodore, etc.)

Formatting places magnetic tracks, invisible to us, on the diskette at specific locations. A typical PC-DOS diskette has 40 tracks. Each track is divided into 9 sectors. This is illustrated in figure 3.9. Within one specific track and sector, DOS places the directory information. When information is requested from the disk, DOS knows precisely where on the disk to find the "directory of information."

The FORMAT command is necessary to set up the tracks and sectors on a blank disk, and to create the preliminary directory.

The FORMAT Command.

PURPOSE: Initializes a diskette or hard disk to a recording format acceptable to DOS. It also analyzes the entire disk for any defective tracks, and prepares the disk to accept DOS files.

FORMAT: FORMAT [d:] [/S] [/V]

The FORMAT command is an essential yet dangerous command, and should be thoroughly understood before you use it. It is possible to destroy valuable information on a diskette or hard disk by using the FORMAT command incorrectly. Since FORMAT initializes the disk and prepares a new directory, *any information already on the disk will be lost.*

The FORMAT command is different from the previous commands, we have examined, in that it is an *external* DOS command. This means that the FORMAT command is really a computer program called FORMAT.COM. In

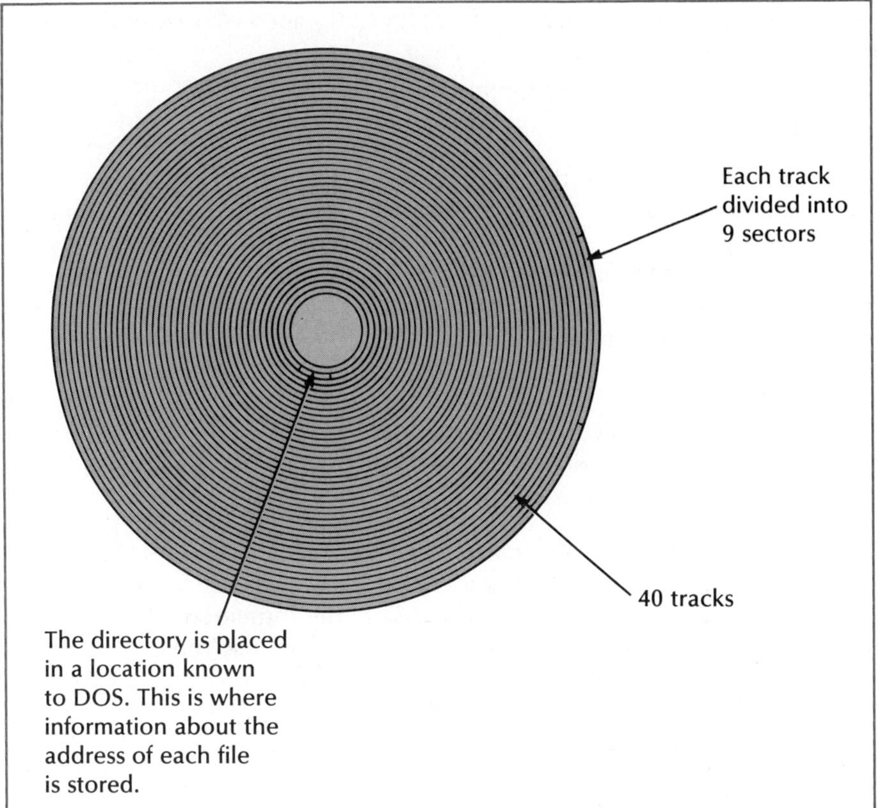
Each track
divided into
9 sectors
40 tracks
The directory is placed
in a location known
to DOS. This is where
information about the
address of each file
is stored.

FIGURE 3.9.
How a double-sided, double-density 360K PC-DOS disk is formatted

order to run the FORMAT command (or program), the file FORMAT.COM must be available on disk. There will be more discussion about external commands later.

Now let's examine a simple example. Suppose you are using a computer with a hard disk drive, and you are logged into the C: drive. The simplest command to FORMAT a new diskette in the A: drive is:

```
C>FORMAT A:
```

When this command is entered, DOS will respond with the message:

```
Insert new diskette for drive A:
and strike ENTER when ready:
```

This gives you a chance to back out of the command if you discover that you really do not want to FORMAT that diskette. If you want to cancel the command at this point, enter CTRL-BREAK. That is, press the CTRL key, and while holding the CTRL key down, press the BREAK key. If you *do* wish to format the diskette in the A: drive, press the ENTER key instead.

Once the FORMAT is complete, the following message is displayed:

```
Format complete
xxxxxxxbytes total disk space
xxxxxxxbytes available on disk
Format another (Y/N)?n
```

The final "n" is your response, stating that you do not wish to format another disk now.

If bad sectors are found on the disk, another line will report:

```
xxxxxxxbytes in bad sectors
```

Bad sectors are defects in the disk found during the FORMAT procedure. These bad sectors cause the diskette to have less storage capacity, but the diskette is still usable.

It is very important to note that if you do not enter the name of the disk drive to initialize, the FORMAT command assumes disk is in the default drive. Thus, if you enter the command

```
C>FORMAT
```

The FORMAT command will assume that you want to FORMAT the Hard Disk Drive C:! Be careful not to do this! (Unless you really want to erase everything on your hard disk.)

Options for the FORMAT Command. In the description of the FORMAT command above, two options were given: "/S" and "/V". The "/V" option allows you to give a *volume name* to the disk being formatted. To FORMAT a disk on the A: drive and give it the name "MYDISK", use the command:

```
C>FORMAT A:/V
```

DOS will prompt with the message

```
Volume label (11 characters, ENTER for none)?
```

Type MYDISK at the prompt. You may want to name your diskettes as a way of uniquely identifying the disk. Some people put their initials and date; others may put the name of a company to signify the ownership of the disk.

The other FORMAT option listed is the "/S" option, which is the "System" option. This creates a system disk, one that contains the files necessary to boot the computer. A system disk has the DOS information required by the computer to start up. A diskette formatted without this option does not have that information, and cannot be used to boot the computer.

The two options can be used together. The command to FORMAT the disk in drive A: with a label and with the system boot information is:

```
C>FORMAT A:/S/V
```

This time, when the FORMAT is finished, the following messages are displayed:

```
Format complete
System transferred

xxxxxxx bytes total disk space
 xxxxxx bytes used by system
xxxxxxx bytes available on disk

Format another (Y/N)?n
```

The DOS system takes about 30,000 to 60,000 bytes of space, depending on which version of PC-DOS or MS-DOS you are using. If you are using IBM PC-DOS, a disk formatted with the "/S" option will contain the file

"COMMAND.COM", and two "hidden" files, IBMBIO.COM and IBMDOS.COM. MS-DOS systems create the files IO.SYS and MSDOS.SYS. These hidden files are on disk, but do not show up when a DIR command is used. A complete format session is illustrated in figure 3.10.

To Format With or Without /S. There is no need to format a disk with the system option (/S) if the disk is going to be used only to store information, such as word processing files. The DOS system takes up a large amount of disk space, which would give you less storage capacity. Thus, if the disk is going to be used only for information storage, do *not* use the /S option. If the disk is going to be used as a boot disk, use the /S option. If you are using a hard-disk machine, DOS is stored on the hard drive, and you will virtually never need to create another boot disk.

You may want to create a system disk that also contains your application program. With both items on the same disk, you can boot the computer and run the program without having to switch disks.

Occasionally a problem occurs in formatting a disk. One type in particular is worth mentioning, having to do with damaged disks. To understand this type of error, you need to know a little more about how DOS stores information on disks.

The FAT Table. Files are sometimes stored in pieces on disk, with the beginning of the file located in one place on the disk, the next part located somewhere else, and so on. The "File Allocation Table" or FAT table, keeps track of those pieces. Thus when DOS wants to find the information for the file REPORT.TXT on disk, it looks in the disk directory, finds its starting

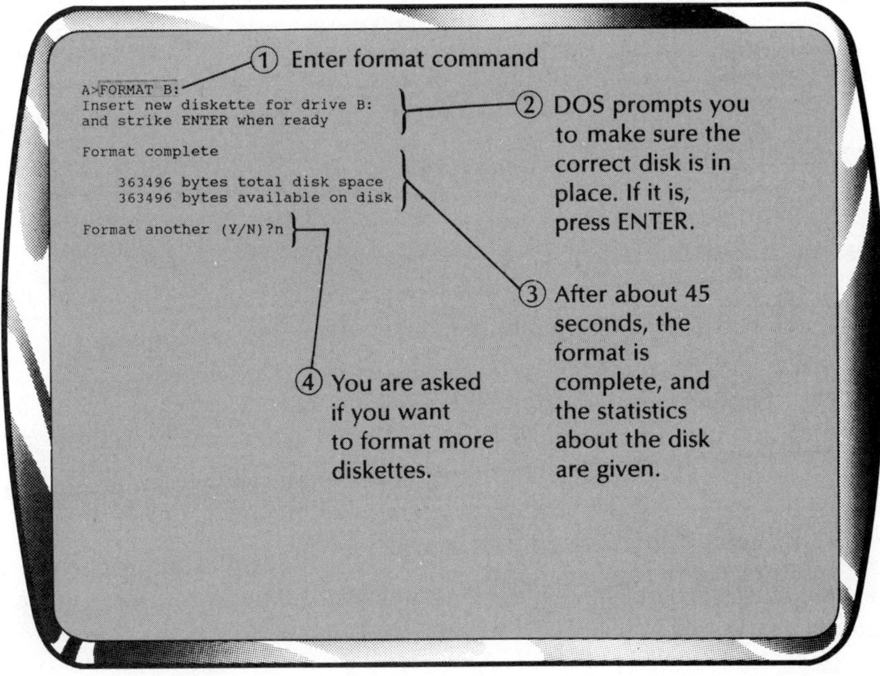

A>FORMAT B:
Insert new diskette for drive B:
and strike ENTER when ready
Format complete
363496 bytes total disk space
363496 bytes available on disk
Format another (Y/N)?n
① Enter format command
② DOS prompts you to make sure the correct disk is in place. If it is, press ENTER.
③ After about 45 seconds, the format is complete, and the statistics about the disk are given.
④ You are asked if you want to format more diskettes.

FIGURE 3.10.
A format session

address (e.g., track 4, sector 5), and then reads the information from the disk, according to information in the FAT table. Users rarely have to know anything about the FAT table. However, if you see a warning message from DOS such as:

```
Disk error reading FAT
```

or

```
Disk error writing FAT
```

It may mean serious problems for your disk files. DOS will try to recover. If it does, you should copy the usable files from this disk to a new disk. You may also refer to programs such as the Norton Utilities to recover lost files. Problems with the FAT table may occur if there is a power failure while the computer is accessing a file on disk, or if you turn off the computer while it is still accessing a file in a program. If a FAT error occurs on a disk, you may need to reformat the disk to make it usable, after you have recovered all usable files.

INTERNAL AND EXTERNAL DOS COMMANDS

DOS consists of a number of commands. These commands are categorized into two types, *internal* and *external* commands. Internal DOS commands are copied into the computer's memory when DOS is loaded as the computer is booted. These commands stay in memory until the computer is turned off, and may be used whenever the DOS prompt appears on the screen. Some common internal commands include DIR, ERASE, DEL, RENAME, TIME, DATE, and COPY.

Some DOS commands are not copied into the computer's memory at boot time. They are stored on disk in a file until they are needed. The reason is that if every DOS command were stored in memory, there would not be enough memory left for application programs. These DOS commands on disk are usually identified by the ".COM" extension. The FORMAT command, for example, is stored on the DOS diskette as the file "FORMAT.COM".

If an external command is to be used, it must be available on disk. When the FORMAT command is entered, for example, DOS looks on the default (logged in) disk to find the file FORMAT.COM. If the file is not found, the message

```
Bad command or file name
```

appears on the screen. This error message tells you that the command you requested was not found on disk.

In the DOS manual, commands are indicated as internal or external by their "Type". As commands are introduced, we will point out whether the command is an internal or external command. A list of internal and external DOS commands is included in the next chapter.

In order for an external command to work, a copy of the command file, i.e., FORMAT.COM, must be in the default drive. Another way to make external commands available—PATH will be discussed later.

CHANGING THE DEFAULT DRIVE

The "logged-in" disk drive has been mentioned in previous sections, but no mention has yet been made of how to log into a disk. The command is simple: to log onto a new disk drive, enter its name. Thus if you are currently logged into the A: drive, and want to be logged into the C: drive, enter the command

```
A>C:
```

Notice that the prompt will change to

```
C>
```

If you are logged into the B: disk and want to change to the A: disk, enter the command:

```
B>A:
```

which changes the prompt to

```
A>
```

SUMMARY

This chapter introduced the function of PC-DOS/MS-DOS, the syntax of DOS commands, and the most commonly used DOS commands. DOS manages the disk resources of the computer, under the direction of you, the computer operator. There have been several versions of DOS, and most features are upwardly compatible to the new versions. DOS is necessary to boot the computer, and the CORE of DOS (the internal commands) is stored in RAM when the computer is booted.

All information on disk is stored in files. A file specification consists of a filename and an optional extension of up to three characters.

DOS is a command language. Some of the most commonly used DOS commands include DIR, ERASE (DEL), RENAME, COPY, and FORMAT. Commands are of two types, internal and external. Internal commands are stored in the computer's memory, and may be used any time. External commands must be available on disk when they are used.

KEY TERMS

DOS

Upwardly compatible

Booting

ROM and RAM

Filename

File specification

Global file character

Default

Formatted disk

Internal DOS command

External DOS command

QUESTIONS

1. What is the purpose of DOS? What are the two brands of DOS that are virtually identical? If you have access to a machine, what version of DOS is it using?

2. What happens when a computer is "booted"?
3. What is a file specification, and what are the limitations on file names and extensions for DOS?
4. What are global file characters, and how are they used? Give an example.
5. What are the two basic rules of DOS command syntax mentioned in the text?
6. What does the DIR command do? Explain the purpose of the /P and /W options.
7. What does the ERASE command do? What is its twin command? What happens if you enter the "ERASE *.*" command?
8. What does the RENAME command do? Why can't you rename a file in disk A: to a new name in disk B:?
9. What does the COPY command do? If a destination is not specified in the COPY command, to where does DOS try to copy the source file?
10. What does the FORMAT command do? How can it be dangerous? What do the /V and /S options do? What happens if you do not specify a disk drive letter in the FORMAT command? What is a bad sector?
11. How does the FORMAT command differ from the other commands mentioned in the chapter?
12. How do you change the logged-in disk drive?
13. Why do the following two commands do the same thing?

```
A>COPY C:MYFILE.TXT
C>COPY MYFILE.TXT A:
```

14. Indicate which file specifications are correct, and which are incorrect, and why:

```
123.4567
REPORT.$$$
THISISAFILE.TXT
C:MYFILE.TXT
B:BATMAN
H:ELP
A:JA7/85.RPT
```

15. Suppose you are logged into the B: drive, and you wish to copy a file named BUDGET.DAT from the C: drive to the A: drive. Write down the command, including the DOS prompt, for this copy.
16. Why is it important to choose the names of files and extensions carefully? Name three extensions that have special meanings to DOS.
17. What is the difference between an internal and an external DOS command? What happens when you type the name of an external DOS command when the program file for that command is not on the logged-in disk?

LABORATORY EXERCISES

Lab Exercise 1. *(The FORMAT Command)* Perform the following tasks and record the results as indicated. If you are using a floppy-based system, you will need to have a copy of your DOS diskette in the A: drive. You will also need a diskette that can be formatted (remember that all information already on the diskette will be lost).

a. Format a blank diskette using no options. Which drive contains the disk to be formatted? What command must be used?

b. Record the number of bytes available on the diskette. Are there any bad sectors on the disk?

Lab Exercise 2. (The FORMAT Command)

a. Format a blank diskette using the option to place the system on the disk. Which drive contains the disk to be formatted? What command must be used?

b. Record the number of bytes available on the diskette. Are there any bad sectors on the disk?

c. Compare the number of bytes available on this diskette as compared to the diskette in Exercise 1. What is the difference?

Lab Exercise 3. (The FORMAT Command)

a. Format a blank diskette using the option to place a volume name on the disk. Which drive contains the disk to be formatted? What command must be used?

b. Record the number of bytes available on the diskette. Are there any bad sectors on the disk? Where does the volume name appear?

c. Is the number of bytes any different from Exercise 1 or Exercise 2?

For the following exercises using FLOPPY-DISK computers, use the Text Examples Diskette in the A: drive and another formatted diskette in the B: drive.

For the following exercises using HARD-DISK computers, use the text examples diskette in the A: drive, and use C: where B: is called for in the exercises.

Always use a backup copy of the original Text Examples Disk.

Lab Exercise 4. (The DIR Command)

a. Make the A: drive the default (logged-in) drive. What command do you use? How can you tell it succeeded?

b. Enter the directory command to get a list of files on the A: drive. What command did you use? Do the same command with the /W option. What is the difference in what is listed on the screen?

c. Enter the directory command to get a list of files on the B: drive (C: drive for hard disk). What command did you use?

d. Enter a command to list all of the files on the A: drive with a file extension that begins with the letter "T". What command did you use?

Lab Exercise 5. (The COPY Command)

a. With A: as the default drive, copy the file EXAMPLE.TXT from the Text Examples Disk to the diskette in drive B: (or C: if using a hard disk). What is the command to use?

b. Copy the file on the A: diskette named EXAMPLE.TXT to a new file called TEMP on the same diskette. What is the command to use?

c. Copy the file on the A: diskette named EXAMPLE.TXT to a file on the diskette in drive B: (or C: if using a hard disk) named TEMP2. What is the command to use?

d. Copy the file named TEMP2 from the B: or C: disk to the A: disk. Record first the full version of the command, then enter the same command in abbreviated form (leave off the destination).

Lab Exercise 6. ***(The RENAME and ERASE Commands)*** This exercise assumes that you have already performed Exercise 5.

a. RENAME the file A:TEMP to a file named TMP.XXX. RENAME the file named A:TEMP2 to TEMP.XXX. What commands do you use?

b. ERASE the file named TEMP. Then erase the file named TEMP2. What commands do you use?

c. ERASE the files named TMP.XXX and TEMP.XXX both in one command. What command do you use?

CHAPTER 4

Introduction to DOS, PART II

CHAPTER OVERVIEW. This is the second of two chapters to discuss the disk operating system PC-DOS, or its equivalent MS-DOS. In the previous chapter, the most common DOS commands were discussed. In this chapter, additional commands will be introduced, including those dealing with the use of DOS on a hard-disk system. Even though many students may not have access to a hard-disk system in a university lab setting, the commands illustrated in the text may be used on a floppy-disk system. In most business and professional offices personal computers are equipped with hard disks.

CHAPTER OBJECTIVES

Upon completion of this chapter, you will be able to:

- Describe and use the commands CHKDSK, DISKCOPY, PRINT, and TYPE, along with other common DOS commands.
- Describe the differences between using a computer with floppy disks, and one with a hard disk system.
- Describe what new tasks the user must perform when using a hard-disk system.
- Make a new directory.
- Switch from directory to directory.
- Remove a directory
- Describe the function of the AUTOEXEC. BAT and CONFIG. SYS files.
- Describe and know how to set up path names.
- Use the PATH and TREE commands.
- Reboot the computer without turning off the power.
- Describe a method of backing up the hard-disk.

COMMONLY USED DOS COMMANDS

The DOS commands presented in the previous chapter are sufficient for most of the work done on the personal computer. However, they represent only about ten percent of the available DOS commands. Some other DOS commands that are commonly used are presented here. A summary of all of the DOS commands covered in the last two chapters appears at the end of the chapter.

The CHKDSK (Check Disk) Command

The CHKDSK command allows the user to examine a diskette or hard disk to determine how much space is being used, and if the disk has any problems. For example, if there are problems with the FAT table, they may show up with the CHKDSK command. CHKDSK is an external DOS command.

The CHKDSK Command.

PURPOSE: Summarizes how much space has been used on the disk drive, and how much internal memory is available in the computer.

FORMAT: CHKDSK [d:]
Where "d:" specifies the diskette or hard disk to check.

An example of the use of this command to check the disk in drive B: would be:

```
A>CHKDSK B:
```

and the result would be a report similar to the one in figure 4.1.

The first set of numbers reports the allocation of space on the disk or diskette being checked. In this case, the diskette being checked is a 360K diskette, which currently has one file on disk. There are 325,632 bytes of usable space still remaining on this diskette.

The second set of numbers from CHKDSK is a report on the internal RAM memory in the computer. The "total memory" is how much RAM is in the computer, while the "bytes free" is how much RAM is left over after DOS has been loaded. Some people find this confusing, but keep in mind that the first group of numbers refers to *DISK* memory, and the second group of numbers refers to *internal* computer memory. It is important to note that the report on RAM memory may not be exactly correct. DOS can only access 640K of memory at a time. Thus the CHKDSK report will find a maximum of 655,360 bytes even if there is more actual memory in the computer.

The CLS (Clear the Screen) Command

This command is useful if there are items displayed on your screen which you no longer want, or if you want your next command to appear at the top of the screen.

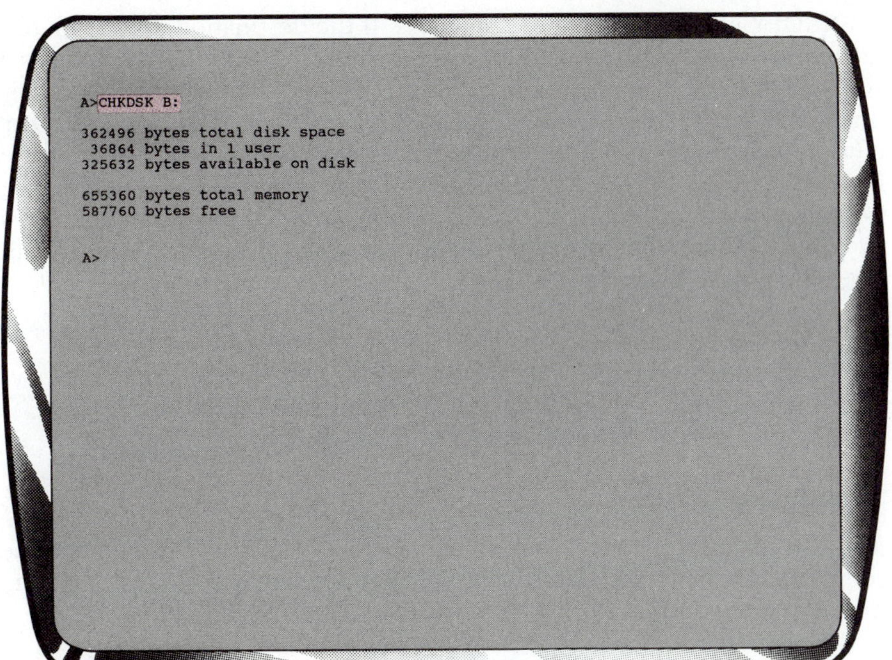
A>CHKDSK B:
362496 bytes total disk space
36864 bytes in 1 user
325632 bytes available on disk
655360 bytes total memory
587760 bytes free
A>

FIGURE 4.1.
A CHKDSK report on disk B:

The CLS Command.

PURPOSE: Blanks out the display screen.

FORMAT: CLS

The DISKCOPY Command: Copying one disk to another.

Many times you want to make an exact copy of a diskette. In fact, when you get new software, it is always a good idea to DISKCOPY all of the original disks, and use copies rather than originals in your work.

The DISKCOPY Command.

PURPOSE OF THE DISKCOPY COMMAND: Used to copy the contents of an entire diskette from one disk to another of equal size.

FORMAT: DISKCOPY d1: d2:
where "d1:" is the source diskette, and "d2:" is the destination diskette.

DISKCOPY is an external DOS command. If the destination disk is not formatted, the DISKCOPY procedure will format it. DISKCOPY makes an exact copy of a diskette. Therefore, if there are any bad sectors on the source or destination diskette, the DISKCOPY procedure may not work. A DISKCOPY must be from and to disks of the same size. You cannot DISKCOPY from the hard disk to a floppy, for instance, since the hard disk is of a different size from the floppy diskette. Usually, the easiest way to DISKCOPY disks is in a two-floppy system. For example, to copy the disk in drive A: to the disk in drive B:, use the command

```
A>DISKCOPY A: B:
```

This is illustrated in figure 4.2.

If you are using a system with only one floppy disk drive, such as an IBM PC XT, you can still perform DISKCOPY. Use the command:

```
A>DISKCOPY A: B:
```

just as you would for a two-disk system. DOS will prompt you to place the source and then the destination diskettes in the drive. You may have to swap diskettes several times during each DISKCOPY.

The PRINT Command: Printing a file to the line printer

You may want to get a printed copy of an ASCII text file on disk. DOS has a command that will allow you to print files. However, note that the files must

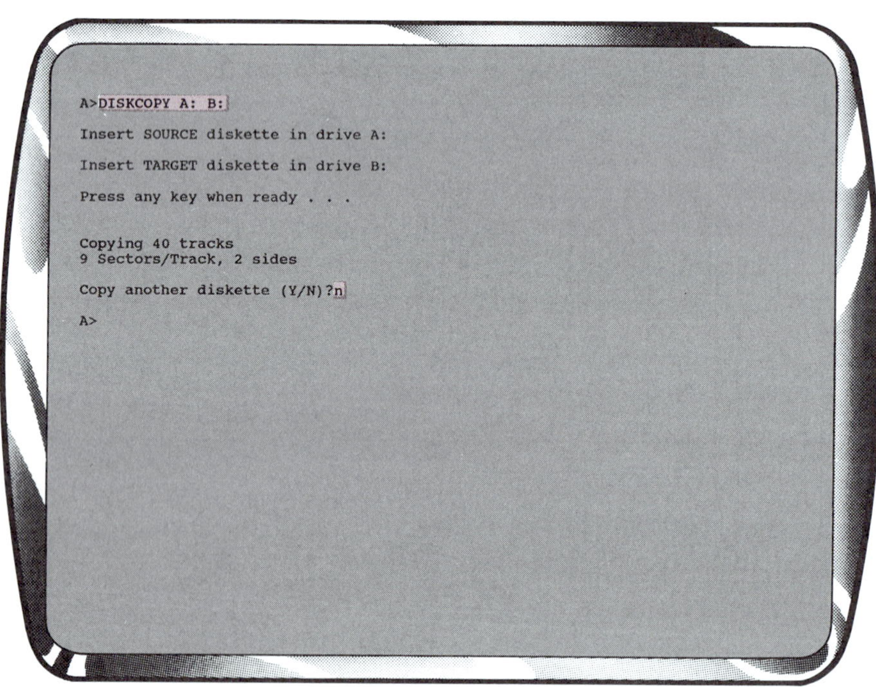

A>DISKCOPY A: B:
Insert SOURCE diskette in drive A:
Insert TARGET diskette in drive B:
Press any key when ready . . .
Copying 40 tracks
9 Sectors/Track, 2 sides
Copy another diskette (Y/N)?n
A>

FIGURE 4.2.
Using the DISKCOPY command.

contain printable information, such as text files. Attempting to print a program file, such as COMMAND.COM, will produce unpredictable results. It may even damage your printer. The Print Command is an external DOS command.

The PRINT Command.

PURPOSE: Prints the contents of a text file to the line printer.

FORMAT: PRINT [d:] filespec [/T]

There are several files on the Text Examples Disk that can be used to demonstrate the PRINT command. For example, to print the file called EXAMPLE.TXT in the B: drive to the line printer, enter the command

```
A>PRINT B:EXAMPLE.TXT
```

The computer will respond

```
Name of list device [PRN]:
```

Pressing the enter key will confirm that you want the file printed to the standard print device (i.e., the printer). If you get the response

```
Bad command or file name
```

it means that the PRINT.COM file was not on disk. Since the PRINT command is an external DOS command, the PRINT program must be available to DOS for the command to work. If you are entering this command while logged in to the A: drive, make sure your DOS diskette is in the A: drive. An example of using PRINT is illustrated in figure 4.3.

You may *queue* several files to be printed at once, and DOS will remember each of them, and print them in the order of the PRINT commands. If you decide that you want the printing of a file to be terminated, use the /T command. For example, to terminate the current PRINT job(s), you would enter the command:

```
A>PRINT /T
```

This terminates all files in the print queue. A cancellation message is displayed; the page in the printer will be advanced to the top of the form, and the printer's buzzer will sound.

The TYPE Command: Typing a file to the monitor

The TYPE command is similar to the PRINT command, but it causes the contents of a file to be displayed on the monitor rather than on the printer. Again, the file to be printed should be a plain ASCII or "text" file.

FIGURE 4.3.
Using the PRINT command

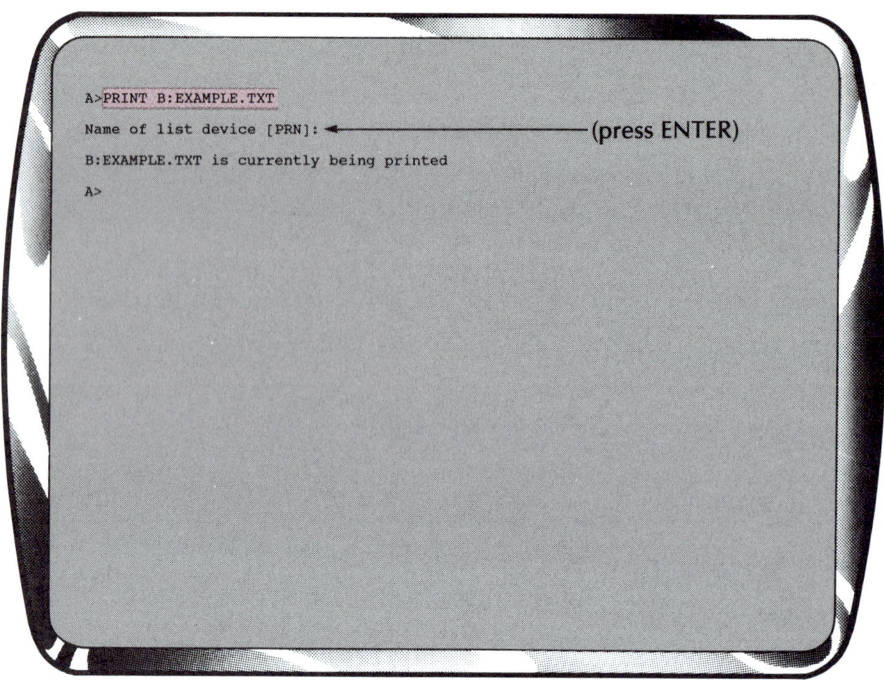

A>PRINT B:EXAMPLE.TXT
Name of list device [PRN]:
(press ENTER)
B:EXAMPLE.TXT is currently being printed
A>

The TYPE Command.

PURPOSE: To display the contents of a file on the monitor.

FORMAT: TYPE [d:] filespec

For example, to display the contents of the EXAMPLE.TXT file (on the Text Examples Disk) in the B: drive on the screen, use the command:

A>**TYPE B:EXAMPLE.TXT**

If you attempt to TYPE the contents of a file that is not an ASCII file, the result will likely be a series of meaningless characters on the screen. Figure 4.4 illustrates the use of the TYPE command.

COMMANDS RELATING TO USING THE HARD DISK

Most microcomputers being sold today include a hard-disk storage device. A hard disk (or fixed disk) is a permanent disk that is usually housed in the computer, and is capable of storing many times more information than a single floppy diskette. The size of most hard disks is measured in megabytes (MB), or millions of bytes. Thus, a 30MB hard disk can store 30 million characters of information.

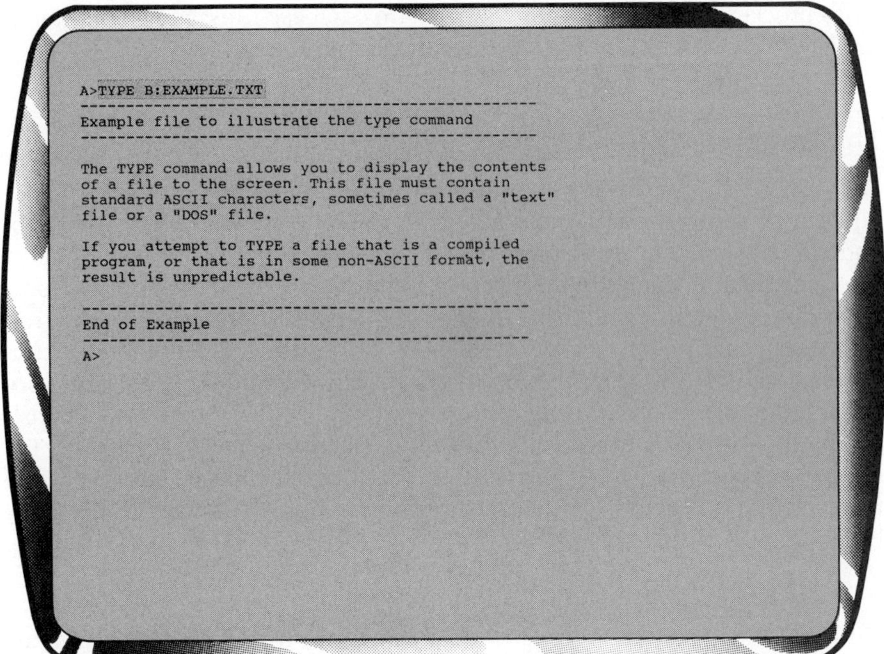

A>TYPE B:EXAMPLE.TXT

Example file to illustrate the type command

The TYPE command allows you to display the contents
of a file to the screen. This file must contain
standard ASCII characters, sometimes called a "text"
file or a "DOS" file.
If you attempt to TYPE a file that is a compiled
program, or that is in some non-ASCII format, the
result is unpredictable.

End of Example

A>

FIGURE 4.4.
Using the TYPE command

If You Are Using a Floppy-Based System

Students who do not have a hard-disk system can still perform the examples in this chapter on a floppy disk. In the chapter, examples of commands related to hard disks use the "C > " prompt to refer to the hard disk drive. If you are using a floppy-based system, you may use the A: or B: drives, and all of the DOS commands discussed will work, with appropriate change of the disk drive names.

Many More Files

Using a computer with a hard disk creates several challenges to the user. The fact that the hard disk can store more information is both a blessing and a curse. It relieves the user from having to keep up with a mile-high stack of floppy diskettes, but it requires more planned organization. A thousand files stored on the hard disk could be awesome. When you entered a "DIR" command, it could take several minutes for the information to scroll by.

Directory Structure

The answer to this dilemma is the ability to divide the hard disk into several directories or *subdirectories,* where each directory contains related information. One directory may contain all of the DOS files. Another may contain word processing files. Another may contain database files, and so on. It is almost as if each directory becomes a separate diskette.

The Root Directory and Beyond

DOS has a particular way to set up directories. When any disk is formatted (including a floppy disk), it automatically contains one directory, called the *root* directory. Other directories may be created to branch off from the root like a family tree. Each directory is given a name. It is up to the user to choose what directories to create, and to choose the philosophy behind the structure. For example, two *trees* are illustrated in figure 4.5. The first directory tree is organized by task. The top directory is the original or root directory. Branching off are directories (or subdirectories) that contain the task-oriented partitions DOS, Word Processing, Database, and Spreadsheet. The second directory tree is organized by person. Tom, Dick, and Harry each have their own subdirectory, with each person having several task directories branching off of his directory.

MANAGING THE DIRECTORIES

How are directories created? How does one move from one directory to another? How do you get rid of a directory? These questions are answered by a series of new DOS commands. As the computer operator, you are given the

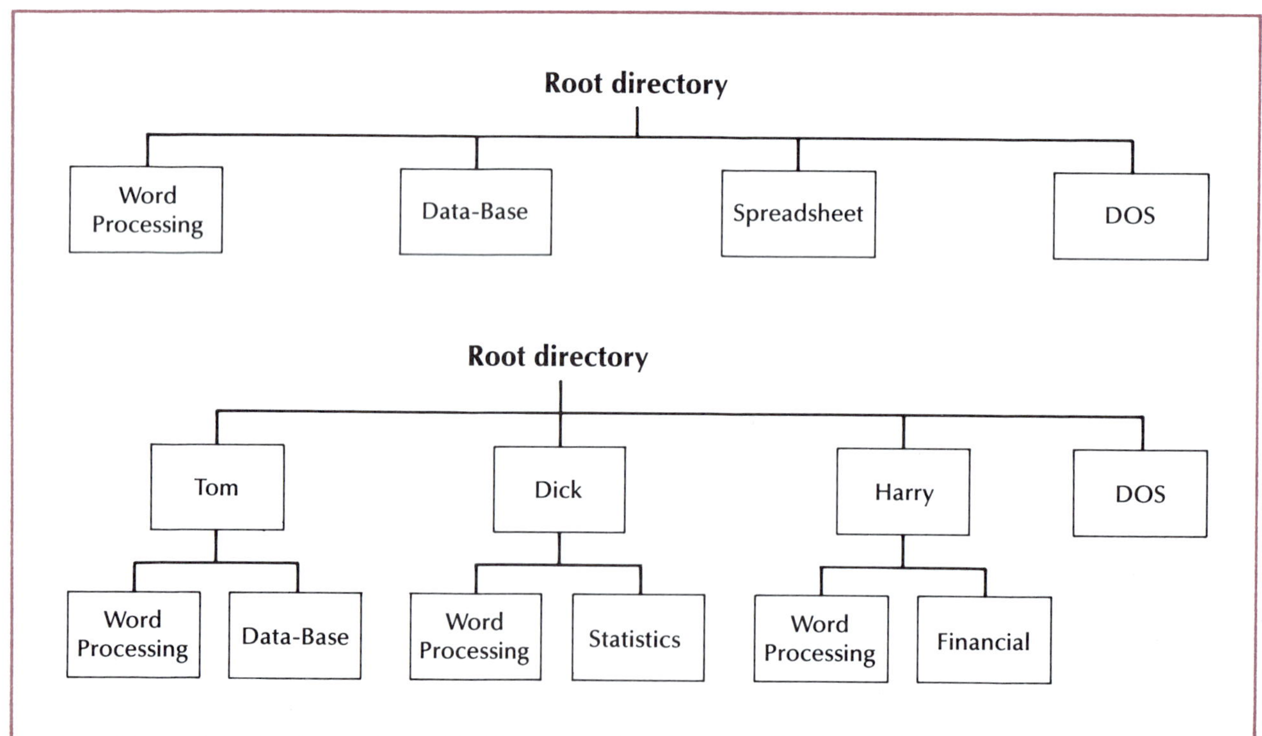

FIGURE 4.5.
Examples of directory trees

opportunity and responsibility to create, use, and remove the directories, as needs arise. You create directories according to your planned "directory tree". If you want to clean up your disk and get rid of a directory, you will need a way to remove it from the disk.

Once the tree is created, you can move from branch to branch according to what directory you wish to use. For example, if you are doing word processing, you will want to be "in" the word processing directory. This gives you access to all of the word processing files. It also separates you from the files in other directories, just as if this directory represented a separate diskette. Thus, if you are in the word processing directory and enter the command "C > DIR", you will get a list of files only in that directory.

These are the three major tasks in managing your hard disk:

1. Create a directory
2. Change from one directory to another
3. Remove a directory

The three commands that will be introduced, MD, CD, and RD, are all internal DOS commands.

Directory Names

Before learning the DOS commands to manage the hard disk, you must understand how the names of the directories are related to file specifications. Each directory has a name. The root directory always has the name "\" (backslash). Subdirectories branching off the root are given names of up to 8 characters. When referring to a subdirectory name, the entire "pedigree" is usually used. That is, the "WP" directory branching off of the root is usually referred to as "\WP". This reference is also called the *path to the WP directory.* The directory "LETTERS" branching off of the "WP" directory is Specified by the path "\WP\LETTERS". Thus, a backslash "\" is used for two purposes:

1. The first backslash "\" specifies the root directory.
2. The backslash "\" is also used to separate the names of successive subdirectories.

These paths become a part of the file specification of any file. Figure 4.6 illustrates how a path is added to the file specification. The path appears between

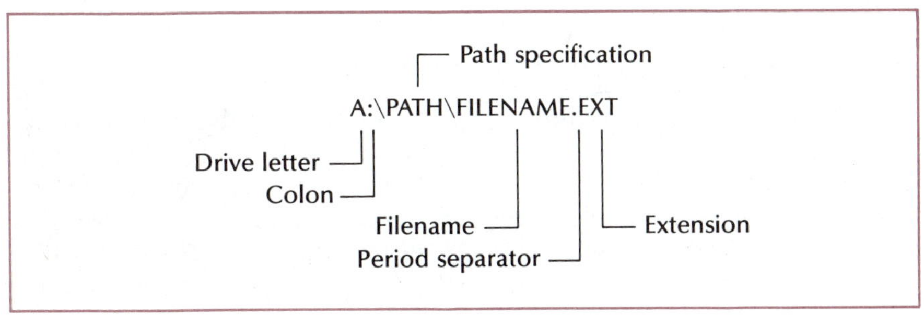

FIGURE 4.6.
A sample file specification containing a path

the drive specification and the filename. It always contains a beginning and ending backslash "\".

How to Create and Use a New Directory

The MKDIR (MD) command is used to make a new directory. "MD" is an allowable abbreviation of the DOS command MKDIR. The abbreviated form will be used in the following examples.

The MKDIR (MD) Command.

PURPOSE: Makes a new directory.

FORMAT: MD path or MKDIR path

For example, the command

```
C>MD \WP      or      C>MKDIR \WP
```

makes a new directory named \WP on disk C:. Technically, a space is not required between the "MD" and " \WP." However, it is a good practice to always place a space after a DOS command and before any parameters or options because the exceptions may be more confusing to remember. If you are using a floppy-based system, and working on the disk drive A:, you could enter the command

```
A>MD \WP      or      A>MKDIR\WP
```

to create a new directory named \WP on the A: drive. The new \WP directory branches directly off of the root directory. The command to make another directory named "LETTERS" that branches off of another \WP would be:

```
C>MD \WP\LETTERS
```

or on a floppy-based system using A:, it would be

```
A>MD \WP\LETTERS
```

Thus, to make any directory, use the MD command followed by the complete path of the new directory you want to create.

Changing From Directory to Directory

Every disk has one or more directories, beginning with the root directory. The CHDIR command, or CD in its abbreviated form, is used to change from the current directory to another directory on the same disk drive. While "in" a particular directory, you may enter commands such as "DIR", "RENAME", etc., that will use only those files in the current directory. This is just like being logged in to one disk drive. What if you want to use files in another directory? As you will eventually see, there are several options. One option is to change to the directory you wish to use.

The CHDIR (CD) Command.

PURPOSE: Changes from the current directory to another directory on the same disk.

FORMAT: CD path or CHDIR PATH

For example, to change to the directory named "\WP", enter the command (for the appropriate drive)

```
C>CD \WP     or     A>CD \WP
```

to go back to your primary (root) directory, enter the command

```
C>CD \     or     A>CD \
```

Using the CD command, you may move from any directory to another directory by entering the command and the complete path of the directory to change to.

Removing an Empty Directory

Sometimes it is necessary to remove a directory from the hard disk to make room for other, more important files. To remove a directory, use the RMDIR (RD) command. In order to remove a directory, the directory must not contain any files or subdirectories; that is, you must ERASE the files and remove all subdirectories first.

The RMDIR (RD) Command.

PURPOSE: Removes an empty directory.

FORMAT: RD path or RMDIR path

For example, the command to remove the directory named \MYDIR would be:

```
C>RD \MYDIR     or     A>RD \MYDIR
```

Using Directories

Once you have decided on a structure for your hard disk, you may create the necessary directories and copy files into those areas. The creation and removal of directories can happen at any time, so you do not need to plan ahead all of the directories you will ever need. You can create them as you need them.

When you are dealing with directories, there are some additional pieces of information needed to use the DOS commands that have already been covered. The commands introduced previously are still valid, but file specifications can not take advantage of DOS directory paths.

When you are using the DIR command, you may specify a path so that you can get a list of files from any directory, for example, suppose you are *not* in the \WP directory, but want a list of files from \WP. The command would be

C>**DIR \WP** or A>**DIR \WP**

To get a listing of only those files in \WP that have a ".TXT" extension, you would use the command

C>**DIR \WP*.TXT**

Remember the extra backslash "\" that appears after the path name and before the file specification. When you request a directory of \WP, you will get a response similar to that in figure 4.7

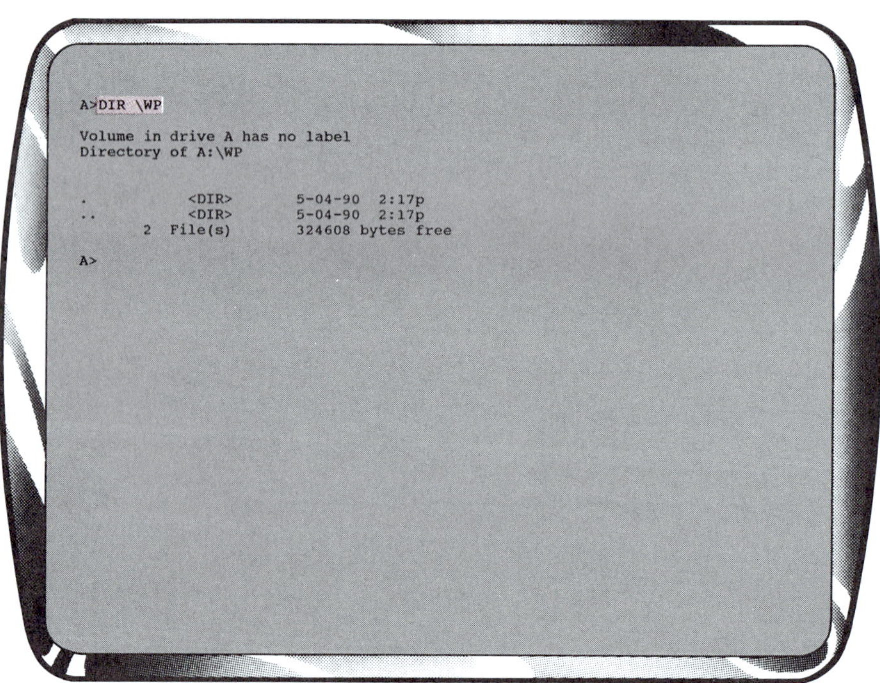
A>DIR \WP
Volume in drive A has no label
Directory of A:\WP
. <DIR> 5-04-90 2:17p
.. <DIR> 5-04-90 2:17p
2 File(s) 324608 bytes free
A>

FIGURE 4.7.
Requesting a directory of the subdirectory \WP

Notice in the directory listing for the \WP directories, two "files" appearing, named "." and ". ." followed by a ⟨DIR⟩ indication where the file extension normally goes. Do not try to get rid of these files—they contain information necessary for DOS to use the directory. You will also notice that in the root directory, the names of directories appear as file names with an extension "⟨DIR⟩", much like these "dot" files in the \WP directory.

In virtually every DOS command that has been learned, the way to use the directory structure is to use the path indication as part of the normal file specification. An example of using a path name in a copy command is:

```
C>COPY \WP\*.TXT A:
```

This command would copy all "*.TXT" files from the \WP directory (source) to the A: diskette (destination). Thus, wherever a file specification can be used in a DOS command, the path simply becomes an additional (and usually optional) part of the file specification.

A Directory of The Directories

Once your hard disk contains a number of directories, you may want to obtain a listing of what directories are available. The DOS command to do that is TREE.

The TREE Command.

PURPOSE: To display a listing of all of the directories on a given disk.

FORMAT: TREE [d:]
Where d: represents any disk drive name

In order to see what directories are on your disk, enter the command:

```
C>TREE
```

TREE is an external DOS command, so it must be available on disk before it can be used. The TREE command is illustrated in figure 4.8.

The PATH Command

The concept of the PATH as a part of a file specification has been discussed. The name PATH is also used for a DOS command. Its purpose is to describe to DOS where to find programs that are not in the current subdirectory. You will need to understand the difference between the two types of paths. Many application programs that you purchase and install on your hard disk will require you to know something about the PATH command.

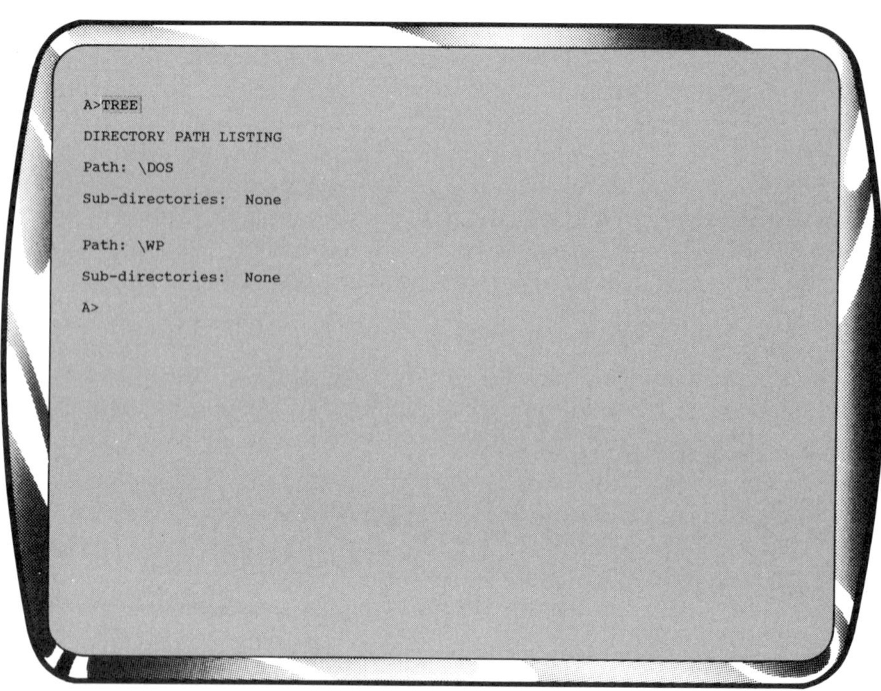

A>TREE
DIRECTORY PATH LISTING
Path: \DOS
Sub-directories: None
Path: \WP
Sub-directories: None
A>

FIGURE 4.8.
Using the TREE command

The PATH Command.

PURPOSE: Defines a search list for DOS to look for commands that are not found in the directory currently logged into.

FORMAT: PATH [\path];[\path]; etc.

For example, the TREE command mentioned above requires that the file TREE.COM be on disk. Under normal circumstances, if you enter the TREE command while you are "logged into" the \WP directory, you would get the message

```
Bad command or file name
```

because the TREE.COM command file was not in the \WP directory, and DOS could not find it in order to execute the command.

To prevent this type of problem, there is a way to tell the computer where to go and find programs when they are requested while in a directory in which they do not reside. This is the function of the PATH command. The PATH command gives the computer a priority, or *Search List,* for searching through the directories on disk to find a program. For example, a common directory setup includes a directory named "\DOS". The \DOS directory would contain all of the DOS files, including all external DOS commands. The command

```
C>PATH \DOS
```

tells DOS that if a command is given while you are logged into any directory, and the command is not found in that directory, it should look in the \DOS directory. Thus, when the command TREE is given while in the \WP directory, the command file TREE.COM will be found in the \DOS directory, and the command will be successful.

Normally, the PATH command will specify several directories (paths) to search in order of priority, separated by semicolons (;). For example, the PATH command may be

```
C>PATH \;\DOS;\WP;\DB
```

In this case, the priority for DOS is to look first in the directory in which the command is given. If the command file is not found there, it will then look in the root directory (\), then in the \DOS directory, then in \WP, then in \DB.

Once a PATH command is given, it remains in effect until the computer is rebooted or until the computer is turned off. Therefore, it is usually only entered once every time the computer is booted. As you will see below in the description of the AUTOEXEC.BAT file, entering the PATH command can be automated so that you do not need to actually enter this command. PATH itself is an internal command. The PATH command only causes DOS to search for three kinds of files, ".COM", ".BAT", and ".EXE", which are command, batch, or program files. (Batch files will be discussed later.) It does *not* apply to data or text files that you create.

The PROMPT Command

You may have noticed that when switching from directory to directory, it is hard to keep track of which directory you are in. One way to solve this problem is to customize the DOS prompt, which is normally "C>", so as to make it give the current directory as well as the current disk drive.

The PROMPT Command.

PURPOSE: To customize the DOS prompt.

FORMAT: PROMPT [message] [$C] [$C] etc.
Where C represents any of these commands:

- **T** **The system time**
- **D** **The system date**
- **P** **The path of the current directory**
- **V** **The version of DOS**
- **N** **The default drive letter**
- **G** **The > sign**
- **L** **The < sign**
- **Q** **The = character**
- **E** **The escape character**
- **B** **The | character**
- **H** **The backspace character**
- **_** **Carriage return and line feed**

Let's look at the optional commands one by one. First, the "message" command represents any message that you want DOS to display on the screen as part of the promp. You could, for instance, tell it to type READY when it is ready for a command. Note that the message should be typed just as you want it to appear on the screen, with no quotes. After the (optional) message, you can request other parts of the prompt using the letters listed. Each of these letters must be preceded by a dollar sign "$", and there should be no spaces between them.
For example, entering the DOS command

```
C>PROMPT $P$G
```

will cause the DOS prompt to include the path of the current directory as a part of the prompt. The "$P" is the prompt command for path and the "$G" is the prompt command for the "greater than" sign. Thus, if you are in the root directory, the prompt becomes:

```
C:\>
```

The "\" between the "C" and the ">" tells you that you are in the root directory. If you change directories by entering the command "CD \DOS", the prompt becomes:

```
C:\DOS>
```

which indicates that you are currently in the DOS directory.

Another example of using the PROMPT command would be:

```
A>PROMPT This Computer Belongs to Bill! $_$P$G
```

This is illustrated in figure 4.9. Notice that the text "This computer belongs to Bill!" will be output literally, since it is not preceded by a "$". The dollar sign-underline ($_) command tells PROMPT to perform a "carriage return, line feed," which means go to the next line. On the next line is the prompt specified by the "PG" PROMPT commands, showing that the current directory is \DOS.

To return to the standard DOS prompt, enter the command PROMPT with no messages or options.

BATCH FILES

Batch files have been mentioned already. A file specification extension. ".BAT" indicates that the file is a batch file. A batch file is a file that contains several DOS commands that you want executed in a particular order. If, for example, you have a series of DOS commands you perform frequently, you can create a file that contains those commands, and cause DOS to execute all of the commands in sequence without retyping them each time. Suppose you often use the two commands:

```
PATH \;\DOS;\WP;\DB
PROMPT $P$G
```

You could place those two commands in a file, named, say, BEGIN.BAT. Then instead of having to remember exactly how to type those commands, you may enter the batch file command, using the file name:

A>PROMPT This Computer Belongs to Bill!$_$P$G
This Computer Belongs to Bill!
A:\DOS>

FIGURE 4.9.
Using the PROMPT command

C>BEGIN

and DOS will automatically execute the two commands in the batch file BEGIN.BAT

Creating a Batch File

There are several ways to create this file. The most common way is to use a file editor. Most word processing programs have the ability to create such files. There is also a simple file editor named EDLIN included as a part of DOS. Another way to create a file without a text editor is the following procedure, which uses the COPY command:

1. Enter a COPY command telling DOS that you will be entering (copying) information from the "CONsole" (the keyboard), and that the information is to be placed in the file named "BEGIN.BAT":

   C>COPY CON BEGIN.BAT

2. Enter the commands you wish to include in this file. Note that *there will be no DOS prompt:*

   PATH \;\DOS;\WP;\DB

   PROMPT PG

   End each line by pressing the ENTER key.

3. End this procedure by pressing the F6 function key, or CTRL-Z, then press Enter. The two lines above are now in the file called BEGIN.BAT

The AUTOEXEC.BAT File: Automating Commands at Boot Time

There is a special batch file called AUTOEXEC.BAT that DOS looks for each time the computer is booted. If you have a series of commands that you want always to occur every time the computer is booted, they should be placed in the AUTOEXEC.BAT file. For example, if you wanted the PATH and PROMPT commands to be activated each time the computer is booted, you could rename the BEGIN.BAT file created above to be AUTOEXEC.BAT. Then, each time you boot your computer, your PATH will automatically be set up, and your prompt will automatically be customized. In fact, these two commands are very commonly included in the AUTOEXEC.BAT file. The contents of a typical AUTOEXEC.BAT file are given in figure 4.10

THE CONFIG.SYS FILE

Another file DOS looks for each time the computer is booted is CONFIG.SYS. Like the AUTOEXEC.BAT file, it is not required that you have one. However, if you do have one in your root directory, DOS looks in the file to see how you want the computer "configured". Users rarely have to decide for themselves what goes into the CONFIG.SYS files, since the software you install will usually have instructions about its requirements for the configuration file.

For example, DOS normally allows software to communicate with 8 files at once on disk. This sounds like a lot, but some complicated programs, such as dBASE III, need more access to the disk than what DOS normally provides. Therefore, the dBASE III installation manual will tell you to place the following lines in your CONFIG.SYS file:

```
FILES = 20
BUFFERS = 15
```

These commands cause DOS to allow more files and more disk buffers than would normally be available. These are the two most common settings in the CONFIG.SYS file. Other items that may be set in this file include:

1. COUNTRY: Specify what country you are in (has to do with how dates are displayed, etc.)
2. DEVICE: Specify certain kinds of output and input devices such as monitors, plotters, memory disks, etc.
3. LASTDRIVE: Specify the maximum number of disk drives on your computer (the normal last drive is E:)

A typical CONFIG.SYS file is illustrated in figure 4.11.This file can be created with a word processor or with the "COPY CON" command, as was illustrated above for batch files.

FIGURE 4.10.
A typical AUTOEXEC.BAT file

```
PROMPT $P$G
PATH \;\DOS;\WP
```

```
FILES = 20
BUFFERS = 15
```

FIGURE 4.11.
A typical CONFIG.SYS file

Note that DOS only looks for the AUTOEXEC.BAT and CONFIG.SYS files at boot time. If you change one of these files, you must then reboot the computer if you want the information in the new files to take effect.

THE WARM BOOT

At times you may need to reboot the computer. One obvious way to do that is to turn the machine off, then turn it back on. This is called a "cold boot". However, electronic equipment is particularly sensitive to being turned on and off. The computer's electronics have to stabilize each time the power is turned on. Many times if there is going to be a failure, it will occur when the computer is first turned on, when it gets the initial burst of power.

Because of this fact, there is a built-in way to restart the computer without turning off its power. This method of rebooting is called a "warm boot". To reboot the computer, hold down the CTRL and ALT keys with your left hand. Then press the DEL key (on the keypad) with a finger on your right hand. Let up on all keys, and the computer will re-boot.

Unless you really know what you are doing, you should only reboot (or turn off the computer) when you are at the DOS prompt. If you reboot the computer in the middle of a program, you may lose information. For example, if you are working on a database, and turn the power off or reboot the computer, the information in the computer's RAM memory is lost. However, there may be times when a computer program "freezes", and you cannot get it to respond. Then you may have to reboot the computer just to get back control of the computer.

SAFETY FIRST: DEVELOP AND FOLLOW A BACKUP PROCEDURE

Data on a diskette or hard disk *can* be destroyed! In fact, sometime during your use of the computer, you will be *likely* to lose some data. If you are careful, this will happen only rarely, and if you have a backup procedure, you can recover from the loss with a minimum of grief.

One of the simplest ways of backing up your information is to make multiple copies of everything you do. For example, if you are working on writing a paper, be sure to keep at least two copies, each on a separate disk. If your original copy is on hard disk, copy the file to a floppy each time you finish working on it. Also, save your work often. Never work on a document for hours without making copies. If the electricity went off, or if the computer had problems, you could easily lose an entire day's work! How often should you save your work? That is determined by how much time you are willing to lose. For example, if you are willing to potentially lose an hour's worth of work, save and back up your work every hour.

Remember this: It is not *if* you will lose information on the computer but *when*.

The BACKUP Command

Besides backing up a single file (which you can easily do with the COPY command), there are also procedures for backing up an entire hard disk. The most common way to back up a hard disk is to copy it onto floppy diskettes. All or part of the hard disk may be saved to diskettes. It may take 30 to 50 diskettes to back up an entire hard disk. This procedure is supported by DOS via the BACKUP command.

The BACKUP Command.

PURPOSE: Copies files from the hard disk to any number of floppy disks.

FORMAT: BACKUP source destination [/options]
Some common options are:

/S	**Back up all subdirectories**
/D:mm-dd-yy	**Back up all files modified on or after the specified date**
/A	**Add more files to a set of already-backed up files**
/M	**Backup all files that have been modified since the last backup.**

The simplest form of the BACKUP command is:

```
C>BACKUP C: A:
```

which tells DOS to BACKUP all files on disk C: to floppy disks on drive A:. This will, however, only back up the files from the currently active directory. Once the command is given, the computer will indicate that diskette number 1 should be in drive A:. Information will be copied to the diskette until it is full, and then you will be prompted to place diskette number 2 in the drive. This procedure is repeated until all the files are backed up onto the diskettes.

If you are using DOS version 3.2 or earlier, all backup diskettes must first be formatted. Unfortunately, this means that you must have an idea before you start of how many diskettes will be required for the backup. To back up 10 megabytes to 360K floppy diskettes will take 10,000,000/360,000 = 27.7, or 28 diskettes.

Backing up Selected Files. There is usually no reason to back up the programs from the hard disk, since you have copies of them on their original floppy diskettes that could be reloaded in a crisis. What you really want to back up are the files containing your work. To back up specific files, you may enter the name(s) of those files using global file characters. For example, suppose you wanted to back up all files with the extension ".DAT". The command would be:

```
C>BACKUP C:*.DAT A:
```

Again, this only backs up files in the currently active subdirectory. To back up the ".DAT" files in all directories, add the /S option to the command (S stands for "subdirectories"):

```
C>BACKUP C:*.DAT A:/S
```

To back up *all* files in all directories, use the command

```
C>BACKUP C:\ A:/S
```

The first example backs up files from the *currently active* directory. The second example backs up files beginning in the root. The \ tells the command to begin backup at the root directory rather than the current directory.

Normally, a back up will erase all files on the target diskette before backing up files to that diskette. If the /A option is used, current files on a backup diskette will not be erased, and new files will be backed up to the diskette, as space allows.

The RESTORE Command

If you need to use one or more of the files that have been backed up, you must use the RESTORE command to copy these files from the backup disks back to the hard disk.

The RESTORE Command.

PURPOSE: Copies files from back-up disks to the hard disk.

FORMAT: RESTORE source destinations [/options]
Options:

/S	**Restore all files from all subdirectories**
/P	**Prompt to select file(s) to restore**
	See DOS manual for others.

An example of the RESTORE command is:

```
C>RESTORE A: C:\*.*/S
```

This command restores all files from floppies in disk A: (source) to the fixed disk C: (destination), including all subdirectories. Other options for the RESTORE command are in the DOS manual. One that is particularly helpful is the /P or PROMPT option. This option causes the computer to prompt you before restoring a file, and lets you pick and choose those files to restore.

A Disaster Plan

A procedure should be set up to back up hard disks or portions of hard disks on a regular basis. Here is an example of a thorough procedure that is based on actual procedures used in business.

1. After initially loading your fixed disk, back up the entire fixed disk *twice.*
2. Daily: Do a backup of the entire disk using the /M/A options.
3. Once a week: Back up entire disk. Place the weekly backup in a secure area, away from the office, or have someone take it home.
4. Result: Two backups, one weekly backup away from the office in case of an emergency (fire, flood, etc.), and one "working" backup at the office to be used on a daily basis.

Keep Disks Free of Unneeded Files

Since backups take up so much diskette space, it is a good idea to keep hard disks clear of unneeded files. Unneeded files on a disk can clutter the directories, limit the amount of disk space for other uses, and prolong the backup procedure. It may also be a good idea, along with the backup procedure, to set aside time once a week (or once a month) to erase any unneeded files from the hard disk, or to copy them to floppies (or back them up) on a semipermanent basis.

Alternatives to the DOS Backup Command

There are also alternatives to using the BACKUP command. Commercially available programs such as FASTBACK provide a quicker way to back up your hard disk. Also, there are backup devices such as tape drives and optical disk drives that allow you to back up an entire hard disk to a single tape or disk in a few minutes. See chapter 12 for a discussion of other backup programs.

Backup vs. Copying

What is the difference between backing up a file to a floppy and copying it to a floppy? If you are putting a file on a diskette to be used or transferred to another PC, the COPY command is preferred over BACKUP. Disks made by the BACKUP procedure should be reserved for emergency backup since files on them cannot be used except by the RESTORE command. If you COPY files from a backup floppy diskette back to the hard disk, they will be unuseable. The DOS RESTORE command is the only way to reverse the BACKUP command. It restores files from the floppy diskettes and places them back onto the fixed disk.

SUMMARY

The DOS commands covered in the past two chapters are the most commonly used commands. There are, however, more DOS commands that have not been covered. This summary lists all of the DOS commands covered in these chapters. The "I" in the table indicates that this is an internal command and the "E" indicates that it is an external command.

Summary of DOS Commands

Command	Purpose	Type
BACKUP	back up files from hard disk	E
CHDIR (CD)	change directory	I
CHKDSK	analyze directories on disk	E
CLS	clear the screen	I
COPY	copy files	I
DEL	same as Erase	I
DIR	directory of disk	I
DISKCOPY	copy entire disk to another disk	E
ERASE	deletes files from disk	I
FORMAT	initialize a disk	E
MKDIR (MD)	make a new sub-directory	I
PRINT	prints contents of a file to printer	E
PROMPT	customize the system prompt	I
RENAME	changes name of a file	I
RESTORE	brings back files backed up	E
RMDIR (RD)	removes a directory	I
TREE	a directory of directories	E
TYPE	displays contents of a file to monitor	I

KEY TERMS

Hard disk

Directory structure

Root directory

Subdirectory

Path

Prompt

Warm boot

QUESTIONS

1. What does the CHKDSK command do? What is the difference between figures for the memory on disk and those for RAM memory? How are these numbers useful? Is this an internal or external command?
2. What does the CLS command do? Is this an internal or external command? When would you use it?
3. What does the DISKCOPY command do? What is the difference between the COPY command and the DISKCOPY command? What are the restrictions on the size of disks to be copied from and to? What problem would occur if there were bad sectors on the source diskette? Is DISKCOPY an internal or external command?
4. What does the PRINT command do? What kinds of files can be printed? How do you terminate a print job? Is the PRINT command an internal or external command?
5. What does the TYPE command do? How is it different from PRINT? What kinds of files can be typed? Is the TYPE command an internal or external command?

6. What is a hard disk, and how does it compare in storage capacity to a floppy diskette? What advantages does a hard disk give a user over a floppy-based system?
7. Describe the purpose of the MD, CD, and RD commands. What is the purpose of having subdirectories on a disk?
8. What is the root directory? What is the name of the root directory? Why does every formatted disk or diskette have a root directory? How do you return to the root directory from any other directory?
9. What does the path to a directory indicate? What would be the path for a directory called BUDGET that was a subdirectory of a directory called DB that was a subdirectory of the root directory?
10. Describe the purpose of tree-structured directories, and give two examples of structure types.
11. What does the TREE command do? Is it an internal or external command?
12. What does the PATH command do? What would happen if you attempted to enter the CHKDSK command (which resides in a directory called \DOS), from the \WP directory, when there was no PATH defined? Describe a PATH command that would cause DOS to look in the following directories: The root, \DOS, \WP, and \UTILS. The PATH command causes DOS to look for three kinds of files. What are those kinds of files? Is PATH an internal or external command?
13. What is the difference between the PATH and the CD commands?
14. What does the PROMPT command do? What PROMPT command will cause the system prompt to display the path of the current directory? Suppose you want the prompt to consist of the current directory path followed by the "=" sign. What PROMPT command would you use? Is the PROMPT command an internal or external command?
15. What is a batch file? What extension does a batch file have? What is the special purpose of the AUTOEXEC.BAT file? When does DOS use the AUTOEXEC.BAT file?
16. What is the purpose of the CONFIG.SYS file? When does DOS use this file?
17. What is a warm boot? Why is it often preferable to a cold boot? How do you perform a warm boot on an IBM PC-type computer? Why is it dangerous to reboot the computer while a program is running?
18. Why is it a good idea to back up the information on your hard disk (or floppy disk)? What are the DOS commands to back up and retrieve files? Are these internal or external commands?
19. Suppose you had a business that recorded stock transactions on your computer. If you lost this information, it would cost you about $10,000 per day of revenue. Describe the backup procedure that you would use.

LABORATORY EXERCISES

Lab Exercise 1. (The CHKDSK and DISKCOPY Commands)

a. If you have a two-floppy system, place your DOS disk in the A: drive, and a blank disk in the B: drive. If you have a one-floppy system, place your DOS disk in the A: drive. Make sure the prompt is A:\), and that you are in the root directory.

b. DISKCOPY the DOS disk to the blank disk.

(If you have a one-disk system, you will be prompted to swap diskettes.)

c. Perform a CHKDSK on the DOS diskette, then on the newly copied disk. Record the results. Are the results identical?

Lab Exercise 2. ***(The PRINT, TYPE, and CLS Commands)***

a. With your DOS disk in the A: drive (containing the file PRINT.COM) and the Text Examples Disk in the B: drive, display the contents of the file B: EXAMPLES.TXT to the screen. If you are using a hard disk system, place the Text Examples Disk in the A: drive, and use C: as the logged into drive.)

b. Clear the screen.

c. If your computer is currently attached to a printer, print the content of the B:EXAMPLES.TXT file to the printer.

d. Repeat part c. This time, as soon as it begins printing, enter the command PRINT /T to terminate the printing. On some printers, you may not be fast enough to terminate before it is finished printing, so you need to be quick.

Lab Exercise 3. ***(Creating Directories, Copying Files, the PROMPT Command, and the TREE Command).*** On a floppy disk in drive A: (which works just like a hard disk for this exercise) perform the following exercises:

a. Make the following directories: \DOS, \WP, \WP\LETTERS, and \TEMP. Write down the commands you used.

b. Modify the system prompt to display the current directory and a "greater than" sign. Write down the command you used.

c. Practice moving from directory to directory using the CD command. Write down three commands you used, and the resulting prompts.

d. Place the Text Examples Disk in the B: drive (or whatever drive you have available). With A:\) as the default prompt, copy the file EXAMPLE.TXT into the \WP directory using the COPY command. Write down the command.
Explain why your command performs this task. Copy the same file from the B: drive into the \DOS directory. Copy the file (\WP\EXAMPLE.TXT) from the \WP directory into the \WP\LETTERS directory. Write down the commands you used.

e. Enter the TREE command to examine the current tree structure of the directories on disk. Write down the result.

f. Make sure you are in the root directory by entering a CD command. Write down your command. Attempt to remove the \WP directory with the command:
A:\)RD \WP
Why did it not work? Next, remove the directory named \TEMP using a similar command. Why did it work this time?

Lab Exercise 4. ***(Batch Files)***

a. Create a batch file in the root directory called CDIR.BAT that will clear the screen, then display the directory in the wide format. Use the procedure described in the text, using the COPY command. Write down the commands you used.

b. Enter a command to execute the batch file you have just created. Write down the command and the results.

GUEST ESSAY

Microcomputers in a Medical Office

by Judy Bennett
Office Manager, Neonatal Associates

As a "one-person office" working for a doctor's practice, my time and efficiency were fast running out. The practice began with only one neonatologist and within the first year expanded to include another. Their practice, caring for ill and premature infants in the Neonatal Intensive Care Unit (NICU) was, to say the least, challenging to record, bill, and track.

As the number of accounts increased, the load of insurance claims, monthly statements, and delinquent accounts became too much for my manual accounting system. We had a fairly efficient system; however, with the increase in the patient load there were too many daily entries to make on each account. Since our patients are infants in the intensive care unit, a day's care often includes more than one daily visit plus procedures. I needed a faster, more efficient way to record that information and to reproduce those accounts for monthly statements. Most stock programs for doctor's practices would not accommodate these parameters. With the help of a computer consultant, a program was located that could be customized to suit our needs.

Our new program allowed us to enter patient information, guarantor information (including addresses, phone numbers, place of employment, etc.), and insurance information for two insurance carriers. This information for each outstanding account was entered, along with their "Balance Forward."

Invoicing in the past had required manually typing dates, insurance codes, descriptions of services, and daily charges for those services. The insurance codes for diagnoses and for procedures were previously kept on a list and referred to continually when coding insurance claims. When coding claims now, the codes are at our fingertips! When the code number is typed, the description and charge are automatically brought up on the screen. They can be accepted as stored or changed for that particular patient's situation. Once the patient information is entered, and the daily visits and procedures are entered, then the computer is ready to produce an insurance claim form, a patient account history, an invoice, or a monthly statement, depending on my needs. Having our new computer program provides us with a good sorting and storing method for all this information.

The most overwhelming problem in my manual accounting system had become the delinquent accounts. I had lost a grasp on how many accounts were pending insurance decisions and how many were fast becoming "bad debts." The new computer program had an "account aging" capability that became very useful. On the patient's monthly statement, the account age is automatically listed as current, over 30 days, over 60 days, or over 90 days old. But best of all, there is a new capability to run a list of each account, amounts owing, and the age of that account. I could see at a glance what kind of action I needed to take in each situation.

Another feature of the computer that has become a "plus" in our office is the ability to search for specific patients or information. Even though a patient's name may not be known or other information may be missing, similar patients can be listed and retrieval of that specific account is made possible. This has been very helpful in identifying lost mail or locating files for doctors or people on the phone.

Having all this information stored and readily available gave us the new capability of compiling statistics. The data can be compiled according to type of illness, length of hospital stay, insurance carrier, and numerous other criteria. End-of-period reports can also be run from any beginning and ending date needed. These include monthly transaction reports, account histories, activity reports in any specific area or a combination of areas, or the monthly accounts receivable summary.

The computer's speed and memory have allowed me to eliminate many extra steps in my work. It has also added new tools to help manage the accounts receivable more efficiently. The organization it provides is unmatched.

CHAPTER 5

Introduction to Word Processing

CHAPTER OVERVIEW. This is the first of two chapters that introduce word processing on personal computers. Two word processors, WordPerfect and WordStar Professional, are used as case studies. In addition, examples and exercises provide an opportunity for you to study your own personal selection of word processor. This will be referred to as "your word processor" throughout the chapter. The reader may skip case studies that do not concern the software he or she is using. Or, all of the case studies may be used to compare the operations of several word processors.

The concepts described in this chapter are relevant to most word processing programs. The chapter includes the concepts of entering the text of a document for the first time, editing an existing document, cursor movement, basic word processing commands, saving and printing, working with blocks of text, selecting formatting options, and setting margins. The next chapter will cover some advanced word processing topics.

CHAPTER OBJECTIVES

Upon completion of this chapter, you will be able to:

- Describe the command structure of a word processor.
- Create a new document.
- Edit an existing document.
- Print a document.
- Save a document to disk and retrieve it.
- Cause text to be printed in bold or underlined.
- Describe how to set margins and line spacing.

PRELIMINARIES ABOUT THE SOFTWARE

The software introduced in the chapter may be used either on a hard-disk system or on a floppy-based system. If you are using a dual-floppy system, you may need to swap diskettes occasionally. Also, in the dual-floppy system, documents will probably be stored on the B: drive, and in the hard-disk system they are usually stored on the C: drive. The examples in the text will usually refer to operations on the C: drive. However, with the exceptions mentioned, other operations of the program should remain the same.

CASE STUDY

Word-Perfect, WordStar and Your Word Processor

In this chapter, two word processing programs will be used as examples:

- WordPerfect from WordPerfect Corporation (version 4.2)
- WordStar Professional from Micropro International Corporation (version 4.0)

and, in addition, space will be provided for you to include information about

- Your Word Processor

The concepts and commands covered are similar in nature to many other word processing programs. The user manuals for these programs are usually several hundred pages in length. The purpose of the introduction in this text is not to rewrite the manual, but to give a tutorial introduction to the major components of word processing, and expose the student to the most commonly used aspects of word processing. From this tutorial, you should be comfortable with the general operation of the word processor. However, you should not expect merely to be exposed to the concepts of word processing and then expect to generate polished documents. Learning to use a word processor effectively and efficiently takes time. You have to sit at the computer, use the word processor, and gradually become comfortable with its possibilities.

THE TYPEWRITER GETS A SLOW START

For ages the processing of words was done with quill in hand. Of course, there was Gutenberg, who made the printing of books an easier proposition. But by and large, most documents were written by hand until the middle of the nineteenth century. Ideas for automating the processing of words resulted in a series of patents for typing machines, beginning in 1843. In fact, over fifty inventions were patented that claimed to do typing, before Christopher Sholes came up with both a machine and a marketing plan that really made an impact on industry.

In 1866, Sholes was tinkering with a machine that could automatically number pages, when a businessman named James Desmore suggested that his machine could be expanded to type letters. After Sholes perfected a simple typewriter, Desmore began touring the country looking for buyers. The

Remington Company liked the idea, modified the mechanics of the machine, and began promoting it. Their ideas for how it would be used may seem a bit humorous to us today. They promoted the typewriter with advertisements such as, "Persons traveling by sea can write with it when pen writing is impossible." It took businesses a while, but they finally decided that the typewriter could be a valuable office tool.

The Processing of Words

By the turn of the century, the processing of words was firmly established on the typewriter, and so it remained until the 1970s. The electric typewriter became popular in the 1950s, and such innovations as erasable paper, correction fluid and correction tape were tried to solve the problems of handling typing mistakes and changes.

Computers were not originally designed for the manipulation of words; they were meant to perform numeric calculations. However, as computers became more powerful, and as they evolved from using punched cards to using terminals, the application of computing to word processing emerged. In the 1970s, companies like Wang introduced small computers to the office with the specific function of processing words. Although they were small computers for the time, they were still very expensive, and were used mostly by large companies.

THE ADVENT OF MICROCOMPUTER WORD PROCESSING

When microcomputers were introduced in the early 1970s, they were capable of only the most primitive word processing. Many microcomputer systems could only print uppercase letters. As the microcomputer industry began to mature, software programs such as WordStar provided the ability to do acceptable word processing on a small computer. However, problems with poor quality printers and computers with small amounts of memory still existed, and few businesses used the early word processing capabilities of the microcomputer. With the advent of a more powerful computer, the IBM PC, and with the introduction of "letter-quality" printing devices, microcomputer word processing of the 1980s became a standard office fixture.

The Modern Word Processing System

Word processing goes far beyond "typewriting". Because the words are stored electronically before being printed, they can be manipulated to get the document to look "just right". Spell-checking routines can search through a document and locate all potentially misspelled words, and will usually suggest correct spellings. Programs with the ability to check grammar are still being developed, but there are some programs, such as Grammatik, that will spot obvious misuses of words and phrases. An on-line thesaurus can help the writer find words with similar meanings without having to flip through the pages of *Roget's Thesaurus.* Other routines can let the writer know the word count of a document and can analyze the text's level of reading difficulty.

No longer do secretaries have to write individual letters to each member of a group of people. Names and addresses can be stored on the computer, and then "merged" with a letter to create "individualized" letters. You have probably received letters such as one proclaiming that John Doe (you) of Somewhere, Ohio may have won $10,000,000 dollars.

With new advancements in printer technology, particularly the introduction of laser printers, textual output from the computer can approach typeset quality. Figure 5.1 illustrates various qualities of print and print styles (fonts) available on printers used on microcomputers.

Examples from a Hewlett Packard Laserjet:

Times Roman Font Size 6 points

Times Roman Font size 10 points

Times Roman Font size 14 points

Times Roman Font Size 18 points

Times Roman Font Size 24

Courier font, size 12 points

Line printer font, size 8 points

Example from an 9 pin dot matrix printer:

This is printed on a 9 pin dot matrix printer.

Example from a 24 pin dot matrix printer:

This is from a 24 pin dot matrix printer

Example from an NEC 3550 letter quality printer:

This is printed on an NEC Letter Quality Printer 3550.

FIGURE 5.1.
Example typefaces

In many of the early word processors, various kinds of type styles, called fonts, were selected by placing special codes in the word processing document. For example, to cause the word "**bold**" to appear in boldface type when printed, the word processing user would have to place command codes around the word. A common command code might be a CTRL-B before and after the word to be printed in bold face. The first CTRL-B would turn the boldface "on", and the CTRL-B after the word would turn the boldface "off". These codes would appear on the computer monitor (usually as special characters not on the keyboard) and the user would have to visualize what the document would look like when printed.

Many word processors now have features which allow a document to appear on the screen exactly as it will look when printed. This feature is known as "What You See Is What You Get", and is often abbreviated WYSIWYG (pronounced "Wiz-ee-wig"). A step beyond word processing is a concept known as *desktop publishing,* which is the creation of typeset-quality documents complete with illustrations. Some word processing programs of the late 1980s have begun to include some of the features of desktop publishing, such as incorporating graphics with text. Figure 5.2 illustrates how some of these abilities can be used.

BEFORE YOU USE A WORD PROCESSOR

With all the power that word processing gives, it is not as easy to use as a typewriter. Because word processing is powerful, it takes some time to learn. Most people learn word processing in stages. It is relatively easy to learn how to create and print a one-page letter. The next step in proficiency may involve creating a long document and using other features that change the way text appears on the page—margins, type styles, tables, etc. Some users may want to learn about footnoting, titling, double columns, and other advanced features.

Word processors do not create words on their own. The user must still type the information to create the document. Word processing will take some of the drudgery out of revision and correction. A sentence may be quickly moved from the beginning to the end of a paragraph. A paragraph can be deleted or moved, or copied to another document. Misspelled words can be corrected and similar words can be looked up in the electronic thesaurus. Margins can be changed, page sizes altered, and titles changed, all electronically and in a matter of seconds. Once the bulk of the text is entered into a document, revisions should be much simpler than when a typewriter is used.

THE LANGUAGE OF THE WORD PROCESSOR

Every word processor has its own "language". That is, to tell the word processor to do something, you must instruct it by pressing a particular key sequence on the keyboard, or by selecting a specific item from a menu. To use a word processor you must first learn its language. Many word processors, like other software programs, use control commands to access various features. A control command is typed by holding the CTRL key down and at the same time pressing another key. Control commands are usually written "CTRL-Letter" or " ^Letter". For example, the command "Control B" would be

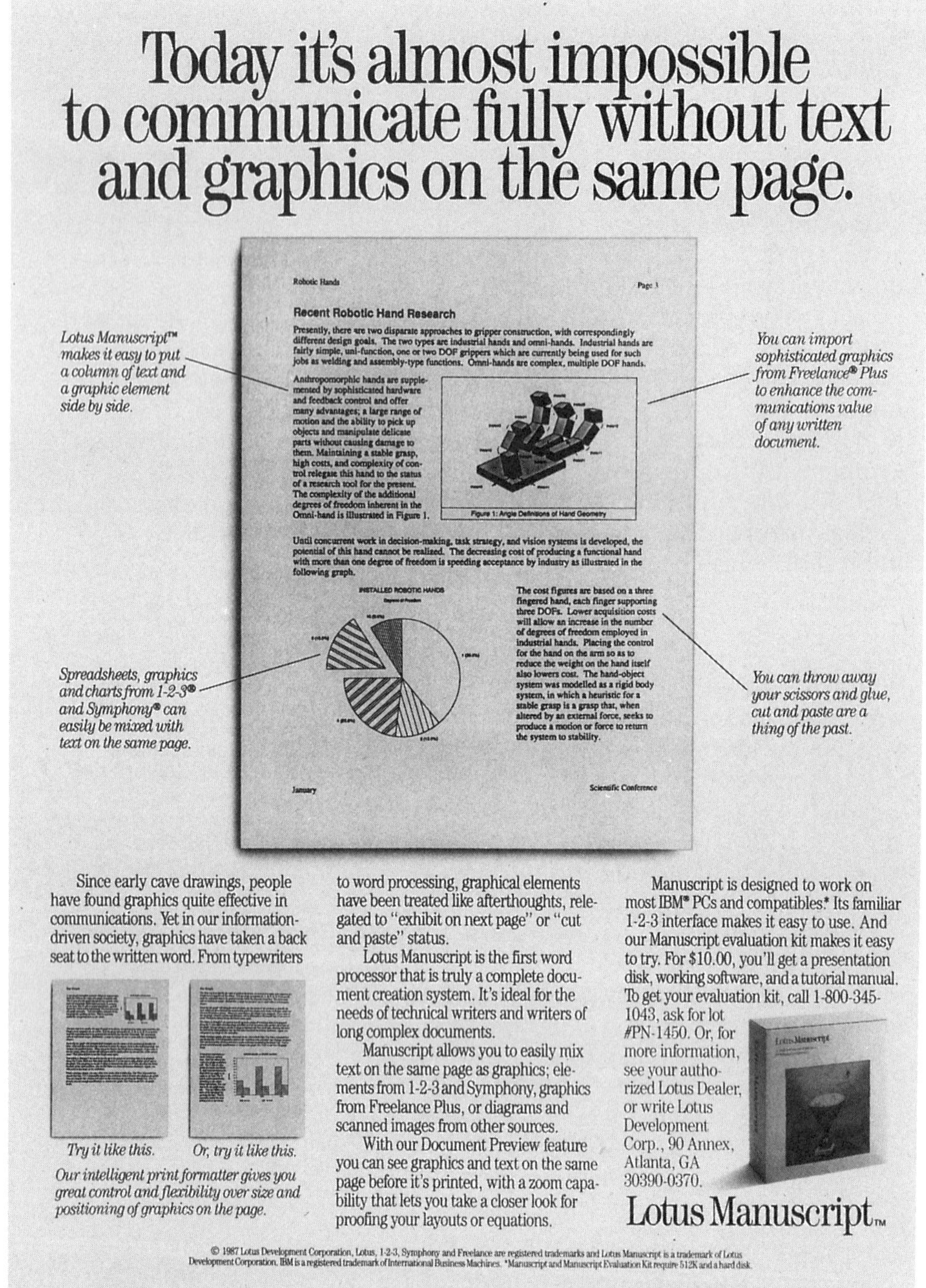

FIGURE 5.2.
Text and graphics produced by a word processor
(From a Lotus ad)

written "CTRL-B" or "ˆB". Another command key that may be used in some programs is the ALT key. This key is used like the CTRL key. The command ALT-B would be given by holding the ALT key down, while at the same time pressing the "B" key. Other commands may be given through the function keys. These keys are labeled F1, F2, . . . , F10 on the keyboard. The function keys may also be used in conjunction with the CTRL, ALT, or SHIFT keys in commands such as CTRL-F1, ALT-F6, or SHIFT-F3.

Some commands may be *embedded* into the text of a document. For example, most word processors automatically pick where they will start a new page by counting the number of lines they have printed on the page. When one page is full of text, the word processor moves the printer to the top of the next sheet of paper. To force the word processor to page at another place might require that a command be placed in the document file. For example, that command might be ".pa", which stands for "page advance". Embedded commands will be introduced as they are used.

CASE STUDY

Word-Perfect—The Command Keys

WordPerfect makes use of the CTRL, SHIFT, and ALT keys to access many of its word processing features. For example, access to the thesaurus is through the command ALT-F1. The spelling checker is accessed by the command CTRL-F1. To help you remember these commands, WordPerfect provides templates that fit around or above the function keys. These are illustrated in figure 5.3. Notice in the illustration that each function key has four meanings. The top meaning is the CTRL command, and is printed in red on the template. The second meaning is in blue, and is an ALT command. The third meaning is in green, and is a SHIFT command. The last meaning, printed in black, is obtained by pressing the function key directly.

CASE STUDY

WordStar Professional—The Command Structure

WordStar operates from a series of menus, with each menu offering a series of options. The opening menu and other WordStar menus are illustrated in figure 5.4. The first menu is called the "Opening Menu", and it allows you to access other menus and features of WordStar. The options on the opening menu are chosen by typing the letter of the desired function. For example, to rename a file, press the "E" key when the opening menu is on the screen. Another WordStar menu is the Edit Menu. Notice that the commands on this menu have a caret or "^" symbol preceding each command letter. This means that these commands are CTRL commands. To type the command "char left", use the keys CTRL-S.

Notice in figure 5.4 that WordStar menus are in layers, with the Opening Menu at the top. From the Opening Menu, you may access other "submenus".

CASE STUDY

Your Word Processor—Commands

If you are using a word processor other than WordPerfect or WordStar, one of the first things you should learn about your word processor is its style of operation. WordPerfect uses the function keys to give commands, WordStar uses mostly control commands, and generally has a menu of available commands on the screen.

How do you enter commands into your word processor? Does it use function key commands, control key commands, menu commands, or a combination of these?

Describe how commands are entered in your word processor:

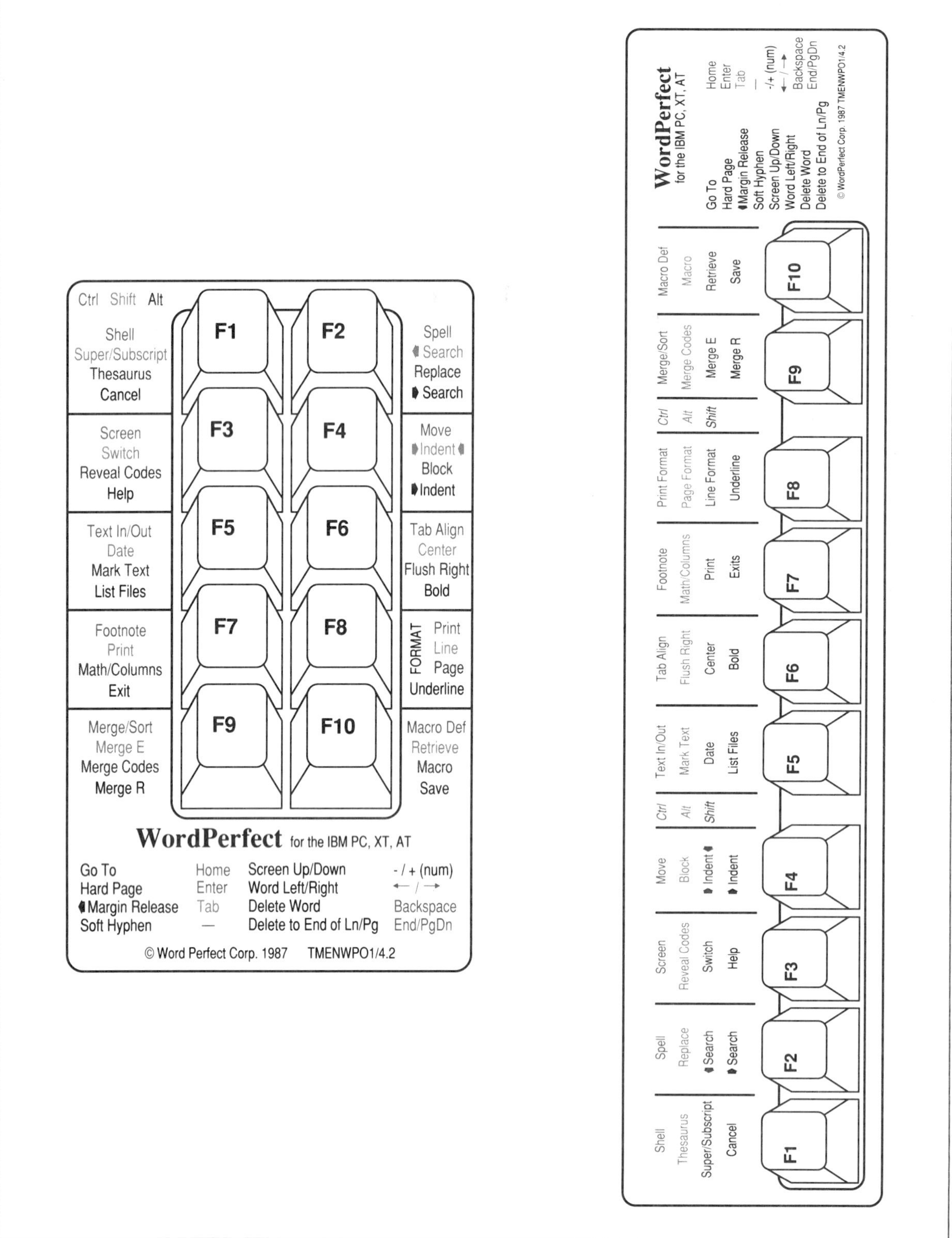

FIGURE 5.3.
WordPerfect Templates

```
                    WordStar Professional Release 4
============================ O P E N I N G   M E N U ============================
      D open a document                     L change logged drive/directory
      N open a nondocument                  C protect a file
      P print a file                        E rename a file
      M merge print a file                  O copy a file
      I index a document                    Y delete a file
      T table of contents                   F turn directory off
      X exit WordStar                     Esc shorthand
      J help                                R run a DOS command

================================ E D I T   M E N U ================================
   CURSOR       SCROLL          ERASE       OTHER                   MENUS
 ^E up         ^W up          ^G char     ^J help                ^O onscreen format
 ^X down       ^Z down        ^T word     ^I tab                 ^K block & save
 ^S left       ^R up screen   ^Y line     ^V turn insert off     ^P print controls
 ^D right      ^C down       Del char     ^B align paragraph     ^Q quick functions
 ^A word left     screen      ^U unerase  ^N split the line     Esc shorthand
 ^F word right                            ^L find/replace again

================== O N S C R E E N   F O R M A T   M E N U ==================
     MARGINS              TYPING                       DISPLAY
   L set left           W turn word wrap off          D turn print controls off
   R set right          J turn right justify off      H turn hyphen help on
   X release            E enter soft hyphen           P turn preview on
   T turn ruler off     G temporary indent            B turn soft space dots off
   F ruler from text    S set line spacing              TABS
   O ruler to text      C center line                 I set tab stop    N clear

====================== B L O C K   &   S A V E   M E N U ======================
    SAVE                           BLOCK                          FILE
 S save & resume edit       B mark begin          C copy       O copy   P print
 D save document            K mark end            V move       E rename
 X save & exit WordStar     H turn display on     Y delete     J erase
 Q quit without saving      W write to disk       M math       L logged drive/dir
     CURSOR                 N turn column mode on              R insert a file
 0-9 set/remove marker      I turn column replace on           F run a DOS command

==================== P R I N T   C O N T R O L S   M E N U ====================
            BEGIN & END                                    OTHER
    B bold              X strike out          H overprint char    O binding space
    S underline         D double strike      <-┘ overprint line   C print pause
    V subscript         Y italics/color       F phantom space     I column tab
    T superscript       K indexing            G phantom rubout    @ fixed position
                                        Q W E R custom            N normal pitch
                                              L form feed         A alternate pitch

============================== Q U I C K   M E N U ==============================
            CURSOR                 FIND              OTHER               SPELL
 E upper left    P previous    F find text     U align paragraphs L check rest
 X lower right   V last find   A find/replace  M math    Q repeat N check word
 S left side     B beg block   G char forward    ERASE            O enter word
 D right side    K end block   H char back     Y line to right      SCROLL
 R beg doc     0-9 marker      I find page   Del line to left     W up, repeat
 C end doc       ? char count    (or line)     T to character     Z down

======================== S H O R T H A N D   M E N U ========================
 ? display and/or change definitions                 ^J help

 = result from last ^QM or ^KM math                  @ today's date
 $ formatted result from last ^QM or ^KM math        ! current time
 # last ^QM math equation
```

FIGURE 5.4.
WordStar Opening Menu and a few other WordStar Menus

WORD PROCESSING VOCABULARY

Word processing has its own vocabulary. As you refer to your own word processing manual, or other books about word processing, you will encounter a number of terms that may be unfamiliar. Below is a list of commonly used terms, many of which will be used in this chapter.

Block: Any number of characters forming one part of the text, from a single letter to an entire document. Blocks are usually used in word processing to designate a portion of text which is to be treated as a single unit.
Cursor: The blinking underline or small box that appears on the screen. In a word processing program, the cursor usually marks the position in the text where text entry or a command will take place.
Default: A standard setting for some characteristic such as the margin or the justification mode. The word processor will automatically use this setting until the user changes it by a command.
Document: Any body of text processed by a word processor, including a page, a letter, or a novel.
Documentation: Supplementary materials, such as manuals, supplied by the manufacturer to explain how to use the word processor.
Flush left, flush right: Even with the left or right margin.
Font: A style of printed characters.
Footer: A block of one or more lines of text that appear at the bottom of each page.
Header: A block of one or more lines of text that appear at the top of each page.
Justify: To cause all lines to line up evenly at the margin. A paragraph that is right-justified contains spaces so that all full lines are the same length and are evenly aligned at the right margin.
Line Spacing: The amount of space that appears between printed lines. Normal line spacing is single spacing. Double spacing puts a full blank line between printed lines. Line spacing can also be in fractional increments, such as 1.5 line spaces, which is halfway between single spacing and double spacing.
Margin: The blank or white spaces on the edges of the printed page. Usually the top, bottom, right, and left margins can all be controlled by a word processing program.
Menu: A list of commands that are currently available, displayed on the screen.
Page Format: The text layout on the page. This may consist of margins, spacing, pitch, font, page numbering, and other similar settings.
Pagination: The division of text into equal pages. Most word processors perform automatic pagination, in which the word processor "figures out" where in a document to begin the next page.
Pitch: The size of characters, usually measured in number of characters per inch (cpi). The most common are 10 cpi and 12 cpi, called pica and elite respectively.
Ragged Right Edge: A format such as a typewriter produces, with each line of text being a different length; the opposite of right-justified.
Spelling Checker: A word processing feature that checks the spelling of words, and usually suggests alternatives for suspect words.

Thesaurus: A feature in some word processors that displays synonyms to a chosen word.
Word Wrap: A word processing feature that causes words that are being typed past the right margin to automatically be moved intact to the next line.

SELF-PACED TUTORIALS

The first part of the WordPerfect and WordStar manuals contain tutorials to help you learn the product. For both WordPerfect and WordStar the section in the manual is called "Learning". These tutorials may be used to reinforce the material covered here. If you are using another word processing program, look in the manual's table of contents. Does it contain a tutorial that you can go through to familiarize yourself with the program?

BEGINNING THE WORD PROCESSING PROGRAM

The word processing programs discussed here may be used on hard-disk or floppy-based systems. The examples in this text will commonly use the "C>" prompt, which implies using the program from the hard-disk drive. Dual-floppy disk systems will use the prompt "A″", with the information created by the word processor stored on the B: drive.

CASE STUDY

Word-Perfect—Beginning the Program

To begin the WordPerfect program, enter the command:

```
C>WP
```

The WordPerfect program's initial screen is mostly blank, with a small **status line** in the lower right corner. This line tells you which document is being edited, the page, the line number, and the position of the cursor. This screen is illustrated in figure 5.5.

CASE STUDY

WordStar—Beginning the Program

To begin the WordStar program, enter the command:

```
C>WS
```

The WordStar program will display the Opening Menu on its initial screen, as illustrated in figure 5.6.

FIGURE 5.5.
Initial WordPerfect screen

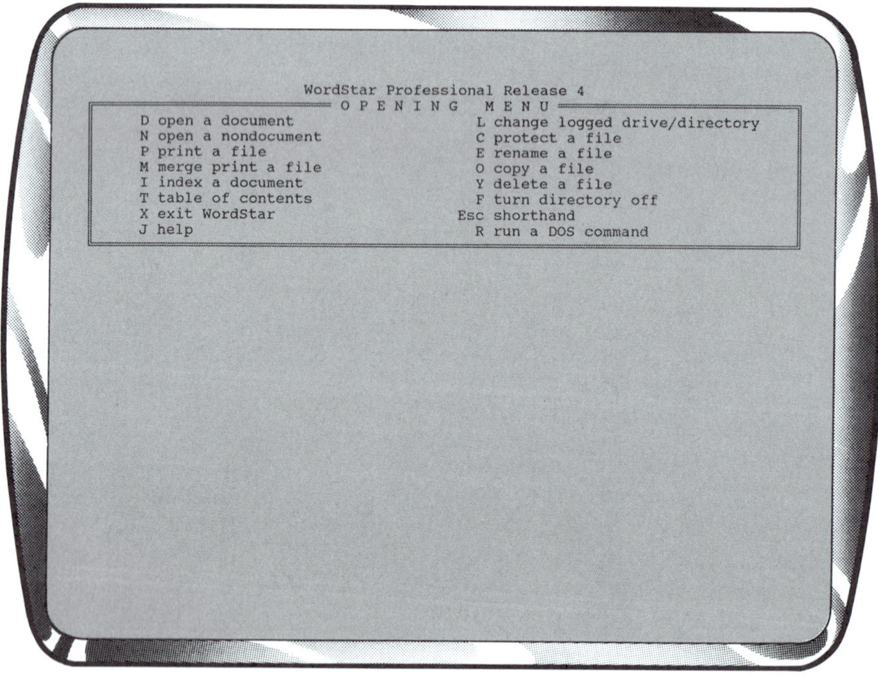

FIGURE 5.6.
Initial WordStar screen

CASE STUDY

Your Word Processor—Beginning the Program

If you are using another word processing program, what is the command to begin the program from DOS?

C>______________________________

SETTING UP THE WORD PROCESSOR FOR YOUR DOCUMENT

The way text appears on the printed page has to do with the way the word processor handles the right, left, top, and bottom margins, headers, footers, and line spacing. Different word processors may have different standard (*default*) settings for these items. Figure 5.7 illustrates many of the common settings that you must consider when working with a word processor. That is, when you begin using the word processor, your document will be situated on the printed page in a certain pre-specified way unless you use some command or alternate setup to change the page format. The initial examples in the text will use the standard page settings. Later, techniques of altering the page format will be covered.

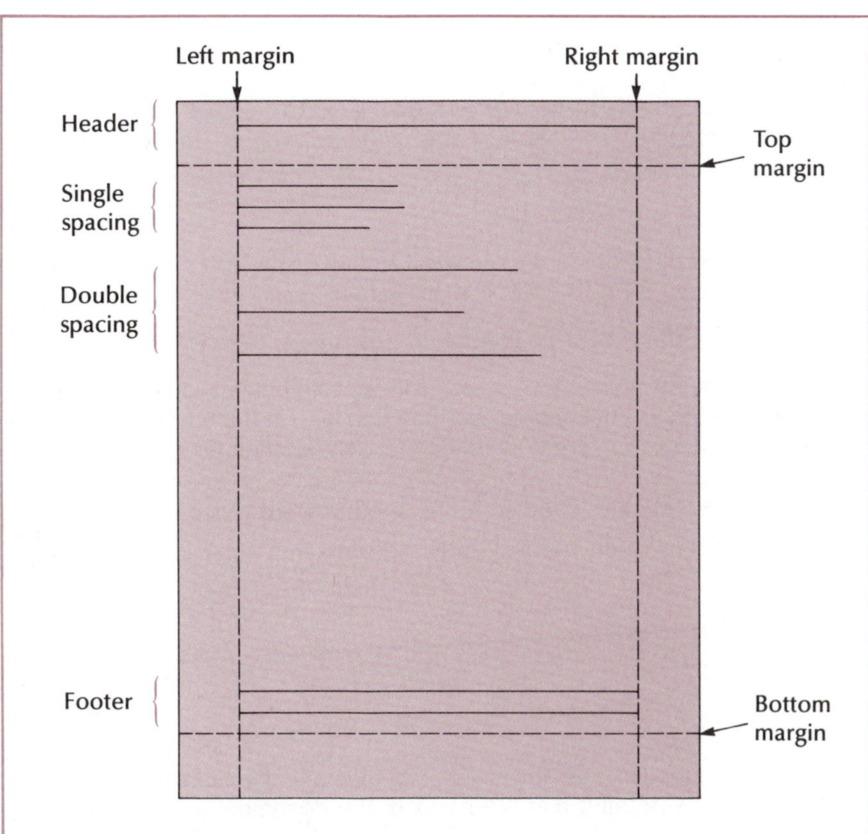

FIGURE 5.7.
Typical page format

Creating a New Document

Word processors may be used to create new documents or to change old documents. (The word *document* refers to any kind of writing created on the word processor, such as a letter, a report, a novel, or a memo.) The creation of a new document occurs when you begin entering information into a blank file. Each document must be given a name. This is the filename used when storing and retrieving the information on a disk. Some word processing programs require you to name the document before you begin entering text. Others allow you to enter information first, and name it later. The name of a document usually follows the same requirements as a DOS file name, since the word processing file is usually stored on disk using the name you have selected for the document.

CASE STUDIES

Word Perfect, WordStar, and your Word Processor—Entering Text

Word Perfect. Once you have started the WordPerfect program, you may immediately begin entering text onto the blank screen, without naming the document.

WordStar. In WordStar, you must choose the "D" option from the Opening Menu. This option is "open a document". After choosing "D", the program will prompt you with the question

```
Document to open?
```

In response, type the file name. For example, if "EXCEL.DOC" is the name you have chosen for the document, enter your answer to the command as indicated:

```
Document to open?EXCEL.DOC
```

Include drive and directory in the file specification if they are different from the current default (e.g., B:EXCEL.DOC). WordStar will respond with the message

```
Can't find that file. Create a new one? (Y/N)
```

After you respond by typing "Y", a screen will appear containing the Edit Menu at the top, an entry area in the middle, and function keys at the bottom. This was illustrated in figure 5.6. You are now ready to begin entering text.

Your Word Processor. If you are using another word processor:

- 1. What happens when you first enter the program? What screen or screens appear?

- 2. Are you required to enter the name of the document to be created or edited? How would you tell it that the name of the document to be created was *EXCEL.DOC*?

- 3. Are there any other steps you must go through before you can begin entering text?

The document that will be used as the first example is the letter pictured in figure 5.8. Several of the most common commands will be illustrated in creating and editing this letter.

FIGURE 5.8
Sample letter

Jane Lavater Consulting, Inc.
1028 Madison Avenue
New York, New York 10016

January 8, 1989

Sir Joshua Reynolds
111 Whatever St.
Place City, NY 11111

Dear Joe,

The modern world is full of instant this and instant that. We want what we want right away. Good character traits cannot be bought off the shelf.

We have all heard about excellence, and somehow we want it right away. <u>This is not possible.</u>

Excellence is never granted, but is the reward of labor. It argues, indeed, no small strength of mind to persevere in the habits of industry, without perceiving those advantages which, like the hands of a clock, while they make hourly approaches to their point, yet proceed so slowly as to escape observation.

Sincerely,

Jane Lavater

IMPORTANT KEYSTROKES

Before actually entering text, you should become familiar with the keyboard. You should already be familiar with the "typewriter" keys, and how some special keys such as the CTRL and ALT keys are used. Other important keys include the SHIFT key(s), the backspace key, the ESC key, the TAB key, the function keys, the ENTER or RETURN key, and the cursor keys. These keys were introduced when you learned how to use DOS. All of the standard typewriter keys and many of the special keys will operate in the same manner in your word processing program as they did when entering DOS commands. Some exceptions are the cursor keys, the CTRL key, the ALT key, and the function keys.

Perhaps the most frequently used keys in word processing are the cursor keys. These arrow keys allow you to move about within the document and change, add, or delete text in specific locations. The PgUp and PgDn keys allow you to scroll through the document. On the original IBM PC-style keyboards, the cursor keys are found on the numeric pad. Newer IBM PC (PS/2) keyboards have cursor keys in an upside-down "T" pattern separate from the numeric keypad. If you are using the cursor keys in the numeric keypad, you must be sure that the pad is in cursor mode and not numeric mode. Otherwise, when you press the up-arrow key you will get the number 8 instead of moving the cursor.

CASE STUDY

Word-Perfect Cursor Control

In WordPerfect, the arrow keys move the cursor one character to the right or left, or up or down one line. These keys have no effect until some text is entered into the document. The arrow keys will not allow you to move to a part of a document where there is no text already defined. When you do have text in your document, the Home Key can be used in combination with the arrow keys to move the cursor to any edge of the screen or any edge of the whole document. The End Key will take you to the end of a line.

The cursor commands are summarized below.

Summary of WordPerfect Cursor Control Commands

Arrow keys: Moves the cursor one character or one line in direction of the arrow.

Home-arrow: Moves the cursor to the edge of the screen in the direction of the arrow.

Home-Home-arrow: Moves the cursor to the extreme edge of the document in the direction of the arrow.

Home-Home-Home-left arrow: Moves the cursor to the beginning of a line before any codes.

End: Moves the cursor to the end of the line.

Escape-#-arrow (# is any number): Moves the cursor a specified number of characters in a line, or a number of lines or pages. For example, ESC-8-down arrow moves the cursor down 8 lines.

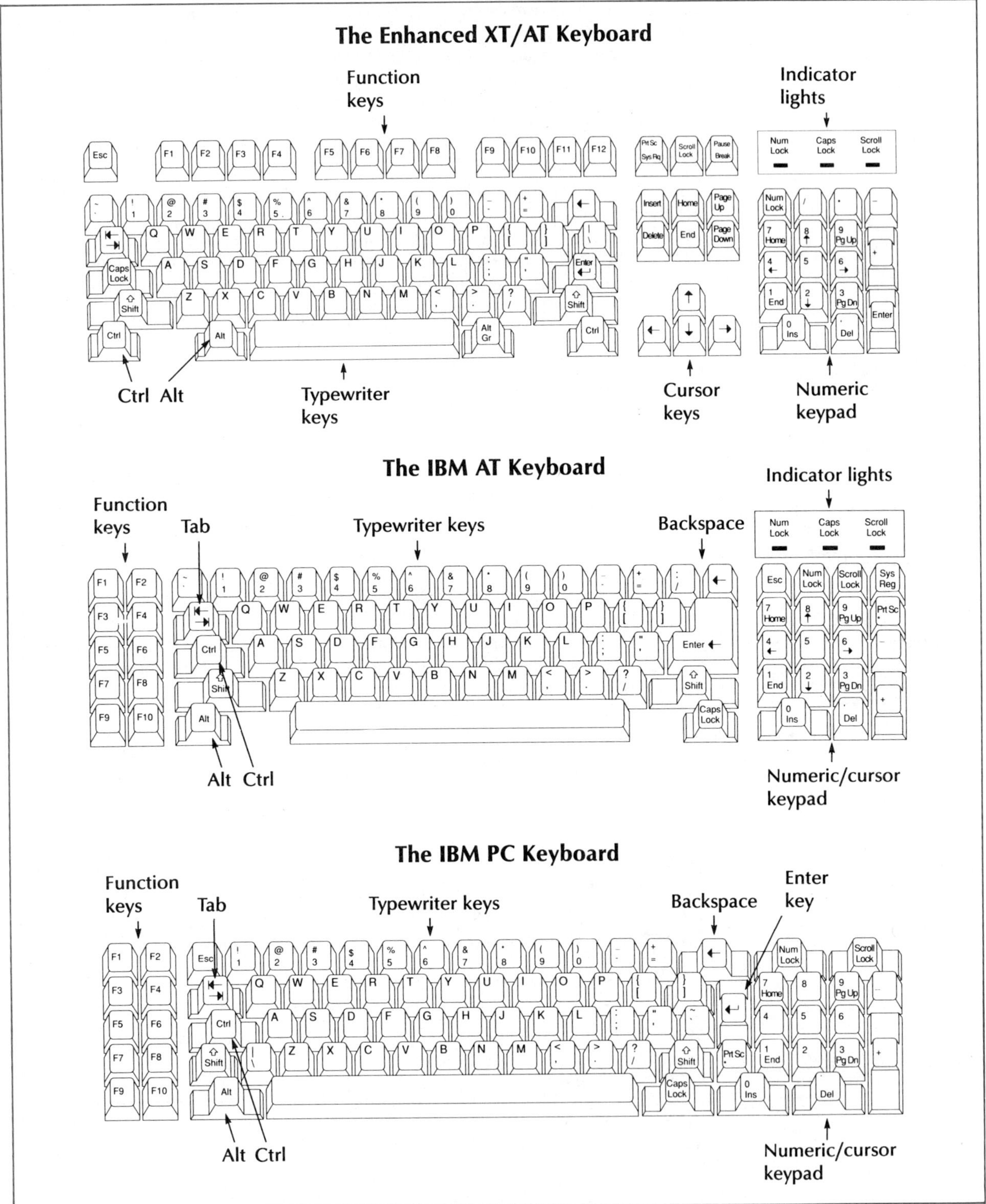

FIGURE 5.9. Review of important keys

CTRL-Home-position: Moves the cursor to a specified position.
Examples:
^Home-character: Moves cursor forward to that character
^Home-number: Moves to that page
^Home-up arrow: Moves to top of page
^Home-block (ALT-F4): Moves to marked block

PgUp/Dn: Moves to the previous or next page.

Another important part of cursor control is *typeover* and *insert* modes, controlled by the Ins key. When WordPerfect is in typeover or strikeover mode, the word "typeover" will appear on the screen in the lower left corner. This means that any character you type will replace the one indicated by the cursor. To remove a character, press the Del key while in typeover mode. Pressing the Ins key will switch over to insert mode, which means that whatever you type will be inserted just *before* the cursor.

CASE STUDY

WordStar Cursor Control

In WordStar, the arrow keys also move the cursor one character to the right or left, or up or down one line. You can combine the CTRL and the arrow keys to move through the document one word at a time. To move by larger steps, use PgUp, PgDn, Home, and End. Some users prefer to use the control commands in lieu of the arrow keys. This came about because many of the earlier keyboards did not have arrow keys. The directional control commands are called the "control diamond". Cursor commands, including diamond control commands, are summarized below and illustrated in Figure 5.10.

Summary of WordStar Cursor Control Commands

Arrow keys (^E, ^X, ^D, ^S): Move the cursor one character or one line in the direction of the arrow.

Home (^QE): Moves the cursor to column 1 on the first onscreen line.

^Home (^QR): Moves the cursor to the beginning of the file.

PgUp/Dn (^R/ ^C): Moves the cursor to the previous or next screen.

^PgUp/Dn (^W/ ^Z): Scrolls up or down one line at a time.

^Right arrow (^F): Moves the cursor right one word.

^Left arrow (^A): Moves the cursor left one word.

End (^QX): Moves the cursor to the end of the last onscreen line.

^End (^QC): Moves the cursor to the end of the file.

As with WordPerfect, WordStar uses the strikeover and insert modes, controlled by the Ins key. When in insert mode, the word "Insert" will appear in the middle of the status line at the top of the WordStar screen, and what you type will be inserted just before the cursor. In strikeover mode, what you type will replace the character indicated by the cursor. To delete a character, use the Del key.

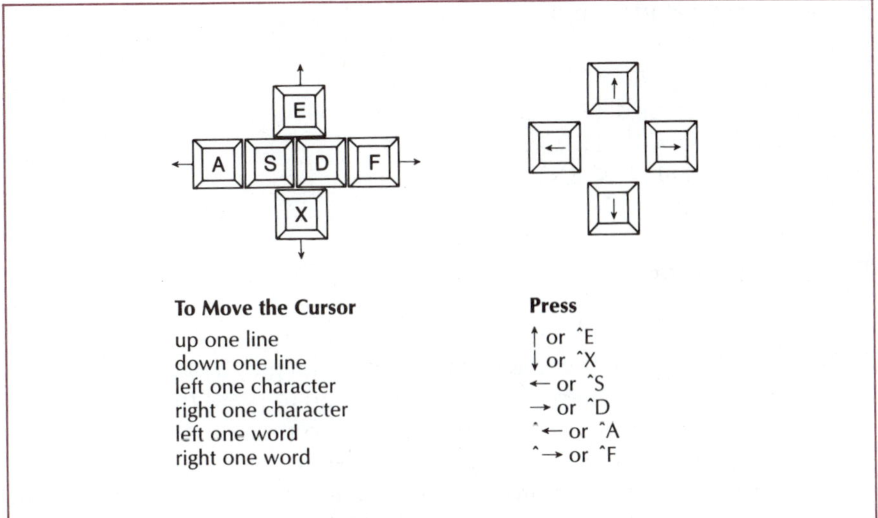

To Move the Cursor	Press
up one line	↑ or ^E
down one line	↓ or ^X
left one character	← or ^S
right one character	→ or ^D
left one word	^← or ^A
right one word	^→ or ^F

FIGURE 5.10. WordStar diamond cursor controls

CASE STUDY

Your Word Processor—Cursor Movement

If you are using another word processor, you need to familiarize yourself with the commands to perform the most common word processing tasks, such as moving the cursor around the document. Fill in the blanks in the following table:

Command	Keystroke(s)
Move right, left one character	______________________
Move up, down one line	______________________
Move right, left one word	______________________
Page Up, Page Down (Scroll) (How many lines at a time?)	______________________
Go to top of document	______________________
Go to bottom of document	______________________

SAMPLE LETTER

As a first example of how to use a word processor, you will enter the text for a letter. Then the letter will be modified in several ways to illustrate how some of the common editing features work. The specific keystrokes are described for each feature.

In the sample letter, you will first enter the date, a few blank lines, the address, more blank lines, and the salutation. As you are entering the first few lines in the letter, you will type in the information for one line and then press the ENTER key to move to the next line on the "page." To create blank lines, simply press the ENTER key, and the cursor will go down one line. If you make mistakes while entering information, move the cursor to the location of the mistake using the arrow keys, and type in the correction, using the strike-over or insert modes, as described earlier. The text to enter is as follows:

January 8, 1989 <ENTER>
<ENTER>
<ENTER>
Sir Joshua Reynolds <ENTER>
111 Whatever St. <ENTER>
Place City, NY 11111 <ENTER>
<ENTER>
<ENTER>
Dear Joe, <ENTER>
<ENTER>

The body of the letter comes next. When a paragraph or a sentence more than one line long is entered, you will not need to press the ENTER key as often. As you enter the text and approach the right side of the screen, the word processor will automatically sense when a line has passed the right margin, and will move the word being entered to the next line. This is called *word wrapping*. Thus, you only press the ENTER key when you have reached the end of the paragraph. Two paragraphs of the sample letter are entered as follows. Notice that <ENTER> occurs only at the end of each paragraph, and when a blank line is desired between paragraphs.

We have all heard about excellence, and somehow we want it right away. This is not possible. <ENTER>
<ENTER>
Excellence is never granted, but is the reward of labor. It argues, indeed, no small strength of mind to persevere in the habits of industry, without perceiving those advantages which, like the hands of a clock, whilst they make hourly approaches to their point, yet proceed so slowly as to escape observation. <ENTER>
<ENTER>
<ENTER>
<ENTER>
Sincerely, <ENTER>
<ENTER>
<ENTER>
<ENTER>
Jane Lavater <ENTER>

After the paragraphs are entered, the ending is added. If you notice mistakes in your typing, you can move the cursor to the location of the errors with the arrow keys on the cursor pad, and type in the corrections. You may need to use the Del key to delete extraneous characters, or the Ins key to insert extra characters, depending on how your word processor handles strikeovers and inserts. Figure 5.11 illustrates what the screen should look like in WordPerfect and WordStar after this text has been properly entered. Notice that the entire letter is not generally visible on one screen of either word processor.

Depending on how your copy of WordStar was installed, you may notice small dots appearing between some words. This indicates the spaces added by WordStar in order to justify the text. They will not show up when the document is printed.

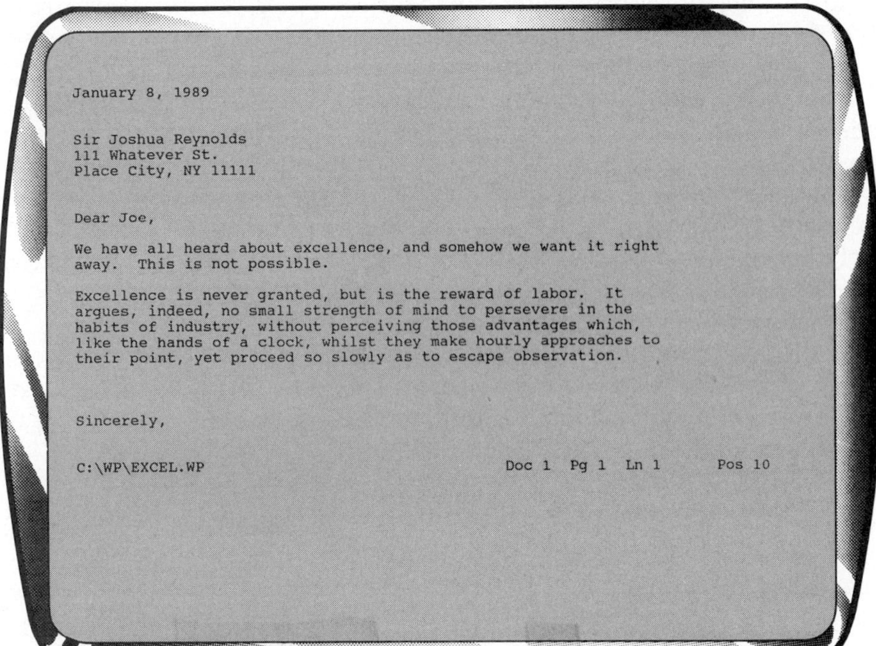

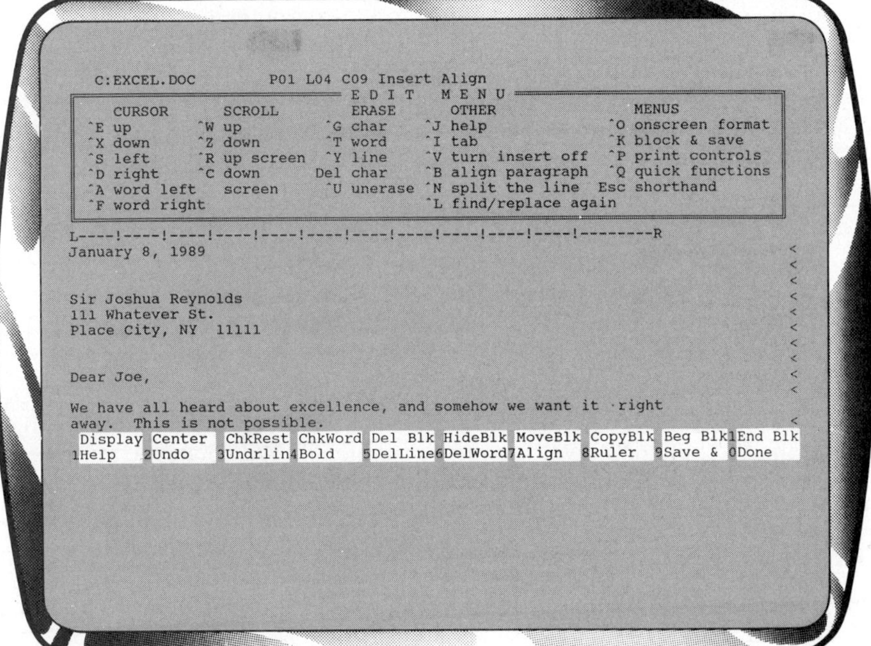

FIGURE 5.11.
WordPerfect and WordStar screens after text is entered

Make This Simple Correction

Suppose you decide you don't like "Old English", so you want to change the word "whilst" to "while". Move the cursor to this location and make this change before proceeding.

SAVING AND PRINTING THE DOCUMENT

Once a document has been entered into the computer, you may want to save it for future reference. Saving it places a copy of the document in a file on disk. If you enter a document into the computer, and then turn the computer off without saving the document, it will not be saved since the electronic memory is erased when the electricity is turned off. If you are working on a long document, you may want to save the document often (i.e., every ten or twenty minutes). Then, if the power goes off, or you accidentally disconnect the power cord, you will not lose hours' worth of work.

Printing a document requires that a printer be attached to the computer, and that the word processing program be *installed* for that printer. The specific steps for installing a printer are covered in each manual. Since each printer manufacturer makes printers that behave in different ways, the word processor must be prepared for the particular printer that is being used. Attempting to print a document on a printer that has not been installed may lead to unpredictable results.

CASE STUDY

Word-Perfect—Saving and Printing

The necessary keystrokes to print the letter are SHIFT-F7, then "1". THE SHIFT-F7 keystroke is the Print command. The "1" command selects the menu option that the entire document ("Full Text") will be printed. Once the "1" is pressed, the document should start printing. If this does not happen, your printer may be turned off, out of paper, or not properly attached to the computer.

To save the document, first press the function key F10, which is the Save command. You will be asked to name the document to save. Enter the name "EXCEL.DOC", and press ENTER. If you need to save the file on a drive other than the default drive, enter the drive name as a part of the file specification, such as "B:EXCEL.DOC"

CASE STUDY

WordStar—Saving and Printing

Before you may print a document in WordStar, you *must* save it. To save the document, enter the command ^K (CTRL-K) to get to the Block and Save Menu, then choose the "D" option to save. To print a document in WordStar, you must be on the Opening Menu. Choose the "P" option from the menu. You will be prompted with the question

```
Document to print?
```

Enter the name "EXCEL. DOC" (or "B:EXCEL.DOC"). Next, the following question will appear on the screen:

```
Number of copies?
```

Press the ESC key to skip the remaining questions, and the document should begin printing. If this does not happen, your printer may be turned off, out of paper, or not properly attached to the computer.

CASE STUDY

Your Word Processor—Saving and Printing

If you are using another word processor, describe the process needed to save the letter just entered into the file named EXCEL, and how to print the letter:

Figure 5.12 compares the output of the sample letter from two word processing programs, printed on an HP Laserjet Series II printer. Notice that the output looks very similar, but there are some differences, having to do with the default settings in each program. Both the WordPerfect and WordStar programs automatically justify the text. That is, each full line of text is adjusted so that it extends out to the right margin. This is particularly noticeable in the second paragraph, where the ends of the lines all line up on the right side. Notice that the letter produced with WordStar has a page number at the bottom. The margins are also set differently. The top margin on the WordStar page is 3/4 inch, and on WordPerfect it is one inch. The right and left margins also differ slightly. All of these conditions can be altered within the program, and sometimes are affected by the type of printer used.

If you are using another word processor, print out the letter and compare it to the sample printouts from WordPerfect and WordStar. How does it differ? What are the widths of the margins?

ENDING THE PROGRAM

Once you have finished your work, you need to know how to end the word processing program. This is a very important point. If you simply turned the computer off without ending the program, you might accidentally lose information (i.e., a letter) that is in the computer's memory, but has not been saved to disk. A good rule of thumb is never to turn the computer off until you are back at the DOS prompt (either "C>", "A>", or "B>").

CASE STUDY

WordPerfect—Ending the Program

To end a WordPerfect session press the F7 function key. You may be prompted with the question

```
Save Document? (Y/N) Y
```

If you have already saved the document with the F10 command, you can answer with "N"; otherwise pressing ENTER will accept the default "Y". If you answer "N" to the "Save Document" question you will be prompted with

```
Exit WP? (Y/N) N
```

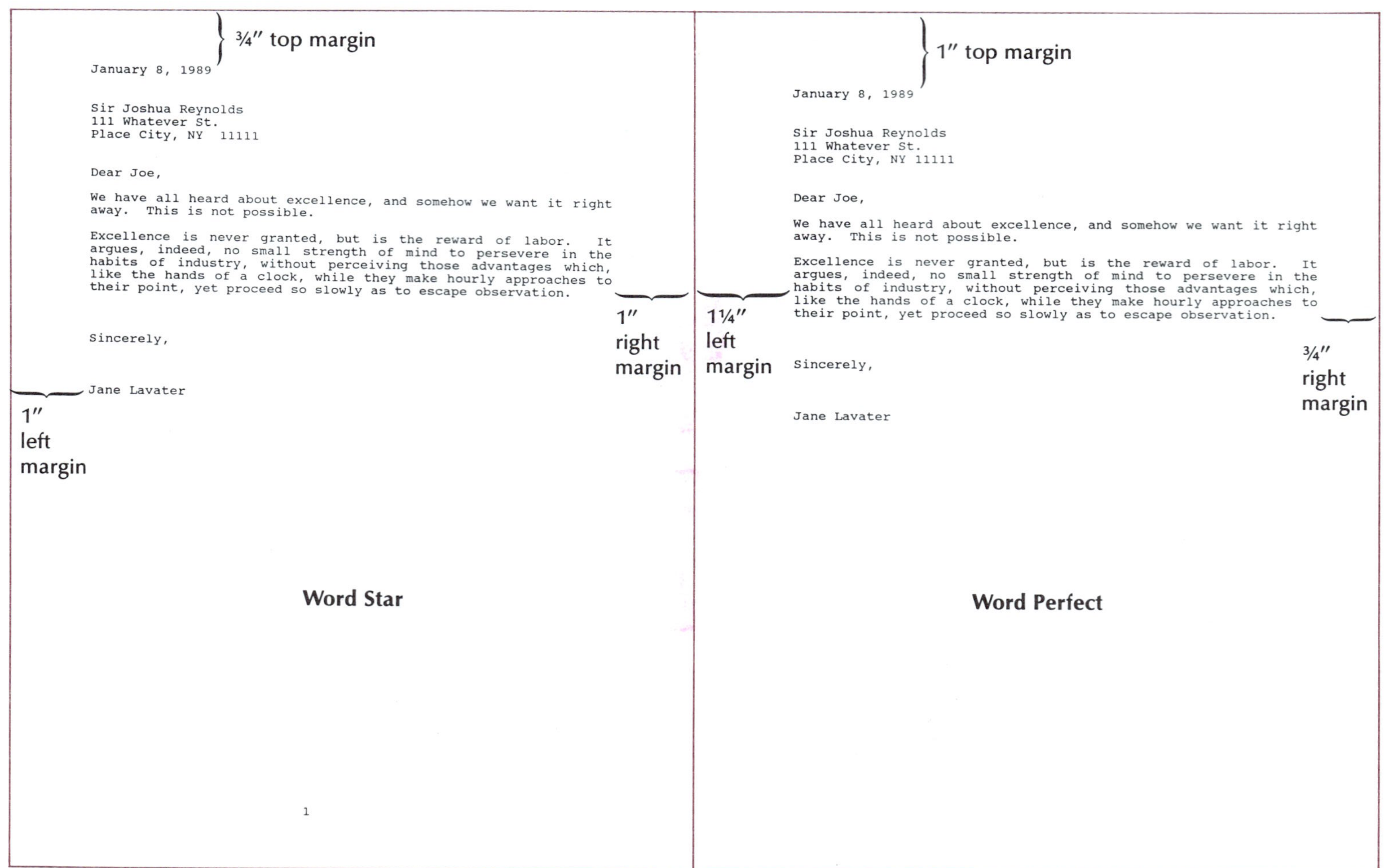

¾″ top margin

January 8, 1989

Sir Joshua Reynolds
111 Whatever St.
Place City, NY 11111

Dear Joe,

We have all heard about excellence, and somehow we want it right away. This is not possible.

Excellence is never granted, but is the reward of labor. It argues, indeed, no small strength of mind to persevere in the habits of industry, without perceiving those advantages which, like the hands of a clock, while they make hourly approaches to their point, yet proceed so slowly as to escape observation.

Sincerely,

Jane Lavater

1″ left margin

1″ right margin

Word Star

1

1″ top margin

January 8, 1989

Sir Joshua Reynolds
111 Whatever St.
Place City, NY 11111

Dear Joe,

We have all heard about excellence, and somehow we want it right away. This is not possible.

Excellence is never granted, but is the reward of labor. It argues, indeed, no small strength of mind to persevere in the habits of industry, without perceiving those advantages which, like the hands of a clock, while they make hourly approaches to their point, yet proceed so slowly as to escape observation.

Sincerely,

Jane Lavater

1¼″ left margin

¾″ right margin

Word Perfect

FIGURE 5.12. Comparison of letters printed with WordStar and WordPerfect

Pressing ENTER will cancel the exit, and pressing "Y" will exit from WordPerfect and return you to the DOS prompt.

If you answer "Y" to the "Save Document" question you will be given a chance to enter a filename for the document. If the filename you choose is the same as a file already on disk, you will be asked

```
Replace file? (Y/N) N
```

You must enter a "Y" to replace the document already on disk. Otherwise pressing ENTER will cancel the save. Either way, you will then be prompted

```
Exit WP? (Y/N) N
```

Pressing ENTER will cancel the exit, and pressing "Y" will exit from WordPerfect and return you to the DOS prompt.

CASE STUDY

WordStar—Ending the Program

To save your document and exit the WordStar program, enter the command "^KD". That is, enter CTRL-K followed immediately by a "D" command. To exit WordStar *without* saving the document, enter the command ^KQX. That is, enter CTRL-K followed immediately by typing a "Q" and an "X".

CASE STUDY

Your Word Processor—Ending the Program

If you are using another word processor, describe how to end the program, with or without saving the document.

MAKING CHANGES TO THE DOCUMENT

It is not uncommon for you to want to change a document after its initial printing. You may want to change a sentence, or make some words boldfaced, centered, or underlined. Word processors allow you to return to a previously saved document, make changes, and reprint it. The EXCEL.DOC letter will be used to illustrate how several text manipulation features work. The changes to be made to this letter include putting a letterhead at the top, centered and bold, setting the date flush left, and adding the following paragraph between the first and second paragraphs:

> The modern world is full of instant this and instant that. We want what we want right away. Good character traits cannot be bought off the shelf.

CASE STUDY

Word-Perfect—Editing an Existing Document

The first time WordPerfect was used, a new document was created. If a document is already on disk, there are two ways of bringing it back into the program to edit. If you are at the DOS prompt, enter the command "WP" followed by a space and the name of the document to edit.

```
C>WP EXCEL.DOC
```

If you are already in WordPerfect, use the SHIFT-F10 (Retrieve) command. This command will prompt you for the name of the file to edit:

```
Document to be Retrieved:
```

Enter EXCEL.DOC (or B:EXCEL.DOC) at the prompt. The EXCEL.DOC. letter will appear on the screen.

The first change to make is the addition of a letterhead. To make some room at the top, move the cursor to the top left of the screen, and press the ENTER key three times. (The insert mode must be on.) Move the cursor back up to the top left. Press the command keys to begin centering and boldfacing. Use SHIFT-F6 (center), then F6 (bold), then enter the lines of the letterhead. Notice that the cursor moves to the center of the screen. As text is entered, it is centered. The bold condition will stay in effect until it is toggled off with another F6. Enter SHIFT-F6 at the beginning of each line to center it.

<SHIFT-F6> <F6> Jane Lavater Consulting, Inc. <ENTER>
<SHIFT-F6> 1028 Madison Avenue <ENTER>
<SHIFT-F6> New York, New York 10016 <ENTER>
<ENTER>
<F6>

If your program is installed correctly, this text should appear in a different color, signifying that the entry is bold. The text should also appear in the center of the screen.

The next change to the letter is to move the date so that it is *flush right* (even with the right margin). If you are entering it from scratch, the process is similar to centering: you would press the command ALT-F6, then enter the date. Since the date is already entered, place the cursor at the first character of the line (on the "J" in "January"). Enter the command ALT-F6, and the date will be moved to the far right. Move the cursor off the line by pressing the down-arrow key once, and the date will adjust to flush right.

The new paragraph will be placed between the first and second paragraphs. Make sure you are in insert mode. Move the cursor to the blank line between the two current paragraphs, and press the ENTER key twice to make more space to insert the new text. Then, leaving one blank line below the first paragraph, enter the new paragraph:

> The modern world is full of instant this and instant that. We want what we want right away. Good character traits cannot be bought off the shelf.

See Figure 5.13 for an illustration of how the text should look on the screen.

Once you have made all the corrections, you may want to print this document again. To print, use the SHIFT-F7 Print command, as before. Also, be sure to save the file before ending the WordPerfect program.

WordPerfect Hidden Codes. When special codes such as F6 (boldface) are entered into the text, they tell the word processor to perform some change in the way text is printed. Sometimes, as in the case of boldface, you can see the results of these codes on the screen. Other times, you do not see their results until the document is printed. As you edit a document, you may need to make changes that affect the codes. For example, you may want to get rid of some boldfacing. In WordPerfect, you can reveal these hidden codes with the command ALT-F3 (Reveal Codes). Figure 5.14 illustrates the document with hidden codes revealed. Using the cursor keys, you may move to and delete, add, or change these codes as needed to correct any problems with your document.

At the top of the screen is the normal way you see the text. Below the line of triangles is a duplication of the lines at the top of the screen. However, this time there are hidden codes appearing around some of the text. Notice the "[C] [B]" in front of "Jane". These are the codes for centering and boldface. The [c] at the end of the line ends the centering for that line. The [HRt] is called a "hard carriage return". This indicates that the ENTER key was pressed at the end of this line as it was entered. Figure 5.15 lists some of the hidden codes used in WordPerfect.

As you move the cursor in the hidden area, you will notice that each hidden code is like a single character—it takes only one arrow key to skip past one of them. You may delete unwanted hidden codes with the Del key, and perform some editing. To exit the 'Reveal Codes" mode, press the F1 (Cancel) function key.

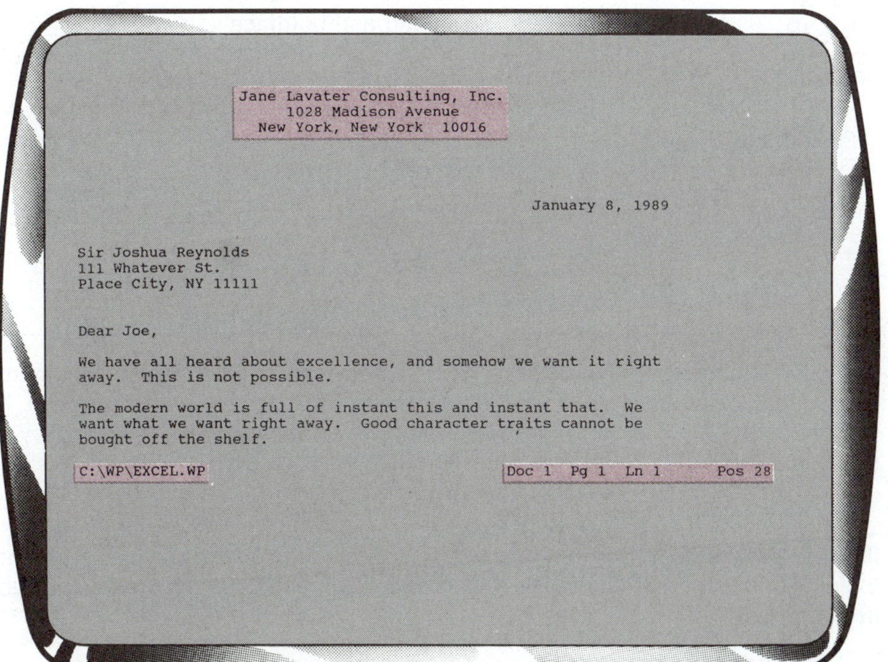

FIGURE 5.13.
WordPerfect original document with new text added

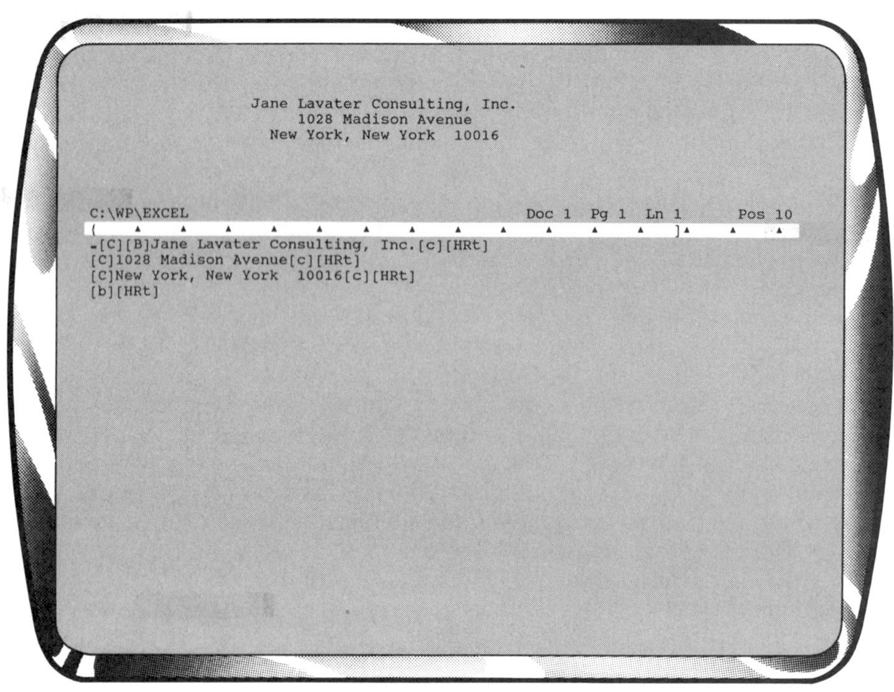

Jane Lavater Consulting, Inc.
1028 Madison Avenue
New York, New York 10016
C:\WP\EXCEL
Doc 1 Pg 1 Ln 1 Pos 10
[C][B]Jane Lavater Consulting, Inc.[c][HRt]
[C]1028 Madison Avenue[c][HRt]
[C]New York, New York 10016[c][HRt]
[b][HRt]

FIGURE 5.14.
Hidden codes in WordPerfect revealed

FIGURE 5.15.
Some WordPerfect hidden codes and their meanings

[C] [c]	Begin and end centering
[B] [b]	Begin and end boldface
[U] [u]	Begin and end underline
[HRt]	Hard carriage return (ENTER key)
[SRt]	Soft return (at a word wrap)
[Pg Lnth:66,72]	Page length
[LPI:10]	Lines per inch
[Margin Set:12,89]	Margin settings

CASE STUDY

WordStar—Editing an Existing Document

You have already used WordStar to create a new document and your document is now on disk. There are two ways of bringing it back into the program to edit. If you are at the DOS prompt, you can enter the command "WS" followed by a space and the name of the document to edit, as shown here:

```
C>WS EXCEL.DOC
```

If you enter WordStar by using "WS" without specifying the name of the document to edit, choose the "D" command (Open a File) from the Opening Menu. You will be prompted with:

```
Document to open?
```

Enter the name EXCEL.DOC, and the previous version of the document will appear on the edit screen.

The first change to make is to add a letterhead. To make some room at the top, make sure the cursor is at the top left of the screen, and press ^N (CTRL-N) three times. This inserts three blank lines. In WordStar, you then enter a line, and then tell WordStar to center it. On the top line of the document, enter the first line of the letterhead, "Jane Lavater Consulting, Inc." To center this text, enter the control command ^O to get the Onscreen Format Menu; then press "C" to center the line. Enter the next two lines of the letterhead in the same way. The entire sequence is as follows:

Jane Lavater Consulting, Inc. <^ O> <C> <ENTER>
1028 Madison Avenue <^ O> <C> <ENTER>
New York, New York 10016 <^ O> <C> <ENTER>
<ENTER>

To make the letterhead print boldfaced, you must place a print control marker at the beginning and ending of the letterhead. Move the cursor to the "J" in "Jane", and enter the control command ^P, which initiates the Print Control Menu. Enter the "B" command (Bold). Move the cursor to the end of the text, after the "6" in the zip code, and enter the bold command again (^PB). The indication "^B" will appear at the start and end of the boldfaced text, indicating that the text will be printed in boldfaced type.

The next alteration to the letter is to set the date flush right, even with the right margin. Move the cursor to the "J" in "January". Make sure you are in insert mode. Enter a series of blank spaces with the space bar, which will move the date toward the right margin. Line up the last character of the date with the "R" in the margin ruler (the line of dashes above the text).

A new paragraph will now be placed between the first and second paragraphs. Move the cursor to the blank line between the two current paragraphs, and press the ENTER key twice to give you more space. Then, leaving one blank line below the first paragraph, enter the new paragraph:

> The modern world is full of instant this and instant that. We want what we want right away. Good character traits cannot be bought off the shelf.

Figure 5.16 illustrates what the corrected text should look like on the WordStar screen.

Once you have made all these corrections, you may want to print this document again, to look at it on the printed page. To print, use the ^KD command to save the document; then choose the "P" command to print as was done previously.

CASE STUDY

Your Word Processor—Editing an Existing Document

If you are using another word processing program, describe how to begin the program from DOS, and begin editing the existing letter named EXCEL.DOC on disk:

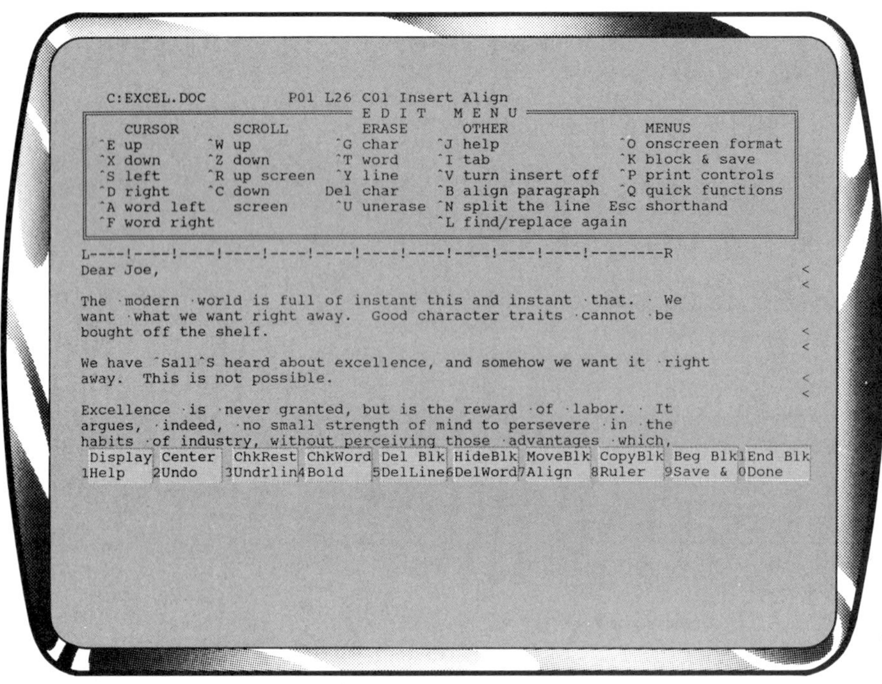
C:EXCEL.DOC P01 L26 C01 Insert Align
E D I T M E N U
CURSOR SCROLL ERASE OTHER MENUS
^E up ^W up ^G char ^J help ^O onscreen format
^X down ^Z down ^T word ^I tab ^K block & save
^S left ^R up screen ^Y line ^V turn insert off ^P print controls
^D right ^C down Del char ^B align paragraph ^Q quick functions
^A word left screen ^U unerase ^N split the line Esc shorthand
^F word right ^L find/replace again
L----!----!----!----!----!----!----!----!----!----!----!--------R
Dear Joe,
The modern world is full of instant this and instant that. We
want what we want right away. Good character traits cannot be
bought off the shelf.
We have ^Sall^S heard about excellence, and somehow we want it right
away. This is not possible.
Excellence is never granted, but is the reward of labor. It
argues, indeed, no small strength of mind to persevere in the
habits of industry, without perceiving those advantages which,
Display Center ChkRest ChkWord Del Blk HideBlk MoveBlk CopyBlk Beg Blk End Blk
1Help 2Undo 3Undrlin 4Bold 5DelLine 6DelWord 7Align 8Ruler 9Save & 0Done

FIGURE 5.16. WordStar version of expanded letter

In your word processor, what commands are required to center the following lines and make them print in boldface characters? Use the descriptions for WordPerfect and WordStar as examples.

Jane Lavater Consulting, Inc.
1028 Madison Avenue
New York, New York 10016

In your word processor, what command can be used to place the date flush left on the page?

In your word processor, you want to enter the following paragraph placed between the first and second paragraphs. How do you place your word processor in insert mode? What must you do to enter this paragraph?

The modern world is full of instant this and instant that. We want what we want right away. Good character traits cannot be bought off the shelf.

Once you have made all these corrections, you may want to print this document again, to look at it on the printed page. Review your previous notes on printing a document using your word processor.

WORKING WITH BLOCKS AND SECTIONS OF TEXT

Many times you may want to perform a function on several characters or words at the same time. Perhaps you want to boldface them, delete them, or move them to some other part of the document. It is often easiest to do this by marking the block of text first, then telling the word processor what to do with the designated block.

CASE STUDY

Word-Perfect—Block Functions

In WordPerfect, a block of text is marked to be moved by using the CTRL-F4 (Move) command. We will now use the block method to move the first paragraph of the letter to a position between the second and third paragraphs. Move the cursor to the "W" in "We", and begin the block mark by pressing the control command ^F4. A menu will appear at the bottom of the screen indicating the kinds of blocks that are possible:

```
Move 1 Sentence; 2 Paragraph;3 Page; Retrieve 4 Column;5 Text;6 Rectangle:0
```

The first three choices are "Move" choices, in which you may select to move a sentence, a paragraph, or a page of text at a time. Since you want to move a paragraph, select "2", and the paragraph will be highlighted. Another menu appears:

```
1 Cut; 2 Copy; 3 Delete :0
```

Choosing "1" (Cut) removes the text from its present location, and stores it in memory awaiting the move. The option "2" (Copy) leaves the text on the screen, and temporarily stores a copy of it awaiting the move, and "3" (Delete) deletes the blocked text. For this example, choose the Cut option (1). Notice that the paragraph vanished—but it is still in the memory of the word processor. Move the cursor to the area between the two remaining paragraphs, and press the ^F4 key again. The same menu will appear as before. This time, select the "5" option (Retrieve text), and the paragraph in memory will be retrieved and placed at the position of the cursor. You may have to add a blank line before or after the moved paragraph to make it appear correctly.

Another way to work with blocks of text in WordPerfect is to use the ALT-F4 (Block) command. As an example, we will make the sentence "This is not possible" appear underlined. To do this, move the cursor to the "T" at the beginning of the sentence and press the ALT-F4 command. Notice the blinking indication "Block

On". Move the cursor to the end of the sentence using the arrow keys. Once a block is highlighted, you may perform a number of tasks on the text. These options are listed in Figure 5.17. For this example, press the F8 (Underline) key. Depending on your monitor, the text will either appear underlined on the screen, or it may appear in a different color, indicating that it will appear with an underline when printed.

Once you have made changes, you may want to print this document again. To print, use the SHIFT-F7 Print command as before.

With a block of text highlighted, you may perform these operations on the text:

FIGURE 5.17. Block options in WordPerfect

Operation	Command	Operation	Command
Bold	F6	Move	CTRL-F4
Center	SHIFT-F6	Append	
Delete	Del	Copy	
Flush Rt	ALT-F6	Cut/Copy Column	
Mark Text	ALT-F5	Cut/Copy Rectangle	
Index		Print	SHIFT-F7
List		Replace	ALT-F2
Redline		Save	F10
Strikeout		Sort	CTRL-F9
Table of Cont.		Spell	CTRL-F2
		Super/Subscript	SHIFT-F1
		Underline	F8
		Upper/Lowercase	SHIFT-F3

See the WordPerfect manual for complete instructions

CASE STUDY

WordStar—Block Functions

In WordStar, blocks are created in the "Block & Save" menu, which is brought up with the ^K command. To place the first paragraph of the letter between the second and third paragraphs, you must first block the text, then move it. Move the cursor to the "W" in the word "We". To begin the blocking, press the command ^K to see the Block & Save menu, then press the "B" key to mark the beginning of the block. Move the cursor to the end of the paragraph using the arrow keys, then enter the command ^K to bring back the Block & Save menu, and press "K" to mark the end of the block. The marked block is highlighted on the screen. (Alternate commands for ^KB and ^KK are SHIFT-F9 and SHIFT-F10.) Move the cursor to the blank line between the second and third paragraphs, and enter the command ^KV (Move). The paragraph is now between the two other paragraphs. You may have to add a blank line above or below the paragraph to make it appear correctly.

Another way to alter sections of text at a time is to mark a beginning and ending point for a certain feature, such as underlining, boldface, subscript, superscript, strikeout, double strike, and italics. These are all options on the Print Controls Menu, which is entered by the command ^P. As an example, to underline the sentence, "This is not possible", move the cursor to the "T", enter the command ^PS, move the cursor to the end of the sentence, and enter ^PS again. The text will appear either underlined or highlighted, depending on the type of monitor you are using. Other block operations for WordStar are listed in Figure 5.18. Once you have made the changes, you may want to print this document again.

Operation	Command(s)	
Mark block beginning	^KB	or SHIFT F9
Mark block end	^KK	or SHIFT F10
Copy block	^KC	or SHIFT F8
Delete block	^KY	or SHIFT F5
Move block	^KV	or SHIFT F7
Convert to lowercase	^K'	
Convert to uppercase	^K"	
Write block to disk	^KW	
Use the following commands at the start and end of the section to alter		
Bold text	^PB	
Double strike text	^PD	
Underline text	^PS	
Strikeout text	^PX	
Subscript text	^PV	
Superscript text	^PT	
Italics/color	^PY	
See the WordStar manual for complete instructions.		

FIGURE 5.18.
Block options and other commands in WordStar

CASE STUDY

Your Word Processor—Block Functions

If you are using another word processor, examine its ability to work with blocks. Describe the commands to work with blocks. How do you select a block of text to work with in your word processor? What are the limitations (if any) on length?

How are the following block functions supported in your word processor? (if they are supported):

Feature	Commands Required
Delete the block:	____________
Copy the block:	____________
Move the block:	____________
Make text all caps:	____________
Make text all italics:	____________
Make text all bold:	____________
Make text all underlined:	____________
Make text superscript:	____________
Make text subscript:	____________
Make text strikeout:	____________

DOCUMENT FORMATTING

Thus far, examples have used the default or standard settings for how a document will appear on the printed page. However, one of the nice features of word processing is the ability to easily adjust the format, or layout, of the document. For example, in WordPerfect and WordStar, on the EXCEL letter, notice that the ends of all the lines in the paragraphs line up on the right edge. This is often called *right justification.* The effect is created by embedding extra spaces in the line to make all lines the same length. When paragraphs do not use this feature, but have lines ending as they would on a normal typewriter, the effect is called a *ragged right edge.* Right-justified paragraphs are considered to be a more formal technique than those with ragged right edges. This is purely a matter of your own choice.

Another item that must be considered when printing a page are the top, bottom, right, and left margins. On most word processors, these default settings cause the printed page to have a margin of about 1 inch around the entire page. This setting may be altered for the entire document, or it may be altered for only a portion of a document.

CASE STUDY

Word-Perfect—Formatting and Margins

If you are not already in WordPerfect, you may begin editing the EXCEL.DOC document again with the command:

```
C>WP EXCEL.DOC
```

After looking at the letter, suppose you decide that having the paragraphs right-justified is too formal, and you want to change that setting. The command to alter the "Print Format" is the ^F8 (CTRL-F8) command. Before entering that command, make sure your cursor is at the beginning of the document, in the upper left corner. When ^F8 is chosen, the menu illustrated in figure 5.19 will appear on the screen. Choose the "3" option, and press the ENTER key. This will turn off right justification, and the latter will be printed with a ragged right edge. You may notice that in WordPerfect the text on the screen looks the same if right justification is on or off.

The next items you wish to change are the right and left margins, so that they are about 1.5 inches from the paper's edge. Press the ALT-F8 command to display the Page Format menu. This menu is illustrated in Figure 5.20. Select menu item "3", which allows you to choose the right and left margins. To figure the margins, you need to know that the current setting for pitch is 10, which means that there are 10 characters printed per inch. If the page is 8.5 inches wide (85 characters), then a margin of 1.5 inches (15 characters) is selected by setting the left margin to 15 characters, and the right margin at 70 characters. This leaves a space equal to 15 characters (or 1.5 inch) on the left and right margins. Select 15 and 70 for the left and right margins. Once you have made changes, you may want to print this document again.

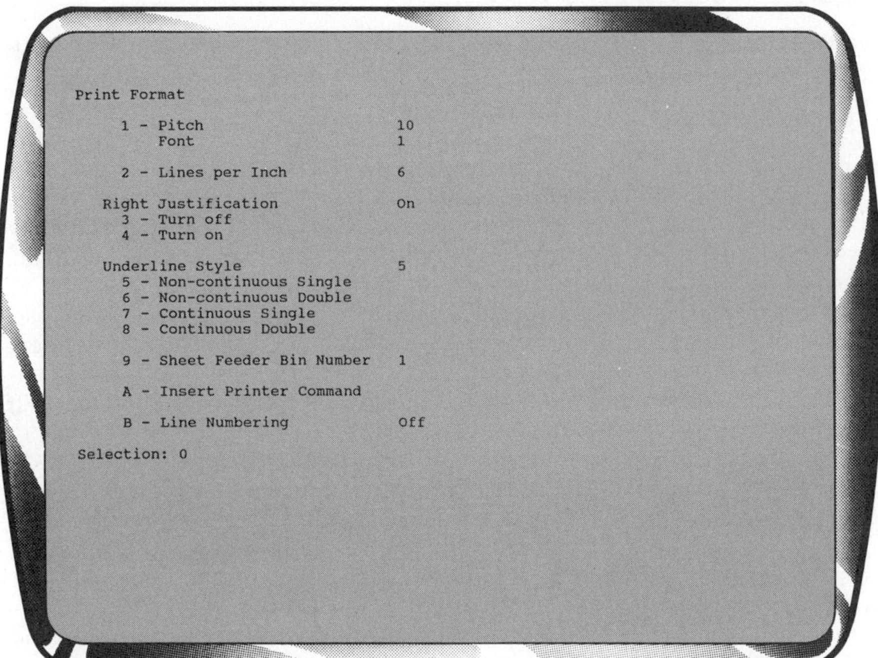

Print Format
1 - Pitch 10
Font 1
2 - Lines per Inch 6
Right Justification On
3 - Turn off
4 - Turn on
Underline Style 5
5 - Non-continuous Single
6 - Non-continuous Double
7 - Continuous Single
8 - Continuous Double
9 - Sheet Feeder Bin Number 1
A - Insert Printer Command
B - Line Numbering Off
Selection: 0

FIGURE 5.19.
WordPerfect Print Format menu

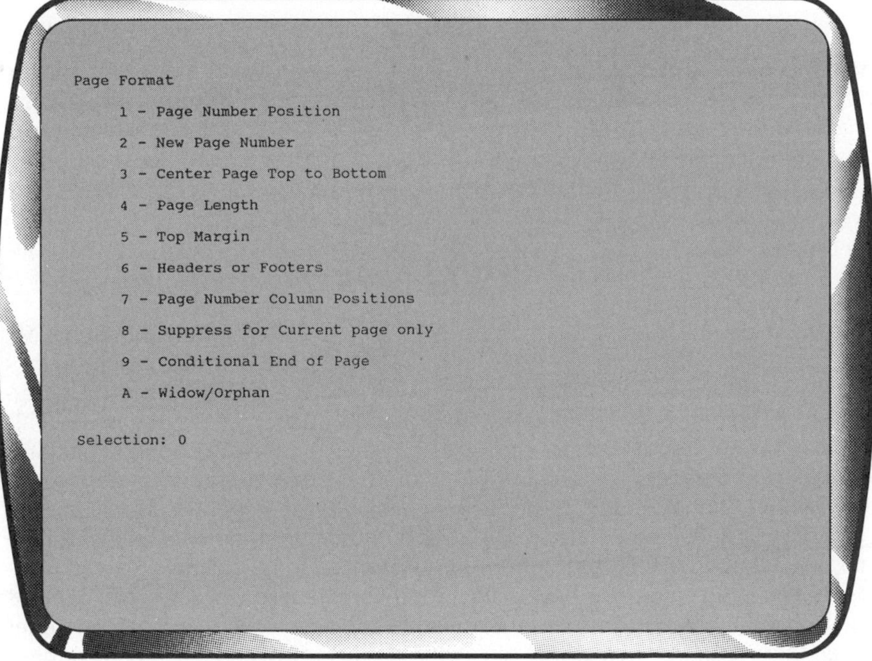

Page Format
1 - Page Number Position
2 - New Page Number
3 - Center Page Top to Bottom
4 - Page Length
5 - Top Margin
6 - Headers or Footers
7 - Page Number Column Positions
8 - Suppress for Current page only
9 - Conditional End of Page
A - Widow/Orphan
Selection: 0

FIGURE 5.20.
WordPerfect Page Format menu

CASE STUDY

WordStar—Formatting and Margins

If you are not already in WordStar, you may begin editing the EXCEL.DOC document with the command:

```
C>WS EXCEL.DOC
```

Suppose that after looking at the letter, you decide that having the paragraphs right-justified is too formal, and you want to use a ragged right edge instead. The menu needed to specify text format is the Onscreen Format Menu, obtained by pressing ^O. Figure 5.20 illustrated this menu. Move the cursor to the beginning of the first paragraph in the letter, and press ^O to get to the menu. Select the "J" option to turn right justification off. Next, press the ^B command to cause the paragraph to be reformatted on the screen. The justification will appear on the screen. (You may see small dots in the place of spaces between words. These will not appear when the document is printed.) You must change the justification for each paragraph separately.

If you want to turn right justification off for the entire document, you may do so with a dot "." command. Dot commands are not selected from menus. Instead, they are entered directly into the document. Dot commands are always placed on a separate line with a dot "." in column 1. They are followed by a two-letter code, and sometimes a space and more information. The dot command to turn off right justification for a document is ".OJ".

To turn off right justification for your letter, you may place the dot command ".OJ" on a separate line at the top of the document. The dot command is stored with the document and appears on the screen, but it will not appear when the document is printed.

In WordStar, right and left margins are set on a "Ruler Line". This line contains information about the right and left margins, and tab stops. It looks like this:

```
L----!----!----!----!----!----!----!----!----!---------R
```

and appears at the top of the document on the screen. The "L" is the left margin and the "R" is the right margin. The exclamation marks are the current tab settings, usually set every five spaces. The default right and left margins are set at columns 1 and 65. Margins may be set either by changing the ruler or by using dot commands. To reset the left margin on the ruler, use the command ^O to select the Onscreen Format Menu, and press "L" for "set left margin". The command ^OR resets the right margin. When you enter the command ^OR or ^OL, WordStar displays the current margin, and prompts you to enter a new margin. To set the margin, enter a column number and press ENTER.

To figure the margins, you need to know that the current setting for pitch is 10, which means that there are 10 characters printed per inch. If the page is 8.5 inches wide (85 characters), then a margin of 1.5 inches (15 characters) is selected by setting the left margin to 15 characters, and the right margin at 70 characters. This leaves a space equal to 15 characters (or 1.5 inches) on the left and right margins. Although the ruler is set at margins 1 and 65 on the screen, the printed page includes an additional margin of 8 characters (called the page offset) making the printing begin in column 9 (8+1). The total number of printed characters in a line is 65, making the last column print on the page at column 73 (8+65).

These margins must also be considered in conjunction with how the paper is actually printed on the printer. For example, on the Hewlett-Packard Laserjet printer, there is an automatic page offset of 2 characters, making the actual printed page offset 10 characters (8+2) and a printed left margin of one inch. The last column printed will be 75 (10+65) giving a right margin of one inch, since the total page width is 85 characters.

To make the printed margins 15 and 70, you must therefore set the left ruler margin to 5 (that is, 15−10), and the right ruler margin to 60, which is 70−10.

An alternate way to set margins is with the dot commands ".LM" and ".RM", which stand for left margin and right margin. These dot commands may be inserted into the document either by entering them manually, or by using the commands ^F5 for ".LM" and ^F6 for ".RM". For example, to set the left margin at 8, enter the command ".LM 8" at the top of the document. To set the right margin, enter the command ".RM 62". Notice that there is a space between the dot command and the setting. Remember that dot commands must begin in column 1, and they should be alone on the line.

Once you have made the changes, you may want to print this document again, to check the margins on the printed page.

CASE STUDY

Your Word Processor—Formatting and Margins

If you are using another word processor, examine the commands that allow you to change the margins for printing the document on the page, and learn how formatting is controlled. How do you cause text to be printed with a ragged right edge, or in justified mode? What commands will set up the EXCEL letter to print in ragged right edge mode?

How do you set the right, left, top, and bottom margins? How would you set up the EXCEL letter to print with a 1.5-inch margin on both sides?

After resetting the margins, print the letter and compare it with your previous printouts.

SUMMARY

Word processing has replaced many of the functions done previously by the typewriter. It is particularly useful for documents that need revising and editing.

Each word processor has its own language of commands, often using the function keys, control commands, or menus. Commands are supplied to enter the program, retrieve a document, move the cursor, make corrections, save and print documents, and exit from the program.

Most word processors also include means of adding special features such as underlines and boldfacing. They can also mark blocks of text to be moved or acted on in other ways. Each word processor has certain default settings that cause documents to be printed with particular margins and with or without right justification. You may change these defaults for each document.

KEY TERMS

Define the following terms in your own words:

Word processing

Block

Default settings

Cursor movement

Document

Justification

Margins

Page format

Word wrap

Status line

QUESTIONS

Fill in the blanks.

1. The word processing feature that causes words that are being typed over the right margin to automatically be moved intact to the next line is called ______________.
2. The process of moving a paragraph from one place in a document to another is commonly called__________________________.
3. When typing a document, the ______________ key should be pressed only at the end of a paragraph or to insert a blank line.
4. If words on the right margin of a document (as well as on the left margin) are aligned, the document is said to be __________________________.
5. The __________________text entry mode causes characters typed at the keyboard to replace characters that are currently on the screen.
6. List the keystrokes used by your word processing program to perform each of the following functions:

   a. Cursor movement

      one character to the right __________

      one character to the left __________

      one line character up __________

      one line character down __________

one word to the right ________
one word to the left ________
top of the screen ________
bottom of the screen ________
beginning of the line ________
end of the line ________
top of the document ________
end of the document ________

b. Text deletion

delete character at cursor ________
delete character to left of cursor ________
delete word at cursor ________
delete entire line ________

Write a short answer in your own words for each of the following questions. Base your answers on the word processing program you used for this chapter.

7. Briefly describe how the CTRL, ALT, SHIFT, and function keys are used to access program commands.
8. Outline the procedure for accessing the general editing screen (i.e., the screen for entering a new document).
9. Outline the procedure for retrieving a previously created document.
10. Describe the function of each of the following keys: Del, backspace, Ins, arrow keys, Home, End, PgUp, PgDn, Esc, Num Lock.
11. Outline the procedure for printing (a) a document that is in memory (b) a document that is on disk.
12. Outline the procedure for saving a document to disk.
13. Outline the procedure for exiting the word processing program and returning to DOS.
14. Explain the difference between typeover and insert text entry modes.
15. List two situations where the ENTER key is always used.
16. Outline the procedure for moving a block of text (e.g., a paragraph) from one part of a document to another.
17. Describe the difference between a ragged right margin and a justified right margin. Outline the procedure for turning justification on and off.
18. Outline the procedure for changing the right and left margin settings.
19. Outline the procedure for (a) boldfacing one or more words (b) underlining one or more words.

LABORATORY EXERCISES

Lab Exercise 1. This exercise is a summary of the tutorial material in this chapter. You will use your word processing program to create a document called EXCEL2.DOC. Try to do the exercise without referring to the instructions in the chapter.

1. Start up your word processing program and get to the main editing or text entry screen.
2. Enter the following text exactly as it appears:

```
January 8, 1990

Sir Joshua Reynolds
111 Whatever St.
Place City, NY 11111

Dear Joe,

We have all heard about excellence, and somehow we want it
right away. This is not possible.

Excellence is never granted, but is the reward of labor.
It argues, indeed, no small strength of mind to persevere
in the habits of industry, without perceiving those
advantages which, like the hands of a clock, whilst they
make hourly approaches to their point, yet proceed so
slowly as to escape observation.

Sincerely,

Jane Lavater
```

3. Move the cursor to the word "whilst" in paragraph two and use the typeover mode to change it to "while". Read over the document and correct any typographical errors.
4. Save the document (use the filename EXCEL2.DOC).
5. Print a copy of the document. Make sure your printer is connected and on line before executing the print command.
6. Exit your word processing program and return to the DOS prompt.

Lab Exercise 2. 1. Start up your word processing program and retrieve the document called EXCEL2.DOC, created in Lab Exercise 1.

2. Make sure the cursor is at the very top of the document and enter the following letterhead:

```
Jane Lavater Consulting, Inc.
1028 Madison Avenue
New York, New York 10016
```

The letterhead should be centered between the left and right margins and should be boldfaced. You may perform these operations while entering the text or after the text is entered.

3. Move the date so that the zero of 1990 is flush with the right margin of the page.
4. Enter the following paragraph between the first and second paragraphs.

```
The modern world is full of instant this and that.
We want what we want right away. Good character traits
cannot be bought off the shelf.
```

5. Save and print a copy of the revised document.

Lab Exercise 3. Use the revised file EXCEL2.DOC saved in Lab Exercise 2.

1. Make sure the document is on the screen.

   Use block operations to move the first paragraph of the letter to a position between the second and third paragraphs. Correct any changes in spacing caused by the block move.

   Note: Make certain the cursor is in the correct position before marking the block.

2. Underline the sentence in paragraph two which reads:

   ```
   ''This is not possible.''
   ```

3. Save and print a copy of the revised document.

Lab Exercise 4. Use the EXCEL2.DOC saved in Lab Exercise 3.

1. Make sure the document is on the screen. Turn off justification so that the letter will print with a ragged right margin.

   Note: The cursor should be at the top of the document.

2. Change the left and right margins to 1 1/2 inches (i.e., 15 characters on each side for 10 pitch). Remember the page offset if you are using WordStar.

   Note 1: The cursor should be at the top of the document.

3. Save and print the final copy of the document. Your final letter should look like Figure 5.8

Lab Exercise 5. In this exercise, you will use your word processing program to create a document called MEMO.DOC.

1. Start your word processing program and enter the following text exactly as it appears:

   ```
   MEMORANDUM

   TO:               George Humphrey, Business Office
   FROM:             Alice Hunicutt, Data Processing Services
   DATE:             January 25, 1990
   SUBJECT:          Telephone installation

   Melissa Johnson in Technical Services and Alan Summer
   in Media Services have each received IBM personal
   computers. Internal modems were supplied with each computer
   to permit communication with the library automation system.
   Please arrange for the installation of additional telephone
   lines in their offices.
   ```

2. Center and boldface the word "Memorandum" at the top of the document.
3. Boldface the names "Melissa Johnson" and 'Alan Summer" in the first sentence of the paragraph.
4. Underline the words "Internal modems" in the second sentence of the paragraph.
5. Set page formatting to the following:
   Top margin = 2 inches (12 lines from the top)
   Left margin = 1 1/2 inches (15 characters in 10 pitch)
   Right margin = 1 1/2 inches (15 characters in 10 pitch)
   Justification off (ragged right margin)
6. Save and print the document.

Lab Exercise 6. In this exercise, you will use your word processing program to create a document called MEMO.DOC. You will enter a list of names and addresses and practice rearranging them using block operations.

1. Start your word processing program and enter the following list of names and addresses exactly as they appear:

```
James Jones
1212 East Street
Austin, TX 78704

Earl Roberts
P.O. Box 2275
Houston, TX 78230

Nancy Adams
456 Elm Avenue
New York, NY 10016

Larry Miller
2910 West 28th Street
Austin, TX 78703

Margaret Swanson
Route 2, Box 223
San Antonio, TX 78333
```

2. Use block operations to rearrange the names into alphabetical order by last name. Make corrections to line spacing as necessary.
3. Enter a centered and boldfaced title at the top of the page which reads "Mailing List".
4. Set page formatting to the following:
   Top margin = 1 inch (6 lines)
   Right margin = 1 inch (10 characters in 10 pitch)
   Left margin = 1 inch (10 characters in 10 pitch)
5. Save and print the document.

Lab Exercise 7. In this exercise, you will use your word processing program to create a document called SAMPLE.DOC.

1. Start your word processing program and enter the following document.

```
The Line format key in WordPerfect lets you set new left
and right margins. Margins may be set to any value between 0
and 250.

Select the Margins feature by pressing SHIFT F8 and then 3.

Enter the new left margin.

Enter the new right margin.

From that point in your document the margins are changed
to the new settings.
```

```
If your cursor is not at the left margin when
setting margins, a Hard Return [HRt] is inserted
before the setting.

When you want to check the current setting of
margins in your document, use the Tab Ruler (see Tab
Ruler in this section for details).

You should adjust the margins when using different
fonts and pitches. For example, when using 10 pitch
you should set the margins at 10 and 74 for 1-inch
margins; for 12 pitch, set the margins to 12 and
89. You may need to change the tab settings
when you change margins.
```

2. Add a centered and boldfaced title to the document which reads "MARGINS". Insert two blank lines after the title.
3. Move the paragraph which begins "When you want to check. . . ." to the end of the document.
4. Underline the word "WordPerfect" in the first paragraph.
5. Set page formatting to the following:
   Top margin = 2 inches (12 lines)
   Left margin = 1 1/2 inches (15 characters in 10 pitch)
   Right margin = 1 1/2 inches (15 characters in 10 pitch)
   Justification on
6. Save and print the document.

The author wishes to acknowledge the contribution of Richard L. Smith, Ph.D., for his valued assistance in the preparation of the end-of-chapter activities on chapters 5, 6, 7, 8, 9 and 10.

CHAPTER 6

Word Processing, Part II

CHAPTER OVERVIEW. This chapter introduces some advanced word processing features, including search and replace operations; choosing pitch, font, and line spacing; using headers and footers; and using a spelling checker or an on-line thesaurus. Case studies use the same packages as in the previous chapter: WordPerfect, WordStar Professional, and your word processor.

CHAPTER OBJECTIVES

Upon completion of this chapter, you will be able to:

- Describe and use the search and replace functions of the word processor.
- Describe and use the concepts of pitch, fonts, and line spacing.
- Describe the particular problems associated with long documents.
- Describe and use page numbering and paging.
- Describe and use headers and footers.
- Describe how a spelling checker is used.
- Describe how an on-line thesaurus is used.
- Describe some of the special features of the word processing program of your choice.

THE TEXT EXAMPLES DISK

The letter EXCEL.DOC that was created in chapter 5 will be used for more examples in this chapter. You may use the document file you created in the previous chapter, or use a copy of the letter on the Text Examples Disk. If you are going to use the letter on the Text Examples Disk, you must copy the original version from the Text Examples Disk to a file called EXCEL.DOC on your word processor document disk. On the Text Examples Disk, the WordPerfect version of the letter is named EXCEL.WP, the WordStar version of the letter is named EXCEL.WS, and an ASCII version of the letter is named EXCEL.TXT. Use the DOS COPY command to copy the appropriate version of the file to the disk that you are using for your word processing files. For example, to copy the WordPerfect file EXCEL.WP from the Text Examples Disk in the A: drive to the C:\WP subdirectory on a hard disk, you would use the command:

```
C>COPY A:EXCEL.WP C:\WP\EXCEL.DOC
```

To copy the file from the A: drive to a disk in the B: drive, you would use the command:

```
A>COPY  EXCEL.WP B:EXCEL.DOC
```

THE SEARCH AND REPLACE COMMANDS

The ability to search for words and phrases and replace them with others is one especially useful feature of word processors. The search feature is used to locate a particular word or collection of characters, called a *string.* Searching can often help you to move quickly to a specific location in a long document. For example, if you are writing the great American novel, and you want to rewrite a paragraph that had to do with radishes, but you do not remember exactly where that paragraph was in the document, you could use a search to go directly to that location.

Some word processors will find string matches regardless of whether characters are upper- or lowercase. Other word processors will not match the same words in different cases. For example, if you search for the word "radish", it may not find the word "Radish" because the first letter in one is lowercase, and the first letter in the other is uppercase. Uppercase and lowercase characters look very different to the computer. Some word processors can handle this problem, and will find the word even when the case does not match. Others allow you to specify whether the match should be made regardless of case. If your word processor does not match differing cases, you might search for "adishes" rather than "radishes". Then, either "Radishes" or "radishes" could be located by the search.

The Replace feature is used to replace a specific word or string of characters with a new string of characters. For example, suppose you wrote a report about Edgar Allen Poe, but throughout the document, you spelled his middle name "Alan". You could go through the document and change the spelling over and over again, or you could use the Replace command to replace all occurrences of "Alan" with "Allen". The same problems with upper- and lowercase may apply to Replace commands, so you need to be aware of how your word processor handles them.

CASE STUDY

WordPerfect—Search and Replace

WordPerfect has the ability to perform both forward and reverse searches. The forward search uses the F2 command, and the reverse search uses the SHIFT-F2 command. The search begins where your cursor is located in the document, and proceeds either forward or backward in the document until it finds the designated characters. Once the search command is given, you will be prompted to enter the word or string of characters to search for. After entering the search, press the F2 command key again, and the search will begin. When a match is found, the cursor will be placed at that location in the document. In WordPerfect, lowercase characters will match both lowercase and UPPERCASE characters. However, UPPERCASE characters will only match UPPERCASE characters. Therefore, a search using the string "radish" will locate "Radish", but a search for "RADISH" will not match "Radish".

The Replace feature of WordPerfect allows you to replace a word or string of characters in a document with another word or string. The Replace command works only in the forward direction. A Replace is activated with the command ALT-F2. You will then be prompted to choose whether to confirm each replacement, or to allow WordPerfect to replace all of the matching strings automatically. You must first enter the word or string of characters that you want to replace. After entering this, press F2, and you will see the prompt "Replace with:" on the screen. Enter the new word or string, and press F2 to begin replacing.

As an example, retrieve the letter named EXCEL.DOC that was created in the last chapter, and use the Replace feature to replace the word "labor" in the letter with the words "hard work".

CASE STUDY

WordStar—Search and Replace

In WordStar, a search is invoked by the Find command. From the Quick menu, which is displayed with the command ^Q, choose the "F" or "find text" option. (The Quick menu was illustrated in figure 5.4.) You will be prompted with the question "Find what?" Enter the word or phrase you want to find, and press the ENTER key. You will then be prompted for "Option(s)?" The options prompt allows you to specify several characteristics of the search. Each option is triggered by a single letter typed at the prompt. For example, to choose the W and U options, you would type:

```
Option(s)?WU
```

Here is an explanation of some of the options:

W—Searches for whole words only. For example, if the search is for "ring", specifying the W option will cause WordStar to ignore the word "bring" and find only the word "ring". If the W option is not chosen, both "ring" and "bring" would be found.

U—Causes WordStar to ignore case. If the U option is selected, the search "radish" will find both "Radish and "RADISH". If the U option is not chosen, WordStar will not find "Radish" when searching for "radish."

B—Searches backwards from the position of the cursor.

?—Treats the character "?" in a search string as a "wild card"; that is, it will match any character. It is like the blank tile in a Scrabble® game. For example, with this option, the search "Su??" will match "Suzy", "Susy", "Susi", and any other four letter string with "Su" plus any two characters.

See the WordStar manual for a complete list of options.

Unless the backward option has been specified, a WordStar Find operation begins at the location of the cursor and moves forward in the document. When the character string is located, the cursor is positioned at that spot, and editing resumes normally at that location. The command ^L causes WordStar to repeat the same Find. Thus, you can continue with a Find until you locate all instances of the specified string.

The Find/Replace option is also located on the Quick Menu (seen with the ^Q command), and is the "A" option on the menu. This command works much like the Find option. After answering the question "Find what?", you will then be prompted with "Replace what?" WordStar will find the first occurrence of the specified character string, and ask if you want to make the replacement. Answer "Y" to make the replacement or "N" to cancel the replacement. The ^L command will move the cursor to the next occurrence of the character string. To cause WordStar to replace the character string without asking each time, enter an "N" at the options prompt. The option "G" will cause the find/replace to be global, that is, to occur throughout the entire document. Thus, the response "GN" at the options prompt will cause all occurrences of the specified string to be replaced automatically without confirmation.

Open the file EXCEL.DOC that was created in the last chapter, and use the Replace feature to replace the word "labor" in the letter with the words "hard work".

CASE STUDY

Your Word Processor—Search and Replace

Describe how the search command is performed in your word processor:

Describe how the replace command is performed in your word processor:

How does your word processor handle the problem of lower- and uppercase?

Can your word processor search and replace both backward and forward in the text? If so, what are the commands?

Open the file EXCEL.DOC that was created in the last chapter, and use the Replace feature to replace the word "labor" in the letter with the words "hard work".

PITCHES, FONTS, AND LINE SPACING

Advancements in printer technology have given the word processor many more printing options than are available on a typewriter. Many printers can produce documents in several pitches and fonts. *Pitch* refers to the number of characters printed per inch. The most common pitch is 10 cpi (characters per inch), commonly known as *pica*. For more information per line, 12 pitch *(elite)* is often used. Dot matrix and laser printers can also create very small letters at about 16 cpi, or larger characters at 5 cpi. The most versatile printers can create an almost infinite number of pitches.

Another term used in selection of type style is *font*. A font is a letter design. Figure 6.1 illustrates several fonts in various sizes. The height of the characters is often measured in *points*. A 20-point character will be twice as tall as a 10-point character. Many fonts can be printed normally, in bold type, in italics, or underlined. Several type sizes are illustrated in Figure 6.1. The word processing program and the printer work together to provide various pitches and fonts to the user. Note that not every printer or every word processor can take advantage of all fonts and pitches.

Another important factor in controlling the way type appears on the printed page is to adjust line spacing. The two most common types of line spacing are single spacing and double spacing. However, many microcomputer word processing programs give you many more choices. For example, spacing can be set at 6 lines per inch (the normal setting) or 8 lines per inch to get more onto a page. Some programs can set line spacing to the nearest fraction of an inch or millimeter. Double spacing places a full blank line between each printed line, but with many programs, you may choose other options such as 1.5-line spacing, which is a half a line between lines of type, or other multiples or fractions of lines.

When changing pitch, fonts, or spacing, you may need to adjust top, bottom, left, and right margins. The number of characters that can be printed on the page can be determined with the following formula:

Number of characters that can be printed across a page = Pitch × Width of page

For example, if pitch (in characters per inch) is 10, and the width of the page is 8.5 inches (a normal piece of typing paper), the number of characters that can be printed across the page is

Pitch × Width of page = 10 × 8.5 = 85 characters

Usually, you will leave a margin on each side, meaning that the actual number of characters you will print across the page is the total number minus the margins. For example, if you have a one-inch margin, each margin (one inch) will take up:

Pitch × Width of margin = 10 × 1 = 10 characters

Therefore, each margin will take up 10 characters or 20 characters total, leaving 65 characters across the page for actual type.

Times Roman Font, 6 points.

Line printer font, 8 points

Courier Font, 12 points

Times Roman Font, 14 points

Times Roman Font , 18 points

Times Roman, 24 points

Script Font ,30 points

Modern, 48 pts

Modern, 75

FIGURE 6.1.
Some type fonts and sizes

You Try It

When the pitch is 12, the number of characters that can be printed across an 8.5-inch page increases to 102 characters. Can you verify it with the following formula?

Pitch × **Width of page** = ________ × ________ = 102

If margins of 1 inch will be set on each side of the paper, how many characters will need to be subtracted from 102 to give the total number of characters that will be printed across the page with margins? Use the following formulas to determine this answer:

Pitch × Width of margin = 12 × 1 = ________ characters per margin.

The number of characters that can be printed across the page, adjusting for both margins, is:

102 − ________ = ________ characters

If your answer is not 78 characters, refigure the above calculation until you understand how to get that answer.

CASE STUDY
WordPerfect—Changing Pitch and Line Spacing

Note that some printers do not support pitch changes. If yours does not, you will still be able to change line spacing. Retrieve the document named EXCEL.DOC for use in this case study. Before making a pitch or spacing change for an entire document, make sure your cursor is at the top left of the document.

Changing Pitch. Suppose you want to change the pitch for the entire document from 10 pitch to 12. Selection of pitch is made from the Print Format menu (displayed by CTRL-F8). Enter ^F8, and the Print Format menu (Figure 5.19) will appear with the prompt.

```
Selection: 0
```

at the bottom of the screen. Enter a "1" to choose to change pitch. The cursor will move to the current setting (probably 10). Enter a "12", and the cursor will move to the font prompt. If your printer supports multiple fonts, you would choose one by number at this prompt. For this exercise, press the ENTER key again, and you will return to the "Selection" prompt at the bottom of the screen. Press ENTER again, and you will be back at the document editing screen.

Changing to Double Spacing. Change to double spacing by using SHIFT-F8 to get the Line Format Menu. After pressing SHIFT-F8, the following menu will appear at the bottom of the screen:

```
1 2 Tabs; 3 Margins; 4 Spacing; 5 Hyphenation; 6 Align Char: 0
```

Choose option 4 from the menu, and the following prompt will appear:

```
[Spacing Set] 1
```

Type 2 for double spacing and press ENTER, which will return you to the document. Notice that the document on the screen is now double spaced. Once you have made changes, you may want to print the document again.

CASE STUDY
WordStar—Changing Pitch and Line Spacing

Your printers may or may not support pitch changes. If not, you will only be able to change line spacing. Retrieve the document named EXCEL.DOC to use in this case study.

Changing Pitch. In this exercise you will change the pitch for the entire document from 10 pitch to 12. Selection of pitch is made from the Print Controls Menu, displayed by the ^P command. The default pitch setting for WordStar is 10 cpi (pica), and an alternate setting is 12 cpi (elite). The command ^PA chooses the alternate (12 cpi) setting, and ^PN chooses the normal setting. Character width setting can also be set with the ".CW" (character width) dot command. How these are supported depends on which printer is being used. Other selections for pitch and fonts may be changed with the WSCHANGE program, which is used to customize WordStar to your particular computer and printer.

Changing to Double Spacing. Line spacing in WordStar is set using the ^O command to display the Onscreen Format Menu, and selecting the option "S" for spacing. You will then be prompted to select spacing from 1 to 9. Choose 2 to select double spacing. However, you must still reformat each of the paragraphs in the document as double spaced by placing the cursor at the beginning of each paragraph and typing the ^B (align paragraph) command.

Line spacing can also be set with the dot command ".LS" inserted at the top of the file. For example, the command

```
.LS 2
```

sets all following lines to print double spaced. Another dot command that can be used is ".LH" or line height. Using the ".LH" command, you may specify line spacing to the nearest 1/48th of an inch. The default is a line height of 8 (8/48), which prints at 6 lines per inch. Thus, the command

```
.LH 16
```

would cause standard double spacing, and the command

```
.LH 12
```

would cause 1 1/2 line spacing. Once you have made these changes, you may want to print this document again, to look at it on the printed page.

CASE STUDY

Your Word Processor—Choosing Pitch and Line Spacing

Remember that some printers do not support pitch changes. Determine whether yours does. If not, you will still be able to change line spacing. Retrieve the document named EXCEL.DOC for this exercise. Change from 10 to 12 pitch in your word processor. What is the default pitch? Describe how it can be changed:

Change the line spacing from single spacing to double spacing in your word processor. Describe how this can be done:

After you have made these changes, you may want to print this document again, to see it on the printed page.

CASE STUDY

Word-Perfect—Boldface, Underlining, and Italics

Although they were used briefly in the previous chapter, this discussion covers more generally how to use boldfacing, underline, and italics in WordPerfect. Almost every printer is able to support the printing of boldfaced and underlined characters. Some printers are not able to print italics. In WordPerfect, boldface and underlining are selected by function key commands F6 and F8 respectively. They may be used in two ways. First, you may press F6 or F8 to begin the enhancement, then enter the text you want enhanced. This is how the letterhead was made bold in chapter 5.) Or, you can block a section of existing text and then press F6 or F8 to cause the entire block of text to be enhanced, as was done in Chapter 5 to underline a sentence.

Italics and other print fonts are selected from the Print Format menu, shown by the function key command CTRL-F8. Place the cursor where you want the font to begin, then choose CTRL-F8, and "1" for the Pitch/Font menu. Here you may select the pitch and font. You must know ahead of time the number of the font that you want. For example, if your printer is set up with italics as font number 4, you would type "4" in the font position. Text following the location of the cursor would be printed in font 4 until you turn it off by choosing another font in another location.

If your printer supports italics, use the Print Format menu to cause the word "cannot" in the EXCEL.DOC letter to be printed in the italic font.

CASE STUDY

WordStar—Boldface, Underlining, and Italics

Boldface and underlining in WordStar were discussed in the previous chapter. This section will review those commands, and add the command for italic type. Boldface and underlining are available on most printers, but italics may not be. In WordStar, boldface, underlining and other print enhancements are available by typing ^P for the Print Controls Menu (Figure 5.4). To cause a portion of the text to be printed in bold type, place the cursor at the beginning of the text and enter the command ^PB. Move the cursor to the end of the text to be boldfaced, and enter ^PB again. The same procedure is used for underlining using the command ^PS. Italic font, which is the only special font normally available in WordStar, is specified in the same way, using the command ^PY. Other fonts include ^V-subscript, ^T-superscript, ^X-strikeout, ^D-Double strike.

If your printer supports italics, cause the word "cannot" in the EXCEL.DOC letter to be printed in the italic font.

CASE STUDY

Your Word Processor—Boldface, Underlining, and Italics

Your printer will almost certainly support bold and underlined characters, but may not support italics. You will need to determine which of these options are available. What command do you use in your word processor to underline and to print in boldface and italics? Can block commands be used?

If your printer supports italics, cause the word "cannot" in the EXCEL.DOC letter to be printed in the italic font.

WORKING WITH LONG DOCUMENTS

Word processors are used for more than single-page letters and documents. When multi-page documents are to be created, there are a few more factors to consider, such as the number of lines to be printed per page, page numbers, titles, headers, footers, and more. Most word processors perform automatic paging when a document gets too long to print on a single page. This *automatic pagination* may occur at a place in a report or document that you don't like. Therefore, there has to be a way to override the automatic paging and either force paging at a particular point, or to ask for conditional paging.

Widows and Orphans

When pagination occurs leaving only the first line of a paragraph on a page, it is referred to as a *widow,* and when the last line of a paragraph appears at the top of a page, it is referred to as an *orphan.* Most word processors have a variety of ways to help you prevent widows and orphans, which are considered bad style. Conditional paging is one of the most common ways to help prevent this malady.

Conditional Paging

Conditional paging is used to keep a block of text together. For example, you may want to specify that if there is only enough room for the first line of a paragraph to appear on the bottom of the page, the word processor should go to the next page to begin printing the paragraph. This is particularly useful to prevent widows. Conditional paging may help with an orphan problem also, but oftentimes rewording of the paragraph to make it longer or shorter is used to solve the problem.

Page Numbering

Page numbers can be placed in a variety of locations on the printed page, according to the type of document you are printing. A common place to have the page number is at the center top or center bottom of the printed page. If the document is to be printed on both sides of the paper and bound into a book, you may want the page numbers on alternating left and right corners, so that the page number is always on the outside edge. If the document is to be printed on single sides and bound, you may want the page number always to appear on the right side of the page.

Sample Multi-Page Document

Figure 6.2 contains the document that will be used to illustrate some of the features associated with multi-page documents. It is a simple report with titles, headings, and references. This document is on the Text Examples Disk under the following names:

- WordPerfect version LEADER.WP
- WordStar version LEADER.WS
- ASCII text version LEADER.TXT

Copy this file from the Text Examples Disk to the disk you are using to store your word processing documents. Use the name LEADER.DOC.

CASE STUDY

Word-Perfect—Page Numbers and Paging

WordPerfect is preset to print no page numbers. Therefore, if you want page numbers, you must specifically tell WordPerfect to add them. This is achieved by selecting the Page Format menu (ALT-F8), illustrated in figure 5.20 in the previous chapter. Once in the menu, you choose option "1", which is the Page Number Position Menu. There are nine options for page number positions. If you are not satisfied with where the numbers are printed on the page, there are further adjustments that can be made using the "Page Number Column Positions" option that is number "7" on the Page Format Menu. You must set the page numbering options at the very beginning of the document.

Placing Page Numbers at Bottom Center. Make the necessary changes in LEADER.DOC to print the page number at the bottom center of each page. To do this, place the cursor at the very beginning of the document. Choose the ALT-F8 command and specify the option "7 – Bottom center of every page." Print the document to verify that this worked.

Creating a "Hard Page". To create a *hard page*—(that is, to force a page break exactly where you want it), use the command CTRL-ENTER. The hard page break is displayed as a line of equal signs (=) on the screen. A conditional page break is set up by the Page Format Menu (ALT-F8). You must have your cursor at the place where you want the conditional page break. Enter the ALT-F8 command, then choose the "9" option, to keep a number of lines together. For example, if you wish to keep the next five lines together, choose "5." When you end this option and move the cursor up or down, you should see the page break line on the screen adjust to reflect the command. Then if you later delete one or more of the five lines

Thoughts about Leadership

There are many ways to skin a cat. There are, it seems, as many ways to define what factors makes a person a leader. The word "leadership" came into the English language less than two hundred years ago, and has only been studied in detail in this century. However, the concept has been intensely investigated. Gordon (1977) cites one survey of leadership that records over 3000 studies, with a bibliography covering 150 pages. With this abundance of material, this phenomenon of leadership is not even now fully understood. It is something that many people recognize when they see it, but have a hard time explaining how it came about.

In his attempt at defining the "Art of Leadership" Tead (1935) gives a reasonable definition of what leadership should accomplish:

Leadership is the activity of influencing people to cooperate toward some goal which they have come to find desirable.

The part that is the most difficult about this definition is the how. How does that influence take place? What causes some person to be able to take a group of people, convince them that an outcome is desirable, and then lead them toward the successful completion of the task? There is no easy answer. Leaders are neither all charismatic, nor all well-schooled, nor all born into the mold. As a result of this fact, researchers have attempted to develop theories of leadership to explain what causes leadership to occur. Each theory tries to examine the personages of the leaders, and/or the situations that nurture leadership.

The possibility that leaders are simply born has never been given much credence. Most researchers assume that leaders can be developed. If this is the case, knowing that a people's intellectual, behavioral, and physical abilities vary, and that their early environment molds their personalities, how can potential leaders be discovered and developed in a logical, effective manner? If some people have traits that can be molded into leadership abilities, then those traits need to be identified. Identification tests need to be utilized, if they exist, or developed if they do not exist. Once the possibility of leadership is identified in individuals, training techniques need to be defined that can bring out those qualities that promote leadership skills. Perhaps leaders can come from all reasonably sane people with the proper training and nurture. If this is the case, is there one way to train a leader, or are different types of leaders and different types of training techniques required for different situations?

1

Review of the Literature

People of many persuasions function as leaders in many varied situations. In an effort to categorize those items that may influence the leadership capacity of an individual, researchers have identified several factors which may be important in discovering who will be a leader. These factors include personal traits, behavior, situation, causality, and substitutes for leadership. Stogdill's Handbook of Leadership (1974) is an often-cited source of findings concerning the importance of leadership traits. In a recent attempt to discover leadership traits, Bennis (1984) interviewed 90 of the most effective leaders in the United States, 60 from business and 30 from the public sector, in search for those common traits that could set this group apart from the ordinary. He found much diversity, but managed to identify several traits that he felt were common. Bennis made an important distinction between a manager and a leader. "Leaders are people who do the right thing; managers are people who do things right." By this he means that leaders are people who affect the culture, who change the very nature of organization, and who create and maintain values. Managers, on the other hand, simply make the machine work well in its current state of affairs. The traits of leadership which Bennis identified include the ability of the leader to draw others to himself; they are able to communicate their dreams and to persuade others to believe in the dream, they have constancy, which means that they have a known philosophy that does not change, and they are able to manage their own skills effectively.

The literature is a sea of conflicting ideas and theories of why leadership happens, and how it can be promoted. However, some consistent threads emerge. First, leadership cannot be explained by traits alone. Genetic or environmental factors, or both, may be responsible for the appearance of leadership traits in some individuals. However, it is not impossible to take a non-leader, and instill in that person some leadership traits or behaviors.

REFERENCES

Bennis, W. (1984), "Good managers and good leaders", Across the Board, October 1984, pp. 7-11.

Gordon, T. (1977), Leader Effectiveness Training, Bantam Books, Toronto.

Stogdill, R. M. (1974), Handbook of Leadership: A Survey of Theory and Research, The Free Press, New York.

Tead, O. (1935), The Art of Leadership, McGraw-Hill, New York.

2

FIGURE 6.2.
Example multi-page document

following the point where you set up the conditional page break, WordPerfect will still keep the next five remaining lines together.

Pagination is normally performed when WordPerfect sees that the maximum number of lines have been allocated for a page. On the edit screen you will see a line of dashes (–) automatically drawn between pages. This is called a *soft page*. If paging does not occur where you want, you may either force an earlier paging, or set conditional paging.

CASE STUDY

WordStar—Page Numbers and Paging

WordStar is preset to print page numbers at the bottom center of each page. Therefore, if you want to omit page numbers or to choose another location for them to appear, you must specifically tell WordStar what to do. Page numbers are regulated by a series of dot commands. To turn off paging, use the command ".OP". To turn page numbering back on, use the ".PG" command. The command ".PC #" prints the page number in a specified column. Thus the command ".PC 40" will print the page number in column 40 of the page. The command ".PN #" specifies which number to begin using. Thus if the command ".PN 20" is located at the top of the document, the page numbering will begin at 20. This is useful if a document is a continuation of another document. Page numbers may also be specified in footers, as will be discussed shortly.

In summary, dot commands that control page numbering are:

.OP	Omit page numbering
.PG	Begin page numbering (turn it back on)
.PC ##	Print page number in column "##"
.PN ##	Begin paging with page number "##"

Make the necessary changes to LEADER.DOC for the page number to print out at the bottom right of each page. To do this, use the .PC ## command. At the beginning of the document, include the command ".PC 70". This will cause the page number to be placed in column 70 at the bottom of each page. Print the document to verify that the change worked.

A new page is normally started when WordStar sees that the maximum number of lines for a page has been entered. On the edit screen you will see a line of dashes "–" automatically drawn between pages. If paging does not occur where you want, you may either force a new page, or set conditional paging. To force a page break to occur at a particular point, you can use the dot command ".PA". A conditional page break is set up with the ".CP #" command. For example, to make sure the next five lines are kept together, use the command ".CP 5". Then, if a page break would normally occur in the middle of those five lines, the page break will be moved so the lines will all be printed together on the next page.

CASE STUDY

Your Word Processor—Page Numbers and Paging

Is your word processor preset to print numbers on the page or not? How do you turn on page numbers and turn them off?

In your word processor, how can you choose where to place the page number?

Does your word processor support hard page breaks or conditional paging? If so, what are the commands?

Make the necessary changes to LEADER.DOC for the page number to print out at the bottom center of each page.

HEADERS AND FOOTERS

When working with multi-page documents, you will often want to place a title or *header* at the top of each page, and/or a *footer* at the bottom of each page. Depending on the word processor, headers and titles may be the same, or they may mean different things, but they always appear at the top of the page. Many books have *running headers* on each page, giving the chapter title, for instance. Footers should not be confused with footnotes. Footers are typically text that appears at the bottom of each page. Footnotes are references that often appear at the bottom of a specific page. Often, the same footer will appear throughout the document. For example, you may want the message "Confidential Document—Do Not Copy" to appear on the bottom of each page of a report, or perhaps you want the date to appear on the bottom of each page. You would create a footer to perform this function. Defining headers and footers means that you do not have to retype your running title at the beginning of each page, as you would if you were using a typewriter.

CASE STUDY

Word-Perfect—Headers and Footers

WordPerfect offers the capability to define a header or footer to appear on each page, using the ALT-F8 Page Format Menu. Option 6 on this menu is the Headers and Footers Menu. You may create a header or footer so that it appears on every page, every odd page, or every even page. An edit screen will appear for you to enter the text of the header or footer. The WordPerfect manual suggests that you begin a header or footer with a hard page break (CTRL-ENTER) at the beginning of the header lines. While creating a header or footer, you may use the print enhancement commands to center, boldface, underline, and so on. After creating a header or footer, use the F7 key and ENTER to exit the menu.

Headers and footers may be changed at any point in the document. For example, if you do not want the header or footer to begin until the second page, make sure your cursor is at the second page before creating the header or footer. If you want a different header or footer at another section in the document, place your cursor on the first page of that section before creating the next header or footer.

A page number may be embedded in a header or footer. Within the definition of the header or footer, at the place where you want the page number to occur, enter a ^B (CTRL-B). WordPerfect will automatically add page numbers at that point.

For LEADER.DOC, define a three-line header that is positioned at the top left of each page, with the text "A Look at Leadership", enclosed by two blank lines. Be sure that you define the header at the beginning of the document so that it will appear on all pages beginning with the first page. Define a footer so the page number appears at the bottom center of each page.

CASE STUDY

WordStar—Headers and Footers

In WordStar, headers and footers may be up to three lines long. They are created using a series of dot commands: .H1, .H2, and .H3 for headers, and .F1, .F2, and .F3 for footers. For example, to create a three-line header, you would place these commands in the first few lines of your document:

```
.H1 This is the first header line
.H2 This is the second header line
.H3 This is the third header line
```

You may use print controls such as ^PB (boldface) or ^PS (underlining) in a footer or header line.

When a footer is created, it automatically turns off the page number that normally appears at the bottom of the page. The page number may be embedded in a header or footer with the symbol "#". Wherever the # appears, the page number will be printed. For example:

```
.F1 Page #
```

would cause the page number to be printed on the first line of the footer, flush left on the page.

For LEADER.DOC, define a three-line header that is flush left at the top of each page with the text "A Look at Leadership" on the second line, enclosed by two blank lines. Be sure that you define the header on the first page of the document so that it will appear on all pages beginning with the first page.

CASE STUDY

Your Word Processor— Headers and Footers

Does your word processor support headers and footers? If so, describe the commands to cause a header to be placed at the top of each page:

Describe the command to cause a footer to be placed at the bottom of each page:

Can page numbers be embedded in a header or footer? If so, describe how

For LEADER.DOC, define a three-line header that is positioned at the top left of each page with the text "A Look at Leadership", enclosed by two blank lines. Be sure that you define the header at the beginning of the document so that it will appear on all pages beginning with the first page. Define a footer so the page number appears at the bottom center of each page.

USING A SPELLING CHECKER

A very popular feature with word processors is the spelling checker. Usually, this procedure allows you to check individual words, or all the words in an entire document. Spelling checkers often know the correct spelling of 40,000 or more words. Even then, some words that you use often may not be in its vocabulary. Most spelling checkers allow you to enter your own list of words that will be added to the dictionary.

CASE STUDY

WordPerfect—Spelling Checker

In WordPerfect, you may check the spelling of a single word, a block of words, or an entire document. The spelling checker is accessed with the ^F2 command. The following menu will appear at the bottom of the page:

```
Check 1 Word; 2 Page; 3 Document; 4 Change Dictionary; 5 Look Up; 6 Count
```

To check the spelling in the entire document, choose option 2. When spell-checking an entire document, WordPerfect will display any suspect word, and give you the choices:

```
1 Skip once; 2 Skip; 3 Add word; 4 Edit; 5 Look up; 6 Phonetic
```

"Skip once" means to skip that word, and look for the next suspect. "Skip" means to ignore that word for the rest of the document. "Add Word" means to save the word in a supplemental dictionary. "Edit" allows you to edit the suspect word, and "Look up" will display similar words. "Phonetic" looks up words in the dictionary that sound like the word in question.

For example, in LEADER.DOC a check of the entire document would find the word "Gordon", which is not in the dictionary. The screen is illustrated in figure 6.3. Notice that the word "Gordon" is highlighted, and several words are listed as possible spellings. To choose a correct spelling, type the letter of the word that is correct. In this case, Gordon is correct, and you would probably choose 2 (Skip), since if the word "Gordon" appears again in the text, you want the spelling checker to ignore it.

CASE STUDY

WordStar—Spelling Checker

In WordStar, spell-checking is available on the Quick Menu, which is accessed with the ^Q command. Options are as follow:

- L Check rest
- N Check word
- O Enter word

Option L checks the spelling in the rest of the document. Option N checks the word at the cursor position. Option O checks the spelling of a word you type. When checking the spelling in a document, WordStar searches for suspect words. When a suspect word is found, it is displayed below the Spelling Check Menu, along with suggestions of correct spellings.

For example, in LEADER.DOC, the spelling checker found the word "Gordon" as a suspect word. The resulting screen is illustrated in figure 6.4. The Spelling Check Menu contains options "I" Ignore the current word and go on to the next suspect, "A" Add that word to the supplemental dictionary, "B" Bypass that word this time only, "E" Enter a correction to the word, "T" Turn auto-align on or off (which causes paragraphs to be reformatted when a word is changed), and "G" Global replacement on or off. When global replacement is on, WordStar replaces all occurrences of one spelling with the one you choose. When the "E" Enter option is chosen, you will be prompted to enter the correct spelling.

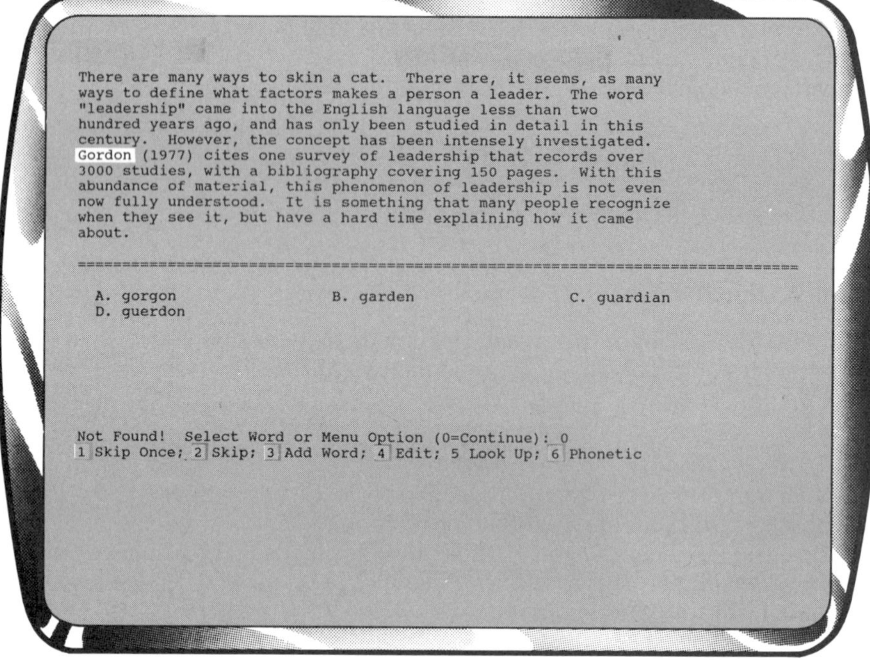
There are many ways to skin a cat. There are, it seems, as many ways to define what factors makes a person a leader. The word "leadership" came into the English language less than two hundred years ago, and has only been studied in detail in this century. However, the concept has been intensely investigated. Gordon (1977) cites one survey of leadership that records over 3000 studies, with a bibliography covering 150 pages. With this abundance of material, this phenomenon of leadership is not even now fully understood. It is something that many people recognize when they see it, but have a hard time explaining how it came about.
A. gorgon
B. garden
C. guardian
D. guerdon
Not Found! Select Word or Menu Option (0=Continue): 0
1 Skip Once; 2 Skip; 3 Add Word; 4 Edit; 5 Look Up; 6 Phonetic

FIGURE 6.3.
WordPerfect spelling checker

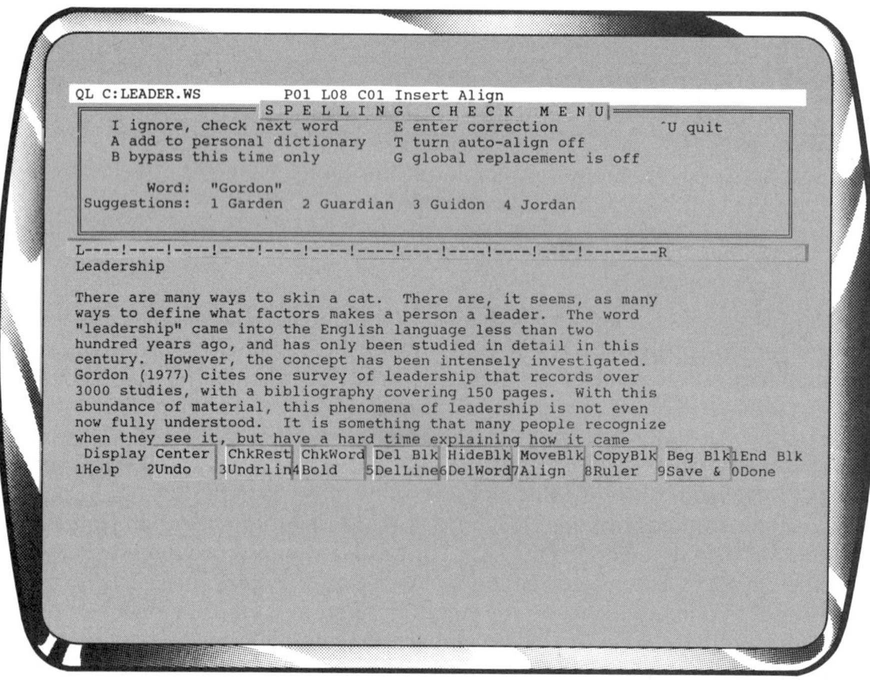
QL C:LEADER.WS P01 L08 C01 Insert Align
S P E L L I N G C H E C K M E N U
I ignore, check next word
E enter correction
^U quit
A add to personal dictionary
T turn auto-align off
B bypass this time only
G global replacement is off
Word: "Gordon"
Suggestions: 1 Garden 2 Guardian 3 Guidon 4 Jordan
L----!----!----!----!----!----!----!----!----!----!----!--------R
Leadership
There are many ways to skin a cat. There are, it seems, as many ways to define what factors makes a person a leader. The word "leadership" came into the English language less than two hundred years ago, and has only been studied in detail in this century. However, the concept has been intensely investigated. Gordon (1977) cites one survey of leadership that records over 3000 studies, with a bibliography covering 150 pages. With this abundance of material, this phenomena of leadership is not even now fully understood. It is something that many people recognize when they see it, but have a hard time explaining how it came
Display Center ChkRest ChkWord Del Blk HideBlk MoveBlk CopyBlk Beg Blk End Blk
1Help 2Undo 3Undrlin 4Bold 5DelLine 6DelWord 7Align 8Ruler 9Save & 0Done

FIGURE 6.4.
WordStar spelling checker

USING AN ON-LINE THESAURUS

Anyone who has written essays, papers, or reports knows that sometimes the right word for a sentence escapes memory. Both WordPerfect and WordStar have capabilities that allow you to look up similar words in order to find that word you need.

CASE STUDY

Word-Perfect—On-Line Thesaurus

In WordPerfect, move the cursor to the word you want to look up, then choose the ALT-F1 command. A Thesaurus Menu will appear at the bottom of the screen:

```
1 Replace Word; 2 View Doc; 3 Look Up Word; 4 Clear Column:
```

and a list of possible words will appear, designated with the letters A, B, C, etc. For example, in LEADER.DOC, if the cursor is moved to "concept", and ALT-F1 is pressed, the Thesaurus screen will appear (see figure 6.5). Some possible substitutes for "concept" are given:

```
A  .idea
B  .notion
C  .philosophy
D  .theory
E  .abstraction
F  .impression
G  .perception
H  .thought
```

To replace "concept" with "notion", choose menu option 1, then type the letter next to the chosen word, "B", and the word "concept" is replaced with "notion".

The option "View Doc" is used if you need to see more of your document on screen. Notice the dot in front of some of the words in the list. This means that these words are "headwords", having their own thesaurus entries. The (3) "Look up word" option allows you to look up another list of synonyms for one of the headwords.

CASE STUDY

WordStar—On-Line Thesaurus

WordStar includes a supplemental program, Word Finder that must be loaded before WordStar is entered. The Word Finder program is loaded with the command:

```
C>WF
```

Once this program is run, it stays in memory until the computer is turned off, so when WordStar is run, the Word Finder program is ready when you need it. To use the Word Finder, move the cursor to the word to look up. Enter the command ALT-1. This will bring up a Word Finder "window". It lists synonyms from which to select the word you want. You can move up and down within the Word Finder list with the PgUp and PgDn keys. To select a word, move the cursor to the word in the Word Finder window. Press the ENTER key, and the word you have selected will replace the word in your document. A sample Word Finder menu is illustrated in figure 6.6.

FIGURE 6.5.
Example Thesaurus screen in WordPerfect

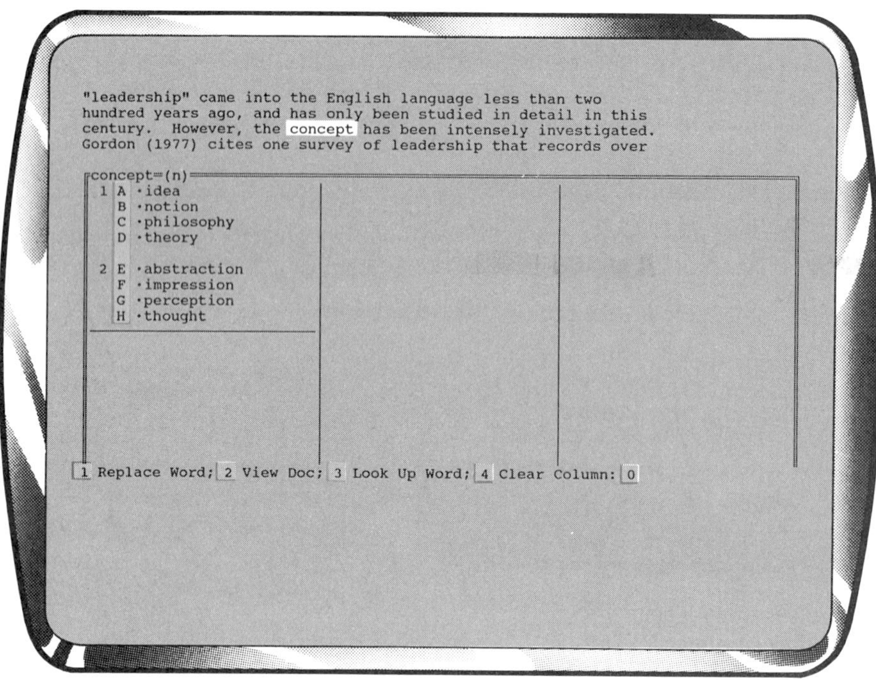
"leadership" came into the English language less than two
hundred years ago, and has only been studied in detail in this
century. However, the concept has been intensely investigated.
Gordon (1977) cites one survey of leadership that records over
concept=(n)
1 A ·idea
B ·notion
C ·philosophy
D ·theory
2 E ·abstraction
F ·impression
G ·perception
H ·thought
1 Replace Word; 2 View Doc; 3 Look Up Word; 4 Clear Column: 0

FIGURE 6.6.
Example WordStar Word Finder screen

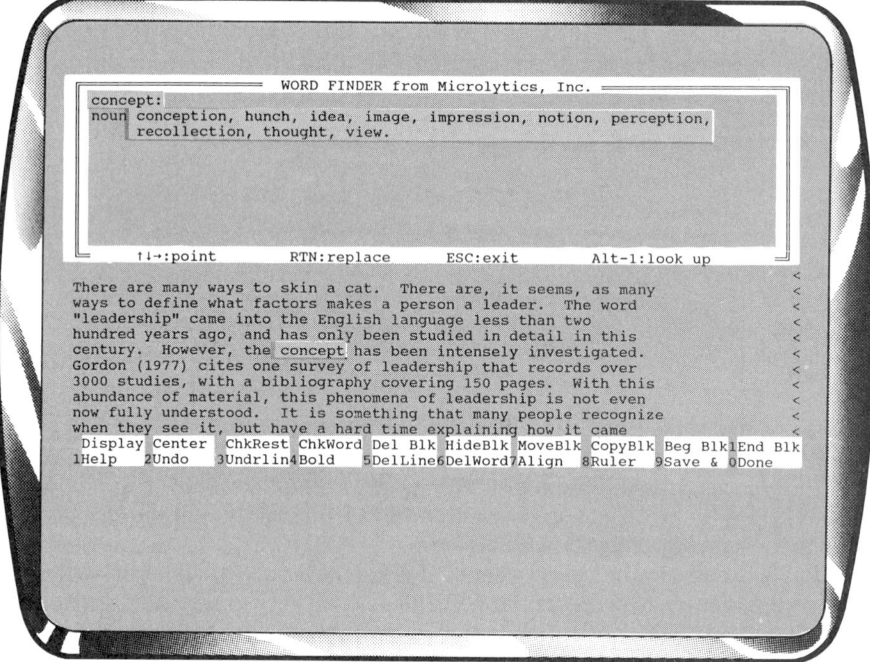
WORD FINDER from Microlytics, Inc.
concept:
noun conception, hunch, idea, image, impression, notion, perception,
recollection, thought, view.
↑↓→:point RTN:replace ESC:exit Alt-1:look up
There are many ways to skin a cat. There are, it seems, as many
ways to define what factors makes a person a leader. The word
"leadership" came into the English language less than two
hundred years ago, and has only been studied in detail in this
century. However, the concept has been intensely investigated.
Gordon (1977) cites one survey of leadership that records over
3000 studies, with a bibliography covering 150 pages. With this
abundance of material, this phenomena of leadership is not even
now fully understood. It is something that many people recognize
when they see it, but have a hard time explaining how it came
Display Center ChkRest ChkWord Del Blk HideBlk MoveBlk CopyBlk Beg Blk End Blk
1Help 2Undo 3Undrlin 4Bold 5DelLine 6DelWord 7Align 8Ruler 9Save & 0Done

CASE STUDY

Your Word Processor—On-Line Spelling Checker and Thesaurus

If your word processor has a spelling checker or thesaurus, describe how they are accessed. How is the spelling checker accessed in your word processor?

How is the thesaurus accessed in your word processor?

ADDITIONAL NOTES ABOUT WORD PROCESSORS

Since every word processor is different, there are features and functions in each word processor that are not necessarily comparable with those found in others. A few of the common features of these word processors have been covered in the last two chapters, but there are some others that deserve mention.

Other WordPerfect Features

One feature popular with those writing papers is automatic footnoting. Footnoting is done with the command CTRL-F7. At the place where you want a footnote to appear, press CTRL-F7. A menu will appear, where the choice "1" will create a footnote. Your cursor will be placed in a small editing space, where you can enter the text for the footnote. The footnotes will be automatically numbered as they are entered.

Other special features of WordPerfect include the ability to create text in a two-column format, like a newspaper. *Redlining* is a word processing feature that is often used by lawyers and others to highlight text by printing a vertical line at the side of the page. WordPerfect also has an outlining feature, can align numbers for numeric typing, and can do simple math. The Merge command allows text from another source to be merged into a document. *Macros* are stored sequences of commands that allow you to create new commands by "programming" a sequence of keystrokes.

WordPerfect 5.0, introduced in 1988, introduced several enhancements into the WordPerfect Word Processor. The most notable addition is the ability to integrate graphics with text. For example, you can include a graph created in Lotus 1-2-3 directly into a report or letter. This gives WordPerfect capabilities similar to some desktop publishing software. Most other features are enhancements of current capabilities, such as support for more types of printers.

Other WordStar Features

One of the most useful features of WordStar is its ability to do *mail-merge*. This feature allows you to write a letter and create a list of names and addresses, then merge the names and addresses with the letter text to print out any number of "personalized" letters. You can also merge in numbers and have WordStar add them up as the document is printed. Another feature that comes in handy is chaining files. This allows you to combine smaller files together in one print job to print out a document that consists of text from more than one file. Other features include automatic indexing, tables of contents, column mode, numeric alignment, and macros. *Macros* are stored sequences of commands that can be used instead of repeating a frequently used pattern of keystrokes. Another version of WordStar (WordStar 2000) includes the feature of combining graphic images such as charts and photographs with text.

SUMMARY

Word processors such as WordPerfect and WordStar include many features that make it possible to produce professional quality documents. The layout and appearance of the text on the page can be enhanced by specifying the font (style of type), pitch (size of type), and the spacing between lines. Headers and/or footers—a title or other text appearing on each page—can be added, along with page numbers. The placement of page breaks can be controlled to avoid awkward layouts.

Other features make editing and revision easier, such as the Search and Replace command or the spelling checker, which help the user to locate and correct particular words easily. An on-line thesaurus is handy for finding just the right word.

KEY TERMS

Define the following terms in your own words:

Pitch	**Header**
Font	**Footer**
Widow	**Pagination**
Orphan	**Conditional paging**

QUESTIONS

Fill in the blanks. Base your answers on the word processing program you used in this chapter.

1. The ____________ feature is used to locate a particular word or string of characters in a document.
2. The ______________________________ feature provides the most appropriate and convenient method for correcting multiple occurrences of a misspelled name.
3. Styles of type may also be called ____________.
4. The height of a printed character is often measured in ____________.
5. The ______________________________ and ________________ work together to provide various pitches and fonts.
6. On an 8 1/2 × 11-inch sheet of paper, you can print _______ characters across the page when pitch is set to 10.
7. On an 8 1/2 × 11-inch sheet of paper, you can print _______ characters across the page when pitch is set to 12.
8. When a page break leaves only the first line of a paragraph at the bottom of a page, it is called a(n) ____________.
9. To help prevent page breaks in the middle of a block of text, we can use the ____ feature.
10. To force a page break, use the command ________________.
11. A ________________ is text that appears at the bottom of every page of the document (e.g., a chapter title).
12. To turn off page numbering, use the ________________ command.

Write a short answer in your own words for each of the following questions. Base your answers on the word processing program you used in this chapter.

1. Outline the procedure for replacing all of the occurrences of a misspelled name with the correct spelling.
2. Why is pitch an important consideration in page formatting?
3. Outline the procedure for changing the pitch from 10 cpi to 12 cpi.
4. Outline the procedure for calculating the number of characters which will appear on a line, when paper width = 8.5 inches, pitch = 10 cpi, left margin = 1 inch, and right margin = 1 inch.
5. Outline the procedure for changing line spacing from single to double.
6. Briefly describe the difference between a soft page break and a hard page break.
7. Describe a situation where you might want to use a conditional page break.
8. Outline the procedure for placing a page number (a) in the right corner of the bottom margin of every page (b) in the center of the bottom margin of every page.
9. Briefly describe the difference between a header and a footer.
10. Outline the procedure for defining (a) a footer (b) header.

LABORATORY EXERCISES

Lab Exercise 1. In this exercise, you will use the LEADER.DOC file from the Text Examples Disk.

1. Start up your word processing program and retrieve the LEADER.DOC file from your data disk.
2. Place a centered and boldfaced title at the top of the document. Use the word "Leadership" as your title. The title should be 2 inches (12 lines) from the top of the page. Skip 4 lines after the title.
3. Boldface the section titles: "Thoughts about Leadership" and "Review of the Literature."
4. Define a header that contains the title "Leadership". The header should print automatically on each page of the document.
5. Set up page numbering so that numbers will print in the center of the bottom margin.
6. Underline all book titles throughout the document.
7. Use the following page formatting settings:
   Left margin = 1 inch (10 cpi)
   Right margin = 1 inch (10 cpi)
   Justification off
   Line spacing double
8. Save and print the revised document under a different name.
9. If your printer supports 12 pitch type, re-format the document for 12 pitch. Save and print the document.

Lab Exercise 2. In this exercise, you will create a document called GLOSSARY.DOC.

1. Start up your word processing program and type the document given below.

   WordStar Key Terms Glossary
   Block Marker: A marker in WS used to define a block or unit of text so that the unit can be moved, deleted, copied, or saved for use in other documents.
   Boiler Plating: Using similar parts to create a unique product.
   Dot Commands: WS commands used to format the printed version of the text.
   Editing: In WS, revising data by changing the written content of the text.
   Formatting: In WS, making changes that deal with the appearance of text.
   Menu Commands: WS commands that accomplish all editing and most formatting.
   Page Break: A line of dashes that WS displays on the screen to indicate that the user has typed a full page of printed text and a new page is about to begin.
   Ruler Line: A dashed line that appears under the WS menu indicating where the current left and right margins are set for text being entered or re-formatted.

Word Wrap: A feature of **WS** that automatically begins a new line when the right margin of the current line is reached.
Toggle Command: A command that turns on and off certain **WS** features.
Scroll: The vertical movement of lines of type on a monitor.

2. Save and print the document entered in step 1. Now make the following changes to the GLOSSARY.DOC file:
3. Center and boldface the title at the top of the page.
4. Insert the following term into the glossary at the appropriate location (i.e., between "Menu Commands" and "Page Break").

   Opening: In **WS**, the act that allows the user to enter or edit data in the file while it is held in **RAM** memory. Equivalent to loading.

5. Delete the term "Boiler Plating" and its definition from the glossary.
6. Boldface each glossary term.
7. Insert a blank line between each of the terms.
8. FIND all occurrences of the term "WS" and REPLACE with the term "WordStar".
9. Use block operations to rearrange the last three glossary items into alphabetical order.
10. Check for typographical and spelling errors and make any necessary operations.
11. Use the following page formatting settings:
    Top margin = 1 inch
    Left margin = 1 1/2 inch
    Right margin = 1 inch
    Line spacing single
    Justification off
    Page numbering off
12. Save and print the revised document.

Lab Exercise 3. In this exercise, you will create a document called LOTUS.DOC.

1. Start up your word processing program and enter the following text.

```
                         Lotus 1-2-3 Workshop
                        Reference Handout #1
                            The Keyboard
CONTROL KEYS
Slash key:          Calls Lotus's main menu of commands.
ENTER key:          Enters the current line into memory for
                    Lotus to act upon.
Escape key:         Cancels current line or operation and
                    ''backs up'' one step.
FUNCTION KEYS
F1  HELP            Accesses 1-2-3's on-line help facility.
                    Help screens appear in context.
F2  EDIT            Allows contents of current cell to be
                    edited.
```

```
F3  NAME        Displays the list of current range names
                while in the POINT mode.
F4  ABS         Permits defining absolute cell addresses
                while pointing to them during formula
                creation.
F5  GOTO        Moves the pointer to the specified cell.
F6  WINDOW      Moves the pointer from one window to
                another.
F7  QUERY       Repeats the last Data Query operation.
F8  TABLE       Repeats the last Data Table operation.
F9  CALC        Recalculates the spreadsheet.
F10 GRAPH       Redraws the graph currently defined.
```

```
POINTER KEYS
Pointer Control Keys: Move the pointer one cell at a
time in the direction of the pointer arrow.
Home Key: Moves pointer to the top left corner of the
spreadsheet (A1), or ''to the beginning of'' in modes
other than READY.
PgUp Key: Shifts screen and pointer one page up at a
time.
PgDn Key: Shifts screen and pointer one page down at a
time.
Tab Key: Shifts screen one page to the right (lowercase)
or one page to the left (uppercase) at a time.
Scroll Lock Key: When SCROLL is toggled on with this key,
scrolling of the spreadsheet occurs one row or column at
a time.
Period Key: Anchors a range to begin pointing to it, or
shifts the anchor while pointing to a range.
```

2. Boldface and double space the three-line title. Add a hard page break after the title. The title should print 20 lines from the top of the page. No page number should print on this page. (The three-line title should print on a page by itself and will serve as the title page for the document.)
3. Underline the subheadings: CONTROL KEYS, FUNCTION KEYS, and POINTER KEYS.
4. Boldface each of the glossary terms.
5. Check for typographical and spelling errors and make any necessary corrections.
6. Use the following page formatting settings for the second page of the document:
   Top margin = 1 inch
   Left margin = 1 inch
   Right margin = 1 inch
   Line spacing single
   Justification off
   Page numbering on
   Page number to print on second page = 1
7. Save and print the document.

Lab Exercise 4. In this exercise, you will use your word processing program to create a document called RESUME.DOC. Using the format of the resumé in figure 6.7, create your own resumé.

1. Center, boldface, and underline the appropriate text (e.g., your name, headings, etc.)
2. Use the following page formatting settings
   Margins = default settings
   Justification off (ragged right edge)
   Page numbering off
3. Save and print the document.

FIGURE 6.7.
Example resumé

ANNETTE G. WEESE
812 Rosa Place
Cedar Hill, Texas 75104
(214) 555-1212

OBJECTIVE

To find a teaching position in an elementary school in grades one to four, either in a traditional classroom setting or as a teacher of children with special needs.

EDUCATION

Dallas Baptist College: 1981, earned a Bachelor of Arts Degree in education with emphasis in speech. Maintained a 3.5 GPA.

Mountain View Community College: 1975 to 1979

WORK EXPERIENCE

1988 to present: Part-time positions while raising two children. Volunteer work in community and church organizations.

1985 to 1987: Teacher for Dallas Independent School District teaching special students, fourth and first grades.

1981 to 1984: Teacher for Clayton County ISD, Clayton, Georgia, sixth grade.

1976 to 1980: Part-time positions including retail sales at Sears and Lane Bryant, day camp coordinator, library assistant.

OTHER EXPERIENCE

Proficient in using computers. Have had experience using Apple II computers and IBM PCs. Served in college senate and and established a volunteer ''adopt a school'' program for education majors.

ACTIVITIES

Have served as an officer in community revitalization program and in the local crime watch commission.

REFERENCES

Credentials and references available upon request.

CHAPTER 7

Introduction to Spreadsheets

CHAPTER OVERVIEW. This is the first of two chapters discussing electronic spreadsheet software. The purpose behind spreadsheets, their common applications, and basic skills for using spreadsheets are covered using Lotus 1-2-3 for examples. Descriptions in the chapter are also relevant to other Lotus-like spreadsheet programs such as The Twin or VP-Planner.

CHAPTER OBJECTIVES

Upon completion of this chapter, you will be able to:

- Describe the basic concepts and terminology of spreadsheets.
- Describe some common applications for spreadsheet programs.
- Describe the structure of a spreadsheet.
- Describe and use labels, mathematical expressions, and functions.
- Construct simple spreadsheets.
- Save and print spreadsheets.

CASE STUDY

Lotus 1-2-3 and Your Spreadsheet Program

In this chapter, Lotus 1-2-3 from Lotus Development will be the spreadsheet program used to illustrate the concepts. Although most of the illustrations will use release 2.01, the examples will be valid for earlier versions of 1-2-3. The concepts and commands covered are virtually identical to several other spreadsheet programs such as The Twin and VP-Planner. In addition, there will be case studies that will enable you to enter information about your own spreadsheet program, even if it is not Lotus 1-2-3.

PENCILS AND ERASERS

Dan Bricklin was like many college students—he wanted to find some short cuts to doing homework. The particular homework he had in mind was the use of business spreadsheets: large worksheets ruled for adding up many rows and columns of numbers. They are used in accounting for doing budgets, and for lots of other chores where numbers have to be totaled up. You can imagine the problem of writing down a proposed budget, only to have to consider "what if rents were raised 10% and sales were raised 11%?" Out comes the eraser, and after the numbers are changed, everything has to be retotaled to calculate the bottom line. After a few of these changes, the paper becomes so thin from erasures that you have to start all over again.

Fortunately for Bricklin, the microcomputer age had begun, and he figured he would let the computer do some of his calculations. He wrote a program that would mimic a large spreadsheet. Columns of numbers could be entered onto the screen, and the program could be told to total certain rows and columns, to increase certain numbers by a given percentage, and perform other mathematical functions. The nice thing about his program was that when one number on the spreadsheet was changed, all other related numbers were automatically changed to reflect the difference. Bricklin called his program VisiCalc, and it was marketed for the Apple II computer beginning in 1979.

In *The Naked Computer*, Jack B. Rochester and John Glantz refer to the introduction of VisiCalc as one of nine "Great Moments in Software." They describe it as "the first program an inexperienced computer user could really use." This one program is the main reason that the Apple II computer took over the market place from the better-funded Radio Shack and Commodore microcomputer manufacturers. However, even though VisiCalc dominated microcomputing for a while, it was eventually challenged by considerable competition. After the introduction of the IBM PC in 1981, a new and more powerful spreadsheet program was introduced. Almost from its introduction, the Lotus 1-2-3 spreadsheet program outsold every other application program available on personal computers.

The Software That Sells Computers

Keeping track of numbers has always been a substantial task in business. However, working with numbers and budgets is not only for business. You probably keep some kind of personal budget. Perhaps you have examined your income and expenses to determine if you can afford to buy that new Porsche, or whether you'll have to settle for the used Yugo.

Figure 7.1 shows how that analysis might work. You list all of your income and expenses, and then compare your leftover money to various monthly payments for cars. However, it may not be that simple. What if you moved from your expensive $350-a-month apartment to a smaller $255 apartment? Then you could afford a more expensive car. What if you cancelled the newspaper, cut down on bowling, and ate at less-expensive restaurants? How would that change your financial picture? These kinds of questions mean that your financial analysis is no longer a simple budget. Out comes the eraser... You can see that financial analysis in business, dealing with hundreds of variables, can be overwhelming unless you have some help from the computer. It didn't take long for the business public to discover how an inexpensive spreadsheet program could solve a lot of number-crunching problems.

Budget for Fall Semester

Revenue	Sept.	Oct.	Nov.	Dec.
From Parents	500	500	500	500
Part-time Job #1	750	750	750	600
Part-time Job #2	100	100	100	100
Total	1350	1350	1350	1100
Expenses				
Rent	350	350	350	350
Phone	35	35	35	35
Football Tickets	20	40	40	20
Food (Groceries)	200	200	200	230
Auto Payment	257	257	257	257
Furn. Rental	120	120	120	120
Entertainment	260	260	260	320
Car Insurance	95	95	95	95
Misc. Entertainment	100	100	100	150
Total	1437	1437	1437	1577
Difference	−87	−87	−87	−477
Cash Balance (Beginning is $1,000)	913	826	739	262

FIGURE 7.1.
Hand-drawn spreadsheet

Because of the power of spreadsheet programs, they have been one of the primary reasons that businesses have invested in microcomputers. Few substantial businesses could be properly managed today without having assistance from computers to do budgets, plan future growth, and keep up with the hundreds of numerical tasks required by regulations and good business practice.

SPREADSHEET PROGRAMS

There are several spreadsheet programs currently available on microcomputers. Although Lotus 1-2-3 is currently the dominant program, there are other programs trying to replace Lotus, as Lotus replaced VisiCalc. Other software packages available on the IBM PC family of computers include SuperCalc, Microsoft Multiplan, Quattro, Excel, The Twin, and VP-Planner. The spreadsheet market for the Apple Macintosh family is dominated by the Microsoft Excel spreadsheet program.

What a Spreadsheet Program Can Do

Like the spreadsheets and budgets created by hand on a sheet of paper, spreadsheet programs enable you to analyze budgets, loans, cost estimates, etc., on the computer screen. After the numerical relationships between the rows and columns have been programmed into the spreadsheet, changing one or more numbers will cause all related numbers to be recalculated automatically. This gives you the power to quickly answer questions about "What if a certain number were different?"

Description of the Spreadsheet

The word *spreadsheet* is a business term. When budgets are calculated, accounting work performed, or inventories kept, numbers are often written on specialized sheets of paper preprinted with lines for rows and columns. These forms make it easy to line up columns of numbers, and to add them together.

An *electronic spreadsheet*, pictured in figure 7.2, is like a blank sheet of paper with columns and rows. Each intersection of a column and row is called a *cell*. In each cell, you may place numbers, formulas, or text. The computer may be instructed to add up columns or rows of the numbers in these cells. If a number in a particular row or column is changed, the program can automatically update the affected calculations in other cells.

Each cell is designated by the letter and number of the column and row it lies in. At the intersection of column B and row 4 is the cell B4. Cell locations will be used to define mathematical computations. You may want to refer to a single cell or a range of cells. A single cell has a name such as B4, and a range of cells is designated with a beginning cell, one or more dots (.), and an ending cell, such as A1.A5 or B1. . D1. The dot (.) means "through." Thus, the designation A1.A5 can be read "cells A1 through A5." You may choose to use either one or more dots to define a range. For consistency, this text will use two dots in referring to a range (e.g. A1. . B4).

		Columns			
		A	B	C	D
Rows	1	cell			
	2				
	3				
	4		B4		
	5				

FIGURE 7.2
Rows, columns, and cells in a spreadsheet.

The range A1 . . A5 refers to a vertical group of cells in column A, while the range B1 . . D1 refers to a horizontal block of cells in row 1. The range A1 . . D4 refers to a rectangular block of cells with the upper left corner being A1 and the lower right corner being D4. Figure 7.3 shows these three ranges.

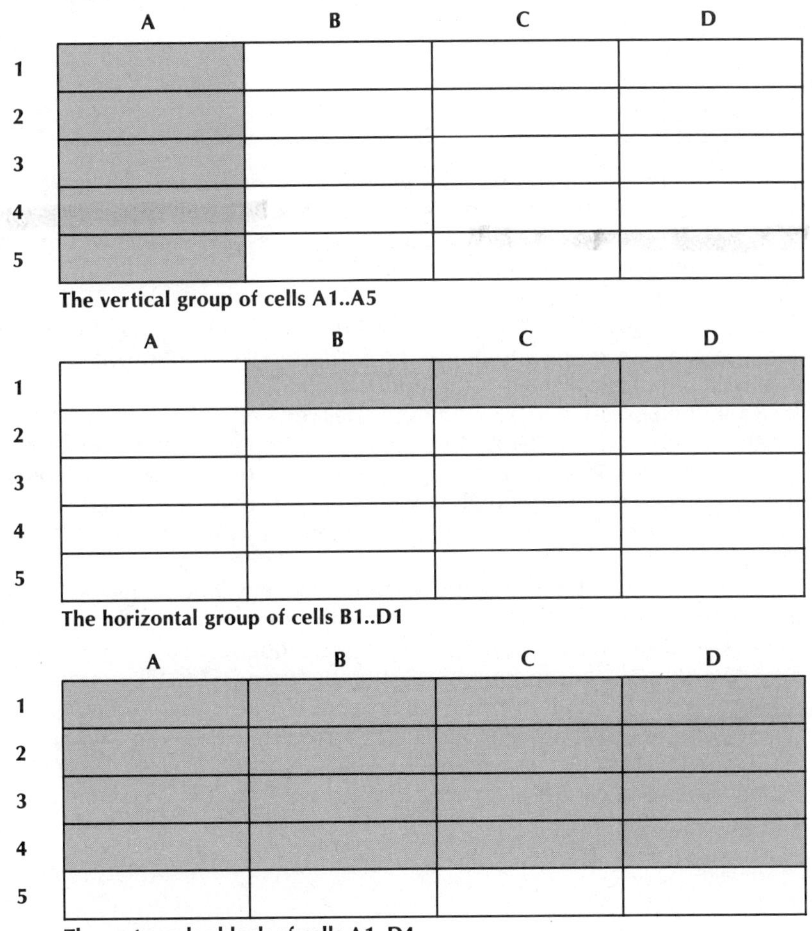

FIGURE 7.3.
Referring to groups of cells

The Structure of the Spreadsheet

In Lotus 1-2-3 version 1A, columns are lettered from A to Z, then AA, AB, AC, out to column IV, for a total of 256 columns. Rows are numbered from 1 to 2048. In Lotus 1-2-3 release 2.01, the number of rows was increased to 8,192. Only a portion of the spreadsheet is displayed on the screen at any time.

The structure of a spreadsheet has to do with the relationships between numbers and formulas in the rows and columns of the spreadsheet. In other words, one spreadsheet structure may be for a yearly budget, while another spreadsheet is structured to calculate grades in a course. This type of structure is also called a spreadsheet *model* or *template.*

COMMANDS IN A SPREADSHEET PROGRAM

Spreadsheet programs use commands, much like the word processors that were discussed in previous chapters. Spreadsheet commands perform editing functions such as moving part of a spreadsheet to another location, or causing numbers to be printed as integers rather than to two decimal places. Some commands are accessed by a single keystroke, such as pressing the function key F1. Other commands may be a series of selections from menus.

CASE STUDY

How Lotus Commands Are Given

Lotus 1-2-3 is a command-menu oriented program. A command is a sequence of keys that tells the program to perform some task. All commands are begun by first typing the slash "/" character. When the "/" is pressed, a menu will appear on the screen like the one illustrated in figure 7.4.

The first line of the menu gives you the options available. "Worksheet" is the first option, followed by "Range" and others. To choose one of these options, either press the key corresponding to the first letter of the option, or move the selection marker (which highlights the option picked) by pressing a right or left arrow key, and then pressing ENTER when the desired option is highlighted. Notice that when the selection marker is moved, the second line of the menu changes to tell you what options are available if the highlighted choice is selected. In other words, the second line is a sub-menu belonging to the highlighted option on the current menu. After selecting an option, another menu or a question may then appear on the screen.

Thus, when you type a command sequence, it will be written with a slash followed by one or more letters designating the subsequent options. For example, the designation /WGF means the keystroke sequence: command slash "/", item "W" (Worksheet) chosen from the first menu, then "G" (Global) from the second menu, then "F" (Format) from the third menu. This keystroke sequence will not appear on the screen: only the menus will appear.

Figure 7.5 illustrates the sub-menus that appear for each of the options on the main menu. Figure 7.6 illustrates the screens resulting from the selection of Worksheet, then Global, then Format, and onwards.

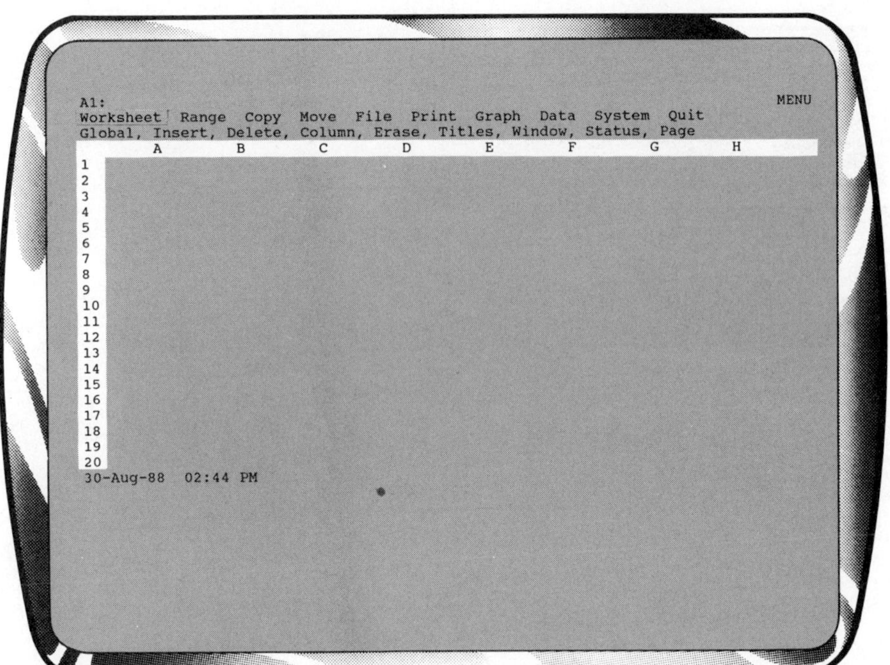

FIGURE 7.4.
Lotus worksheet menu

```
Worksheet Range Copy Move File Print Graph Data System Quit
Global, Insert, Delete, Column, Erase, Titles, Window, Status, Page

Worksheet Range Copy Move File Print Graph Data System Quit
Format, Label, Erase, Name, Justify, Protect, Unprotect, Input, Value, Transpose

Worksheet Range Copy Move File Print Graph Data System Quit
Copy a cell or range of cells

Worksheet Range Copy Move File Print Graph Data System Quit
Move a cell or range of cells

Worksheet Range Copy Move File Print Graph Data System Quit
Retrieve, Save, Combine, Xtract, Erase, List, Import, Directory

Worksheet Range Copy Move File Print Graph Data System Quit
Output a range to the printer or a print file

Worksheet Range Copy Move File Print Graph Data System Quit
Create a graph

Worksheet Range Copy Move File Print Graph Data System Quit
Fill, Table, Sort, Query, Distribution, Matrix, Regression, Parse

Worksheet Range Copy Move File Print Graph Data System Quit
Invoke the DOS Command Interpreter

Worksheet Range Copy Move File Print Graph Data System Quit
End 1-2-3 session (Have you saved your work ?)
```

FIGURE 7.5.
Lotus main menu items and their related sub-menus

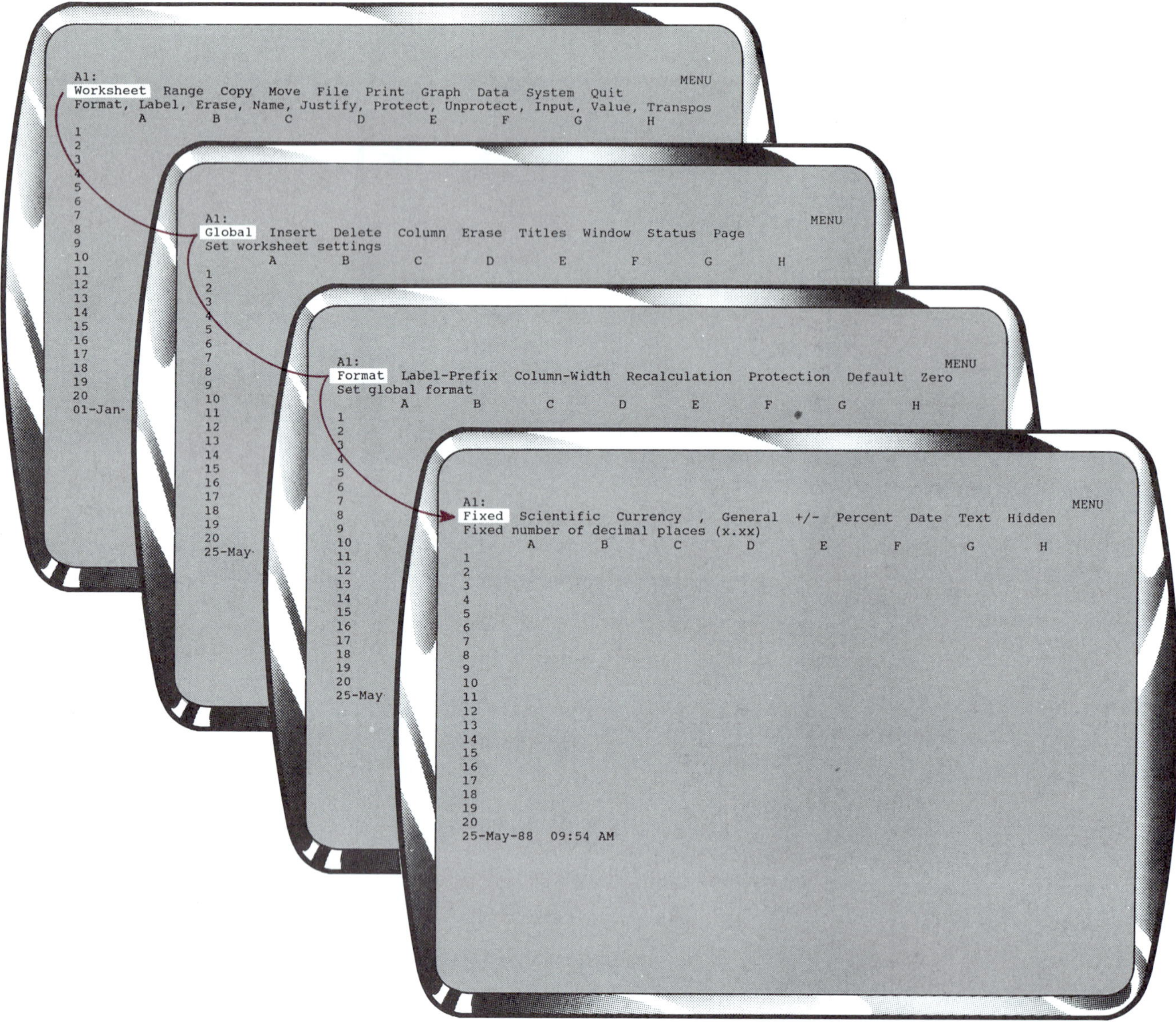

FIGURE 7.6.
Example of the menu screens for the command sequence /WGF (Worksheet, Global, Format)

Commands on the Lotus 1-2-3 Worksheet Menu

There are literally thousands of command combinations possible in Lotus 1-2-3, so it is impossible to cover all options. The ones illustrated here are meant to represent the kinds of common procedures you need to operate the program successfully. The following definitions describe the major roles of the main menu commands:

- Worksheet: This command is invoked when changing something that affects the entire spreadsheet—for example, changing the way numbers appear on the screen (Format), changing the way calculations take place (automatic or manual), inserting or deleting columns or rows, changing column widths, or erasing the entire spreadsheet.

- Range: This command is used to specify a range of cells on which to perform a procedure. For example, Range is used when erasing a range, changing the format in a range, naming ranges, etc.
- Copy and Move: These commands allow you to copy or move a cell or a range of cells to another location in the spreadsheet.
- File: This command allows you to enter information from a file on disk, save information to disk, erase files, or get a listing of files on disk.
- Print: This command is used to output information from your spreadsheet to a printer or to a file on disk.
- Graph: This command allows you to create a variety of graphic representations of the data in your spreadsheet, including bar graphs, line graphs, and pie charts.
- Data: This command is used to access the database feature of 1-2-3, which is not covered in this text.
- System: This command invokes the DOS command interpreter. You can then issue DOS commands without leaving Lotus 1-2-3.
- Quit: End the program.

Another way to access commands in Lotus 1-2-3 is by the function keys. Each function key is assigned a particular meaning. For example, the function key F1 is a Help key. It displays a help menu on the screen. The function key F2 is used to edit entries in cells. Specific uses of the command menus and the function keys will be covered later. Other function keys that will be discussed include the F3 key which allows you to name a range of cells, the F5 key that allows you to go to any cell in the table, the F6 key which is used to go from one windowed area to another, the F9 key that is used in manual recalculation, and the F10 key that is used to display a graph.

CASE STUDY

Your Spreadsheet Program—How Commands Are Given

How are commands accessed in your spreadsheet program? Do you use keystroke commands such as F1 or CTRL-B to access the functions of the program, or are there menus on the screen from which to choose options, or is there a combination of commands and menus?

If there is a main menu of options (such as the Worksheet menu in Lotus), list those options and what general function they perform. If control commands are used, list them, and describe what command they perform. Are the function keys used as commands? If so, list their meanings.

BASIC SPREADSHEET OPERATIONS

Like a word processing program, spreadsheet programs have a particular way of allowing the user to move around the document or spreadsheet, enter new information, and edit old information. In most word processing programs, the arrow keys are used to move over one character at a time, or from line to line. In a spreadsheet program, you move from column to column or from row to row.

CASE STUDY

The Basics of Lotus 1-2-3

You may begin Lotus 1-2-3 from a general menu called the Access Menu with the command LOTUS. (The Access Menu is illustrated in figure 7.7.) Lotus 1-2-3 may also be begun directly from the DOS prompt with the command:

```
C>123          (or          A>123)
```

If you are on a hard-disk system, the prompt will probably be "C>". Some versions of 1-2-3 require that the Lotus system diskette be in drive A: for the program to operate. If you begin 1-2-3, and nothing happens, you may not have the system disk in the A: drive. This system disk requirement is not true of some other spreadsheet programs, and newer versions of Lotus 1-2-3 do not have this requirement.

Once you have begun the program, a title screen will appear. Press any key and a blank spreadsheet will appear, as in figure 7.8.

Moving Around in 1-2-3

Locate the arrow keys on the right side of the keyboard. Press the down-arrow key a couple of times, and you will notice that the highlighted cell in the spreadsheet will move from cell A1 to cell A2, then to cell A3. Pressing the right-arrow key will move the highlight to the right. Pressing PgDn and PgUp moves up and down the spreadsheet 20 rows at a time. Pressing the Home key places you back in "home" position in cell A1.

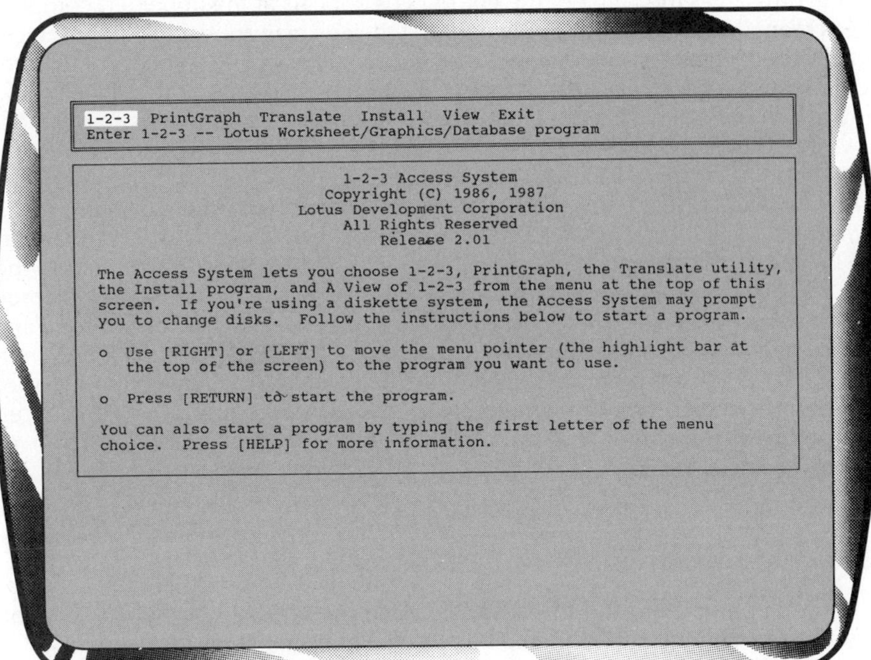

1-2-3 PrintGraph Translate Install View Exit
Enter 1-2-3 -- Lotus Worksheet/Graphics/Database program
1-2-3 Access System
Copyright (C) 1986, 1987
Lotus Development Corporation
All Rights Reserved
Release 2.01
The Access System lets you choose 1-2-3, PrintGraph, the Translate utility, the Install program, and A View of 1-2-3 from the menu at the top of this screen. If you're using a diskette system, the Access System may prompt you to change disks. Follow the instructions below to start a program.
o Use [RIGHT] or [LEFT] to move the menu pointer (the highlight bar at the top of the screen) to the program you want to use.
o Press [RETURN] to start the program.
You can also start a program by typing the first letter of the menu choice. Press [HELP] for more information.

FIGURE 7.7.
The Lotus 1-2-3 Access Menu

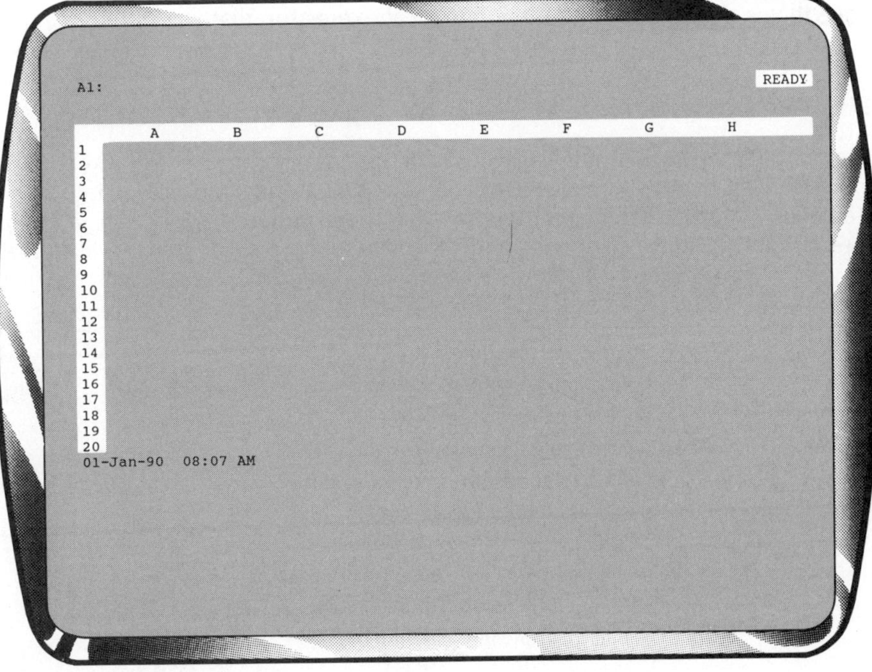

FIGURE 7.8.
A Lotus 1-2-3 screen

In Lotus 1-2-3 the name of the current cell appears at the upper left corner of the screen. (In clones of 1-2-3, the name of the cell may appear in different locations.) The highlighted cell is where the "action" takes place. If you want to enter something in a particular cell, you must first move the pointer (the highlight box) to that cell before making the entry. Figure 7.9 illustrates the pointer movement keys for Lotus 1-2-3.

When the cursor is in the far right column on the screen, pressing the right-arrow key will cause the spreadsheet to move so as to display more columns to the right (until the limit is reached). Likewise, moving the cursor to the left and pressing the left-arrow key again will cause the spreadsheet to move horizontally to the left. Pressing the up- or down-arrow keys while at the edge of the display will force the spreadsheet to scroll up or down one row at a time. An express route to any particular cell in the spreadsheet is the use of the F5 "goto" function key. When you press F5, you are prompted to enter the name of a cell where you want to go. For example, if you enter N50, the spreadsheet will then be displayed with the cell N50 at the top left corner. In large spreadsheets, this method is faster than movement with the arrow keys.

Entering Information into 1-2-3

To make an entry into the spreadsheet, place the highlight at the cell location where you want the information to be placed. For example, place the highlight in the A1 cell, and type the entry:

```
1+2
```

As you type, the entry appears not in the highlighted cell, but on the entry line at the top of the screen. It is not until you press the ENTER key that the result of your entry is placed in the spreadsheet. In this case, the number 3 appears in cell A1, since that is the answer to the mathematical expression that was entered.

The Ready Indicator in 1-2-3

The word READY will usually appear in the upper right corner of the screen. This tells you that Lotus 1-2-3 is ready for you to begin entering information into a cell. However, when a command or value has been entered for a cell, and the spreadsheet program is working on the problem, the message "WAIT" will appear.

FIGURE 7.9.
Lotus 1-2-3 pointer keys

↑ [Up]	Moves pointer one row up
← [Left]	Moves pointer one column to the left
↓ [Down]	Moves pointer one row down
→ [Right]	Moves pointer one column to the right
[Home]	Moves pointer to upper left corner of worksheet
[End]	Moves pointer to "end" of block of cells
[PgUp]	Moves pointer up by one screenful or page
[PgDn]	Moves pointer down by one screenful or page
⇤	Moves pointer left by one screenful or page
⇥	Moves pointer right by one screenful or page

NOTE: If you begin pressing the arrow keys, and numbers appear on the screen, pressing the NUM LOCK key once will take the cursor pad out of numeric mode.

During this time, text is being stored, or calculations are being performed. You must wait for the ready indicator before you resume entering information. If an illegal entry is made, such as "(1 + 2", which has a missing parenthesis, the program may place you into Edit mode, which allows you to correct the mistake.

Correcting Entries in 1-2-3

While you are entering information into a spreadsheet cell, and before you press ENTER, you may use the backspace key (located just above the ENTER key), to back up and make corrections. You should not use the arrow keys on the cursor keypad, as this will end the entry and move you to the next cell instead.

If you notice a mistake after pressing ENTER, place the pointer on that entry and press the F2 function key to enter the Edit mode. During an edit, you *may* use the right- and left-arrow keys, as well as the Home key, to move around in the entry and make corrections. The Del key may be used to delete characters. In Lotus, you are automatically in Insert mode during an edit, so you can move the cursor to a position within the text of the entry and insert new characters. To cancel an entry or an edit, press the ESC key. To end the procedure normally, press the ENTER key.

CASE STUDY

The Basics of Your Spreadsheet Program

Describe the keystrokes used to move around in your spreadsheet program. How do you move up and down? What happens if you attempt to move the cursor off the side of the screen, or past the bottom of the screen?

Is there a place on the screen that always indicates the name of the cell that the cursor is in? Is there an indication such as "READY" that lets you know that the program is ready to receive a command?

How do you enter information into a cell? Does the entry appear in the cell as you type it, or does it appear somewhere else on the screen until you press the ENTER key? How do you correct information in a cell?

THE CONTENTS OF CELLS

Each cell of a spreadsheet can contain one of several kinds of information such as numbers, text, or formulas. Numbers are perhaps the most obvious contents of a cell. Textual contents of cells often are used as labels for rows and columns, to describe the numbers in a table. Formulas are used to calculate results. Formulas are usually mathematical, such as a formula to calculate the sum of several numbers. However, there are other kinds of formulas (e.g. macros) that are not covered here. Since a formula usually produces a numeric value, the contents of cells are often referred to as either text (labels) or as values.

CASE STUDY

Text and Values in Lotus 1-2-3

When you enter information into a cell, the program must decide if the information is numeric (a value) or textual in nature. In Lotus 1-2-3 a *value* (or *numeric expression*) is an entry which begins with a numeric digit (i.e., 0,1,2, etc.), or with one of the following characters: (, +, −, ., $, @ or). Any entry beginning with a letter, such as E1 + 2, is not recognized as a value. However, the entry + E1 + 2 is recognized as a value. The " + " in front of the "E1" means that the program is to use the value stored in cell location E1 in calculating the mathematical expression "E1 + 2".

If an entry is not a value, it is recognized as a *text* entry. Text entries can be used to label rows and columns. Text is automatically left-justified in the cell. That is, the text is positioned at the leftmost edge of the cell. However, placing a double quote in front of an entry forces the text to be right-justified in the cell. That is, the text is positioned with the last character at the rightmost edge of the cell. Prefixing the text with a caret "^" forces the text to be centered in the cell. If text is wider than the cell width, the result is always left justification. Using a back slash "\" as the first character makes text repeat itself within the width of the cell. That is, the entry \- would result in a cell filled with dashes (a good way to underline). The entry \Hi would result in a cell containing "HiHiHiHiH" (filling a 9-character cell). To force an entry to be considered text when it might otherwise look like a number, prefix the entry with a single quote (') or one of the other formatting prefixes. Thus, the entry '120 would be treated as text. These prefixes are summarized in figure 7.10.

CASE STUDY

Text and Values in Your Spreadsheet Program

When you enter information into a cell, the program must decide if the information is numeric (a value) or textual in nature. Usually, the program examines the first character in the entry to make that decision. What criteria does your spreadsheet program use to decide if an entry into a cell is text or a value?

Examine the prefixes used by Lotus 1-2-3 in figure 7.10. Are there similar ways in your spreadsheet program to format a text entry in a cell? Describe how the following formats are indicated in your spreadsheet program. Which one is the default?

1. Left justification of text in a cell

2. Right justification of text in a cell

3. Centering of text in a cell

4. Repeated text in a cell

Prefix	Result
'	Left justification (default)
"	Right justification
^	Centered text
\	Repeated text

FIGURE 7.10.
Textual prefixes for cell entries

ARITHMETIC OPERATORS

As mentioned earlier, a cell may contain a formula, or *expression*, instead of a number or label. Mathematical (numeric) expressions are entered into a spreadsheet cell to describe how other cells are to be totaled, multiplied, divided, etc. These expressions are entered into a spreadsheet cell by using *arithmetic operators* and *functions*, just as in writing an algebra problem. For example, if the cell A1 contains the value 1, and the cell A2 contains the value 2, then by using their location addresses, the expression

```
A1 + A2
```

in a cell would calculate the answer 3. If the values of cells A1 and A2 were changed, the resulting answer in this cell would automatically be changed too.

CASE STUDY

Arithmetic Operators in Lotus 1-2-3

The arithmetic operators supported in Lotus 1-2-3 are listed in Figure 7.11. Three examples are given for each operator. Example 1 uses named cell locations in the expression, such as A1 and B4. Example 2 uses numbers, and Example 3 mixes numbers and variable names. The variable names A1 and B4 are cell locations and represent the numerical values in those cells. Thus, the variable A1 is equal to the number in the spreadsheet cell named A1. Notice that if a mathematical expression begins with the name of a cell, it must be preceded by a mathematical symbol such as the plus " + " or minus " − " sign to indicate to the program that the expression is a formula rather than text. Using a plus sign will not affect the meaning of the formula.

CASE STUDY

Arithmetic Operators in Your Spreadsheet Program

Examine the arithmetic operators listed in figure 7.11. List the corresponding operators for your spreadsheet program, and give an example of how each operator is used in a mathematical expression:

Addition:

Subtraction:

Multiplication:

Division:

Exponentiation:

FIGURE 7.11.
Arithmetic operators in Lotus 1-2-3

Operator		Example 1	Example 2	Example 3
+	Addition	+A1+B4	4+3	+A1+3
−	Subtraction	+A1−B4	4−3	4−B4
*	Multiplication	+A1*B4	4*3	+A1*3
/	Division	+A1/B4	4/3	4/B4
^	Exponentiation	+A1^B4	4^3	+A1^3

FORMATTING NUMBERS IN CELLS

When numbers are typed into a spreadsheet cell, or when they are calculated by a formula, the results appear in that cell. Usually, the program decides the format of how to print a number. For example, the number 100 could be printed as 100, 100.00, $100.00, or in a variety of other ways. Usually, a spreadsheet program will allow you to choose a numeric format for the entire spreadsheet (e.g., print all numbers to two decimal places) and will also let you choose a format for a particular cell or range of cells (e.g., print all numbers in the range D1..D10 as integers).

CASE STUDY

Formatting Numbers in Lotus 1-2-3

In Lotus1-2-3, the format for the entire spreadsheet is called the *global format.* The global format is defined using the command sequence /WGF (Worksheet, Global, Format). To define a format for a range of cells, use the command sequence /RF (Range Format).

Some of the command format options in Lotus 1-2-3 are fixed, currency, comma, and percent. The meanings of these formats are:

- Fixed Format: This format causes a value to be printed with a constant number of decimal places, from 0 (for integers) to 15 decimal places. Examples of a fixed format with two decimal places: 100.00, −0.23, 1.23, and 123456.78.
- Currency format: This format causes the currency sign ($) to appear before each entry. It also causes a comma to appear between thousands. Negative values appear in parentheses with no minus sign. You may specify a fixed number of decimal places. Examples: $1.23, ($1.23), $1,234.56.
- Comma Format: This format places commas between thousands. Negative values appear in parentheses with no minus sign. You may choose a fixed number of decimal places. Examples: 1,234, (1,234.00).
- Percent Format: This format displays a value after multiplying it by 100, followed by a percent sign. You may choose a fixed number of decimal places. Examples: 1234.56%, 98.44%, −1.23%.

For example, to change the global format to Fixed with two decimal places, enter the command sequence /WGF. The FORMAT menu will appear:

```
Fixed Scientific Currency , General +/- Percent Date Text
Hidden
```

Choose "F" (fixed) from the format menu by pressing "F". You will be prompted to enter how many decimal places to use:

```
Enter number of decimal places (0..15): 2
```

You may specify from 0 to 15 decimal places. Choose to have the numbers printed out with two decimal places by entering "2". Try the command sequence again, this time choosing "currency" with 2 decimal places.

If the intention is to change the format for only a range of cells, the command "/RF" (Range Format) could be used. For example, enter the command /RF. After you choose the format you want, you will be prompted with

```
Enter range to format:
```

To cause the format to affect only certain cell locations you could enter the range Cl..C4 at the prompt.

CASE STUDY

Formatting Numbers in Your Spreadsheet Program

Describe the kinds of numeric format options available in your spreadsheet program. Use the ones previously described for 1-2-3 as examples.

Describe the procedure for setting a global numeric format in you spreadsheet program.

Describe the procedure for setting a numeric format for a range of cells in your spreadsheet program.

COLUMN WIDTHS

Most spreadsheet programs have a set column width for every column, such as 8 or 10 characters wide. However, there are times when it is necessary to change this width to accommodate a particular spreadsheet application. For example, if the entries in your cells are always integers from 0 to 9, then columns 9 characters wide would be too big. If you could make the columns only 2 to 3 characters wide, more would appear on the screen at one time, letting you view a larger portion of the spreadsheet. On the other hand, perhaps you are calculating a precise engineering measurement, and you want the resulting answer to be printed to 15 decimal places. Such a number would not fit into a cell only 9 characters wide, so you would want to reset the width of that column to perhaps 16 to 18 characters wide.

CASE STUDY

Changing Column Widths in Lotus 1-2-3

The default width for columns in 1-2-3 is 9 characters wide. However, many times you may want wider or narrower columns for a particular application. This can be done with the command /WC (Worksheet, Column). To set the column width for a particular column, say column C, you place the cursor in the column to be affected, then enter the /WC command. You will be asked to specify the width. The following menu will appear:

```
Set-Width Reset-Width Hide Display
```

Choose the Set-Width option, and the prompt

```
Enter column width (1..240): 9
```

will appear. Type 11, and press ENTER. The spreadsheet will now be displayed with column C having a width of 11 characters. The Reset-Width option is used to reset the column width back to 9. The Hide option allows you to hide columns. They will not be displayed on the screen, but they are not erased permanently. The Display option allows you to re-display hidden columns. The Hide and Display options are available beginning in Lotus 1-2-3 version 2.01.

To change the column width globally, use the command sequence /WGC (Worksheet, Global, Column). Changing the width using this command will affect all columns, except those that have been set by the /WC command. For example, suppose you wish to change the widths of all columns to 11. To do this, enter the /WGC command sequence. The following menu will appear:

```
Set-Width Reset-Width Hide Display
```

Choose the Set-Width option, and the prompt

```
Enter global column width (1..240): 9
```

will appear. Type 11, and press ENTER. The spreadsheet will now be displayed with each column changed to a width of 11 characters.

CASE STUDY

Changing Column Widths in Your Spreadsheet Program

What is the default width of cells in your spreadsheet program? How do you change column widths for all of the columns in the entire spreadsheet?

How do you change column widths for a single column in the spreadsheet?

ORDER OF CALCULATION

Most spreadsheet programs calculate numeric expressions in what is called a natural sequence. That is, an expression is not calculated until all cells which that expression depends on have already been calculated. For example, if cell A1 contains the number 5, cell A2 contains the expression A1 + 1, and cell A3 contains the expression A2 + 2, the spreadsheet program will always calculate the expression in cell A2 before calculating the expression in A3, since the expression "A2 + 2" depends on A2 being calculated first. It is possible to create circular relations, where natural sequencing cannot take place. For example, if the cell A1 contains the expression A1 + 1, and the cell A2 contains the expression A1 + 1, the spreadsheet program cannot tell which cell to calculate first, since they both depend on each other. In cases where circular expressions are defined, an error message is usually displayed.

There are other calculation order options available in some spreadsheet programs, such as top to bottom (rowwise) and left to right (columnwise), but natural sequencing is by far the most common technique.

CASE STUDY

Calculation Order for Lotus 1-2-3

The 1-2-3 program, like many spreadsheet programs, calculates all numeric expressions in natural sequence. If a circular relation is defined, where natural sequencing cannot take place, 1-2-3 will display the error message "CIRC".

Calculation sequence may be changed with the "/WGR" (Worksheet, Global, Recalculation) command. Menu options for recalculation are

```
Natural Columnwise Rowwise Automatic Manual Iteration
```

If you choose to set calculation to Manual, this means that the spreadsheet will *not* automatically change numbers in the cells when other related numbers are altered in the spreadsheet. You must press the F9 key each time you want a calculation to take place.

CASE STUDY

Calculation Order for Your Spreadsheet Program

Does your spreadsheet program perform calculations in natural sequence, as described above? If so, what happens if a circular expression is defined?

What other calculation sequences are available in your spreadsheet program?

Does your spreadsheet program have both manual and automatic calculation? If so, how do you place it in manual mode? When it is in manual mode, how do you tell it to perform the spreadsheet-wide calculations?

PRINTING SPREADSHEET RESULTS

Once you have created a spreadsheet, you may want to have a printed copy of the results. Most spreadsheet programs permit printing the results to a printer or to a file. When the spreadsheet is printed to a file, the results can usually be merged as a text file into a word processing program, allowing you to include spreadsheet results in a report or letter.

CASE STUDY

Output to a Printer or to a File in Lotus 1-2-3

The command sequence to display the Print command menu is /P. From this menu you may choose to print your spreadsheet to a printer or to a file. When you press /P, you will be prompted with the sub-menu

```
Printer File
```

Choose "Printer" to print to a line printer, or "File" to output a copy (a standard ASCII text file) of the spreadsheet to disk. If you choose File, you will be asked to give the name of an output file. (The extension ".PRN" is automatically affixed). The Print sub-menu is:

```
Range Line Page Options Clear Align Go Quit
```

Explanations of these options are listed in Figure 7.12. You must specify the range of cells to be printed. Therefore, the Range option is usually the first option you would choose form this menu. A range marks the upper left corner and bottom right corner of the rectangular portion of the spreadsheet to print. When asked for a range, you may either enter the range manually, or you may specify the range by moving the cursor.

To specify the range by cursor moves, enter the command /PPR (Print, Printer, Range). A prompt will ask for the range to be specified, and the current cursor position will appear after the prompt (see figure 7.13). Move the cursor to A1, which is the upper left corner of what you want to print. Enter a ".", then move the cursor to the cell C4. Notice that as you move, the area is highlighted. Once the highlighted area specifies what you want to print, press the ENTER key, and the print range is defined. Alternately, you may type the range indication A1..C4 when asked to enter the range.

Other options in the Print menu allow you to control the printer, or to define the way the output will appear on the printed page. The Print sub-menu "Options" allows you to create a header to appear at the top of each printed page or a footer to appear at the bottom of each printed page; to set the right, left, top, and bottom margins and the page length; and to send the printer a special code (Set-up).

Once settings of range, margins, etc., are made for a particular spreadsheet, these are remembered by the program and need not be reset again unless a change is desired. If the spreadsheet is too wide for the printer, it is printed in parts. The width of the printout is established in the Options menu.

To print the spreadsheet to the printer, press "G" for the Go command. You may then want to press the "P" for Page to move the paper to the top of the page. Finally, press "Q" to quit the print procedure and return to the "Ready" mode.

CASE STUDY

Printing to a Printer or File in Your Spreadsheet Program

Describe the procedure for printing a spreadsheet, including how you specify the following options:

1. What range to print:

2. Print to a printer or to a file:

3. Set margins and page length:

FIGURE 7.12
Lotus 1-2-3 Print sub-menu

Range allows you to choose the range of the cells to print.

Line advances the printer one line.

Page advances the printer to top of form.

Align allows you to set the paper at the top of the form.

Go begins printing (or outputting to the file)

Quit ends the print procedure.

Options brings up the sub-sub-menu for designating header, footer, margins, page length, and printer code settings:

```
Header Footer Margins Borders Page-Length Set-up Other Quit
```

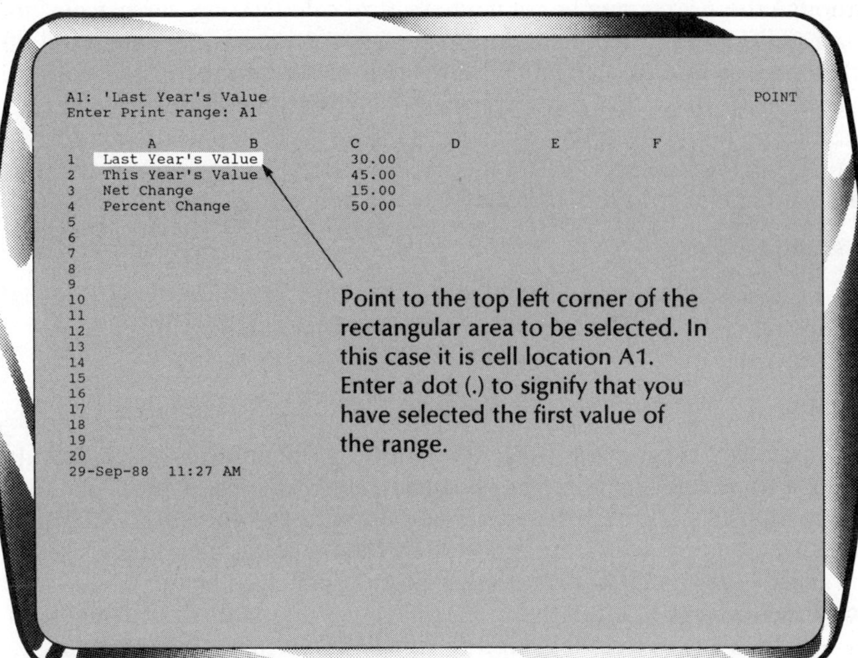
A1: 'Last Year's Value
POINT
Enter Print range: A1
A B C D E F
1 Last Year's Value 30.00
2 This Year's Value 45.00
3 Net Change 15.00
4 Percent Change 50.00
5
6
7
8
9
10
11
12
13
14
15
16
17
18
19
20
29-Sep-88 11:27 AM
Point to the top left corner of the rectangular area to be selected. In this case it is cell location A1. Enter a dot (.) to signify that you have selected the first value of the range.

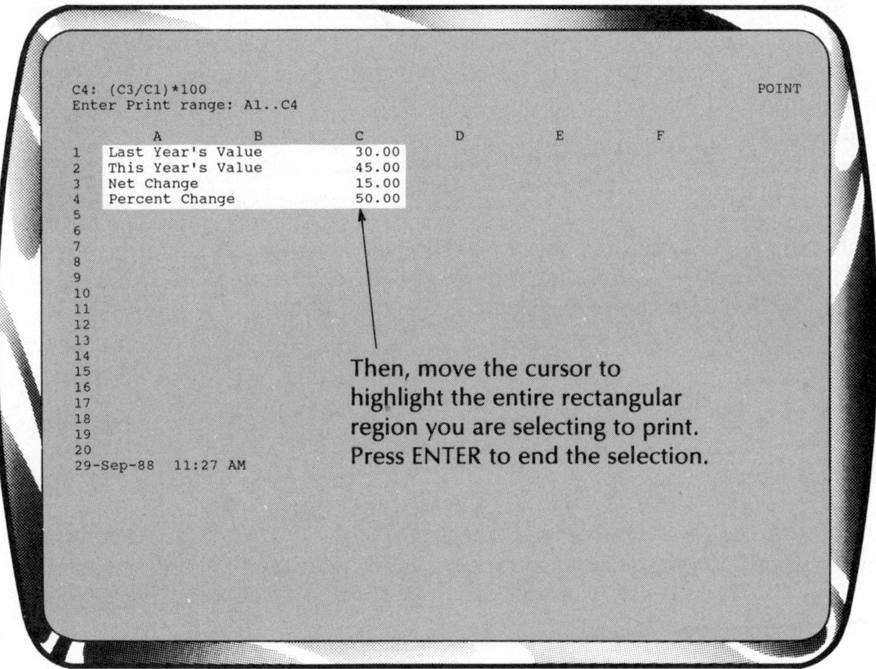
C4: (C3/C1)*100
POINT
Enter Print range: A1..C4
A B C D E F
1 Last Year's Value 30.00
2 This Year's Value 45.00
3 Net Change 15.00
4 Percent Change 50.00
5
6
7
8
9
10
11
12
13
14
15
16
17
18
19
20
29-Sep-88 11:27 AM
Then, move the cursor to highlight the entire rectangular region you are selecting to print. Press ENTER to end the selection.

FIGURE 7.13.
Specifying a Print range

USE OF FUNCTIONS

Although there are a number of mathematical calculations you may perform using addition, subtraction, multiplication, and division, there are some calculations that require more flexibility. This is where functions are useful. Mathematical functions allow you to calculate arithmetic expressions not possible or not convenient with the standard operators. For example, in Lotus 1-2-3, the function @SUM ( ) could be used. To designate a cell location that contains the sum of cells A1 to A5, you would enter

```
@SUM(A1..A5)
```

Functions can often be used within expressions, combined with numbers and operators. For example, 3 times the sum of the numbers in cell locations A1 to A5 would be:

```
@SUM(A1..A5)*3
```

Most spreadsheet programs support a variety of functions that allow calculation of arithmetic, trigonometric, financial, and statistical expressions.

Functions usually require one or more inputs or ***arguments.*** These arguments are numbers which are required by the function to calculate a result. The arguments appear in parentheses after the function name. When entering a function into a cell in the spreadsheet, the argument is an actual number (e.g., 3, 3.14) or a cell location (e.g., A1, X3). When 1-2-3 calculates the value for that cell, it will perform the function using either the number you typed or the number contained in the given cell. Then the cell where the function appears will be filled with the result of the calculation. Note that some arguments may be ranges such as A1..B3, or numbers. When a range or a list of arguments may be used, "list" is given in the function description.

CASE STUDY

Use of Functions in Lotus 1-2-3

A list of some common functions in 1-2-3 is given in figure 7.14. Refer to the manual for a complete list. Lotus functions always begin with the @ (at) sign, followed by the function name and the argument(s) in parentheses.

A function expression may be used just like a number. For example, the above function calculation may be part of a bigger expression:

((@SUM(Al..A5))/B4)*B1

Notice that parentheses may be used in expressions to specify the order in which calculations will take place without parentheses, the order of precedence is:

First: Expressions within parentheses ( )

Function	Purpose and Arguments
@ROUND(x,n)	Round a number, x, to n decimal places
@SQRT(arg)	Square root of x
@AVG(list)	Average of items in list
@COUNT(list)	Counts number of items in list
@MAX(list)	Finds maximum of values in list
@MIN(list)	Finds minimum of values in list
@SUM(list)	Sum of numbers in list
@FV(pmt,int,term)	Future value of an annuity pmt = payment made each period int = interest per period term = number of periods
@IRR(guess,list)	Internal rate of return guess = initial guess (usually 0 to 1.) list = cash flows
@NPV(x, list)	Net present value x = per-period interest rate list = cash flows
@PMT(prn,int,term)	Mortgage payment per period prn = beginning principal int = per-period interest rate term = number of payments to be made
@PV(pmt,int,term)	Present value of an ordinary annuity pmt = payment per period int = interest per period term = number of periods

@ERR designates a value of ERR (error). A cell with value ERR will cause subsequent functions using that cell to return a value of ERR.

FIGURE 7.14.
Some functions in Lotus 1-2-3

Next: Evaluate functions
Mathematical operators ^, *, and /

Last: Mathematical operators + and −

CASE STUDY

Use of Functions in Your Spreadsheet Program

Describe how to use a function to calculate a sum of numbers in a column of your spreadsheet program:

Using the list of functions for 1-2-3, describe which similar functions are supported in your spreadsheet program.

DESCRIPTION	FUNCTION
Round a number	
Square root	
Average of items in list	
Counts number of items in list	
Maximum of values in list	
Minimum of values in list	
Sum of numbers in list	
Future value of an annuity	
Internal rate of return	
Net present value	
Mortgage payment per period	
Present value of an ordinary annuity	

CREATING A SPREADSHEET EXAMPLE

The following example leads you through the steps of creating a simple spreadsheet. The example uses a Lotus 1-2-3 spreadsheet, but is general enough that you could also use it to create a similar spreadsheet in almost any spreadsheet program.

Suppose you want to know how much (proportionally) an item such as a rare coin has increased in value over the past year. You know the value last year, and the value this year. First, make sure you are beginning with a new spreadsheet. (In 1-2-3, enter the command sequence /WEY). Place the cursor in cell A1, and type "Last Year's Value". As you enter information, it will appear at the top of the screen, not directly in the cell. You can make corrections during entry. Once you press the ENTER key, the entry will appear in the spreadsheet itself. Notice that the entry is longer than the normal cell width and the text "spills over" into cell B1.

Move the cursor to the A2 cell and enter "This Year's Value". In A3 enter the text "Net change", and in A4 enter "Proportion Change". The formula for the proportion of change is

$$\frac{\textbf{This Year's Value} - \textbf{Last Year's Value}}{\textbf{Last Year's Value}}$$

Assuming that last year's value for the coin was $100, enter the number 100 in cell C1 by moving the cursor to cell C1. Type the entry

```
100
```

and press ENTER. This year's value is $125. Locate the cursor in cell C2 and enter the number 125. To calculate Net Change in cell C3, move the cursor to cell C3 and enter the expression

```
+C2−C1.
```

This is the numerator for the formula we wish to calculate. The plus "+" *must* be entered before the cell name "C2" to tell the program that this is a numeric expression that is being entered, and not text. The number 25 will appear in cell C3. To calculate the proportion of change in cell C4, move the cursor to cell C4. Enter the relation

```
+C3/C1
```

and 0.25 will apperar in cell location C4. The completed spreadsheet should look like the one in figure 7.15

Changing Values

If the numeric entry in cell C1 (Last Year's Value) or C2 (This Year's Value) is changed, the resulting calculated values in cells C3 (Net Change) and C4 (Proportion Change) will automatically be recalculated. For instance, you could replace this year's value with the value 175 by moving the cursor to cell location C2, entering 175, and pressing ENTER. Observe the changes in the values in the Net Change and Proportion Change cells.

Editing an Entry

To calculate percentages rather than proportions, you can edit the formula in cell C4 by moving the cursor to cell location C4. In 1-2-3, press the F2 (Edit) key to edit this field. The old expression appears on the screen:

```
+C3/C1
```

The new expression should be +(C3/C1)*100.To make this change in 1-2-3:

1. Press the Home key. This places the cursor on the "+" in the expression.
2. Move the cursor one space to the right using the right arrow key, and press the left parenthesis key (don't forget to use the SHIFT key). This inserts a left parenthesis between the "+" and the "C". (You are automatically in insert mode.)
3. Move the cursor to the end of the expression with the right-arrow key and type

```
)*100
```

	A	B	C
1	Last Year's Value		100
2	This Year's Value		125
3	Net Change		25
4	Proportion Change		0.25

FIGURE 7.15.
Rare coin spreadsheet

The new expression should look like this:

```
+(C3/C1)*100
```

4. Press the ENTER key, and the spreadsheet will reflect the change.
   We should also change the label in cell A4 from "Proportion Change" to "Percent Change", to match the change in the numeric expression. To do this, move the cursor to A4, then type in "Percent Change". This will replace the label that is currently in that cell. The altered spreadsheet should look like figure 7.16.

To continue with the example, we could change last year's value to 30 and this year's value to 45, and the spreadsheet will look like figure 7.17.

MORTGAGE EXAMPLE

The next example is a spreadsheet which figures the amount of periodic payments on an amortized loan. The labels and formulas for this spreadsheet are given in figure 7.18.

The mortgage spreadsheet is on the Text Examples Disk. To retrieve this spreadsheet use the command sequence /FR (File, Retrieve), then enter the name of the file to retrieve: MORTGAGE. If your Text Examples Disk is in the B: drive, you must enter "B:MORTGAGE". When you retrieve a file in 1-2-3, any existing information in your spreadsheet is replaced by the new spreadsheet you retrieve.

Notice that the entries for cells E11 to E17 are formulas. You can verify the contents of formulas by moving the cursor to a particular cell location and observing the contents of the cell, displayed at which are the upper left of the screen. The way the spreadsheet appears on the screen is illustrated in figure 7.19. Notice that the number in cell E17 appears as −0.00 because of a slight rounding of some numbers in the calculations. Usually this is of little concern. However, if very large or very small numbers are involved (millions or millionths) then rounding can cause substantial accuracy problems.

FIGURE 7.16. Revised rare coin spreadsheet

```
     A        B          C
1  Last Year's Value     100
2  This Year's Value     175
3  Net Change             75
4  Percent Change         75
```

FIGURE 7.17. Third version of rare coin spreadsheet

```
     A        B          C
1  Last Year's Value     30
2  This Year's Value     45
3  Net Change            15
4  Percent Change        50
```

FIGURE 7.18.
Mortgage example with formulas listed

```
   A        B          C          D          E

 1      LOAN ANALYSIS FOR AN AMORTIZED LOAN
 2
 3 Description                        Amounts
 4 ==============================
 5 Enter amount of loan              65000.00
 6 Enter interest rate per year         12.75
 7 Enter number of payments per year    12.00
 8 Enter number of years                30.00
 9 Enter number of payments made         0.00
10 ------------------------------
11 Total number of payments                        +E7*E8
12 Amount of payment               @PMT(E5,E6/(100*E7),E11)
13 Number of payments remaining                   +E11-E9
14 Payoff balance remaining         @PV(E12,E6/(100*E7),E13)
15 Total amount paid to date                      +E12*E9
16 Principal paid to date                         +E5-E14
17 Interest paid to date                         +E15-E16
18 ---------------------------------------------
```

The spreadsheet as it first appears shows the monthly payment required to pay off a $65,000 loan in 30 years. It also shows the total principal and interest paid. Note that all of the rows above the single dashed line contain values designed for you to enter into the spreadsheet. You can then obtain all of the information below the line for a variety of loan amounts, interest rates, lengths of loan, etc. To illustrate this, change the loan above from monthly payments (12 payments a year) to quarterly payments (4 payments per year) by changing the number in cell E7 (number of payments per year) from 12 to 4. Notice how this changes the values in rows 11 to 17.

Enter Your Favorite Loan

Use this spreadsheet to enter a loan amount that interests you. It could be used to calculate the payments for a new car, a new house, or any other loan that is paid back at periodic intervals over a fixed period of time at a fixed interest rate. Recall that you should only change numbers *above* the dashed line. Changing values below that line will destroy the relationships set up to perform these calculations.

Enter This Table Yourself

As an exercise, enter this spreadsheet yourself on a blank spreadsheet. You may first erase the current spreadsheet from memory (this does not affect the copy stored on disk) by entering the command sequence /WEY (Worksheet, Erase, Yes).

Enter the information on the spreadsheet as indicated in figure 7.18. Notice that the numbers in figure 7.19 all appear with two decimal places. If your numbers do not appear with two decimal places, you may set the global format with the /WGF command sequence. Choose the fixed format with 2 decimal places.

Saving the Table

You may wish to save your version of the spreadsheet for future use. To do this, enter the command /FS (File, Save). You will be asked to name the file. Enter any legal DOS file name. The program will automatically add the extension ".WKS" (or perhaps something else if you are using a 1-2-3 clone or a newer version of 1-2-3). For example, use the name "LOAN" to save this spreadsheet. If a file is already on disk by that name, you will be asked if the old file should be replaced with the new. If you replace the old file, it is gone forever, and only the new spreadsheet is saved under that name. Once a working copy of the spreadsheet is on disk, you may retrieve it at any time. Changing items within the program does not change the file on disk (unless you save those changes).

The Formulas in the Mortgage Table

This spreadsheet makes use of the PMT( ) and PV( ) functions. The PMT( ) function calculates the payment amount for a loan, given the amount of the

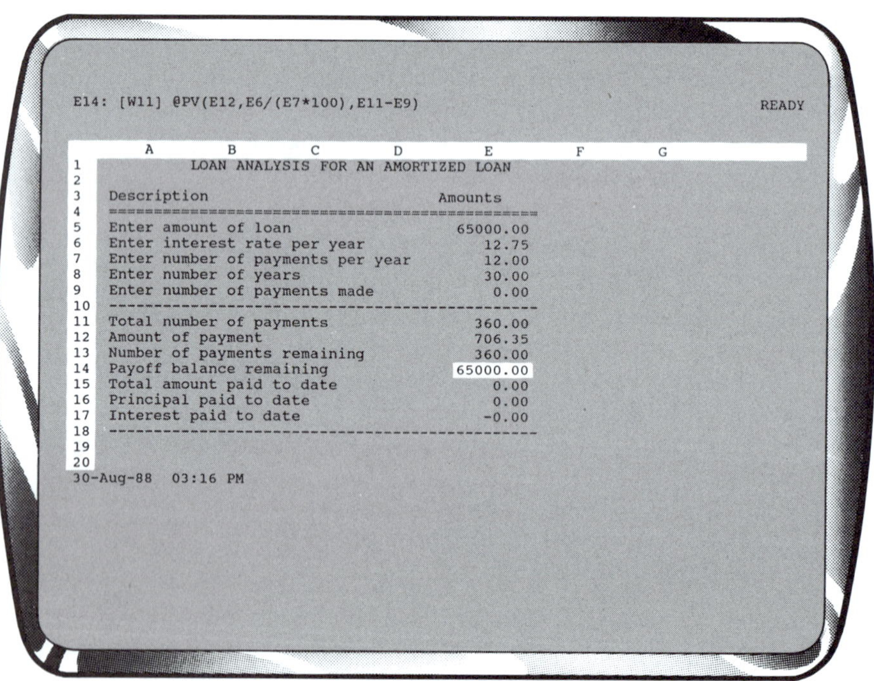

FIGURE 7.19.
Mortgage example as it appears on the screen

loan, the interest rate per period, and the number of payments. As listed in figure 7.14, the PMT( ) function has three arguments:

- Argument 1: Beginning principal (E5)
- Argument 2: Per-period interest rate (E6/(100*E7))
- Argument 3: Number of payments to be made (E11)

The formula in the E12 cell location is therefore

```
@PMT(E5,E6/(100*E7),E11)
```

The cell location E5 contains argument 1, the amount of the loan, or the beginning principal. The per-period interest rate, which is argument 2, depends on the annual interest rate and the number of payments made per year. Since the intrest rate is entered as a percent, it must be divided by 100 to get the actual rate. It must also be divided by the number of payments per year to get the interest rate per period.The cell E11 contains argument 2, the total number of payments to be made, which is the number of payments per year times the total number of years.

Cell E14, the remaining balance, uses the function for the present value of an ordinary annuity. The present value function uses a financial formula to determine the current (present) value of a flow of payments, and thus can be used for the remaining balance of a loan at any point in time. The expression

```
@PV(E12,E6/(100*E7),E13)
```

uses the PV (Present Value) function with three arguments. The first argument is E12, the calculated payment per period for the loan. The second argument E6/(100*E7) is the interest rate per period, which was explained above. The final argument is E13, the number of payments remaining to be made.

BUDGET EXAMPLE

The next example shows how you could plan a budget using 1-2-3. The labels and formulas for this spreadsheet are given in figure 7.20. Start with an empty spreadsheet (/WEY), and enter the information. The resulting spreadsheet should look like figure 7.21. You will learn an easy way to copy similar formulas like those in cells C7 to F7 in the next chapter. For now, enter each formula individually.

The BUDGET spreadsheet is an example of a four-quarter budget with totals. The bottom line gives the profit—the difference between revenues and expenses. All of the totals in column G were performed with the @SUM( ) function. Totals in row 7 were simply adding two numbers (e.g., +C5+C6). The profit figures come from subtracting the total expenses in row 16 from the total revenues in row 7 (e.g., +C7−C16).

Once such a spreadsheet is defined, you can ask "what if" questions. For example, what if sales were $5,000 less each quarter than projected? How would that affect the total profit? Change the numbers in "Sales" to answer that question for yourself. You may wish to save this spreadsheet for future use.

```
      A              B              C              D              E              F              G
 1                                     BUDGET EXAMPLE (IN $1000's)
 2
 3  Revenues                          Q1             Q2             Q3             Q4          Total
 4  ---------------------------------------------------------------------------------------------
 5  Sales                            134            154            166            175   @SUM(C5.F5)
 6  Interest                          12             14             16             18   @SUM(C6.F6)
 7  Total                         +C5+C6         +D5+D6         +E5+E6         +F5+F6   @SUM(C7.F7)
 8
 9  Expenses
10  ---------------------------------------------------------------------------------------------
11  Rent                              44             44             46             46 @SUM(C11.F11)
12  Utilities                          5              5              5              5 @SUM(C12.F12)
13  Salaries                          88             90             92             94 @SUM(C13.F13)
14  Travel                             3              6              3              6 @SUM(C14.F14)
15  Misc                              12             14             16             17 @SUM(C15.F15)
16  Total    @SUM(C11.C15) @SUM(D11.D15) @SUM(E11.E15) @SUM(F11.F15) @SUM(C16.F16) @SUM(C18.F18)
17  ---------------------------------------------------------------------------------------------
18  Profit                       +C7-C16        +D7-D16        +E7-E16        +F7-F16
19  ---------------------------------------------------------------------------------------------
```

FIGURE 7.20.
Labels and formulas for budget example

C5: 134 READY

	A	B	C	D	E	F	G	H
1			BUDGET EXAMPLE IN $1000					
2								
3	Revenues		Q1	Q2	Q3	Q4	Total	
4	------------		------	------	------	------	------	
5	Sales		134	154	166	175	629	
6	Interest		12	14	16	18	60	
7	Total		146	168	182	193	689	
8								
9	Expenses							
10	------------		------	------	------	------	------	
11	Rent		44	44	46	46	180	
12	Utilities		5	5	5	5	20	
13	Salaries		88	90	92	94	364	
14	Travel		3	6	3	6	18	
15	Misc		12	14	16	17	59	
16	Total		152	159	162	168	641	
17	------------		------	------	------	------	------	
18	Profit		-6	9	20	25	48	
19	------------		------	------	------	------	------	
20								

30-Aug-88 03:17 PM

FIGURE 7.21.
Budget on screen

SUMMARY

Spreadsheets are powerful tools, used for accounting, inventory, budgeting, data analysis, and a host of other tasks.

A spreadsheet is composed of rows and columns of cells. Different parts of the spreadsheet can be displayed using the cursor control keys. Each cell may contain text (a label), a numeric value, or a formula based on numbers in other cells. Formulas may use functions such as @SUM to perform more involved calculations. The widths of the cells and the format for numbers can be altered for ranges of cells or globally. The spreadsheet program can be instructed to recalculate formulas automatically as numbers are changed, or only at a manual command.

A completed spreadsheet can be printed on a printer, saved in a disk file, or printed as an ASCII text file for use in a word processing program.

KEY TERMS

Define the following terms in your own words:

Spreadsheet

Cell

Active cell

Range

Scroll

Numeric expression

Arithmetic operator

Format

Recalculation

Function

Argument

QUESTIONS

Fill in the blanks.

1. The cell address for the intersection of the third column and the fifth row would be ________.
2. The types of entries which can be placed into a spreadsheet cell include ________________, ________________, and ________________.
3. A ____________ of cells is designated with a beginning cell address, a period, and an ending cell address.
4. Numeric relationships are entered into a cell using ________________ ________________ and ________________________.
5. If a numeric expression begins with a cell address, it must be preceded by a ________________.
6. The command menu may be accessed by typing ________.
7. A label (i.e., text) typed on the entry line is placed in the highlighted (or active) cell when the ________ key is pressed.
8. To cancel an entry or back out of a command, press the ________ key.
9. A label preceded by a ____________ will be centered in a cell.
10. A backslash "\" as the first character in a cell signifies a ____________ ____________.
11. Pressing the ________________________ key moves the pointer (i.e., the cursor) to cell A1.
12. Typing the key sequence /WGF means ________________________ __________.
13. The default width for columns is ________ characters.
14. To save a worksheet, type the command sequence ________.
15. To exit Lotus 1-2-3, type the command sequence ________.

Write a short answer in your own words for each of the following questions.

16. List the common arithmetic operators used in spreadsheets and indicate their order of precedence in performing calculations.
17. Describe the three types of cell groupings which can make up a cell range.
18. Describe two methods for accessing commands from the command menu.
19. Outline the procedure for editing a cell entry using the Edit command.
20. Briefly describe the difference between a label (i.e., a text entry) and a numeric entry.
21. Outline the procedure for formatting the numbers in a single column of a spreadsheet to have a dollar sign and two decimal places (e.g., $###.##).
22. What is a function and why are they used in spreadsheets?
23. Outline the procedure for setting the width of column D to 12 characters.
24. Outline the procedure for printing a spreadsheet on the printer.
25. Why are some spreadsheet commands referred to as global?
26. Describe how the four label prefixes would affect the text entry "JAN" in a cell that was 9 characters wide.
27. Given below is a spreadsheet screen from Lotus 1-2-3.

```
B4: 2000                                                  READY

        A            B         C         D         E         F
1
2                   Jan       Feb       Mar       Apr       May
3   -----------------------------------------------------------
4  Income         2000.00   2000.00   2000.00   2000.00   2000.00
5
6  Expenses
7    Mortgage      500.00    500.00    500.00    500.00    500.00
8    Auto          250.00    250.00    250.00    250.00    250.00
9    Utilities     100.00    115.00    125.00     95.00    110.00
10   Food          375.00    325.00    350.00    330.00    395.00
11   Other         500.00    575.00    625.00    540.00    750.00
12  -----------------------------------------------------------
13 Totals:
14
15 Balance:
16  -----------------------------------------------------------
17
18
19
20
12-Jun-88  10:55 PM
```

Use the spreadsheet given above to answer the following questions.

a. You want to total the expense figures in column B. What would the formula look like and in what cell would you place the results?

b. You want to calculate the balance between your income (row 4) and your expenses (rows 7–11) for column D. What would the formula look like and in what cell would you place the results?

c. You want to calculate the average amount of money spent on food during the months of January through May. What function would you use and how would the formula be written?

d. The names of the months in Row 2 are centered in the cells. What procedure would you use to reposition the names at the right side of the cells (i.e., right justified)?

e. The numbers in the worksheet are all displayed with a decimal and two zeros (i.e., 2000.00). How was this accomplished?

LABORATORY EXERCISES

Lab Exercise 1. In this exercise you will create a spreadsheet called COINS using Lotus 1-2-3. This exercise is a summary of the tutorial used in this chapter. Try to complete the exercise without referring to the instructions in the chapter.

1. Start up Lotus 1-2-3 and get to the worksheet screen.
2. Enter the following labels in column A:

```
A1   Last Year's Value
A2   This Year's Value
A3   Net Change
A4   Proportion Change
```

3. Enter the following numeric constants in column C:

   ```
   C1   100
   C2   125
   ```

4. Calculate Net Change and place the formula in cell C3.
   Hint: Net Change = This Year's Value − Last Year's Value
5. Calculate Proportion Change and place the formula in cell C4.
   Hint: Proportion Change = Net Change / Last Year's Value
   You may check your answers by referring to figure 7.15.
6. Change this year's value to 175 and write down the changes in the Net Change and Proportion Change cells.
7. Add the following label to column A:

   ```
   A5   Percent Change
   ```

8. Calculate the Percent change and place the formula in cell C5.
   Hint: Percent Change = (Net Change / Last Year's Value) * 100
9. Make the following changes to the worksheet and write down the changes that occur in cells C3..C5.

   ```
   C1   30
   C2   45
   ```

10. Change the format of the numeric values in cells C1..C3 to Currency format with 2 decimal places.
11. Save the worksheet using the /FS command sequence and name the worksheet COINS.
12. Print the worksheet using the /PPRAG command sequence. Quit the Print Menu.
13. Clear the worksheet from memory using the /WEY sequence.

Lab Exercise 2. In this exercise you will create a spreadsheet called MORT2 using Lotus 1-2-3. This exercise is a summary of the tutorial used in this chapter. Try to complete the exercise without referring to the instructions in the chapter.

1. If you are not already in Lotus 1-2-3, start up the program and get to the worksheet screen.
2. Enter a title for your worksheet in row 1 which reads:

   ```
   LOAN ANALYSIS FOR AN AMORTIZED LOAN
   ```

3. Enter the following labels into the worksheet:

   ```
   A3    Description
   A4    (Create double dashed line from A4..E4–use
         the equal sign)
   A5    Enter amount of loan
   A6    Enter interest rate per year
   A7    Enter number of payments per year
   A8    Enter number of years
   A9    Enter number of payments made
   A10   (Create dashed line from A10..E10)
   A11   Total number of payments
   A12   Amount of payment
   A13   Number of payments remaining
   ```

```
A14   Payoff balance remaining
A15   Total amount paid to date
A16   Principal paid to date
A17   Interest paid to date
E3    Amounts
```

4. Enter the following numeric values in column E:

```
E5    65000
E6    12.75
E7    12
E8    30
E9    0
E11   +E7*E8
E12   @PMT(E5,E6/(100*E7),E11)
E13   +E11-E9
E14   @PV(E12,E6/(100*E7),E13)
E15   +E12*E9
E16   +E5-E14
E17   +E15-E16
```

5. Format all numbers to appropriate formats (e.g., dollar amounts should be formatted as currency, etc.).
6. Change the values in cells E5. . E8 so they calculate a new car loan based on the following data:

   Amount of loan = $18,000
   Interest rate per year = 16.25%
   Number of payments per year = 12
   Number of years = 5

7. Save and print the worksheet.

Lab Exercise 3. In this exercise you will create a spreadsheet called BUDGET using Lotus 1-2-3. This exercise is a summary of the tutorial used in this chapter. Try to complete the exercise without referring to the instructions in the chapter.

1. If you are not already in Lotus 1-2-3, start up the program and get to the worksheet screen.
2. Enter the following information into your worksheet as constant values:

```
           A                B        C        D        E       F

 1 BUDGET EXAMPLE (in $1,000's)
 2
 3 Revenues                Q1       Q2       Q3       Q4   Total
 4 ------------------------------------------------------------
 5 Sales                  134      154      166      175
 6 Interest                12       14       16       18
 7 Total
 8
 9 Expenses
10 ------------------------------------------------------------
11 Rent                    44       44       46       46
12 Utilities                5        5        5        5
13 Salaries                88       90       92       94
```

```
14 Travel          3       6       3       6
15 Misc           12      14      16      17
16 Total
17 -----------------------------------------
18 Profit
19 -----------------------------------------
20
```

3. Enter the following numeric calculations into the worksheet:

C7..F7	Calculate the total revenues Hint: Total = Sales + Interest
C16..F16	Calculate the total expenses using @SUM( ) Hint: Total = Rent + Utilities + Salaries . . .
C18..F18	Calculate profit Hint: Profit = Total Revenues − Total Expenses
G5..G18	Caculate totals for four quarters using @SUM( )

4. Format all numeric values as Currency with no decimals.
5. Save and print the worksheet.

Lab Exercise 4. In the following exercise you will create a worksheet called GRADES. In this exercise, you will practice using some of Lotus's statistical functions.

1. Enter the following labels in the worksheet:

```
A1    Sample Worksheet with Formulas
A3    Grades
D5    Sum of scores
D6    Average of scores
D7    Smallest score
D8    Largest score
D9    Number of scores
D10   Rounded average
```

2. Enter the following numeric constants in columns A5..A14:

```
90.5, 80.9, 70.6, 90.9, 65.4
88.6, 78.6, 98.9, 90.1, 63.7
```

3. Enter the following numeric functions into the worksheet:

```
C5    Sum up the grades in column A
C6    Calculate the average grade
C7    Show the smallest grade in the list
C8    Show the largest grade in the list
C9    Indicate how many grades are in the list
C10   Calculate the average rounded to
      1 decimal place
```

4. You can also use functions to perform other tasks; for example, converting the class average to a letter grade. As a demonstration of the @IF function, type the following formula into cell B16.

```
@IF(C6>=90,''A'',@IF(C6>=80,''B'',@IF(C6>=70,''C'',''F'')))
```

Check that you have entered the correct number of parentheses in the formula. If you have entered all the numbers into the worksheet correctly, cell B16 should display the letter grade "B" for the class average of 81.82.

5. Save and print the worksheet.

CHAPTER 8

Advanced Spreadsheet Topics

CHAPTER OVERVIEW. This chapter continues with the description of the uses of microcomputer spreadsheet software. This chapter will cover some advanced topics in the creation, editing, and manipulation of spreadsheet models. Lotus 1-2-3 is used as the case study. There are several 1-2-3 "look-alike" programs that work almost identically to 1-2-3, and may also be used as the spreadsheet program to do the examples in the text.

CHAPTER OBJECTIVES

Upon completion of this chapter, you will be able to:

- Copy and move portions of the spreadsheet.
- Erase portions of the spreadsheet.
- Insert and delete rows and columns.
- Assign a name to one cell or a range of cells.
- Lock and unlock cells.
- Produce a graph from information in the spreadsheet.

ADVANCED SPREADSHEET TOPICS

The last chapter introduced many fundamental concepts of using spreadsheets. This chapter will discuss some of the more advanced features. One of the necessities in using spreadsheets is the ability to alter and edit them. The last chapter introduced methods of altering the contents of one cell at a time. This chapter will discuss techniques of manipulating ranges of cells. The first commands to be covered are the Copy and Move commands. These commands allow you to copy or move relevant portions of a spreadsheet to other places in the spreadsheet, and are a time saver for duplicating repetitious calculations.

MANIPULATING BLOCKS OF CELLS: MOVE, COPY, AND ERASE

The Move and Copy commands are among the most frequently used commands in spreadsheet programs. The Move command allows you to move blocks of cells to different locations within the spreadsheet, maintaining the same mathematical relationships among individual cells. The information is deleted from the original location in the spreadsheet and placed in a new location. The Copy command duplicates the contents of a block of cells, also retaining the mathematical relationship, but leaves the original block of cells intact.

The Copy and Move commands present something of a dilemma for the spreadsheet program. When a Copy or Move is used, the program needs to know if you want the mathematical relationships to refer to the same *relative* locations of the cells they referred to (e.g., so many cells to the left), or if the relationship should be *absolute,* still pointing to the original cells.

To clarify this issue, consider the spreadsheet in figure 8.1. It has a column of numbers in the A column and some calculations in the B column. (The formulas are shown in the top version, and the bottom version shows the actual values that would appear on the screen.)
Suppose you copy columns A and B (the range A1 . . B3) to columns C and D. Do you want the calculations in column D to remain +A1/2, +A2/2, +A3/2? Probably not. The program assumes that you want the new relations in column D to be +C1/2, +C2/2, and +C3/2, and it makes those changes during the copy (or move). That is, the program assumes that you want the calculations to remain *relative* to the column they are now in. The calculation "+A1/2" in cell B1 referred to the A1 cell that was immediately to its left, so when the formula in cell B1 is copied to D1, the program assumes that you still want the calculation to refer to the cell immediately to the left, which is

FIGURE 8.1.
Original spreadsheet with calculations

	A	B	
1	1.00	+A1/2	**Spreadsheet with formulas — what you enter**
2	2.00	+A2/2	
3	3.00	+A3/2	

	A	B	
1	1.00	0.5	**What appears on the screen.**
2	2.00	1	
3	3.00	1.5	

now cell C1. Therefore the calculation becomes "C1/2" instead of "A1/2". The results of this copy are illustrated in figure 8.2, the top half of the illustration showing formulas and the bottom half showing results.

Absolute and Relative Cell Reference

However, if you do not want the program to make these assumptions about the copy, you can force a reference to retain its *absolute* meaning. In Lotus 1-2-3 this means placing a dollar sign in front of the column or row designator. For example, to force the column designation to stay the same, write the expression "+$A1/2", and to keep the row specification the same, write "+A$1/2". The expression "$A$1/2" would keep them both the same. Thus, in the copy, the new calculation that is moved to cell D1 will not be changed to "C1/2", but it will remain "$A$1/2", no matter where it is moved within the spreadsheet. Examine figure 8.3. The formula in cell B1 contains the formula +$A1/2. Thus, the resulting copy in cell D1 maintains the absolute relationship (pointing to the same cell), while the copies in cells D2 and D3 are copied using the relative relationship (one cell to the left).

If a move or copy forces relations "off the spreadsheet", the resulting formula may produce the error designation "ERR" within a cell. For example, if the information in the cell B1 (the formula "A1/2") is moved to cell A10, then there are no cells to the left of the "A" column, so the formula cannot be adjusted relative to the new cell. In cases like this, the entry for the cell becomes "ERR".

In most spreadsheets, the Erase command will allow you to erase information in cells or ranges of cells in a fashion similar to the Copy and Move commands.

	A	B	C	D
1	1.00	+A1/2	1.00	+C1/2
2	2.00	+A2/2	2.00	+C2/2
3	3.00	+A3/2	3.00	+C3/2

	A	B	C	D
1	1.00	0.5	1.00	0.5
2	2.00	1	2.00	1
3	3.00	1.5	3.00	1.5

FIGURE 8.2. Spreadsheet after copying columns A and B

	A	B	C	D
1	1.00	+$A1/2	1.00	+$A1/2
2	2.00	+A2/2	2.00	+C2/2
3	3.00	+A3/2	3.00	+C3/2

	A	B	C	D
1	1.00	0.5	1.00	0.5
2	2.00	1	2.00	1
3	3.00	1.5	3.00	1.5

FIGURE 8.3. Absolute and relative cell references

CASE STUDY

Move, Copy, and Erase in Lotus 1-2-3

In Lotus 1-2-3, the Copy command is selected with the command /C. When you enter this command, you will be prompted to enter the range for the copy, and the destination. This range may be selected by typing the range of cells at the prompt, or by using the highlight range selection technique explained in the last chapter. In the above example, the ranges for the copy from and to would be:

```
Enter range to copy FROM:
```

Your answer would be A1 . . B. This designates the boundaries of the rectangle that include the area to be copied. For the next prompt,

```
Enter range to copy TO:
```

Your answer would be C1. Notice that you indicate the "Copy TO:" position by giving only the upper left corner of the location, the place where you want the rectangle you specified previously to be located.

The Move command is similar to the Copy command, except that the contents of the range indicated to "move FROM" are erased after being placed in the "TO" location.

Multiple copies of cell ranges or individual cells may also be made. For example, using the sample spreadsheet from figure 8.1, one could enter the copy command /C, and designate the FROM and TO ranges as:

```
Enter range to copy FROM:B1..B3

Enter range to copy to: C1..E1
```

This command will result in the spreadsheet shown in figure 8.4. In this spreadsheet the formulas are shown rather than the actual numbers calculated. Notice that the FROM range of cells (B1 . . B3) was duplicated for each row in the TO range (C1..E1).

An Example Using the Move and Copy Commands

As an exercise, enter the original spreadsheet illustrated in figure 8.1, and save it under the name SAMPLE. Using the copy command /C, copy the cell range A1..B3 to the destination C1, to get the spreadsheet illustrated in figure 8.2. Move your cursor to reveal the formulas in cells D1 to D3 to verify that the copy worked.

Using the /FR command, retrieve the spreadsheet SAMPLE, which is the original spreadsheet as in figure 8.1. Move the cursor to cell location B1 and enter the

FIGURE 8.4.
Multiple copies of column B

	A	B	C	D	E
1	1.00	+A1/2	+B1/2	+C1/2	+D1/2
2	2.00	+A2/2	+B2/2	+C2/2	+D2/2
3	3.00	+A3/2	+B3/2	+C3/2	+D3/2

NOTE: Formulas shown rather than calculated results.

new formula +$A1/2. Now do the same copy as above. What do you notice about the results in row one? Examine the formulas. Why did this happen?

Retrieve the SAMPLE spreadsheet again. This time perform a Move command and move the range of cells A1 . . B3 to the location C1. Compare this to what happened with the Copy command.

Retrieve the SAMPLE spreadsheet again, and this time copy the single column B1..B3 to the range of columns C1 . . E1. This should produce the spreadsheet illustrated in figure 8.4. Examine the resulting formulas in columns C to E.

Erasing Portions of the Table

To erase the information in a portion of the spreadsheet, choose the command sequence /RE (Range, Erase). You will be prompted to `enter the range to erase`. Enter the range of the spreadsheet to be erased, such as A1..F5. The information in those cells will be removed.

Erasing cells may affect calculations you have defined. This can result in undefined calculations such as divisions by zero. After erasing a range, watch for cells with the entry "ERR", and examine these cells to determine the cause of the error.

You may be tempted simply to enter a blank (i.e., pressing the space bar) in a cell to remove some undesired contents. However, this is not as desirable as erasing the cell. When you blank out a cell location by putting a blank character in it, the cell contains information—a blank. If a long label is then entered in a cell to the left of the blanked-out cell, the blank will prevent the text from overflowing into the "blank" cell, making your text truncated.

An Example: Erasing Cells

As an example of erasing a range of cells, retrieve the SAMPLE spreadsheet. Enter the command /RE (Range, Erase) and answer the prompt

```
Enter range to erase:
```

with the range A2..A3. This will erase cells A2 and A3, and affect the calculations in cells B2 and B3. Now move the cursor to cell A5 and enter the following text:

```
This is a very long label for cell A5.
```

Notice that the text spills across into cells B5 and C5.

Now, move the cursor to cell B5 and enter a blank (i.e., press the space bar once, then press ENTER). Notice that this caused the text to vanish beginning at cell B5. All that appears is

```
This is a
```

Use the command /RE to erase only the cell B5, and observe the results. The entire label will appear again.

To erase the entire spreadsheet, enter the command sequence/WEY (Worksheet, Erase, Yes). Be careful that this is really what you want to do. If you erase a spreadsheet without first saving it, you will lose all of the information in the spreadsheet.

CASE STUDY

How to Move, Copy, and Erase in Your Spreadsheet Program

Describe the procedure for copying a range of cells from one location to another in your spreadsheet program. How does the Copy operation affect the formulas in cells that have been moved? Does your spreadsheet program make the same changes that were described for the Lotus 1-2-3 Copy command?

Describe the procedure for moving a range of cells in your spreadsheet program. How does a move affect the formulas in the cells that have been moved?

Describe how to erase the contents of a range of cells in your spreadsheet program. Is there a difference between erasing a cell and placing a blank in a cell?

INSERTING AND DELETING ROWS AND COLUMNS

As you are creating a spreadsheet, you often want to adjust the position of your data in the spreadsheet. Besides the Copy and Move commands, you may also Insert and Delete entire rows and columns. Sometimes in editing an existing spreadsheet you find that you need to make more room at the top (by inserting some rows) or more room at the left (by inserting some columns). For example, you may find that you need three more rows between the present rows 5 and 6. The Insert command will place three new (blank) rows below row 5. All cells in the previous rows 6 and below will be shifted down to row 9 and below, and renumbered.

The Delete command performs the opposite operation. If you delete columns B and C, then the information in those columns will be permanently removed from the spreadsheet, and all the information in columns D and beyond will be shifted two columns to the left and relabeled. That is, the previous column D will now be column B, and so on. This is different from the Erase command because a deletion adjusts the positions of the remaining cells. The Erase command simply empties out specified cells but does not change the position of any cells.

Mathematical expressions in affected cells are adjusted the same way as with the Copy and Move commands. Carefully consider how inserting and/or deleting rows and columns will affect the formulas in your spreadsheet. Although the program will try to adjust the formulas, it may do something you did not have in mind. Double-check everything after making insertions or deletions.

CASE STUDY

Insertions and Deletions in Lotus 1-2-3

Here is a summary of the command sequences required for inserting and deleting columns and rows, all beginning with the "worksheet" menu:

- Insert Rows: /WIR (Worksheet, Insert, Row)
- Insert Columns: /WIC (Worksheet, Insert, Column)
- Delete Rows: /WDR (Worksheet, Delete, Row)
- Delete Columns: /WDC (Worksheet, Delete, Column)

When you enter one of these commands, you will be prompted to enter the range of the deletion or insert. For example, to insert 3 blank rows between rows 5 and 6, enter the range A6. . A8. This causes blank rows to be inserted as rows 6 to 8, and all items on rows 6 and below to be moved down 3 rows. Notice that you could have specified B6. . B8, and the result would have been identical. Insertions and deletions always work with whole rows or columns.

Retrieve the SAMPLE spreadsheet from disk (figure 8.1). Using the command /WIR, and designating the insert range as A1. . A2, insert two rows above the spreadsheet. Examine how this affects the formulas. Insert a column at A1 using the command /WIC, and see how that affects the formulas. Finally, do the reverse: use the /WDC command to delete column A, and use the /WDR command to delete rows 1 and 2. This will revert the spreadsheet back to its original location. Did the formulas survive the movements?

CASE STUDY

Insertions and Deletions in Your Spreadsheet Program

Describe the procedure for inserting one or more rows or columns in a spreadsheet. How are mathematical expressions affected by insertions that move cells containing formulas?

Describe the procedure for deleting one or more rows or columns in a spreadsheet. How are mathematical expressions affected by deletions that move cells containing formulas?

ASSIGNING NAMES TO CELLS

When you are developing a spreadsheet, there may be times when you want to refer to a cell or a range of cells quite often. One problem you may encounter is remembering the range of a particular group of cells. A solution to this is to name the cells with something you can remember. For example, if you are developing a budget, you may define a range of cells called REVENUE1, that contains all of the values for revenue during quarter 1. Somewhere else in the spreadsheet, when you want to calculate the sum of the revenues during quarter 1, you can enter the command @SUM(REVENUE1) rather than trying to remember that the range was F1. . F15. A named range is illustrated in figure 8.5.

FIGURE 8.5.
Example of a named range. The cell range C18. . F18 is named PROFIT

```
F18: +F7-F16                                                  POINT
Enter name: PROFIT                      Enter range: C18..F18

        A         B        C        D        E        F        G        H
1                       BUDGET EXAMPLE IN $1000
2
3    Revenues                 Q1       Q2       Q3       Q4    Total
4    ---------------------------------------------------------------
5    Sales                   134      154      166      175      629
6    Interest                 12       14       16       18       60
7    Total                   146      168      182      193      689
8
9    Expenses
10   ---------------------------------------------------------------
11   Rent                     44       44       46       46      180
12   Utilities                 5        5        5        5       20
13   Salaries                 88       90       92       94      364
14   Travel                    3        6        3        6       18
15   Misc                     12       14       16       17       59
16   Total                   152      159      162      168      641
17   ---------------------------------------------------------------
18   Profit                   -6        9       20       25       48
19   ---------------------------------------------------------------
20
27-May-90  11:22 AM
```

CASE STUDY

Range Names in Lotus 1-2-3

In Lotus 1-2-3, range names are created with the command sequence /RNC, which stands for the commands Range, Name, Create. You must specify a range name (up to 14 characters), and the range, such as B1 . . B3. Once a name is defined, you can use it in place of the cell range in formulas.

An Example of Naming a Range

Retrieve the spreadsheet named SAMPLE from disk (figure 8.1). Using the command /RNC, name the range from B1 to B3 "NUMBERS". The result should be the sum of the numbers from cells B1 . . B3.

There are other options to the /RN (Range, Name) command, including the ability to delete a name, delete all range names (Reset), and more.

CASE STUDY

Range Names in Your Spreadsheet Program

Describe the procedure for naming a range of cells in a spreadsheet. Once you have named a range, can you use this name in formulas and mathematical expressions? In commands? How do you delete a range name?

LOCKING AND UNLOCKING CELLS

As is often the case when you build a spreadsheet, there may be one or more cells that you want to protect from being changed by other users, or accidentally by yourself. For example, you may build a spreadsheet to provide specified calculations. The blank template will be passed on to other people in your organization, and you do not want them to accidentally change the formulas in your spreadsheet. You want to *protect* certain cells from being changed.

CASE STUDY

Protecting Cells in Lotus 1-2-3

Protecting cells in 1-2-3 is a two-step process:

1. Specify the cells to be protected. Use the command sequence /RP (Range, Protect). You will then specify a range to protect. Use the /RU (Range, Unprotect) command sequence to unprotect a range of fields.
2. Enable the protection; that is, turn it "on." This is done with the command sequence /WGPE (Worksheet, Global, Protection, Enable). You may turn off the protection with the /WGPD (Worksheet, Global, Protection, Disable) command.

Normally, as you build a spreadsheet, you will not need to turn on protection. However, after you have finished developing a spreadsheet that you are now going to distribute, you would enable the protection before sending the spreadsheet to other people. This method of protecting cells is not meant to prevent anyone from knowingly altering the spreadsheet. It is mostly for protecting against accidental destruction of formulas in the spreadsheet.

An Example Using Cell Protection

Retrieve the SAMPLE spreadsheet from disk (figure 8.1). Using the /RP command, specify the cells B1 . . B3 to protect. Next, enable protection with the command /WGPE. Now, attempt to edit the formula in cell B1 by moving the cursor to B1 and pressing the F2 (edit) function key. The formula will appear as if you could edit it, but the program will not let you change the formula. If you try, it will display the message "Protected Cell". You also will not be able to delete these protected cells.

CASE STUDY

Protecting Cells in Your Spreadsheet Program

Is there a method for preventing accidental changes to certain cells in your spreadsheet program? If so, describe the procedure for protecting a range of cells from being changed by someone who uses a spreadsheet you have created.

Is there a procedure for turning the protection for cells off and on for the entire spreadsheet in one command? If so, what is the procedure?

GRAPHIC CAPABILITIES

Once information is placed in a spreadsheet, it is often desirable to produce graphs of the results. Most spreadsheet programs give you some simple graphical capabilities, including the ability to create line graphs, bar graphs, pie charts, and other kinds of graphs. Figure 8.6 illustrates some of the graph types available.

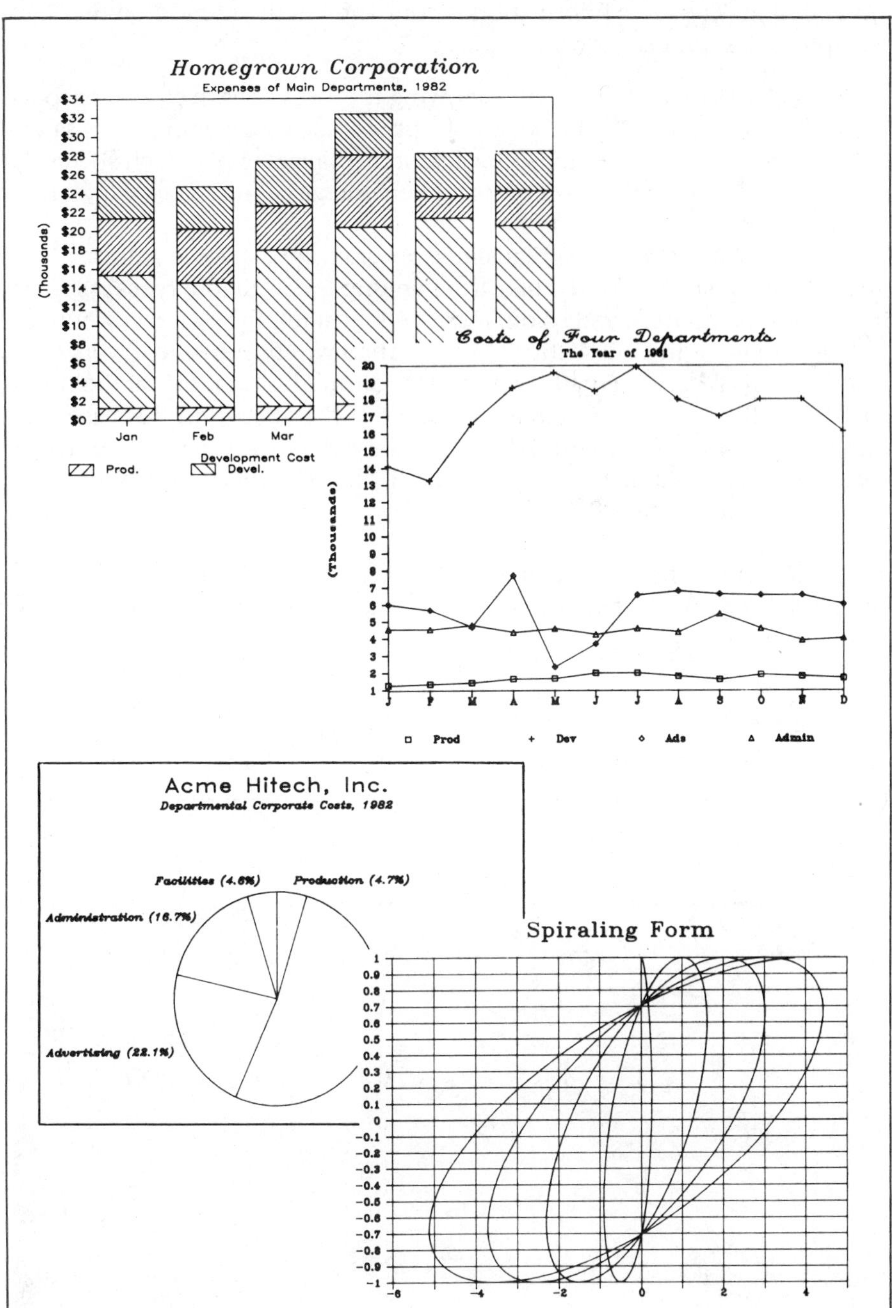

FIGURE 8.6.
Sample graphs

Pie Chart Example

Andy's Pie Company was interested in what pies were selling best, in order to be able to predict what kinds of filling to order from next year's crop of fruit. The kinds of fruit pies Andy makes are Apple, Peach, Banana, Cherry, and Pumpkin. The sales information is contained in the file PIE on the Text Examples Disk, and is shown in figure 8.7.

Andy wishes to have a *pie chart* showing the sales of each type in proportion to the total sales. The pie chart will be a circle representing total sales, divided into "slices" or sections for each of the flavors of pie. Each slice will be labeled with the type of pie and the percentage of total sales which that slice represents.

To draw the chart, the spreadsheet program needs some information. First, you must specify a pie chart from among the available types, such as line graphs, bar graphs, and so on. Next, you must tell the program where to find the labels for the pie sections. Andy's chart will use the pie flavors contained in cells A3. . A7. Finally, you must indicate the locations of the numbers that will be used to calculate the sizes of the slices—in this case, the sales figures, which are in cells B3. . B7. Once you have given instructions on what to put in the graph, the program can display it on the screen. Andy's pie graph is shown in figure 8.8.

The percentages on the chart are calculated automatically as the percent of the sales for that flavor compared to the total sales. For example, the Apple slice contains 34.8% of the sales. This percentage is calculated automatically by the formula:

$$\text{Apple Pie \%} = \frac{5634}{5634 + 2343 + 4323 + 2345 + 1543} * 100$$

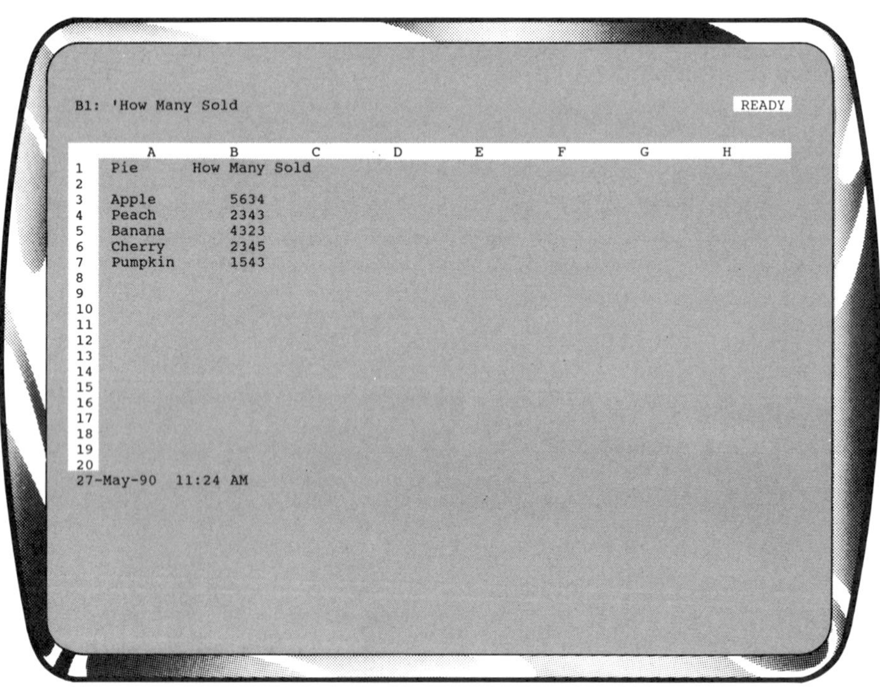

B1: 'How Many Sold
READY
A B C D E F G H
1 Pie How Many Sold
2
3 Apple 5634
4 Peach 2343
5 Banana 4323
6 Cherry 2345
7 Pumpkin 1543
8
9
10
11
12
13
14
15
16
17
18
19
20
27-May-90 11:24 AM

FIGURE 8.7.
Andy's pie data from Text Examples Disk file PIE.

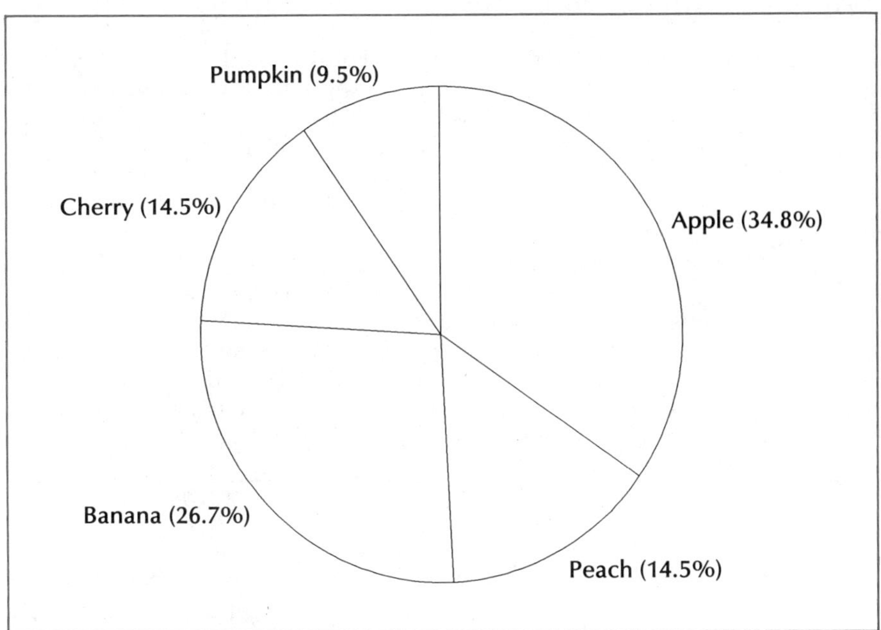

FIGURE 8.8.
Andy's pie chart

CASE STUDY

Creating a Graph in Lotus 1-2-3

Retrieve the spreadsheet PIE from the Text Examples Disk. It contains the information from figure 8.7. To graph it, first enter the Graph menu with the command /G. The Graph menu has these options:

```
Type X A B C D E F Reset View Save Options Name Quit
```

To choose a pie chart, you must select the type option. The choices are:

```
Line Bar XY Stacked-Bar Pie
```

To choose the pie-chart type, enter P, and the original Graph menu will appear again.

Next the labels and numeric values for the pie sections must be specified. The X option on the Graph menu is used to specify the labels. You will then be prompted to enter a range of cells for the labels. In this case, it is A3. . A7, the cells containing the names of the pies. To indicate what numeric values to use for the sizes, select the A option, and enter the range B3. . B7 after the prompt, to specify the sales data. For a pie chart only the X labels and the A numeric values need to be given.

Enter the command V to view the graph. The resulting graph should be similar to the graph in figure 8.8. (Note: You must have a monitor that will display graphs, or the program will not be able to display the pie chart.)

Press the ENTER key to return to the Graph menu, and then exit the Graph menu with the Q (Quit) command. Back in READY mode, you can redisplay the graph quickly by pressing the F10 (graph) function key. After another look you can exit back to Ready mode by pressing the ENTER key. You may want to experiment with other types of graphs, labels, and options to give the graph the appearance you desire.

Printing Graphs in Lotus 1-2-3

There are two ways to print graphs created with Lotus 1-2-3. The first method is to enter the Print Screen command from the PC keyboard by pressing Shift-Print Screen key. For this to work, you must have a printer that will support graphic printing, and you must have entered the Graphics command at the DOS prompt before entering 1-2-3. (The Graphics command is a DOS command that is on the IBM PC-DOS disk.) Some computers may use an alternate command that allows the printing of graphic screens.

A second method of printing a graph is the Lotus Printgraph routine. To print a graph in this way, you must save the graph using the Save command in the Graph menu (this is different from saving the spreadsheet information from the Worksheet menu). Then choose the Printgraph option and select the graph to be printed from those that are saved on disk. For this print method to work, you must have a printer that is supported by the Lotus Printgraph routine. Check your version of Lotus to determine if your printer is supported.

CASE STUDY

Creating a Graph in Your Spreadsheet Program

Determine the procedures for creating graphs in your spreadsheet program. First, describe how the numerical information must be entered into the spreadsheet in order to create a graph.

Describe the kinds of graphs available in your spreadsheet program.

Describe how to create a pie chart using Andy's pie data.

Describe how to print this graph.

OTHER FEATURES OF LOTUS 1-2-3

The last two chapters have described some of the most commonly used features of Lotus 1-2-3. However, there are some other features that are quite useful. This section is an overview of the features not covered in the last two chapters.

Windows

Lotus 1-2-3 allows you to split your spreadsheet into two parts, where each part is a separate window into the same spreadsheet. The command used is /WW (Worksheet, Window). For example, you may have a series of labels at the top of a long spreadsheet. Normally, these labels would scroll off the screen as you scrolled the spreadsheet. You can create a window that holds the first few rows of the spreadsheet in place, while the rest of it scrolls. To move your cursor back and forth between the windows, use the F6 key. Figure 8.9 is an example of a spreadsheet split into two windows.

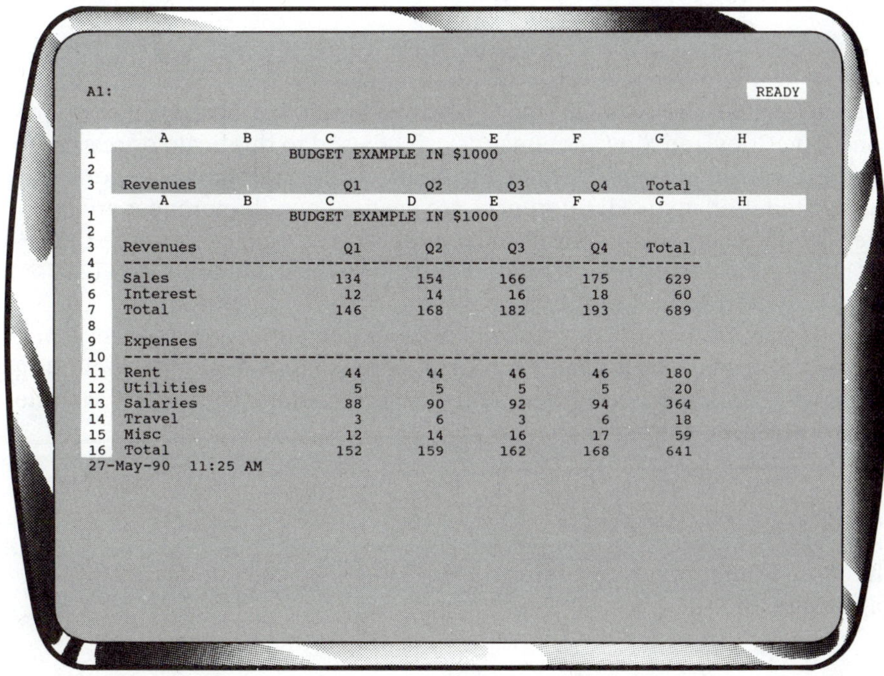

A1:
READY
A B C D E F G H
1 BUDGET EXAMPLE IN $1000
2
3 Revenues Q1 Q2 Q3 Q4 Total
A B C D E F G H
1 BUDGET EXAMPLE IN $1000
2
3 Revenues Q1 Q2 Q3 Q4 Total
4 --
5 Sales 134 154 166 175 629
6 Interest 12 14 16 18 60
7 Total 146 168 182 193 689
8
9 Expenses
10 --
11 Rent 44 44 46 46 180
12 Utilities 5 5 5 5 20
13 Salaries 88 90 92 94 364
14 Travel 3 6 3 6 18
15 Misc 12 14 16 17 59
16 Total 152 159 162 168 641
27-May-90 11:25 AM

FIGURE 8.9.
Screen split into two windows

Macros

A *macro* or *keyboard macro* is a stored sequence of keystrokes. Lotus 1-2-3 allows you to create and store these keystroke sequences to use for tasks that you perform frequently. In fact, you can use this feature to write a program in Lotus. For example, if you frequently use the same set of commands to send various spreadsheets to the printer, you may wish to write a macro to activate all of those options with just one command.

Database

The 1-2-3 in Lotus 1-2-3 stands for Spreadsheet, Graph, and Database. The database portion of 1-2-3 has not been discussed. The database in Lotus is not as powerful and flexible as the databases, discussed later in this text. However, it is convenient for keeping and manipulating lists of information. The Lotus database allows you to store information, sort it, search it, and perform calculations on the fields. It should not be expected to be a substitute for a database management system.

New Versions

Version 1A of Lotus 1-2-3 was a very successful product, and quickly became the best-selling program for IBM PCs. In subsequent versions, Lotus has offered improvements over the original product. This includes LAN (Local Area Network) capabilities; providing ways of breaking the 640K memory barrier in order to create bigger spreadsheets; providing faster speed in recalculation; and providing ways to link spreadsheets, so that numbers from one spreadsheet can be used in another.

SUMMARY

This chapter discussed some more advanced topics in Spreadsheet operations. The Copy and Move commands can be used to duplicate or rearrange groups of cells in the spreadsheet. Mathematical formulas in those cells may be adjusted if relative cell references are used, or not, if references are absolute. The Erase command erases the contents of existing cells, while the Insert and Delete commands create and destroy rows and columns of cells. Formulas may be adjusted in this process also.

Cells may be named, and they can be protected to prevent accidental changes. Spreadsheet programs can draw various kinds of graphs, including pie charts, bar graphs, and line graphs. Newer versions Lotus 1-2-3 include more powerful features.

Lotus 1-2-3 Commands

The most commonly used commands in Lotus 1-2-3 are summarized in the following table.

Operation	Purpose
Help	
F1	Display menu of Help items
Esc	Quit Help menu
Exit Lotus	
/QY	Return to DOS from READY made
Go to cell	
F5, cell location	Move cursor to given cell
Stop calculations	
/WGRM	Put calculations in manual mode for faster data entry
F9	Request recalculation of the Spreadsheet
/WGRA	Return to automatic recalculation
Print to printer	
PP, options, G	Send current spreadsheet to printer with given options, and begin printing
Q	Quit Print menu
Print to a file	
/PF, file name, options	Send current spreadsheet to a disk file with given options. File can be merged into word processor later.
G	Begin printing
Q	Quit Print menu
Edit a cell	
F2	Edit entry at current cursor position
Home, arrow keys	Move cursor within entry
ENTER	Return to READY mode
Copy and Move	
/C, range, location or range	Copy given range to rectangle at given location. Giving a second range makes multiple copies.
/M, range, location or range	Moves given range to rectangle at given location. Giving a second range makes multiple copies.
Erase	
/WEY	Erases all information in current spreadsheet.
/RE, range	Erases contents of given range
Change formats	
/WGF, format options	Change number format throughout entire spreadsheet
/RF, format options	Change number format in given range

Operation	Purpose
Help	
Retrieve file from disk	
/FR, file name	Retrieve a spreadsheet from the given file and display it
Save a spreadsheet	
/FS, file name	Save current spreadsheet to given file
List files on disk	
/FL, option	List files on disk
Options:	
W	List only .WK1 files (spreadsheets)
P	List only .PRN files (printer files)
G	List only .PIC files (graphs)

QUESTIONS

Write a short answer in your own words for each question.

1. Describe the primary difference between the Move command and the Copy command.
2. Describe how formulas are adjusted when the Move or Copy command is used.
3. Describe what happens when a Copy or Move command results in a reference to cells that are off the spreadsheet (e.g., cells to the left of column A).
4. What is the difference between a *relative* cell reference and an *absolute* cell reference? How does Lotus 1-2-3 differentiate between relative and absolute references?
5. Given the following spreadsheet:

```
       A              B         C         D         E          F
1  Revenues          Q1        Q2        Q3        Q4      Total
2  ______________________________________________________________
3  Sales          13400     15400     16600     17500
4  Interest        1200      1400      1600      1800
5  Total         +B3+B4
```

   Outline the procedure for copying the formula in cell B5 to cells C5, D5, and E5.

6. Given the following spreadsheet:

```
       A              B         C         D         E          F
1  Tax Rate=          28%
2                    Jan       Feb       Mar       Apr
3  Gross Income  2000.00   2000.00   2300.00   1900.00
4  Tax Due
5  Net Income
```

   a. Indicate the correct formula for calculating the Tax Due for cell B4. Hint: Use the Tax Rate in cell B1 and the Gross Income in Cell B3.

b. Outline the procedure for copying the formula derived for cell B4 to the remainder of row 4. Think first about relative and absolute cell references!

c. Indicate the formula for calculating Net Income in cell B5 and outline the procedure for copying the formula to the remainder of row 5.

7. Given the following spreadsheet:

	A	B	C	D	E	F
1	Tax Rate=	28%				
2		Jan	Feb	Mar	Apr	
3	Gross Income	2000.00	2000.00	2300.00	1900.00	
4	Tax Due					
5	Net Income					

a. Outline the procedure for erasing the contents of cell B3.

b. Outline the procedure for erasing all the numeric entries for Gross Income.

c. List the commands you would use to erase the entire spreadsheet from the memory of the computer.

8. Given the following spreadsheet:

	A	B	C	D	E	F
1	Revenues	Q1	Q2	Q3	Q4	Total
2						
3	Sales	13400	15400	16600	17500	
4	Interest	1200	1400	1600	1800	
5	Total	+B3+B4				

a. Outline the procedure for inserting a new row between Sales and Interest (i.e., a new row 4).

b. Outline the procedure for inserting a new column between Q4 and Total (i.e., a new column F).

9. Briefly describe how you would assign a name to a range of cells. Why would you want to do this?

10. Given the following spreadsheet:

	A	B	C	D	E	F
1	Revenues	Q1	Q2	Q3	Q4	Total
2						
3	Sales	13400	15400	16600	17500	
4	Interest	1200	1400	1600	1800	
5	Total	+B3+B4				

Outline the procedure for locking (protecting) the numeric entries in cells B3 through E3.

11. Given the following spreadsheet:

	A	B	C	D	E	F
1	Revenues	Q1	Q2	Q3	Q4	Total
2						
3	Sales	13400	15400	16600	17500	
4	Interest	1200	1400	1600	1800	
5	Total	+B3+B4				

Outline the procedure for creating a bar graph of the Sales figures for the four quarters.

LABORATORY EXERCISES

Lab Exercise 1. In this exercise you will create a spreadsheet called BUDGET2.

1. Create the spreadsheet shown below using the labels and numeric constants provided.

	A	B	C	D	E	F	G
1	Household Budget						
2	————————						
3		Jan	Feb	Mar	Totals	% of	Average
4						Income	Expenses
5	————————						
6	Income	1750	1500	1650			
7							
8	Rent	650	650	650			
9	Utilities	175	165	150			
10	Food	250	225	215			
11	Automobile	325	355	315			
12	Savings						
13	————————						
14	Total:						
15							
16	Balance:						

2. Set column widths as follows:

   Column A = 16 Columns B through G = 9

3. Center column headings in rows 3 and 4.
4. Calculate Savings for cell B12 (Savings = Income 8 * .10) and copy to C12..D12.
5. Calculate the total expenses (adding up rows 8 through 12) for each column using the appropriate function, and store in Total (row 14).
6. Calculate the monthly balance (subtract Total from Income) and store in Balance (row 16).
7. Calculate the total for Income and for each row in the expense category (i.e., Rent, etc.) using the appropriate function, and store in Totals (column E).
8. Calculate the percent of your total income spent on each expense category (divide totals by total income) and store in % of Income (column F).
9. Calculate the average amount spent on each expense category using the appropriate function and store in Average Expenses (column G).
10. Numeric values in columns B, C, D, E, and G should be formatted as currency. Numeric values in column F should be formatted as percentages.
11. Save and print the spreadsheet. Use the command sequence /PPRAG.

    You may also want to print out a copy of the cell contents so you can see the formulas and formatting used for each cell. From the printer menu see Options, Other, Cell-Formulas (command sequence /PPROOCQAG). If you have problems, ask your instructor for assistance.

Lab Exercise 2. In this exercise you will design a spreadsheet which could be used as a personal budget manager. The spreadsheet should keep track of income and expenses for a given period of time. Your spreadsheet should have the following features:

1. A general title in Row 1.
2. At least four time periods with appropriate column headings in row 3. The time periods may be weeks, months, quarters, etc.
3. At least ten budget categories with appropriate row labels. You should select your own categories (e.g., rent, utilities, food, insurance, medical, auto, credit cards, etc.) At least two of your categories should have sub-categories; for example:

Utilities:	Automobile:
Electricity	Payment
Gas	Gasoline
Telephone	Insurance
Water	Repairs
Total Utilities:	Total Automobile:
Insurance:	Credit Cards:
Household	Mastercard
Medical	Visa
Auto	Discover
Life	American Express
Total Insurance:	Total Credit Cards:

4. Totals for spending in each time period and for spending in each budget category and sub-category.
5. Average amount spent for at least two of your budget categories.
6. Minimum and maximum amount spent for at least two of your budget categories.
7. An Income category for each time period. The income and expense figures you enter into your spreadsheet do not have to be real, but they should be realistic.
8. A Balance which indicates your expenses subtracted from your income.
9. Appropriate formatting for all labels and numeric values.
10. Once you are sure that your spreadsheet functions correctly, save it as BUDGET3, and print a copy to the printer.
11. You might want to experiment with calculating taxes owed or with savings based on certain interest rates.

Lab Exercise 3. In this exercise you will create a spreadsheet called DRINKS. The spreadsheet will assist you in managing a small business enterprise.

Assume that you own a small business which delivers cold drinks to the dormitory rooms on campus. You charge $1.50 per drink or $6.00 for six drinks. Your profit is 90 cents on a single drink and $3.10 for six drinks. Your sales are as follows:

Month	Singles	Six-Packs
September	23	12
October	34	17
November	39	28
December	36	29
January	44	36
February	47	42

1. Create a spreadsheet based on the above information. Months should be in column A, Singles sales in column B, and Six-Pack sales in column C.
2. Add three more columns, one for each of the following:

Profit for Singles
Profit for Six-Packs
Total Profit

Enter the formulas for September and copy them for the remaining months.

3. Add appropriate formatting for all labels and numeric entries.
4. Save and print the spreadsheet.
5. Create a line graph which shows Singles Profit, Six-Pack Profit and Total Profit.
6. Create a pie chart which shows Total Singles Profit and Total Six-Pack Profit. What new calculations must you add to the spreadsheet before you can construct this graph?
7. Print the graphs created above.

Lab Exercise 4. In this exercise you will create a spreadsheet model which could be used by an instructor for keeping track of grades during the semester. First, you will create the model with appropriate headings and formulas and save it to disk. Next you will enter the names and grades for five students to test the model.

1. Create the following spreadsheet model. All columns are the default width except column A. The grade weights in column D are entered as decimal numbers and formatted as percentages.

```
              A                B          C          D         E         F
 1  Semester Grade Sheet
 2  -------------------
 3                            Test       Test       Test      Test   Exercise
 4  Name                       1          2          3        Avg       1
 5  ====================================================================
 6
 7
 8
 9
10
11  ====================================================================
12  Highest score:
13  Lowest score:
14  Average score:
15  Number of students:
16  --------------------------------------------------------------------
18  Grade Weighting:       Tests =         60%
19                         Exercises =     30%
20                         Homework =      10%


        G          H          I          J          K      L
 1
 2
 3  Exercise   Exercise   Exercise   Homework     Final
 4     2          3         Avg                   Grade
 5  ==========================================================
 6
 7
 8
```

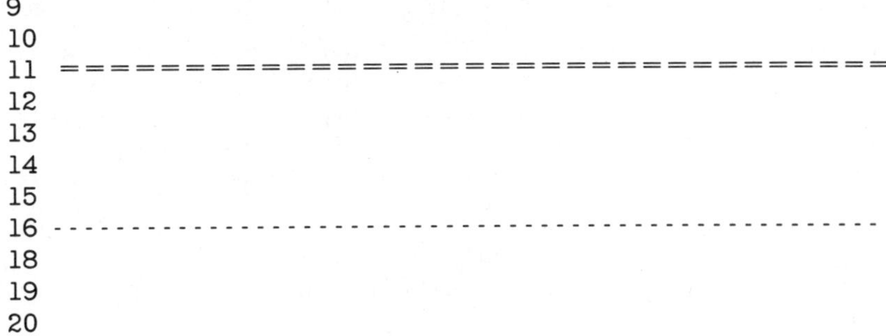

```
9
10
11 ====================================
12
13
14
15
16 -------------------------------------------------------
18
19
20
```

2. In the Test Avg column, use the proper function to average the three test scores.
3. In the Exercise Avg column, use the proper function to average the three exercise scores.
4. In the Final Grade column, create the formula which will assign the final numeric grade to the student. The final grade is based on the test average, the exercise average, and the homework grade. The appropriate grade weights are given in column D. Hint: Final Grade = Test Avg * Test weight + Exercise Avg * Exercise weight, etc. Use cell references throughout the formula and remember absolute references when needed. The final grade should be rounded with no decimal places.

   Note 1: This grading scheme assumes that a perfect score on Tests, Exercises, or Homework would be 100.
5. In the Highest Score row, use the proper function to determine the largest score for each of the activities.
6. In the Lowest Score row, use the proper function to determine the smallest score for each of the activities.
7. In the Average Score row, use the proper function to determine the average score for each of the activities.
8. In the Number of Students position, use the proper function to determine the number of students in the class.
9. Numbers should be formatted appropriately (e.g., fixed to 2 decimal places).
10. Save the spreadsheet model using the name GRADES1. This model may be retrieved and modified as necessary for different classes.

You should now have a spreadsheet model which is suitable for storing the names and grades for five students. Before entering data into the spreadsheet, make the following alterations.

11. Insert enough rows into the spreadsheet at the appropriate location so that the model can accommodate 20 students.
12. Suppose you have two classes of 20 students and you want to keep all grades in the same spreadsheet, but still separated into two classes. To do this, copy the entire spreadsheet so that the top left cell is in field A30.

    Be sure to check all of your formulas after inserting the rows and copying the spreadsheet.
13. Save the modified spreadsheet model using the name GRADES2.

You are now ready to enter test data into your spreadsheet to see if the model functions as it should.

14. Enter the following names and grades into the GRADES2 spreadsheet:

Name	T1	T2	T3	Ex1	Ex2	Ex3	Homework
Alice Avery	98	91	88	100	100	95	87.75
Bob Borland	78	71	66	90	80	70	76.8
Diane Daniels	89	96	93	95	80	80	83.5
Howard Hessman	74	86	87	95	85	95	90.2
Rick Richards	95	92	89	100	90	85	93.25

Check all of the calculated data in your spreadsheet to see if the answers are correct. You may need to go back and edit some of your formulas.

Once you are certain that the spreadsheet is functioning properly, save it as GRADES3.

15. Print a copy of the GRADES3 spreadsheet in condensed type with a right margin of 132. (Note: These settings are accessed from the Printer Menu and will allow the entire spreadsheet to print on one page. If your printer does not support condensed type, you should print the spreadsheet with the default settings.)
16. Print a copy of the Cell-Formulas used in the GRADES3 spreadsheet. (From the printer menu use Options, Other, Cell-Formulas.)

Now that you have saved a copy of the GRADES3 model, you may want to experiment with the spreadsheet by asking some "What if. . ." questions. For example:

17. What if you decide not to give a third test? You could delete that column and see how it affects the other calculations. (Remember to change the appropriate formulas.)
18. What if you decide to give four exercises rather than three? You could insert a new column and see how it affects the other calculations. (Remember again to change the formulas.)
19. What if you decide that homework should count more than 10% on the final grade? You could change the grade weightings in column D (make sure the weights total 100%) and see if the new weightings more accurately reflect class performance.
20. What if you want the letter grade displayed along with the final grade? You could add a column with a nested @IF function to display the letter grade. (See chapter 7, Lab Exercise 4.)

CHAPTER 9

Introduction to Database Management Systems

CHAPTER OVERVIEW. This is the first of two chapters to discuss database management systems on personal computers. This chapter introduces the concept of information storage and retrieval on a PC, and discusses the need for such a system in today's information-glutted society. An example is used to illustrate the questions that need to be asked to design a database. A database is created on the computer, and data is entered. Once the information is in the computer, methods of asking questions using the database are covered. Also, methods of adding, deleting, and editing records are discussed.

CHAPTER OBJECTIVES

Upon completion of this chapter, you will be able to:

- Define a database.
- Give examples of uses for database management systems.
- Describe database fields, records, and files.
- Outline the important questions to be asked in creating a useful database.
- Describe basic database field types.
- Create a database file.
- Enter information into a database.
- Display information from a database.
- Query the database with simple criteria.
- Request on-line help.
- Add records to an existing database.
- Delete records from a database.
- Edit records in a database.
- Exit the database program.

CASE STUDIES

dBASE III Plus and Your Database Program

In this chapter, dBASE III Plus from Ashton-Tate and your database program will be used to illustrate the examples. Virtually all commands and procedures mentioned are identical for the older dBASE III program, and many are the same as in the original dBASE II program. Commands covered for dBASE III Plus in this chapter include Append, Create, Delete, Display, Edit, Go Top, Help, Locate, Pack, Quit, and Recall.

COLLECTING INFORMATION

Elaine Slagle was preparing to write a paper for her English class. It was going to be about American poets. Elaine went to the library and began doing her research. Each time she found information on a poet, she wrote the information on a 3 × 5 card. At the top of the card she put the poet's name: "Poe, Edgar Allen". On the rest of the card, she wrote where the poet was born, when the poet lived, and a list of the poet's major works. Elaine collected over a hundred cards and placed them in a card box in alphabetical order, as shown in figure 9.1. When she began writing her paper, it was easy to find information about a particular poet by looking up the information on the 3 × 5 card.

A hot line called "Poison Control" was recently created to help people determine treatment for a variety of poisons. Sometimes people called in and knew exactly what was ingested by the name of the poison, such as ammonia. Other times people called in with only a brand name of a possible poison, such as "Farmer's Liniment". The poison center had to maintain a huge file of information on thousands of substances and thousands of brand-name products. The center had dozens of file cabinets containing information

FIGURE 9.1.
Elaine Slagle's Poet "Database"

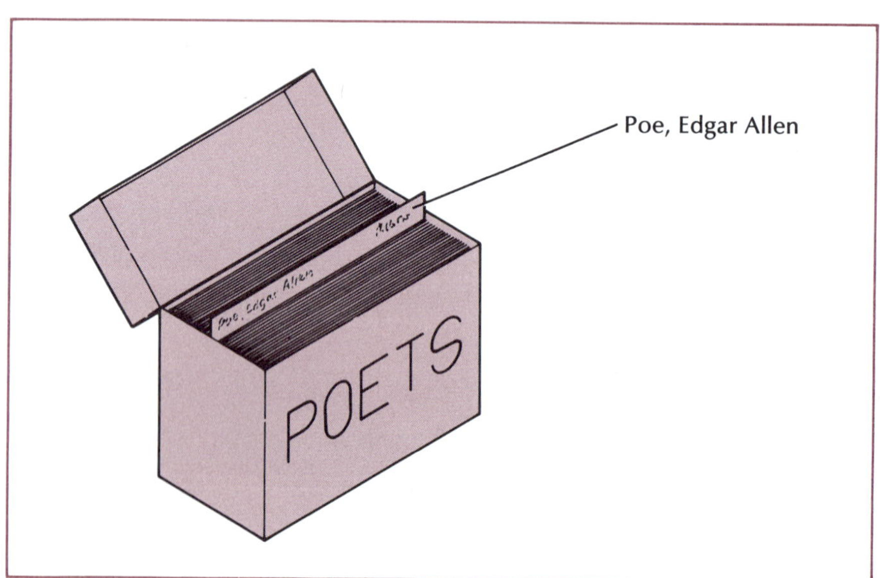

about substances. It was very important to be able to get the correct information as soon as possible, since lives were at stake. If a file had been pulled from the cabinet and misplaced, it slowed the process considerably.

Ron recently opened an auto parts store. Since competition was fierce, Ron wanted to keep enough parts on hand without tying up too much money in inventory that was not selling. If he could make his inventory bring in maximum profit, it would give him a competitive advantage over the other stores in the area. To do this, Ron wanted to develop a tracking system that would let him know how many of each item were sold, how many he had left, and how long it would take to replenish the supply. That way, he could time his ordering so that he would have the most efficient use of his money. He could also quickly detect slow-moving items, and replace them with items that brought in more profit.

The Computer to the Rescue

Before computers, the tasks involving the collection and manipulation of data were mostly done on paper, and required a lot of human labor. Because the information was gathered, stored, and arranged by a variety of workers, it was prone to misplacement and was difficult to manage. This manual manipulation of the data was often too expensive to be worth the effort. One task computers can do very well is to store and retrieve information. Many computing centers are called "Information Systems" to emphasize the role of the computer as a machine that manages knowledge. Although computers cannot guarantee the accuracy of information, they can keep track of the information and provide a quick way to access the information in storage.

Computer systems that are set up to collect information and make that information available to the user are called *database management systems* (DBMS). They will be referred to as *database systems* in this chapter. In such a database system, Elaine could store the same information on computer that she placed on her 3 × 5 cards. With her card system, Elaine's information was only organized by the author's name. What if she wanted to know which poets were from New England? What if she wanted to know which authors lived in the eighteenth century? Searching for that information would require Elaine to look at every card. If the information were properly stored in a computer database, the questions could be answered in a few seconds.

At Poison Control, a desperate mother called up because her child had swallowed some Farmer's Liniment. The people at Poison Control looked through their index of brand names, which described the ingredients of many products. Then they had to look up each ingredient to see what the correct treatment would be, and to determine any interactive effects. If the information were placed in a computer database, the search for that information could be performed in seconds rather than minutes. Each operator could perform searches by entering a question on a computer terminal. With a well-maintained computer database system, data should never be lost or misplaced, and would be available to more than one person at a time.

Ron's inventory system sounded like a good idea, but he had to pay a full-time worker to keep up with the system. This cost more money than he saved, and the system was still too slow. If the information for each sale could be placed automatically in a computer database at the time of sale, Ron could get a printout each day that showed him precisely what was sold, how much of the item was left in inventory, and automatically write up an order for new parts when the quantity slipped below a certain level.

Computers Can Do It Well

From the simple to the complex, the management of information is one of the most significant uses of a computer. Some people have dubbed America in the last part of this century an "Information Society". Businesses, government, and private citizens are consumers of a growing amount of information. In almost every job, and certainly in every profession, quick access to information is no longer just a convenience, it is a necessity. Those who lack information skills will be passed over in favor of those who have them.

DEFINING A DATABASE

A database is an organized collection of related information. The system for storing and retrieving information from the database is called a Database Management System (DBMS) or an Information Collection and Retrieval System. There are many database software packages available on computers. One of the most popular packages for microcomputers is dBASE III Plus. Originally marketed by Ashton-Tate as dBASE II, it was upgraded to dBASE III specifically to take advantage of the IBM PC family of computers, and was subsequently upgraded to dBASE III Plus to take advantage of PC Networks, where several computers can access the same information at once. (In 1988, Ashton-Tate introduced dBASE IV.) Other popular database programs include PFS:File, R:Base, PC-File, Paradox, and Reflex.

USER INTERFACES TO DATABASE PROGRAMS

There are four basic kinds of user interfaces to database software programs. They are *menu-driven, program-driven, command-driven* and *multiple interface* systems. These interfaces refer to how the program interacts with you, the user.

Menu-Driven Database Systems

A menu-driven database program prompts the user with menus on the computer screen. These menus contain the options that are available to you. You may choose the option to create a database, add new data, delete data, issue a report, and so forth. Menu-driven systems can be very easy to learn. However, because many options are preset, these systems can be less flexible than other systems. Even though menu systems tend to be easier to learn than other systems, once you learn them, you may be slowed down by having to answer question after question on a series of menus. However, for many uses a menu-driven database system can contain all the power you need. Figure 9.2 illustrates the opening screen from the popular database program PC-File from Buttonware. PC-File has a good menu-driven user interface, but it also gives the user some flexibility in "programming" what the database system will do.

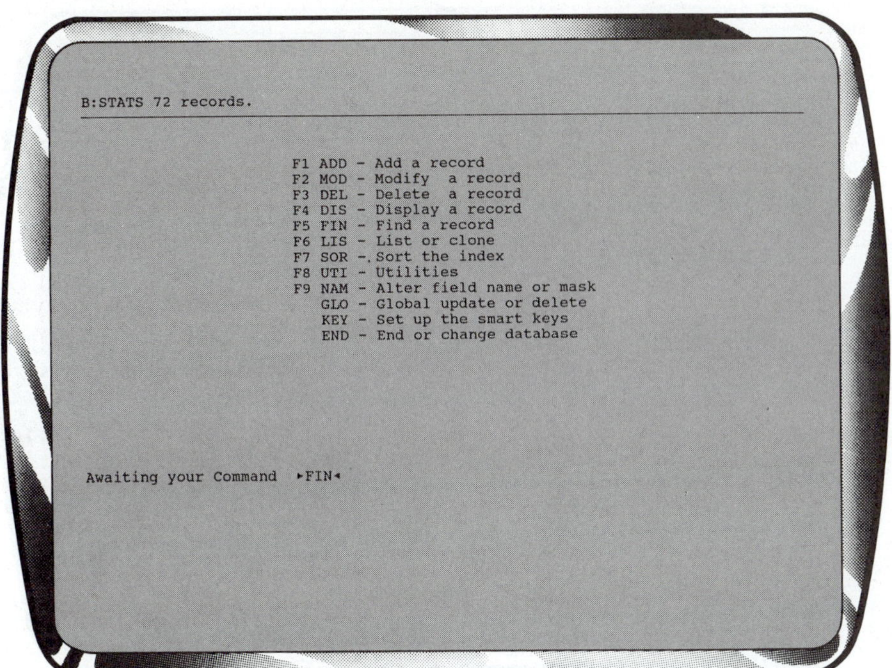

FIGURE 9.2.
Sample menu-driven database screen from PC-File III

Program-Driven Database Systems

A program-driven database system uses a programming-language approach to database management. This means that you, the user, must know a programming language in order to instruct the system to store and retrieve information. Although this is a very flexible approach to data management, it can be very difficult to learn, and usually takes a person with good programming skills to use it properly. Figure 9.3 illustrates a few lines of code from a database programming language.

Command-Driven Database Systems

Command-driven database systems operate much like PC-DOS. At a screen prompt, the user types in a command, and the database software program acts on the command to do some database task. This system is often less complicated than a strict programmed system, but the user must be proficient in the command language to properly create and manage the database. The dBASE III Plus system and other popular databases can be used in a command mode.

Multiple-Interface Database Systems

Many of the more popular database systems have integrated parts of the menu, programming, and command features into a single package. Beginners can operate in the menu-driven mode, while users with more experience may skip the menus in favor of the more direct command approach. Users needing maximum flexibility can use the database in its programming-language mode.

FIGURE 9.3.
Example of programming code from a program-driven database

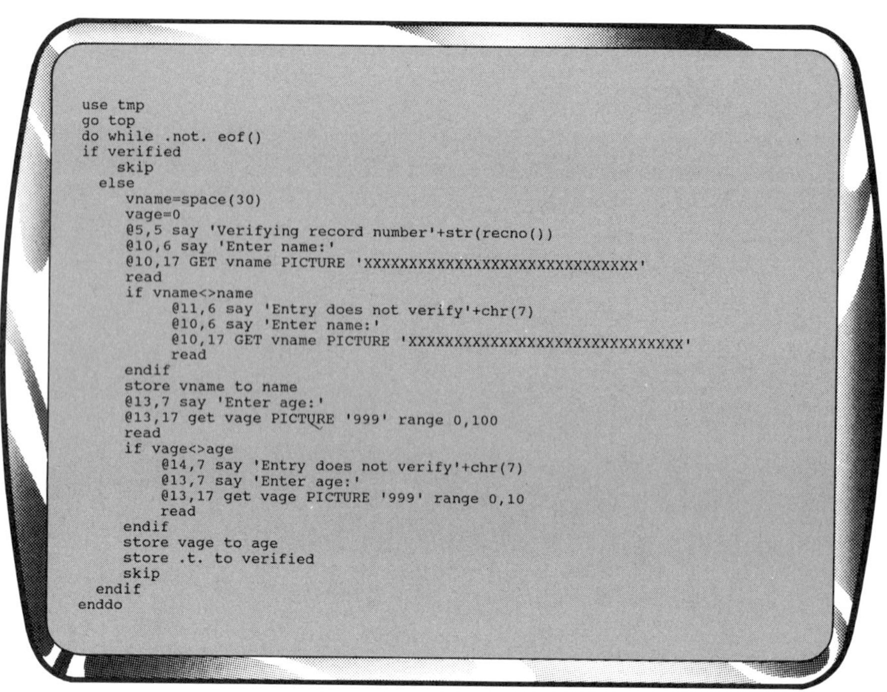

```
use tmp
go top
do while .not. eof()
if verified
    skip
  else
     vname=space(30)
     vage=0
     @5,5 say 'Verifying record number'+str(recno())
     @10,6 say 'Enter name:'
     @10,17 GET vname PICTURE 'XXXXXXXXXXXXXXXXXXXXXXXXXXXXXX'
     read
     if vname<>name
          @11,6 say 'Entry does not verify'+chr(7)
          @10,6 say 'Enter name:'
          @10,17 GET vname PICTURE 'XXXXXXXXXXXXXXXXXXXXXXXXXXXXXX'
          read
     endif
     store vname to name
     @13,7 say 'Enter age:'
     @13,17 get vage PICTURE '999' range 0,100
     read
     if vage<>age
         @14,7 say 'Entry does not verify'+chr(7)
         @13,7 say 'Enter age:'
         @13,17 get vage PICTURE '999' range 0,10
         read
     endif
     store vage to age
     store .t. to verified
     skip
  endif
enddo
```

CASE STUDY
dBASE III Plus

The dBASE III Plus system uses a multiple-interface approach. The menu system in dBASE III Plus is a program called "Assist", which allows the user to choose options from a number of menus. Figure 9.4 illustrates the main Assist menu in dBASE III Plus. In command mode, dBASE places a dot prompt "." on the screen, and the user requests certain actions by entering commands. Finally, dBASE III Plus programs can be written using the dBASE language, which can provide a tremendous amount of flexibility in manipulating and using the information stored in the database. These modes are not three different versions of dBASE; all three modes of dBASE are accessible from the same program.

CASE STUDY
Your Database Program

What type of user interface does your database program have? Does it use menus, commands, a programming language, or all of these?

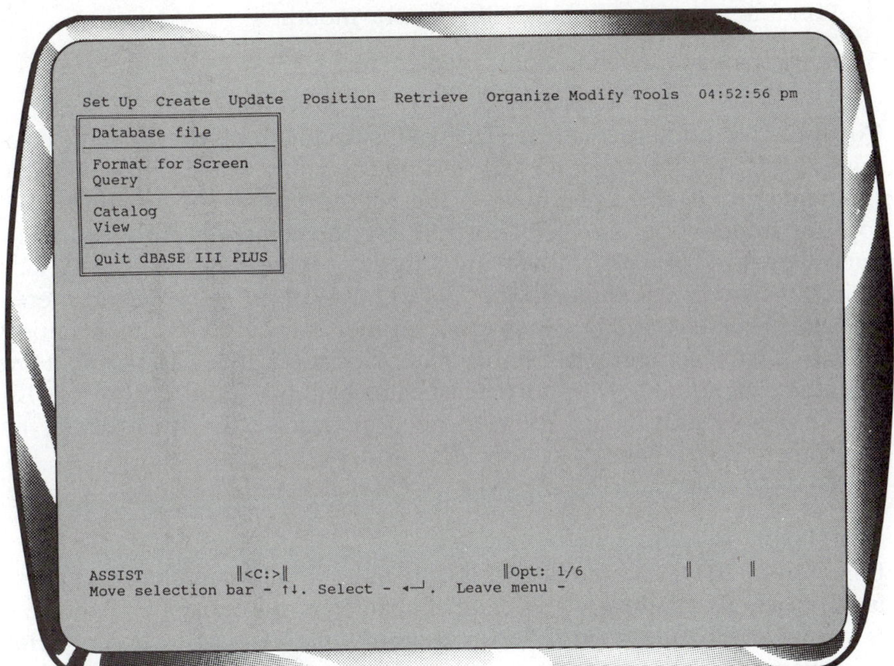

FIGURE 9.4.
Initial Assist menu from dBASE III Plus

PUTTING THE DATABASE TOGETHER

Although each database program uses somewhat different commands and procedures for putting information into the computer, there are some standard definitions and ideas that describe how a database is constructed. An example will be used to describe the makeup of a typical database. John Joiner is president of the campus Glider Club. He wants to keep track of the club's members and place the information on the computer. These are the items he wants to keep track of:

- Name
- Address
- Phone number
- Have they paid annual dues?
- Birthdate
- Number of hours flying

Before entering information into a computer database, John needs to decide how the information will be used. John wants to be able to use his database to help him with the following tasks:

1. Create a list of members and phone numbers alphabetized by name
2. Print out labels sorted by zip code, so he can get a discount on postage when he mails the club's newsletter "Gliding Light"
3. Find out which members have paid their dues

4. Print out a list of members' birthdays by month
5. Keep track of the flying hours by member.

The list of intended uses of a database helps decide the structure of the database; that is, what information will be stored and how. The database software program requires that a precise definition of the database be formulated before any information is actually entered into the computer. Although many database programs allow you to change aspects of your database after the fact, doing so may be very cumbersome. For example, if the full name is entered into the database as a single item ("John Joiner"), it would be almost impossible to ask the computer to list the names alphabetically by last name. How does the computer know where the last name begins? (It could, however, list them alphabetically by first name.) Since John wants a list by last name, the last name must be entered as a separate item in the database.

FIELDS, RECORDS AND FILES

Using dBASE III terminology, each single piece of information in a database is called a *field*. A field is a collection of characters, numeric or alphabetical. It may be a last name, a zip code, or other information. A collection of fields relating to the same person or entry is called a *record*. A group of related records is what makes up the *database file*. The relationship between fields, records, and files is illustrated in figure 9.5.

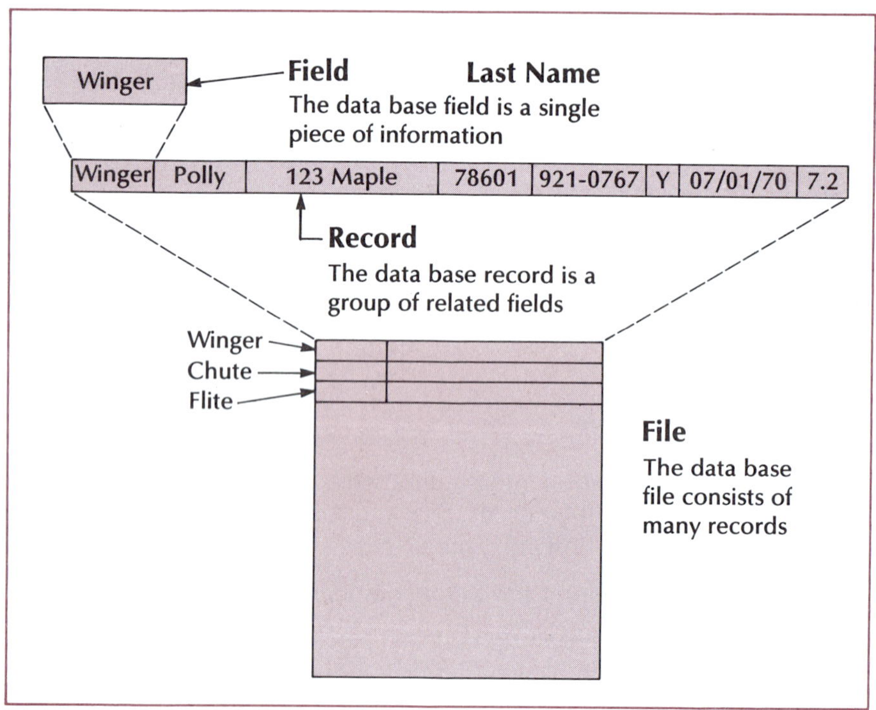

FIGURE 9.5. Relationship between fields, records, and files

Each field contains a piece of information and is given a short name that usually describes the proposed contents of the field. In most database programs, field names can be up to 10 characters in length. Blanks in field names are usually not allowed; however, the underline character "_" may be used as a separator in field names such as DATE_BORN, HOW_OLD, and so on. For the Glider Club database, John has decided to use the fields specified in figure 9.6, in order to do the tasks described above. In the particular example used here, since all members live in the same city and state, only the street address needs to be entered into the database. Since there are three zip codes for the city, zip code is included as a part of the information.

Once field names are defined, the database begins to take shape. However, there are some other components of the database structure that need to be decided upon. Each field must be described by what kind of information will be stored, and the maximum number of characters needed to store the information. The field LASTNAME, for example, will contain the member's last name. John has decided that he will allow a maximum *width* of 10 characters for the field LASTNAME, since that length will be long enough for the longest last name. John may be making a mistake here, since new members' last names may go over 10 characters. If this happens, the database structure will have to be altered. A field *type* must also be indicated. Figure 9.7 lists the five types usually supported in database programs:

Field Name	Description of Field
LASTNAME	Last name
FIRSTNAME	First name and middle initial
ADDRESS	Street address
ZIP	Zip code
PHONE	Phone number
DUES	Have yearly dues been paid?
BIRTHDATE	Date of birth
HOURS	Total flying time

FIGURE 9.6.
Description of the Glider Club Database

Field Type	Description	Allowed Width
Character/Text	Any keyboard character	1 to 254
Numeric	Numbers for mathematical calculations.	1 to 19
Date	Dates	8
Logical	Fields whose contents are Y, N, T, or F, which mean Yes, No, True, or False.	1
Memo	A long field which allows information such as long descriptions or explanations.	1 to 5,000

FIGURE 9.7.
Five Common Field Types

The entire process of thinking through the creation of a database is illustrated in a simple flow chart in figure 9.8. You must first decide what you want the database to be able to do—that is, what questions do you want to "ask" it, or what reports do you want generated? Next you must decide what specific pieces of information will be required to do the tasks you have in mind. Finally, you need to decide on the types, widths, and any decimal places for each field in the database. Logically progressing through this procedure can save time and frustration.

A Structure for the Glider Club Database

In the Glider Club database, most entries are of the character type. However, DUES is a logical type, BIRTHDATE is a date type, and HOURS is a numeric type. Although ZIP and PHONE contain numbers, they are treated as character types since they are never used for mathematical calculations, and in some cases (e.g., Canadian zip codes) contain non-numeric characters. A field is usually defined as numeric only if it will be used in a mathematical calculation. Date fields *could* be called character types. However, as will be discussed later, there are built-in functions in database programs that can manipulate dates to extract information or to calculate time between two dates. Date fields are automatically assigned an 8-character width in dBASE, using the date format "mm/dd/yy" which means month, day, and year. DUES could be a character field rather than a logical field. There are no set answers for what type you must use for every piece of information. The choice depends mostly on what you intend to do with the information once it is in the computer.

Like character fields, numeric fields must be assigned a maximum length. In the case of the HOURS field, records are kept with one decimal place. The maximum time any member has ever recorded is several hundred hours.

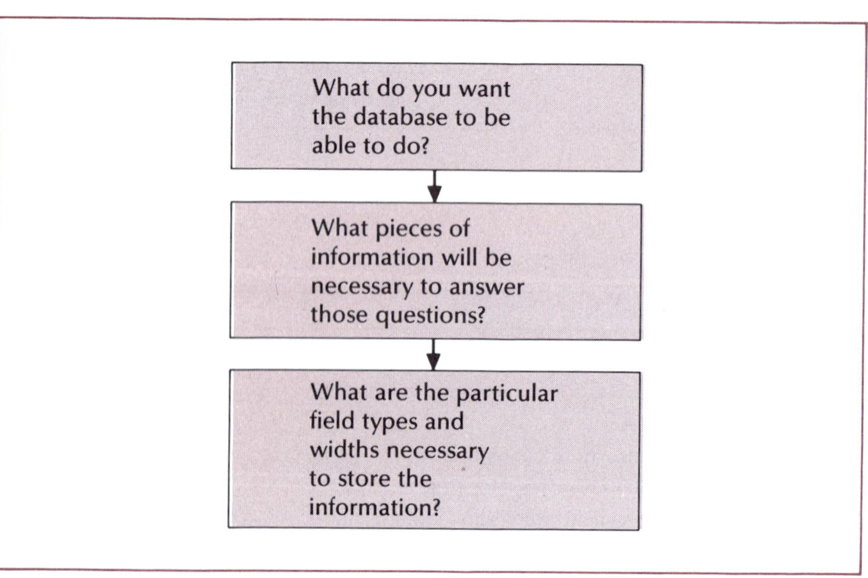

FIGURE 9.8. Flow chart describing the questions that need to be asked before creating a database

Field Name	Type	Width	Decimals
LASTNAME	Character/Text	10	
FIRSTNAME	Character/Text	10	
ADDRESS	Character/Text	10	
ZIP	Character/Text	5	
PHONE	Character/Text	8	
DUES	Logical	1	
BIRTHDATE	Date	8	
HOURS	Numeric	5	1

FIGURE 9.9.
The Glider Club database

Therefore, the database should allow numbers in the range of 0 to 999.9 hours. Notice that the number 999.9 takes up 5 characters, including 1 character after the decimal point. The final structure of the Glider Club database is summarized in figure 9.9.

CASE STUDY

Defining a structure in dBASE III Plus

The main components of John's Glider Club database have been described. However, to make it fit precisely into a dBASE III Plus database, there are some restrictions that must be observed.

1. A field name must begin with a letter (A–Z). Field names are always treated as all uppercase, even if you enter them using lowercase letters. (The actual *contents* of a field may have both upper- and lowercase characters.) Field names can only contain letters, numbers, and the underline character. Examples of legal field names would be A123, HOW_LONG, and QUEST_2. Illegal field names include HOW LONG (contains a blank), WHAT_% (contains an illegal character) and WHATISTHEDATE (too long).

2. Data types in dBASE III Plus include Character/Text, Numeric, Date, Logical, and Memo. Here are the limitations and specifications of each type:

   Character/Text Field: May have a width of up to 254 characters, and can contain any keyboard characters, including blanks and upper- and lowercase characters.

   Numeric Field: May have a length of up to 19 characters. Numeric fields may have decimal places designated. If no decimal places are designated, the number is expected to be an integer. In the definition of a numeric field, a decimal point and a negative sign each count as one character in the field width.

   Examples:

Number range	Width	Decimals
1 to 999.99	6	2
-999.99 to 999.99	7	2
1 to 999 (integers)	3	0

   Date Field: A date field always has a width of 8 characters, and dates are stored in the format mm/dd/yy. The date June 25, 1988 would be stored as "06/25/

88". Notice that if a month or date is less than 10, a zero must precede the number to make it have two digits.

Logical Field: A logical field has a width of 1, and stores only characters representing true/false or yes/no. Thus, the only entries for a logical field are T,F,Y, or N.

Memo Field: A memo field is used to store long blocks of characters, such as a sentence or paragraph. A memo field is of variable size, and may contain up to 5,000 characters.

3. The maximum number of records that dBASE III Plus can store is 1 billion. This is, of course, also restricted by the amount of space available on the computer disk.
4. The maximum number of fields that can be defined for one database is 128. However, later discussion will cover how related database files may be linked to provide increased capacity.
5. The maximum record size, not counting memo fields, is 4,000 characters per record. That is, if the lengths of all fields are added up, the total number of characters assigned to a record cannot exceed 4,000.

CREATION OF THE DATABASE ON THE COMPUTER

It is important to go through the process of deciding what the database should store and what kinds of reports will be required before actually sitting down at the computer and creating a database. Although many database programs allow you to make changes in the database structure after it has been created, it may waste a lot of time that could have been saved with a little planning. Also, if a database is ill-planned, information that is necessary to ask a question or generate a report may be left out of the original database, requiring costly research to get the additional information. Figure 9.10 is a database planning sheet that may be helpful in deciding on the correct structure for your database.

Once you are sure you have planned the contents of the database well, the actual creation of the database structure or skeleton takes only a few minutes. Using the Glider Club example, John started up his database program on the computer and chose the option to create a database. The computer prompted him for the name, type, width, and, where appropriate, the number of decimal places, for each field. On databases that use a strict programming approach, the task of creating a database structure would be more complicated.

Database planning sheet

Indicate what you want the database to do. Be specific about what questions you will ask the database, and what reports are to be generated.

Description of question or report	What fields are necessary to perform this task?

Summary of database fields

Field Name	Type	Width	Decimals	Field Name	Type	Width	Decimals

FIGURE 9.10.
Database planning sheet

CASE STUDY

Defining a Structure in Your Database Program

After defining the components of a database such as John's Glider Club file, you must specify to the database program how the information is to be stored. Most database programs have structures like the field names, data types, and field widths described for dBASE III. For your database program, answer these questions:

What are the limitations on naming a field? What characters can be used in the field name? What is the maximum length for a field name?

What data types are supported? (e.g., character, numeric, date, logical, memo, etc.) What are the definitions and limitations of each data type?

What is the maximum number of records that your database can store? What is the maximum number of fields in one record? What is the maximum number of characters in one record? Can databases be linked?

CASE STUDY

Creating a Database in dBASE III Plus

The dBASE III program may be used on either a floppy-based system or a hard-disk system. This discussion will use the "C > " prompt of a hard-disk system. If you are using a floppy-based system, your prompt will be "A > ". To begin dBASE III Plus from the DOS prompt, enter the command "DBASE":

```
C>DBASE
```

After a few seconds, the dBASE disclaimer will appear on the screen. Press ENTER, and the dBASE dot prompt will appear. The dot prompt is a period "." that indicates when you may enter a dBASE command. The cursor (blinking underline) will appear next to the dot, signifying that this is where characters will appear as they are typed from the keyboard. Figure 9.11 illustrates the initial dBASE III Plus screen.

If You Do Not Get the Dot Prompt

If you do not get the dot prompt, your version of dBASE may be set up to automatically enter the Assist menu. If the Assist menu appears, pressing the ESC key will place you in the command mode with the dot prompt.

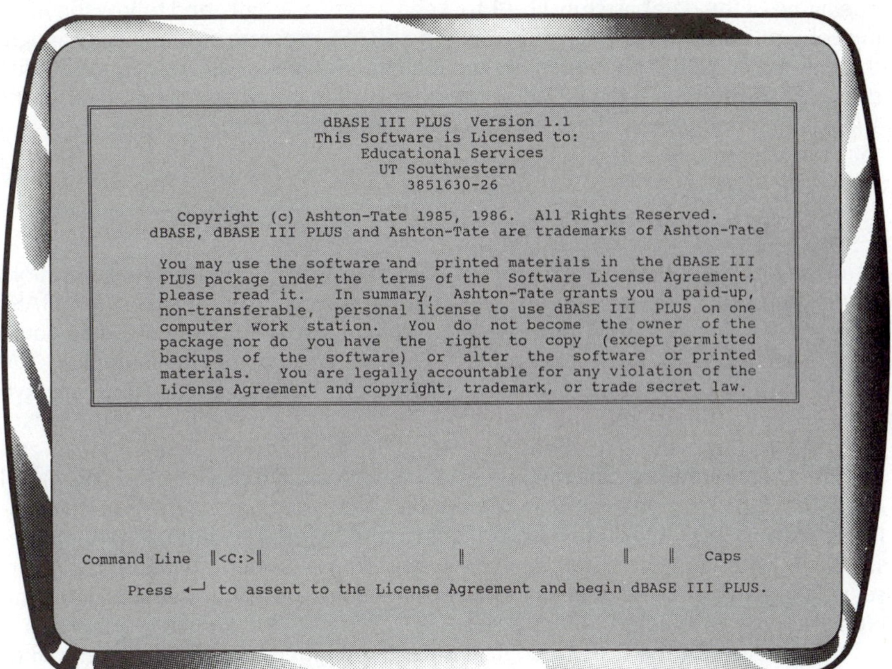

FIGURE 9.11.
Initial dBASE III Plus screen

Stopping dBASE III Plus

From the dBASE dot prompt, the command to return to DOS is "QUIT". *Never* turn off the computer while you are still in the dBASE program. Doing so may cause you to lose information on disk. Always return to the DOS prompt before turning the computer off.

If You Are Using a Floppy-Based System

On a hard-disk system the dBASE program and databases are usually on the C: disk. On a floppy-based system, you usually have the program disk in drive A:, and use the B: drive for the storage of your data. If you are using this system, you must tell dBASE that your database files will be on the B: drive. To do this, enter the following command at the dBASE dot prompt:

```
.SET DEFAULT TO B:
```

This tells dBASE that when you create or access a database, you want it to reside on the B: drive.

Creating a Database

The command to begin creating a dBASE database is "CREATE" plus the name of the database to create. For example, for John to create the database "GLIDER", he enters the command:

```
.CREATE GLIDER
```

The name of the database must be 1 to 8 characters in length, and follow the naming convention for a PC-DOS filename. The dBASE program automatically assigns the extension ".DBF" to the file, so the GLIDER database will appear on the disk directory as the file GLIDER.DBF. When the Create command is typed, a screen such as that in figure 9.12 appears on the computer monitor.

Entering Each Field Description

At the beginning of the creation process, the cursor is in the "Field Name" position. The name of the field may be entered in either lower- or uppercase. The dBASE program will always translate the field name to uppercase. For the first field name John enters "LASTNAME", and presses ENTER. The cursor then jumps to the "TYPE" position. The current (or default) type is Character/Text. There are two ways to select the desired field type. Pressing the space bar will cause the cursor to rotate through the selections Character/Text, Numeric, Date, Logical, and Memo. Alteratively, pressing the first letter of the desired type (T, N, D, L, or M) will cause that type to appear in the type position. Once the correct type is in the position, pressing ENTER will move the cursor to the "Width" position, where the desired field width may be entered. If you are entering a numeric-type field, the cursor will then move to the decimal position. (Decimals are only requested when the Numeric type is selected.)

When selecting the Date or Logical type, the width is automatically set to 8 or 1 respectively.

After entering the information for the LASTNAME field, dBASE prompts for field number 2, where John enters the information for the FIRSTNAME field, and so

FIGURE 9.12.
A dBASE III Plus Create screen

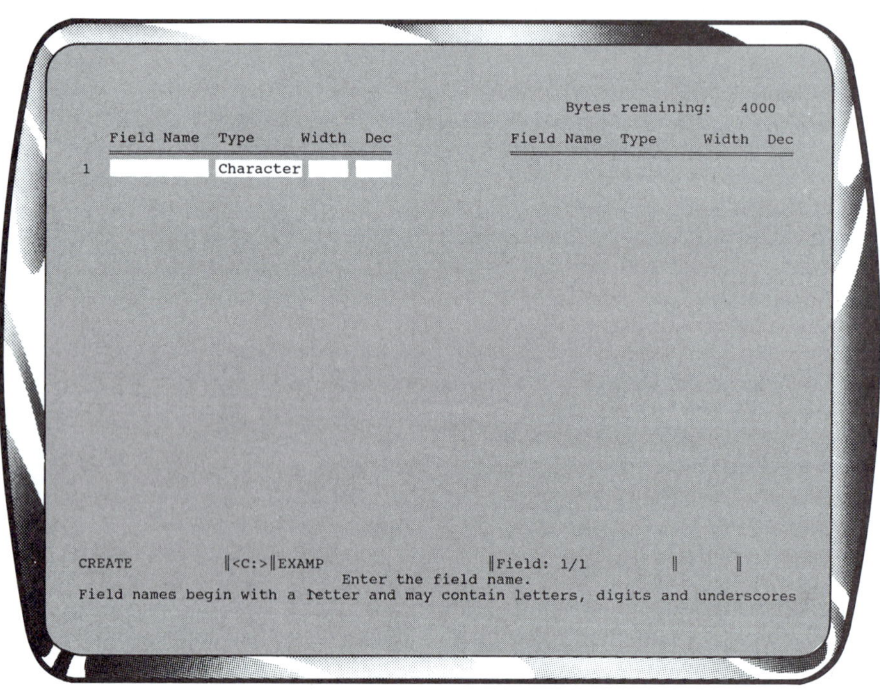

forth until all fields for the GLIDER database have been entered. Figure 9.13 illustrates the completed entry.

Ending the Creation Process

Even after all field definitions are entered, you may still make any necessary changes in the structure before saving it. Using the up and down arrow keys on the keyboard, you may move back to any of the reverse-video entry areas and make changes. Once you are satisfied with the information, make sure your cursor is on the last field (in this case field 11, where *no information* has been entered), and press the ENTER key. This tells dBASE that you are finished with the creation process. Then dBASE will prompt you with the message "Hit RETURN to continue—Any other key to resume". If you want to enter more fields or make changes, press any key other than the ENTER (RETURN) key. If you wish to end the creation process, press the ENTER key.

Another way to exit the creation procedure is by pressing CTRL-End (sometimes written ^END). That is, hold the CTRL key down, and then press the End key on the cursor keypad.

Once you end the creation process, dBASE prompts you with "Input records now? (Y/N)". You may press "Y" to begin data entry, or "N" to postpone data entry until later. John was ready to enter the first six members into the GLIDER database, and he pressed the "Y" key to begin the entry process. Note: If you accidentally get back to the dot prompt, the command to begin or resume the entry procedure is "APPEND".

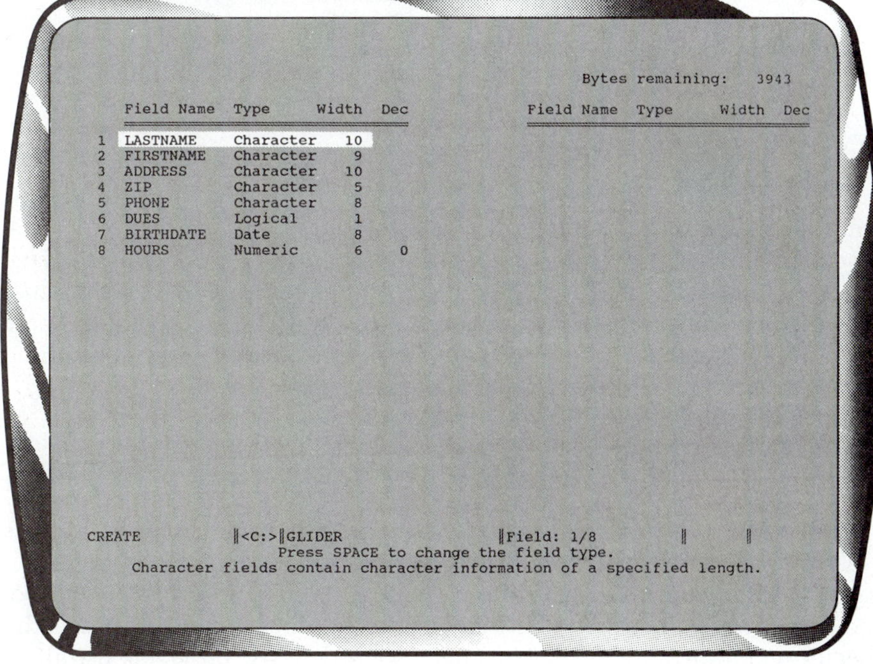

Bytes remaining: 3943
Field Name Type Width Dec
Field Name Type Width Dec
1 LASTNAME Character 10
2 FIRSTNAME Character 9
3 ADDRESS Character 10
4 ZIP Character 5
5 PHONE Character 8
6 DUES Logical 1
7 BIRTHDATE Date 8
8 HOURS Numeric 6 0
CREATE ‖<C:>‖GLIDER ‖Field: 1/8 ‖ ‖
Press SPACE to change the field type.
Character fields contain character information of a specified length.

FIGURE 9.13. Completed Create screen for GLIDER Database

CASE STUDY

Creating a Database in Your Database Program

The following questions relate to creating a new database in your database program:

How do you begin your database program from the DOS prompt?

A>

____

What is the procedure for telling your database program that you want to create a new database? How do you name the database? What is the procedure for entering the specifics of the database structure? (the field names, data types, etc.)

How do you end the creation of the database? Once the structure of the database is created, how do you tell the database that you are ready to begin data entry?

ENTERING INFORMATION INTO THE DATABASE

Once the database structure is defined, information is entered into the database by typing it into the computer. The information for the GLIDER database is shown in figure 9.14. One record at a time is entered. If the number of fields in a database is small, an entire record may be entered on a single screen. If the database has a large number of fields, screens may be required for each record.

Validity Checking Schemes

Most database programs will automatically perform some *validity checking* as information is entered. For example, you cannot enter "$45.00" into a numeric field, since the dollar sign is not a number. Invalid dates are refused, and entries other than Y, N, T, or F are refused in a logical field. Although the specific techniques are not covered here, some database programs also allow *range checking* of entry items. For example, in a study of teenagers, the age

LASTNAME	FIRSTNAME	ADDRESS	ZIP	PHONE	DUES	BIRTHDATE	HOURS
Winger	Polly	123 Maple	78601	921-0767	Y	07/01/70	7.2
Chute	Brian	432 Elm	78602	921-0098	N	12/31/69	10.5
Flite	Vanessa	112 Pecan	78601	921-7654	Y	08/02/70	100.0
Tailspin	Alex	122 Maple	78601	921-0776	Y	04/22/70	15.5
Arrow	Sean	231 Oak	78632	921-3222	N	03/02/70	0.0
Louis	Lindi	332 Pecan	78601	921-2122	Y	04/23/71	75.5

FIGURE 9.14.
Data for the GLIDER database

ıriable could be forced to be between 13 and 19. Any other age would be refused. Other types of validity checking which may be programmed into a database entry procedure include checks to compare zip codes with states, ranges for monetary entries, and amounts of medical doses. Another example of validity checking is to have information entered twice, by different persons, and then compare any differences. It is easy to understand that care must be taken to assure the correctness of information involving money, medical records, or other important data.

CASE STUDY

Data Entry in dBASE III Plus

To begin entry of data at the dBASE dot prompt, enter the command "APPEND". This will begin the procedure to enter new information in the database.

The dBASE program will display an "entry screen", which shows the names of each field and highlights the space, or number of characters, allocated for that information. An entry screen for the GLIDER database is illustrated in Figure 9.15.

Entry Techniques

During the entry of information, you may move the cursor anywhere in the highlighted entry region to make entries or corrections. Notice that when an entry fills an entire field, such as in the ZIP field, dBASE II Plus beeps, and moves the cursor to the next field without your having to press the ENTER key. Also, notice that in the BIRTHDATE field, the date is expected in the format mm/dd/yy, and the slashes "/" are already in the field. If a month or day is a single digit, such as 3 for March, it must be entered with a preceding zero ("03").

Ending the Entry Process

After entering the last record, you must tell dBASE that you are finished with the entry procedure. There are several ways to do this:

1. If your last record is still on the screen, end the entry procedure by typing CTRL—End (^End).
2. If dBASE III Plus has gone to the next blank record, you may exit by entering nothing in the first field, or by pressing the ESC key.

Pressing CTRL-End causes dBASE III Plus to save the entries *including* the one you are currently on, while ESC does *not* save the current record.

FIGURE 9.15.
Entry Screen for GLIDER database

CASE STUDY

Data Entry in Your Database Program

Describe the process for entering data in your database program. Are there any special ways it expects information to be entered in character-type fields? Numeric fields? Other fields? How do you end the entry process? Do you have to tell the program to save the data, or is it automatically saved to disk?

ONCE INFORMATION IS IN THE DATABASE

Creating a database and entering the data are only the first steps in using the power of a database program. In fact, there are many databases already created by other people or companies, that you can now access. But what can you do with all this information? How is it used? Generally, there are three major ways to use information in a database: queries, reports, and data extraction.

Queries: Asking the Database a Question

To *query* a database means to ask it questions. Some people call this a database *search*. For example, John wants to know who has not paid dues. Using a language that the database understands, John enters the command:

```
.DISPLAY ALL LASTNAME,FIRSTNAME FOR .NOT. DUES
```

This means, "Give me a list on the screen of names of those entries in the database for which the logical variable DUES is false." The result of this query in the GLIDER database is shown in figure 9.16.

There are numerous business and commercial databases that are available for searching. When a person uses a credit card, the card number is often entered into the computer by the salesperson. A search of the database of credit card holders takes place until that card number is found. Then it is determined if that person has enough credit available to complete the transaction. A number of public databases may be accessed by telephone. Financial databases may be searched to find information about a particular public company. Medical databases may be queried to get a list of all papers recently written on a particular subject. Legal databases provide lists of cases that pertain to a particular subject. Newspapers and journals from around the world are available by computer as soon as they are published in print. There are literally thousands of databases available, from airline schedules to zoological information, that are available through commercial services over a computer-telephone hookup.

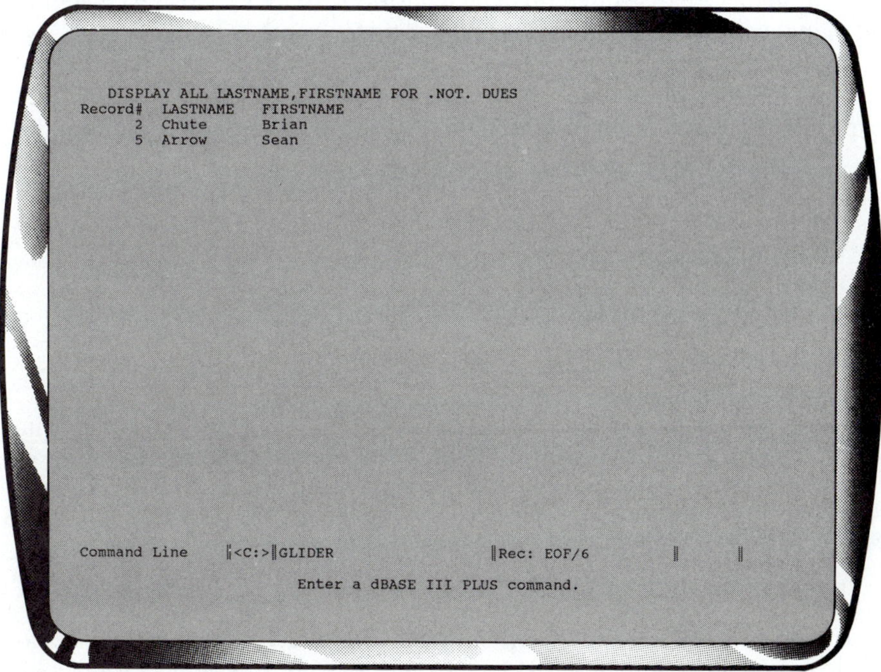

DISPLAY ALL LASTNAME,FIRSTNAME FOR .NOT. DUES
Record# LASTNAME FIRSTNAME
2 Chute Brian
5 Arrow Sean
Command Line
<C:> GLIDER
Rec: EOF/6
Enter a dBASE III PLUS command.

FIGURE 9.16.
Result of querying a database

Reports: Summary Information From the Database

Most private or business databases are used to produce reports. A simple report may be the listing of names and addresses from the club list. It may also be a series of reports that list all of the purchases of each customer, so that they may be sent an invoice at the end of each billing period. A store may print out a daily inventory list to determine if it is time to reorder particular items. A library may print out postcard "reports" that are sent to people with overdue books. The simplest printed report would be a listing of the database to the printer.

As you will learn, you may define a report procedure that will produce a listing based on some criteria you have previously defined. Some databases permit you to create a file of instructions for a standard type of report.

Data Extraction

Reports are usually listings or simple summaries of information. Many times the information in the database needs to be made available for other purposes: The data needs to be *extracted.* Perhaps someone wants to analyze the data with a statistics program to make forecasts, or to make decisions.

Organizations must make many kinds of decisions. Most decisions are based on information. The more accurate and up-to-date the information, the better the decision-making capabilities. Answers are needed to questions such as "Which version of the product is selling best in the test markets?" or "Which drug is being most effective in the study?" The raw information to make these decisions is often collected in a database system. Once the information is collected, it may either be analyzed by a program written in the database language, or it may be extracted from the database and analyzed using other programs. In cases like this, the database system is used as a data entry and management device, to prepare the data for another program.

For example, suppose you have entered data in your database. Now a programmer in the mail-order department wants a copy of the data in a form that his program will read. You might need to "export" the information from the fields NAME, ADDRESS, CITY, STATE, and ZIP to create a file in the form that the programmer needs. Most databases include a procedure for extracting this data and creating the file. The procedure for dBASE will be covered in the following chapter.

CASE STUDY

Examining the database in dBASE III Plus

Once a dBASE III Plus database has been created, and often before you "ask" the database questions, you will want to examine the database to verify that the information is stored correctly. As a command-oriented language, dBASE III Plus has a variety of commands that can be used to look at the database. To see the structure of a database, type in the following command at the dBASE dot prompt:

```
.DISPLAY STRUCTURE
```

The command "DISPLAY STRUCTURE" displays the structure of the current database in use on the screen. It shows the field name, type, and width of each field.

Figure 9.17 illustrates the use of this command.

In the command "DISPLAY STRUCTURE", the command "DISPLAY" is followed by the qualifier "STRUCTURE". There are other things dBASE III Plus can "DISPLAY". For example, to display the actual records now stored in the database, use the same Display command, but with a different qualifier, "ALL", meaning all records. To list the contents of the database to the computer screen, type:

```
DISPLAY ALL
```

The "DISPLAY ALL" command is illustrated in figure 9.18.

The Display command is quite flexible, having a number of types of qualifiers. A particularly useful form is the form "DISPLAY ⟨scope⟩," where ⟨scope⟩ describes which section of the database you wish to see. The scope "ALL", used before, means all of the records in the database. The scope "NEXT 10" means to display the next 10 records, starting from the record where the pointer is now. The command "DISPLAY 19" would display only record 19. These scope descriptions can also be used with other commands, such as List, Delete, and Recall (described later in this chapter).

The Difference Between Display and List

The command "LIST ALL" can used to display all records. List and Display are very similar commands. If a database is long, then the Display command will cause dBASE III Plus to pause when a screenful of information is displayed. A message "Press any key to continue..." will appear at the bottom of the screen. If the List command is used in place of the Display command, all records are listed without pause.

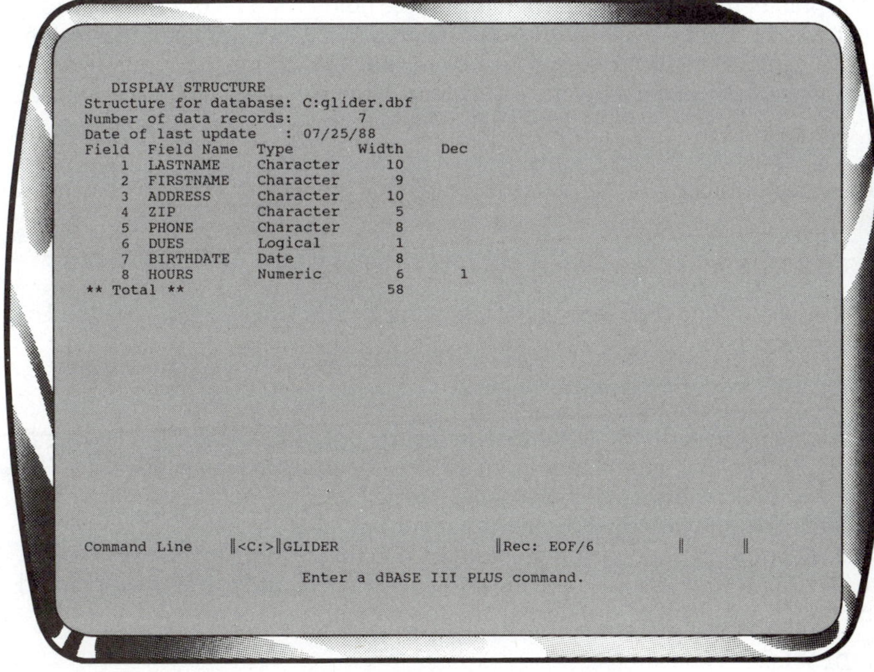

DISPLAY STRUCTURE
Structure for database: C:glider.dbf
Number of data records: 7
Date of last update : 07/25/88
Field Field Name Type Width Dec
1 LASTNAME Character 10
2 FIRSTNAME Character 9
3 ADDRESS Character 10
4 ZIP Character 5
5 PHONE Character 8
6 DUES Logical 1
7 BIRTHDATE Date 8
8 HOURS Numeric 6 1
** Total ** 58
Command Line ‖<C:>‖GLIDER ‖Rec: EOF/6 ‖ ‖
Enter a dBASE III PLUS command.

FIGURE 9.17
The Display Structure command

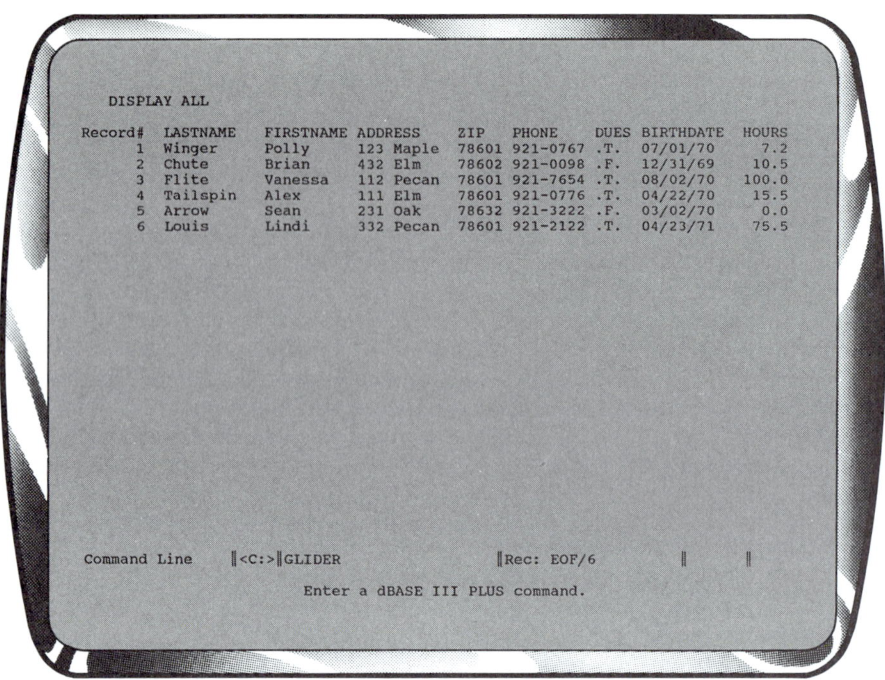

DISPLAY ALL
Record# LASTNAME FIRSTNAME ADDRESS ZIP PHONE DUES BIRTHDATE HOURS
1 Winger Polly 123 Maple 78601 921-0767 .T. 07/01/70 7.2
2 Chute Brian 432 Elm 78602 921-0098 .F. 12/31/69 10.5
3 Flite Vanessa 112 Pecan 78601 921-7654 .T. 08/02/70 100.0
4 Tailspin Alex 111 Elm 78601 921-0776 .T. 04/22/70 15.5
5 Arrow Sean 231 Oak 78632 921-3222 .F. 03/02/70 0.0
6 Louis Lindi 332 Pecan 78601 921-2122 .T. 04/23/71 75.5
Command Line ‖<C:>‖GLIDER ‖Rec: EOF/6 ‖ ‖
Enter a dBASE III PLUS command.

FIGURE 9.18. The Display All command

Searching a Database

Whenever you use a dBASE III Plus database, dBASE keeps a *pointer* to the record it is currently on. When you "ask" dBASE a question about the database, it begins searching at the record where the pointer is currently pointing, and moves down the database. As you move up and down the database looking at records, the dBASE pointer moves with you. Therefore, if the pointer is at record 3, and you ask dBASE to search for a person whose last name is Winger, it will not find a match, since Winger is at record 1. Therefore, before you perform a search, you will probably want to make sure the pointer is at the top of the database with the command:

```
GO TOP
```

The Locate command is then used to search for the desired entry. The general form is

```
.LOCATE FOR [fieldname]=[desired item]
```

For example, to find the record containing the LASTNAME "Arrow", use the Locate command:

```
.LOCATE FOR LASTNAME=''Arrow''
```

This command asks dBASE to locate the first record that contains the last name "Arrow". Notice that upper- and lowercase are important in typing the name. The name "ARROW" will not match the name "Arrow" because of the case difference. If a match is found, dBASE indicates the record number that was found with the notice "Record = 5", and the pointer is moved to that record, but dBASE does not actually display the record. To see the contents of the record that is being pointed to by the dBASE pointer, you display the record with the command:

```
DISPLAY
```

The Display command without any qualifier displays the record currently being pointed to.

What would happen if you entered these commands?

```
.GO TOP
.LOCATE FOR LASTNAME=''ARROW''
```

The record would not be found, since "Arrow" does not match "ARROW", and dBASE gives the message "End of LOCATE Scope." To solve this problem, you can use the UPPER () function. (Functions will be covered in the next chapter.) Try these commands:

```
.GO TOP
.LOCATE FOR UPPER(LASTNAME)=''ARROW''
```

This tells dBASE III Plus to translate the contents of the LASTNAME field to uppercase before doing the comparison. This does not affect the actual contents of the field; the uppercase conversion is only for the comparison. These searches are illustrated in figure 9.19.

Ending dBASE III Plus

Once all the information has been entered in the database, the database file needs to be saved to disk. In dBASE III Plus, all files are saved when the program ends. Therefore, entering the Quit command returns you to DOS, and insures that the information in the database is saved on disk. (Turning off the computer while still in dBASE III Plus can mean that the information may be lost. *Always* return to the DOS prompt before turning off the computer.)

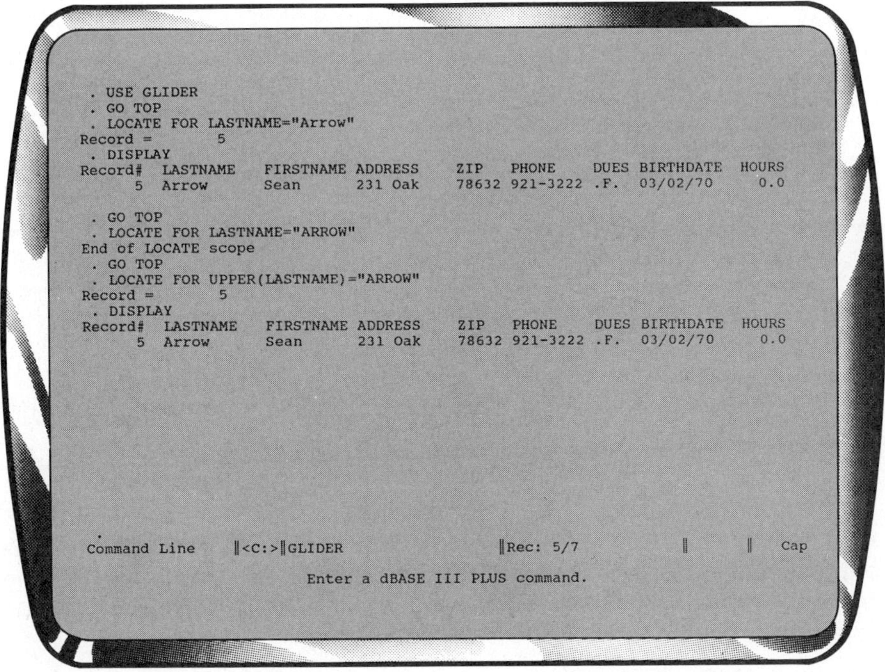

. USE GLIDER
. GO TOP
. LOCATE FOR LASTNAME="Arrow"
Record = 5
. DISPLAY
Record# LASTNAME FIRSTNAME ADDRESS ZIP PHONE DUES BIRTHDATE HOURS
5 Arrow Sean 231 Oak 78632 921-3222 .F. 03/02/70 0.0
. GO TOP
. LOCATE FOR LASTNAME="ARROW"
End of LOCATE scope
. GO TOP
. LOCATE FOR UPPER(LASTNAME)="ARROW"
Record = 5
. DISPLAY
Record# LASTNAME FIRSTNAME ADDRESS ZIP PHONE DUES BIRTHDATE HOURS
5 Arrow Sean 231 Oak 78632 921-3222 .F. 03/02/70 0.0
Command Line ‖<C:>‖GLIDER ‖Rec: 5/7 ‖ ‖ Cap
Enter a dBASE III PLUS command.

FIGURE 9.19.
Examples of the Locate command.

CASE STUDY

Examining the Database in Your Database Program

Once a database has been created, there are usually a variety of ways to examine the information in the database. In your database program, how do you display the structure of the database? (that is, the components such as field names, types, etc., that make up the database)

How do you list the information in the database to the computer screen? Is there more than one way to do this?

Can you search the database for a particular record? For example, how would you search the database for the record that contained the person whose last name was Arrow?

How do you end your database program?

ON-LINE HELP

Most database programs have on-line help facilities. That is, if you forget the particular way to ask the database a question, you can use the Help command or Help key to get information without having to go to the manual

CASE STUDY

The dBASE III Plus Help Facility

The dBASE III Plus on-line help facility uses function key F1 on IBM PC types of computers. Alternately, you may enter the command "HELP", followed by the particular command that you want information about. For instance, to find out about the Display command, enter

```
.HELP DISPLAY
```

The dBASE program responds with a screen of information, including the syntax of the command and a description, as illustrated in figure 9.20. To get back to the dot prompt, press the ESC key, or you can enter another command to see another Help screen. Items in brackets "[]" are optional. Thus, the minimum command is "DISPLAY" with no qualifiers. The options are explained below the syntax line.

CASE STUDY

The Help Facility in Your Database Program

Does your database program have an on-line help facility? That is, can you display information about how to use the program on the screen while you are running the program? If so, explain how it is done.

```
                                                        DISPLAY

                              DISPLAY

Syntax      :  DISPLAY [<scope>] [<expression list>] [FOR <condition>]
                       [WHILE <condition>] [OFF] [TO PRINT]

Description :  Lists the current record.  Use DISPLAY with
               a scope and an expression list to see selected fields or
               a combination of fields.  Use the FOR and WHILE conditions
               to display specific contents of the records.  Use TO PRINT
               to get a hard copy of the list, and use OFF to suppress
               the record numbers.  DISPLAY lists with periodic pauses.

HELP           ║<C:>║GLIDER               ║Rec: 5/7          ║     ║  Cap
 Previous screen - PgUp. Previous menu - F10. Exit with Esc or enter a command.
                ENTER >
```

FIGURE 9.20.
The Help screen for the Display command

ADDING, EDITING, AND DELETING RECORDS

Most databases are never finished. Information is always being added, changed, or deleted. The Gliding Club adds new members, and others leave. In business, personnel records change, credit information is updated, and inventory is hopefully turning over at a rapid pace. In light of these situations, it is important to be able to make these changes in the database.

CASE STUDY

Adding Editing, and Deleting Records in dBASE III Plus

John had some changes to make in the Glider Club database. A new member had been recruited, one member had resigned, and an address had changed for another member.

Adding Records to a Database

The command to tell dBASE III Plus to append (add) records to the GLIDER database is:

```
.APPEND
```

This will cause dBASE III Plus to display an empty record, which we can use to enter new data, just like when we entered the original data. John entered the following information on the new member:

LASTNAME	Flapper
FIRSTNAME	Vivian
ADDRESS	324 Peach
ZIP	78632
PHONE	921-0094
DUES	Y
BIRTHDATE	08/31/71
HOURS	0

Once this information is entered, another blank record is displayed so that more information can be entered. In this case, only one additional record needed to be added to the database. To end the append/entry procedure, with a blank record on the screen, press the ESC key. If a record with information is still on the screen, end the procedure with ^End.

Editing a Record

Alex Tailspin moved to a new address, and John had to edit his record to reflect the change. Alex is record number 4 in the GLIDER database, and the command to change information in that record is

```
.EDIT 4
```

This causes dBASE III Plus to display the entry screen containing the data from record number 4. It looks just like the original entry screen, but with current information appearing in the reverse-video areas. Using the cursor movement keys, John moved to the ADDRESS field and changed the old address to 111 Elm. To edit nearby records, you may use the PgUp and PgDn keys to locate another record to edit. End Edit with ^End. The edit screen for Alex is illustrated in figure 9.21.

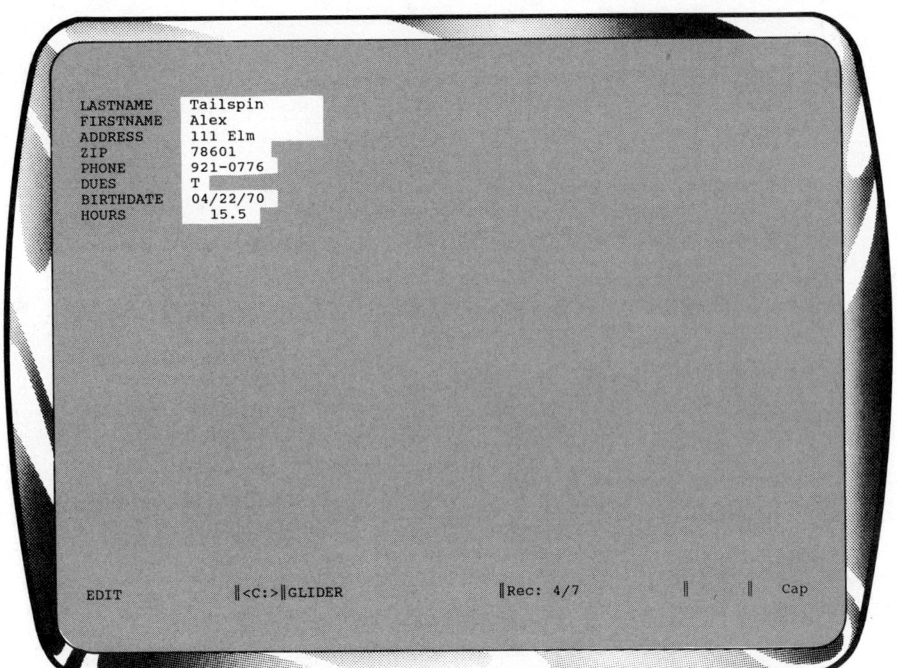

FIGURE 9.21.
Editing a record

Another way to edit is with the Browse command. To enter the Browse mode, place the pointer where you want the Browse to begin, and then enter "BROWSE":

```
.GO TOP
.BROWSE
```

This displays a screenful of records, one to a line. Using the cursor arrows, you may move to the location you wish, making changes in the database. If the total length of the record is too long for the screen, use ^right-arrow and ^left-arrow to move the window to the right or left. The Browse screen is illustrated in Figure 9.22.

Deleting Records

John's final task was to remove Lindi Louis from the Glider Club's roster. This can be done by deleting the record from the database. Getting rid of a record permanently is a two-step procedure. First, the record is marked for deletion; then the database is "packed" to eliminate the deleted records. Until the pack procedure is done, deleted records may be recalled. The dBASE III Plus program has several ways of marking a record for deletion. In the Edit or Browse mode, entering a CTRL-U (^U) marks the current record for deletion. The command

```
.DELETE RECORD 6
```

marks record 6 for deletion. When a "DISPLAY ALL" or "LIST" command is performed, deleted records still appear in the database, but are preceded by an asterisk "*", which signifies that those records are marked for deletion. This is illustrated in figure 9.23.

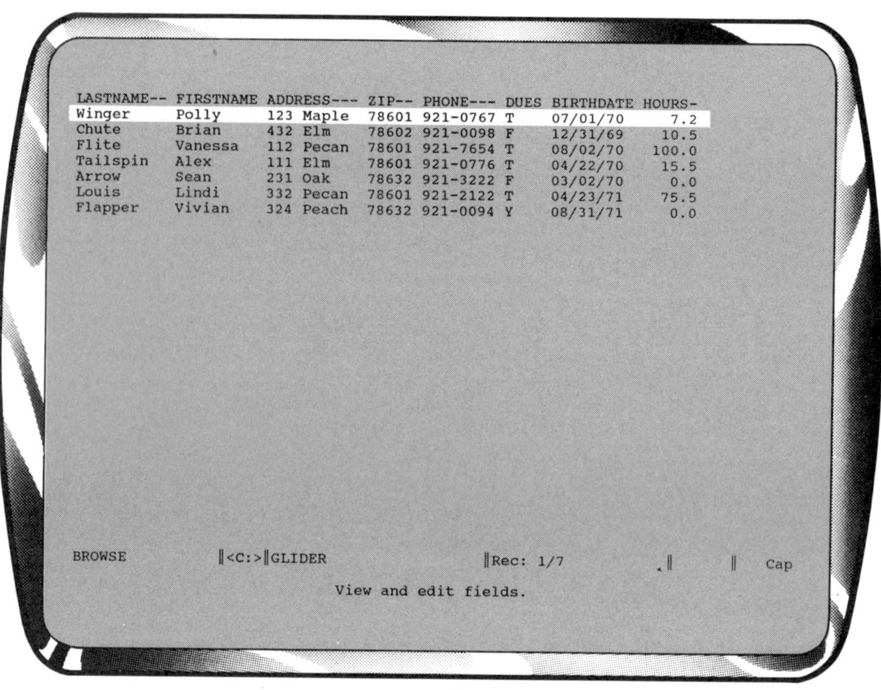

LASTNAME-- FIRSTNAME ADDRESS--- ZIP-- PHONE--- DUES BIRTHDATE HOURS-
Winger Polly 123 Maple 78601 921-0767 T 07/01/70 7.2
Chute Brian 432 Elm 78602 921-0098 F 12/31/69 10.5
Flite Vanessa 112 Pecan 78601 921-7654 T 08/02/70 100.0
Tailspin Alex 111 Elm 78601 921-0776 T 04/22/70 15.5
Arrow Sean 231 Oak 78632 921-3222 F 03/02/70 0.0
Louis Lindi 332 Pecan 78601 921-2122 T 04/23/71 75.5
Flapper Vivian 324 Peach 78632 921-0094 Y 08/31/71 0.0
BROWSE ‖<C:>‖GLIDER ‖Rec: 1/7 ‖ ‖ Cap
View and edit fields.

FIGURE 9.22.
A Browse Screen

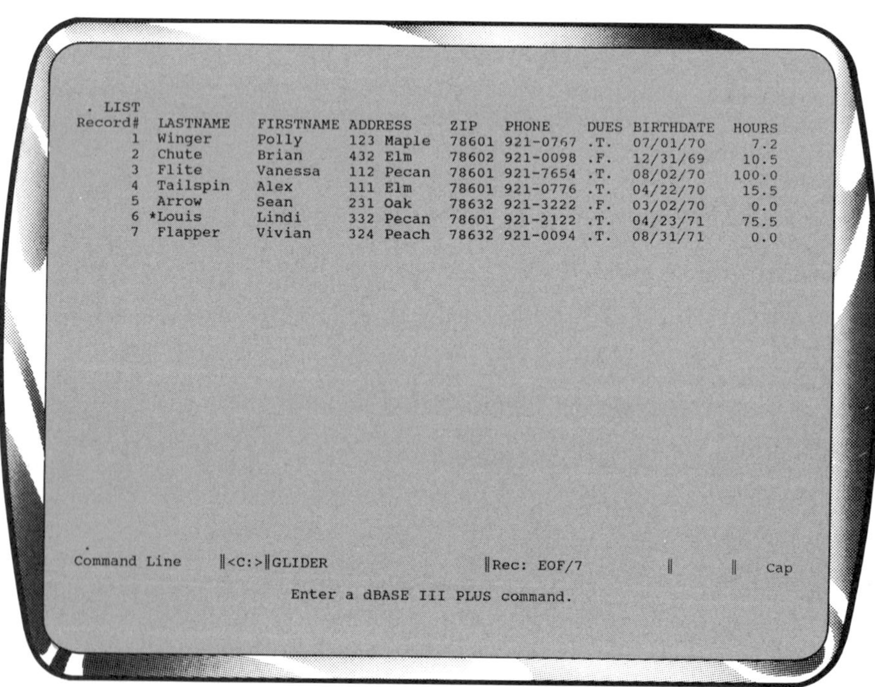

. LIST
Record# LASTNAME FIRSTNAME ADDRESS ZIP PHONE DUES BIRTHDATE HOURS
1 Winger Polly 123 Maple 78601 921-0767 .T. 07/01/70 7.2
2 Chute Brian 432 Elm 78602 921-0098 .F. 12/31/69 10.5
3 Flite Vanessa 112 Pecan 78601 921-7654 .T. 08/02/70 100.0
4 Tailspin Alex 111 Elm 78601 921-0776 .T. 04/22/70 15.5
5 Arrow Sean 231 Oak 78632 921-3222 .F. 03/02/70 0.0
6 *Louis Lindi 332 Pecan 78601 921-2122 .T. 04/23/71 75.5
7 Flapper Vivian 324 Peach 78632 921-0094 .T. 08/31/71 0.0
.
Command Line ‖<C:>‖GLIDER ‖Rec: EOF/7 ‖ ‖ Cap
Enter a dBASE III PLUS command.

FIGURE 9.23.
A display with a deleted record

To cause the deleted records NOT to appear in a List, use the command:

```
.SET DELETED ON
```

Now, a "DISPLAY ALL" or "LIST" does not show any deleted records. However, these records will again show up after using the command

```
.SET DELETED OFF
```

The Delete command may be used to temporarily get rid of records that may be recovered at a later date. To recover records that have been marked for deletion use the Recall command. For example:

```
.RECALL ALL
```

or

```
.RECALL RECORD 6
```

"Set Delete Off" must be active for the Recall command to work. To permanently delete the records so they are no longer recoverable, use the command

```
.PACK
```

The Pack command gets rid of all records marked for deletion. Notice that it may also change record numbers. In the GLIDER database, Lindi Louis was record number 6, and Vivian Flapper was number 7. After record 6 was deleted and packed, Flapper became record 6.

CASE STUDY

Adding, Editing, and Deleting Records in Your Database Program

Once information is in the database, you often need to make changes. For example, John needs to remove one member and add another. How can you add a new record to the database?

How can you edit the contents of a record that has already been entered into the database?

How can you delete records from the database? Is it possible to "mark records for deletion", and temporarily remove them from any reports, and then recover them later? If so, how can you get rid of deleted records permanently?

SUMMARY

This chapter presented reasons for using computers to store and retrieve information. The dBASE III Plus software package was used to illustrate how a database is designed, created, searched, and modified.

Several dBASE III Plus commands were introduced in this chapter, and are listed briefly here. In this list, items in < > are to be filled in according to the particular need. For example <filename> means that a filename should appear in that location in the command.

APPEND: Add new records to the database.

BROWSE: Display records one per line in edit mode.

CREATE <filename>: Begin the creation of a database.

DELETE <scope>: Mark records for deletion.

DISPLAY <scope>: Display records to the screen, pausing after each screenful.

EDIT <record number>: Begin editing the given record.

GO TOP: Move pointer to the first record of the database.

HELP <command>: Display Help screen for given command.

LIST <scope>: List records to screen without pause.

LOCATE <condition>: Search for record that meets condition.

PACK: Get rid of all records marked for deletion.

RECALL <scope>: Recall records that were marked for deletion.

SET DELETE <ON/OFF>: Cause List and Display to ignore or display deleted records.

QUIT: Exit dBASE III Plus and return to DOS prompt, saving the database file.

KEY TERMS

Define the following terms in your own words:

Database

Database management system (DBMS)

Field

Record

File

Database structure

Field type

Query

Report

Search

QUESTIONS

1. A ______________________ is a mechanism for storing and retrieving information in an organized manner.
2. The four basic user interfaces for database software are ______________, ______________, ______________, and ______________.
3. The three types of user interface available in dBASE III Plus include ______________, ______________ and ______________.
4. Before entering information into a computer database, you need to ______________.
5. Each separate item or entry in a database is called a ______________.
6. A collection of fields relating to the same entry is called a ______________.
7. A group of related records is referred to as a ______________.
8. The five types of fields supported by most database programs include ______________, ______________, ______________, ______________ and ______________.
9. The command used to start dBASE III Plus is ______________.
10. The command used to tell dBASE you want to start a new database is ______________.
11. To end record entry while the last record is still on the screen, press ______________.
12. To ______________ a database means to ask it questions.
13. To show all of the database records on the screen type ______________, ______________, or ______________.
14. To exit a dBASE session type ______________.
15. The command used to add records to a database is ______________.
16. To make changes to a particular record in the database type ______________.
17. The two commands necessary to delete a database record during BROWSE or EDIT are ______________ and ______________.
18. To position the record pointer at the beginning of a database file, type ______________.
19. The ________ key can be used to end record entry when dBASE has gone to the next blank record.

20. The __________ command can be used to search for a record that meets a specific condition.

Write a short answer in your own words for each question.

21. Describe three applications for a database management system.
22. Explain the difference between the terms *field, record,* and *file.*
23. What is meant by the term "command-driven" user interface? How does this differ from a menu-driven interface? A program-driven interface?
24. What are the questions to ask when preparing to create a new database? Put them in the correct order.
25. Describe the five different kinds of field types and give the limitations for each in the dBASE III Plus program.
26. Which type would the following fields probably be, and why?

AGE, DATE_BORN, ADDRESS, WEIGHT, ZIPCODE, SBP (Systolic Blood Pressure), SSNO (Social Security Number), DECEASED (Yes/No answer), ROOM_NO, SCORE, PAID (True/False answer).

27. What is validity checking? Give examples of when validity checking would be important in data entry.
28. Why should you always type "QUIT" when ending a dBASE III Plus session?
29. Under what conditions would you use CTRL-End or Esc to end a record entry session?
30. Describe the type of information provided on a dBASE III Plus Help screen.
31. What is the difference between marking a record for deletion and packing the database?
32. Matching: Fill in the correct letter for each operation.

____ Begin the creation of a database	A. APPEND
____ Show records on screen without pause	B. BROWSE
____ Mark records for deletion	C. CREATE <filename>
____ Move pointer to beginning of database	D. DELETE
____ Exit dBASE III Plus	E. DISPLAY
____ Add records to the database	F. EDIT
____ Show records on the screen with pause	G. GO TOP
____ Show records on the screen one per line in edit mode	H. LIST
____ Call up a single record to make changes	I. PACK
____ Delete marked records	J. QUIT

LABORATORY EXERCISES

Lab Exercise 1. In this exercise, you will use dBASE III Plus to create a database called ACCNTS. You will also enter records into the database, display the records on the screen, edit the information in several records, print the database, and exit dBASE. This ACCNTS database will also be used in chapter 10.

1. Use the Create command to create a database called ACCNTS which has the following structure:

Field Name	Type	Width	Decimals
LASTNAME	Character/Text	10	
FIRSTNAME	Character/Text	10	
AMTDUE	Numeric	6	2
PASTDUE	Logical	1	

2. Answer 'N' to the "Enter data now" prompt and examine the structure of the database using the "DISPLAY STRUCTURE" command. If the structure does not look like what is displayed above, ask your instructor to help you change the structure of the database using the "MODIFY STRUCTURE" command (introduced in chapter 10).
3. Enter the following data into the database using the Append command.

LASTNAME	FIRSTNAME	AMTDUE	PASTDUE
Skinner	Albert	397.33	N
Cash	Betsy	111.12	Y
Dollar	Diller	987.63	Y
Nichols	Penny	555.15	N
Bitts	Fred	100.25	Y
Late	Lynda	732.00	Y
Geators	Tom	34.33	N

4. Display the database on the screen using either List or Display.
5. Using Edit, change Betsy Cash's amount due to $30.54, and change her past due status to "N".
6. Using Browse, change Lynda Late's amount due to $32.00.
7. Using the Append command, enter the new customer "Harvey Bucks". Harvey owes $121.00 and is not past due.
8. Diller Dollar has paid off the account, so use the Delete command and the Pack command to eliminate the record from the database.
9. Display the customers' last names, first names, and amounts due if their record is past due.

   Hint: Look at the example under the section on "Querying a Database."
10. Print a copy of the records in the database using the following command:

    .DISPLAY ALL TO PRINT

    Note: First make sure the printer is connected and on line.
11. Exit dBASE using the Quit command.
12. Use the DOS Dir command and look for the ACCNTS.DBF file in the directory listing.

Lab Exercise 2. In this exercise, you will use dBASE III Plus to create a database called GLIDER. You will also enter records into the database, display the records on the screen, delete a record, and print the records to the printer. This GLIDER database will also be used in chapter 10.

1. Use the command to create a database called GLIDER which has the following structure:

Field Name	Type	Width	Decimals
LASTNAME	Character/Text	10	
FIRSTNAME	Character/Text	10	
ADDRESS	Character/Text	12	
ZIP	Character/Text	5	
PHONE	Character/Text	8	
DUES	Logical	1	
BIRTHDATE	Date	8	
HOURS	Numeric	5	1

2. Answer 'N' to the "Enter data now" prompt and examine the structure of the database using the "DISPLAY STRUCTURE" command. If the structure does not look like what is displayed above, ask your instructor to help you change the structure of the database using the "MODIFY STRUCTURE" command (introduced in chapter 10).
3. Enter the following data into the database using the Append command.

LASTNAME	FIRSTNAME	ADDRESS	ZIP	PHONE	DUES	BIRTHDATE	HOURS
Winger	Polly	123 Maple	78601	921-0767	Y	07/01/70	7.2
Chute	Brian	432 Elm	78602	921-0098	N	12/31/69	10.5
Mayday	Ellen	167 Ash	78603	921-9989	Y	11/12/65	33.0
Flite	Vanessa	112 Pecan	78601	921-7654	Y	08/02/70	100.0
Tailspin	Alex	122 Maple	78601	921-0776	Y	04/22/70	15.5
Arrow	Sean	231 Oak	78632	921-3222	N	03/02/70	0.0
Louis	Lindi	332 Pecan	78601	921-2122	Y	04/23/71	75.5

4. Use the "DISPLAY ALL" command to show all the records on the screen. Edit any incorrect entries using the Edit command.
5. Use the Browse command to display the database and mark the following records for deletion: Ellen Mayday, Alex Tailspin, and Lindi Louis.
6. Use the Recall command to unmark the records of Alex Tailspin and Lindi Louis.
7. PACK the database. (The database should now have six records.)
8. Print a copy of the records in the database to the printer using the following command:

   .DISPLAY ALL TO PRINT

   Note: First make sure the printer is connected and is on line.
9. Exit dBASE using the Quit command.
10. Use the Dir command and look for the GLIDER.DBF file in the directory listing.

Lab Exercise 3. Pick one or more of the following possible databases, and fill out a database planning sheet (figure 9.10):

- Mailing list for a church
- List of relatives, friends, and associates

- Customer list
- Stock market investments
- Automobile dealer inventory
- Real estate properties for sale
- Stamp or coin collection
- Recipe file
- Inventory of personal items of worth
- Personal checkbook information
- Others...

CHAPTER 10

Database Management Systems, Part II

CHAPTER OVERVIEW. This chapter continues the discussion of database management systems on personal computers. Topics covered include how to use previously created database files, how to set up the database program environment, more detailed information on conditional searches of the database, sorting and indexing, modifying the structure of the database, functions, and creating reports.

CHAPTER OBJECTIVES

Upon completion of this chapter, you will be able to:

- Use databases that have been previously created.
- Customize the database environment.
- Perform conditional searches and lists using logical and relational operators.
- Sort a database.
- Create an index to a database.
- Modify the structure of a database.
- Use database functions.
- Create simple output reports.

MAKING USE OF THE DATABASE

In the previous chapter a database for the college Glider Club was created on the computer. On any computer, and with any database program, there may be many databases that are accessible by a database program. For example, Ron's Auto Supply keeps not only an inventory database, but also a database on regular clients, an accounting database, and a list of the kids on the Little League soccer team he coaches. At the Poison Control hotline center, the computer not only contains a database of poisons, it also contains a database of volunteers who help run the hotline.

Each database on the computer disk is created just as the GLIDER database was created. They are each given separate names and are stored on disk in separate files. When one database is being accessed by the database program, information from the other database files is generally not available. There are certain occasions when two or more databases *are* related, and information on both can be used at the same time. However, databases containing unrelated information are separate files that do not communicate with one another.

When the database program is first started from DOS, it generally does not know which database to communicate with. Therefore, one of the first things a user must do is to tell the program which database to use.

CASE STUDY

The USE Command in dBASE III Plus

In dBASE III Plus, the command to communicate with a database is the Use command. After beginning dBASE from DOS with the command:

```
C>DBASE
```

the program responds with the dot prompt. It is not presently communicating with any database. If a command such as "DISPLAY ALL" is given, a message will tell the user that no database is in use, but it will then prompt you to enter the name of the database to use. One of the first items of business whenever dBASE is started is to tell it which file to use. To tell dBASE to access the database called GLIDER, type the command

```
.USE GLIDER
```

If the database to be used is on a different disk drive than the default drive, place a drive indicator in front of the database name. For example, to use the database called SOCCER which is in the B: drive, the command would be

```
.USE B:SOCCER
```

(See also the command "SET DEFAULT TO" described in the next section.) Note that the actual name of the GLIDER database on disk is GLIDER.DBF. The dBASE program automatically looks for a "DBF" file when the Use command is given.

CASE STUDY

Using a Database in Your Database Program

When you first begin your database program from the DOS prompt, it usually does not know which of the many database files on disk is the one you wish to use. How do you specify to your program which database to use?

SETTING UP THE DATABASE ENVIRONMENT

Most programs have certain defaults that make the database program react in one way or another without the user having to specify options. For example, dBASE III Plus may be set up to automatically begin the Assist program (a menu-driven interface), or it may be set up in command mode with the dot prompt. It may be set up to display a Help box during information entry, or it may be set up so the Help box does not appear. These and other options are what make up the *program environment.* Other items that may be controlled include colors displayed on the screen, the default disk drive, the number of decimal places to use in printing numbers, and other options.

CASE STUDY

The Set Command in dBASE III Plus

The dBASE III Plus program allows the user to set certain options on the program using the Set command. This command controls the behavior of dBASE III Plus in certain circumstances. For example, in the previous chapter you may have noticed that during the entry of information, when the cursor reached the last character in an entry field, the program beeped, and the cursor automatically went to the next field, without the user having to press the ENTER key. The beep can be turned off with the command "SET BEEP OFF", or it can be turned back on with the command "SET BEEP ON". The command that controls whether or not the cursor automatically goes to the next field is the "SET CONFIRM". To turn off the automatic ENTER that moves the cursor command, use the command "SET CONFIRM OFF", or turn it back on with "SET CONFIRM ON".

If the database information is being stored on a disk other than the DOS default disk, dBASE needs to be told which disk is being used. For example, the command to tell dBASE that the database and related files are to be stored on disk B: is:

```
.SET DEFAULT TO B:
```

There are a number of "SET" commands that allow the user to control the way dBASE acts. Figure 10.1 is a list of the most commonly used SET commands.

Help Menus

One particularly useful Set command relates to the Help facility. The F1 key in dBASE III Plus is set up to be the Help key. Typed at the dot prompt, it causes dBASE to enter a Help menu, where the user can request Help on several topics. When entering, appending, or editing information in a database, or during the creation of a report form F1 turns on and off an on-the-screen Help menu. Figure 10.2

illustrates the Help screen that is displayed when F1 is pressed at the dot prompt, and the Help box that is displayed when in data entry mode. The default for the Help box can be selected using the command "SET HELP ON/OFF".

"DISPLAY STATUS": Set Commands and Function Key Settings

The dBASE III Plus command "DISPLAY STATUS" will display the status of the current database and of all Set commands. Upon entering the command "DISPLAY STATUS" dBASE will display information about the database currently in use. Once you press ENTER, dBASE will then display the current settings of the Set options and the meanings of the function keys. Figure 10.3 illustrates the results of the "DISPLAY STATUS" command.

The function keys can be used to enter dBASE III Plus commands with a single key stroke. For example, the F1 key means "HELP". Pressing the F1 key at the dot prompt is the same as entering

```
.HELP
```

Function keys F2 to F10 are *programmable.* Their initial (default) meanings are given in figure 10.3, but you can change them. To change the command associated with function key F5 to the command "DISPLAY ALL LASTNAME,FIRSTNAME, PHONE" with a carriage return, enter the Set command:

```
.SET FUNCTION 5 TO ''DISPLAY ALL LASTNAME,FIRSTNAME,PHONE;''
```

The semicolon means to enter a carriage return (ENTER) after the command is typed. If the semicolon is left off, the command is typed to the screen, and the user is then expected to ENTER the command. Your new definition of this key will be in effect only until you Quit the dBASE program.

FIGURE 10.1.
Common dBASE III Plus Set commands

SET BELL ON/OFF: Sets bell in data entry

SET CONFIRM ON/OFF: Sets automatic "return" at end of entry line

SET DECIMALS TO #: Sets numbers of decimals reported in calculations to the number of digits specified by #.

SET DEFAULT TO ⟨drive⟩: Determines which drive will be considered the default drive when communicating with a database file.

SET DELETE ON/OFF: Determines whether records marked for deletion will be ignored or not.

SET HELP ON/OFF: Determines if Help screen will appear in various editing situations.

Many other options are described in the dBASE III Plus manual.

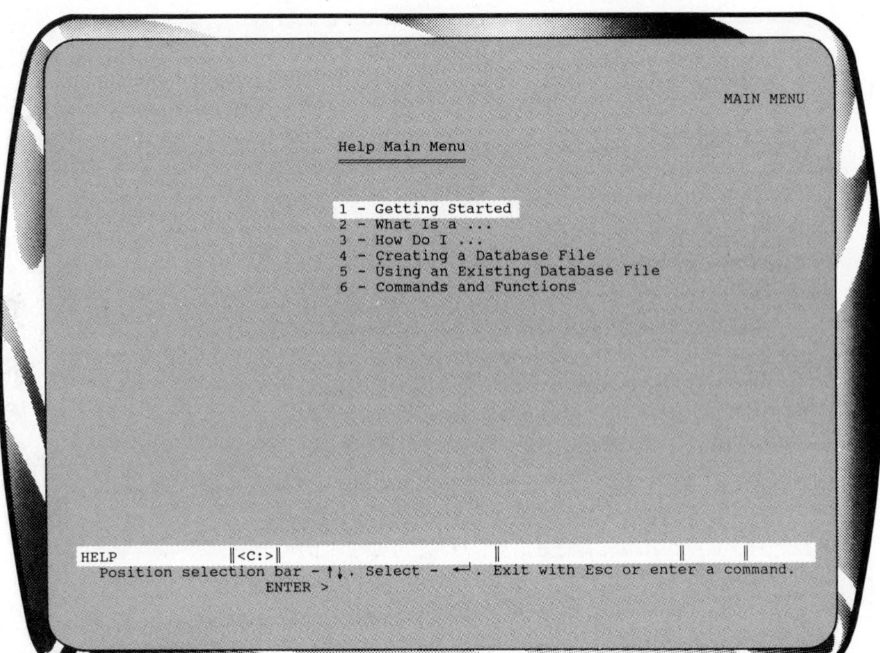

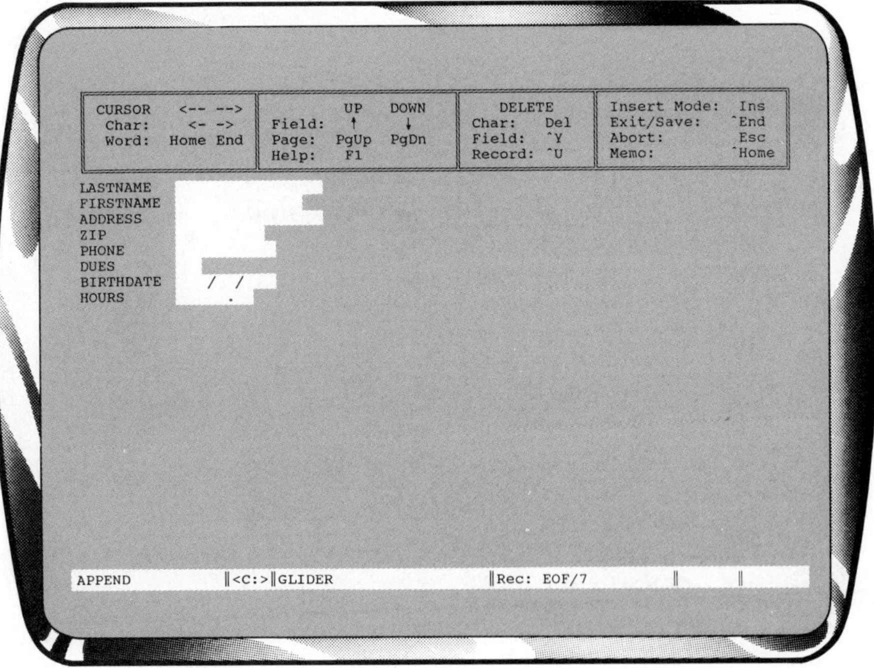

FIGURE 10.2.
Help screens. The first screen is the main Help menu, and the second screen is the Help box displayed in data entry mode.

FIGURE 10.3.
Example of "DISPLAY STATUS" screen

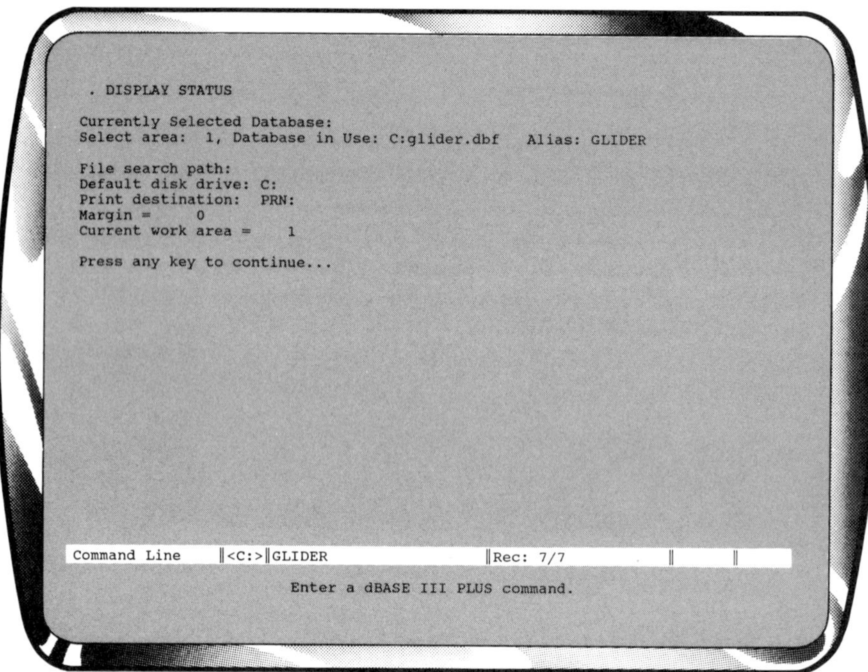

. DISPLAY STATUS
Currently Selected Database:
Select area: 1, Database in Use: C:glider.dbf Alias: GLIDER
File search path:
Default disk drive: C:
Print destination: PRN:
Margin = 0
Current work area = 1
Press any key to continue...
Command Line ‖<C:>‖GLIDER ‖Rec: 7/7 ‖ ‖
Enter a dBASE III PLUS command.

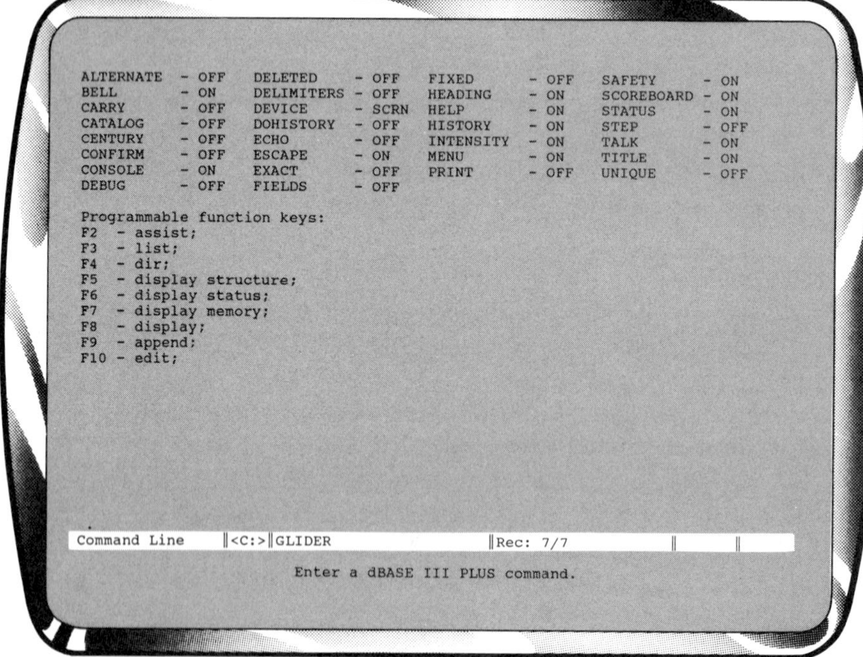

ALTERNATE - OFF DELETED - OFF FIXED - OFF SAFETY - ON
BELL - ON DELIMITERS - OFF HEADING - ON SCOREBOARD - ON
CARRY - OFF DEVICE - SCRN HELP - ON STATUS - ON
CATALOG - OFF DOHISTORY - OFF HISTORY - ON STEP - OFF
CENTURY - OFF ECHO - OFF INTENSITY - ON TALK - ON
CONFIRM - OFF ESCAPE - ON MENU - ON TITLE - ON
CONSOLE - ON EXACT - OFF PRINT - OFF UNIQUE - OFF
DEBUG - OFF FIELDS - OFF
Programmable function keys:
F2 - assist;
F3 - list;
F4 - dir;
F5 - display structure;
F6 - display status;
F7 - display memory;
F8 - display;
F9 - append;
F10 - edit;
Command Line ‖<C:>‖GLIDER ‖Rec: 7/7 ‖ ‖
Enter a dBASE III PLUS command.

CASE STUDY

Setting up the Environment in Your Database Program

Most database programs have options that you can change in order for you to customize the program to fit your personal needs. This is known as "setting up the environment". Specify if the following items can be set by the user in your database program, and how. First, examine the BEEP and CONFIRM options in the dBASE III discussion. Are there similar options in your database program? How are they controlled?

Can you specify to your database program a default disk and path where your data is stored? For example, when the program is running from disk A:, how do you specify that the data is on disk B:?

Can you define the meaning of the function keys (or any other keys) in your database program so that pressing one key will issue a command of your choice? If so, how?

QUERIES: SELECTING OUTPUT WITH CONDITIONAL SEARCHES

In the previous chapter, the concept of asking a database questions was introduced. Often, when a list of information is requested, the user can set conditions that limit the search to certain desired records. There are three basic ways of selecting the output from the database: (1) expression list, (2) scope, and (3) condition.

Selecting Output by Expression List

First, the user may limit the number of fields to be listed or printed. In most cases, the fields to be printed out are listed in the query request. For example, in the GLIDER database, John issues a query to list only the first and last names, using the dBASE command.

```
.DISPLAY ALL FIRSTNAME,LASTNAME
```

Even though there are more fields in the database than FIRSTNAME and LASTNAME, these two alone will be reported on the screen.

Selecting Output by Scope

The second method of selecting output is by *scope*. Scope is selecting a range of records. For example, one might wish to list all the records in the database, or only the first hundred records, or only the next twenty records starting at the present pointer position.

Selecting Output by Condition

Probably the most widely used kind of selection is to select records by condition. This means that a command specifies which records will be listed according to some condition that must be met. For example, the dBASE command:

```
.DISPLAY ALL LASTNAME,HOURS FOR HOURS > 10
```

specifies that only the records where the field HOURS contains a number greater than 10 will be displayed. Notice in this example that the scope is "ALL", and an expression list, "LASTNAME,HOURS" is given. Figure 10.4 illustrates this command with the GLIDER database.

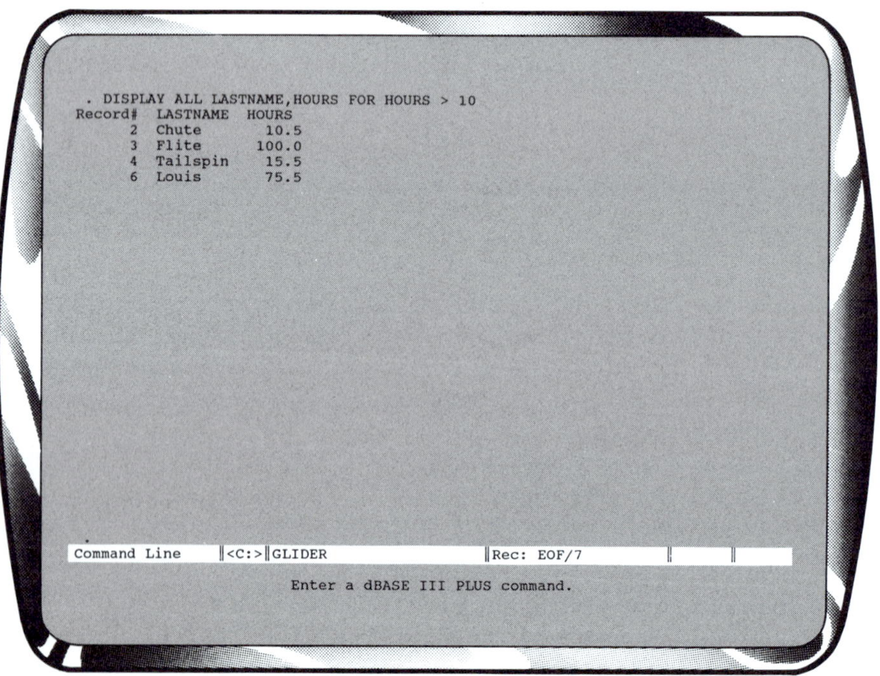

. DISPLAY ALL LASTNAME,HOURS FOR HOURS > 10
Record# LASTNAME HOURS
2 Chute 10.5
3 Flite 100.0
4 Tailspin 15.5
6 Louis 75.5
Command Line
<C:>
GLIDER
Rec: EOF/7
Enter a dBASE III PLUS command.

FIGURE 10.4.
Selecting output by condition

Relational and Logical Operators

To understand how to create conditional phrases, the concepts of relational and logical operators must be discussed. The common relational operators are listed in figure 10.5. They are the same operators you have used in algebraic expressions.

There are some important points to be observed in using these relational operators. In some data bases they may be used with both numeric-type and character-type fields. Using "greater than"(>) or "less than" (<) with character-type fields generally refers to alphabetical order. For example, "APPLE" would be considered less than "ZOO". The two types must never be mixed. An expression in dBASE such as:

```
.DISPLAY ALL FIRSTNAME,LASTNAME FOR AGE < ''THIRTY''
```

has no clear meaning and will cause the program to display an error message, because of the mixing a numeric type (the field name AGE) with a character type expression ("THIRTY").

The relational operator "=" (equal sign) requires an exact match. It should be clear what "equal" means in terms of numbers. However, in character fields, there can be some cause for confusion. Many programs do not match upper- and lowercase when comparing two character variables. For example, "Mary" does not match "MARY".

Care must also be used when specifying the "<=" (less than or equal) or ">=" (greater than or equal) condition rather than the "<" (less than) condition or ">" (greater than) condition. The condition that includes the equal sign includes the test value, whereas the condition without the equal sign does not include the test value. For example, this command:

```
.DISPLAY ALL FIRSTNAME,LASTNAME FOR HOURS > 10
```

does *not* include records where HOURS is exactly 10. To select the records where HOURS is 10 or greater, use the condition:

```
.DISPLAY ALL FIRSTNAME,LASTNAME FOR HOURS >= 10
```

Logical Operators

Relational conditions may be combined to form complex conditions by using the Boolean logic operators "AND", "OR", and "NOT". (Some database programs use additional logic conditions such as "NOR","XOR", "NAND",

Operator	Meaning
=	equal to
<	less than
>	greater than
<=	less than or equal to
>=	greater than or equal to
<>	not equal to

FIGURE 10.5. Relational operators

and others, that will not be covered in this text. The three conditions "AND", "OR", and "NOT" are sufficient for describing all logical conditions.)

The "AND" Condition. The "AND" condition specifies that both of the two conditions must be true before the command is acted upon. An example of this using plain English is "If you go outside AND it is raining, take the umbrella." Using this condition, you would only take the umbrella if both conditions were met. If you go outside and it is not raining, you would not take the umbrella. If it is raining, but you do not go outside, you still do not take the umbrella. It is only under the two conditions "you go outside" AND "it is raining" that you take the umbrella. Using logical terms, you say that it is only when both conditions are "TRUE" that the whole condition is also "TRUE". If either one of the conditions is "FALSE", the total result is a "FALSE" statement.

The "OR" Condition. The "OR" condition specifies that only one condition has to be true before the command is acted upon (that is, before the whole condition is considered "TRUE"). For example, "If it is cloudy OR raining, take your umbrella." In this case, any combination of cloudiness, rain, or both would cause you to take the umbrella.

The "NOT" Condition. The NOT condition reverses the true or false status of the current condition. It says "whatever was stated, do the opposite." For example, the statement "Tell me who is *not* less than 30," is the same as saying "Tell me who *is* 30 or older."

Here is an example of a conditional request using a relational operator. Suppose you wanted to know which members of the Glider Club have flown some, but are not experts. That is, you were interested in members who have some flying time, but less than 30 hours. In dBASE you could use this command:

```
.DISPLAY LASTNAME,HOURS FOR HOURS>0 .AND. HOURS <=30
```

The result of this command is shown in figure 10.6.

FOR and WHILE

Conditional phrases may be a part of many database commands. Generally, conditional phrases in a command are preceded by the word "FOR" or "WHILE." An example in plain English would be, "Make a list of all members FOR whom the zipcode is 78601."

"FOR" indicates that the command will apply to every record in the database for which the condition is true. "WHILE" indicates that the command will be repeated with each record as long as the condition remains true. Whenever one "false" comes up, the command is halted. For example, Elaine Slagle could request that her computer print out all the poets' records "while name <Poe." Then she would see all the poets filed alphabetically before Poe.

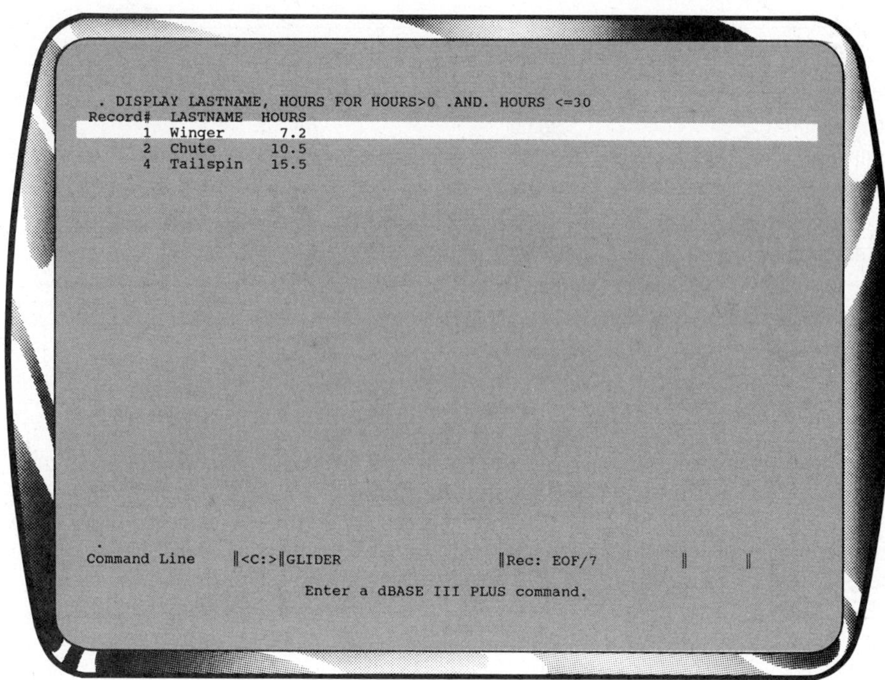
. DISPLAY LASTNAME, HOURS FOR HOURS>0 .AND. HOURS <=30
Record# LASTNAME HOURS
1 Winger 7.2
2 Chute 10.5
4 Tailspin 15.5
Command Line <C:> GLIDER Rec: EOF/7
Enter a dBASE III PLUS command.

FIGURE 10.6.
Example of use of a logical operator

CASE STUDY

Conditional Searches in dBASE III Plus

The dBASE III Plus program uses the relational and logical operators described above to request more-specific queries about a database. As an example of such a conditional search, suppose the GLIDER database is being used. John now wants a listing of all members whose flight time is less than or equal to 20 hours. The command he needs is

```
.DISPLAY ALL LASTNAME,FIRSTNAME FOR HOURS <= 20
```

Now, suppose John needs a listing of members whose flight time is less than or equal to 20 hours AND who have not paid their dues. The command would be

```
.DISPLAY ALL LASTNAME,FIRSTNAME FOR HOURS<=20 .AND. .NOT. DUES
```

Notice that the logical operators are surrounded by periods. Thus, when using AND, OR, or NOT in a dBASE command, they must take the form ".AND.", ".OR.", and ".NOT."

The two previous examples used "FOR" before the conditional expression. This means that every record that met the condition was listed. Suppose there is a database that contains your accounts-receivable information (see figure 10.7.) Notice that this database is listed in order by AMTDUE (amount due). To request a listing of people owing more than $1.00 you could use the dBASE command

```
.DISPLAY ALL NAME,AMTDUE WHILE AMTDUE>1
```

The WHILE specification would cause the display to continue listing all of the records down to Bob Smith, but would then stop at the record where AMTDUE is $1.00, and would *not* display the record for Bob Smith. Note that even if there were a record past this point that had an AMTDUE greater than $1.00, it would still not be listed, since a WHILE condition stops whenever it sees the first non-matching record.

FIGURE 10.7.
Using WHILE to find amounts due greater than $1.00

Name	AMTDUE	Displayed?
Ron Weather	123.22	Yes
Linda Barrett	98.00	Yes
Bill Sun	77.50	Yes
Patsy Mee	21.00	Yes
Bob Smith	1.00	No <--dBase stops looking here
Fred Katz	.34	No

CASE STUDY

Conditional Searches in Your Database Program

A common use of a database program is to create listings based on conditional searches. That is, you want to choose to output only information that meets certain criteria. For example, you may want a listing of all members of the Glider Club whose flight time is less than or equal to 20 hours. Explain how such a listing would be produced in your database program:

PUTTING YOUR RECORDS IN ORDER: SORTING AND INDEXING

Many times when using information in a database, the output needs to be in a particular order. This could be alphabetized—for example by name, by company, or by state; or it could be in numerical order—for example, by amount due or years of service. There are usually two ways of listing output in order: *sorting* and *indexing*. Sorting and indexing work differently. A sort actually changes the position of the records in the database. The record you originally entered as record number 20 may have a new record number after a sort. If you want to maintain the original database, the sorted database must be stored as a separate database file, which may take up lots of valuable space on your computer disk. Indexing preserves the original record numbers and uses an *index file* to keep track of the order in which you want the records accessed. The advantage to indexing is that you can have several indexes to the same file without having to alter the original database. In the long run, indexing is the faster and more efficient approach.

Sorting

Elaine could sort the 3 × 5 cards in her poet database by physically rearranging them into alphabetical order. A sort in a database does the same thing. The records are physically moved in the database so that record 1 is the record containing the first item in the sorted list. Figure 10.8 shows the GLIDER database before and after it is sorted by LASTNAME. Notice that the physical location (record number—RECNO) for each record was changed by the sort.

Indexing

Indexing is a method of outputting records without changing their original record numbers in the database. The index procedure actually creates an index file on disk that contains the information necessary to output the information in the correct order. For example, the index file to output the original GLIDER database in LASTNAME order would look something like figure 10.9.

			Records in Original Order					
RECNO	**LASTNAME**	**FIRSTNAME**	**ADDRESS**	**ZIP**	**PHONE**	**DUES**	**BIRTHDATE**	**HOURS**
1	Winger	Polly	123 Maple	78601	921-0767	Y	07/01/70	7.2
2	Chute	Brian	432 Elm	78602	921-0098	N	12/31/69	10.5
3	Flite	Vanessa	112 Pecan	78601	921-7654	Y	08/02/70	100.0
4	Tailspin	Alex	122 Maple	78601	921-0776	Y	04/22/70	15.5
5	Arrow	Sean	231 Oak	78632	921-3222	N	03/02/70	0.0
6	Louis	Lindi	332 Pecan	78601	921-2122	Y	04/23/71	75.5

			Records in Sorted Order					
RECNO	**LASTNAME**	**FIRSTNAME**	**ADDRESS**	**ZIP**	**PHONE**	**DUES**	**BIRTHDATE**	**HOURS**
1	Arrow	Sean	231 Oak	78632	921-3222	N	03/02/70	0.0
2	Chute	Brian	432 Elm	78602	921-0098	N	12/31/69	10.5
3	Flite	Vanessa	112 Pecan	78601	921-7654	Y	08/02/70	100.0
4	Louis	Lindi	332 Pecan	78601	921-2122	Y	04/23/71	75.5
5	Tailspin	Alex	122 Maple	78601	921-0776	Y	04/22/70	15.5
6	Winger	Polly	123 Maple	78601	921-0767	Y	07/01/70	7.2

FIGURE 10.8.
Sorting the GLIDER database by LASTNAME

Arrow	5
Chute	2
Flite	3
Louis	6
Tailspin	4
Winger	1

FIGURE 10.9.
Index file for GLIDER database

The index file gives the order in which the records must be output to make them come out in alphabetical order. In this case, the records were indexed by LASTNAME. When a listing is requested, the index file is read, and the first record to be displayed is record 5 (Arrow) instead of record 1. The next record to be displayed would be record number 2 (Chute), then 3, 6, 4, and finally record 1. The original database is *not* altered. There would be several index files, each indexing the records in a different order, as will be illustrated later.

CASE STUDY

Sorting and Indexing in dBASE III Plus

The command for sorting a database in dBASE III Plus is

```
.SORT ON ⟨key⟩ TO ⟨newfile⟩
```

The ⟨key⟩ is the field to be used in the sort, and the ⟨newfile⟩ is what file name to call the new sorted database. Using the GLIDER database as an example, the command

```
.SORT ON LASTNAME TO LASTSRT
```

would sort the database in alphabetical order by LASTNAME, as in figure 10.8. The new database would be stored in a database file named LASTSRT.DBF. There are other options to the dBASE Sort command not covered here, such as choosing ascending or descending order, and sorting with conditions. See the dBASE III Plus manual for more information on these options.

The Index command has the general form:

```
.INDEX ON ⟨key⟩ TO ⟨filename⟩
```

To index the active database GLIDER in order of LASTNAME, use the following command:

```
.INDEX ON LASTNAME TO LAST
```

This command creates an index file named LAST.NDX on disk. (The extension NDX is added automatically by dBASE.) The NDX file contains the information needed by dBASE to output the information from the database in the desired order, and is similar to the one shown in figure 10.9.

Now when you issue a Display or Print command, the records will appear in the order given in the current index file, just as if they had actually been sorted.

Another index could be created that arranges the records in ZIPCODE order. That command would be

```
.INDEX ON ZIP TO ZIP
```

Notice that the index file name can be the same as the field name being indexed. In this case ZIP is the field name to be used in indexing, and ZIP.NDX is the name of the index file. Each index file is automatically saved to disk when it is created.

Index fields can be combined to create a more complicated index key. For example, the command to index records first by zip code, and then within zip code by last name, is

```
.INDEX ON ZIP+LASTNAME TO ZIPLAST
```

The plus sign "+" can only be used on two fields, no more. The index key is then ZIP+LASTNAME, and the index file is ZIPLAST.NDX. The result of this index command would be to list the GLIDER database in the order indicated in figure 10.10.

Using Indexes

In this example, we now have three index files, LAST, ZIP, and ZIPLAST. How does dBASE know which index to follow when listing the records? Since the ZIPLAST index was the last one created, dBASE will follow it when listing information from the database. However, the other indexes can be chosen with the command "SET INDEX". To make an index active (for example, the index LAST.NDX), use the command

```
.SET INDEX TO LAST
```

A "DISPLAY ALL" command will verify that the records now appear in LASTNAME order. To make the ZIPLAST index active, use the command:

```
.SET INDEX TO ZIPLAST
```

Again, a "DISPLAY ALL" command will verify that the records now appear in ZIP+LASTNAME order. The dBASE program has the feature that if any change is made in a record while an index is active, the index file is automatically changed to reflect the changed record, keeping the records in indexed order. For example, if a person moves from ZIP area 78601 to 78632, that record will automatically be reindexed to appear toward the bottom of the list.

To make more than one index current, the "SET INDEX" command must list all index files. To make sure dBASE properly updates all index files when you are deleting, editing, or appending records, set all indexes to active by listing them in the "SET INDEX" command, separated by commas:

```
.SET INDEX TO LAST,ZIP,ZIPLAST
```

The first index listed (in this case LAST.NDX) is the active index, but now if a record is changed, all three NDX files will be updated to keep track of the changes.

When first entering dBASE, you may specify which database to use, and which index, all in one command. This is done with the Use command. For example:

```
.USE GLIDER INDEX LAST,ZIP,ZIPLAST
```

This is equivalent to first entering the "USE GLIDER" command followed by a "SET INDEX TO . . ." command.

RECNO	LASTNAME	FIRSTNAME	ADDRESS	ZIP	PHONE	DUES	BIRTHDATE	HOURS
3	Flite	Vanessa	112 Pecan	78601	921-7654	Y	08/02/70	100.0
6	Louis	Lindi	332 Pecan	78601	921-2122	Y	04/23/71	75.5
4	Tailspin	Alex	122 Maple	78601	921-0776	Y	04/22/70	15.5
1	Winger	Polly	123 Maple	78601	921-0767	Y	07/01/70	7.2
2	Chute	Brian	432 Elm	78602	921-0098	N	12/31/69	10.5
5	Arrow	Sean	231 Oak	78632	921-3222	N	03/02/70	0.0

FIGURE 10.10.
Indexing the GLIDER database by ZIP+LASTNAME

CASE STUDY

Sorting and Indexing in Your Database Program

Are sorting and indexing supported in your database program? If so, can you sort the GLIDER database on the LASTNAME field? Does this create a new file? If so, how would you name it LASTSRT?

Can you index the database on the LASTNAME field? Does this create an index file? What is its name? Is it saved automatically, or must you save it?

Can you combine fields for a sort or index key? If so, how would you sort or index on the ZIP and LASTNAME fields at the same time?

How many index files can you have active for a database at one time? How do you change from using one index to using another without re-indexing?

MANIPULATING DATABASE INFORMATION

Many times the information in the database is not in the exact form that you wish to print out, or that you need to make searches or selections. In the previous chapter, an example of the UPPER ( ) function was used to help in the search for the name "Mary" in the FIRSTNAME field. Using the UPPER ( ) function, the contents of the FIRSTNAME field were temporarily altered from "Mary" to "MARY" for the purposes of the search. Database programs often supply a number of functions to manipulate information.

A function must be given some information to work on, such as a field or a number, and then it provides an answer. (The information you supply is called an *argument* and is contained in parentheses after the function name.) Then the function name can be used like a variable name, to stand for the answer. For example, the square root function with an argument of 4 forms the expression SQRT(4), which is equal to 2. Within dBASE there are character, date, and numeric functions.

Functions

Many times during a search or during output, the contents of a field need to be temporarily changed to make comparisons more appropriate. In these temporary changes, the actual contents of the field do not change. For example, suppose a person's birthday is stored as a date, and a listing of all birthdays that occurred on Saturday is needed. The date in the form mm/dd/yy is not readily usable. However, a function that can extract the day of week could be used to help in the search. The dBASE program supplies a day-of-the-week function Dow( ) which extracts the numeric day of week with Sunday = 1, Monday = 2, and so on. To search for people born on Saturday, the dBASE command would be

```
.DISPLAY ALL LASTNAME FOR DOW(BIRTHDAY)=7
```

In this case the function name is "DOW", which stands for "Day of Week." The argument for the function is the field name BIRTHDAY. The Dow( ) function will look at the BIRTHDAY date in each record and calculate its day of the week. If the day is 7 (Saturday), dBASE will then display the LASTNAME in that record. Some functions work with Date-type arguments (as in this case), some work with Character-type arguments, and some work with Numeric arguments. If an incorrect argument is used, the result will be a program error.

CASE STUDY
Functions in dBASE III Plus

There are dozens of functions available in the dBASE III Plus program. A few of the most frequently used ones will be discussed. The functions are categorized by the type of argument they can work on: Date, Character, or Numeric.

Date Functions

Date functions manipulate Date-type fields. Dates are in the form mm/dd/yy. To convert the day part of a date to a character variable, use the CDOW( ) function, which stands for "Character Day of Week". The reason for doing this would be to use the result like a string in a search, in a character replacement, or in the creation of another string field. For example, in output, if you wanted the day of the week for the value of BIRTHDAY=12/03/85, you could use the CDOW( ) function. The result of the statement

```
.? CDOW(BIRTHDAY)
```

would be the character string "Tuesday". (The dBASE command "?" means "print out the result of" whatever follows.) To extract the character name of the month in this date, use the function CMONTH( ). Other portions of BIRTHDAY can be extracted with DAY( ) to get the number of the day of the month, and YEAR( ) to get the year. A summary of Date functions appears in figure 10.11.

As an example, suppose you want to list the BIRTHDATE field from the GLIDER database using the name of the month, the day of the month, and the year. This could be done with the command:

```
.LIST LASTNAME,CMONTH(BIRTHDATE),DAY(BIRTHDATE),YEAR(BIRTHDATE)
```

The results of this command are illustrated in figure 10.12.

FIGURE 10.11.
Date functions for dBASE III Plus

Function	Description
CDOW( )	Returns character day of week. (e.g., "Tuesday")
CMONTH( )	Returns character month. (e.g., "May")
CTOD( )	Converts a character-string date to the date format mm/dd/yy.
DATE( )	Returns system date (date on your computer).
DAY( )	Returns numeric day of month.
DOW( )	Returns numeric day of week (1, 2, 3, 4, 5, 6, or 7).
DTOC( )	Converts a date to a character string.
MONTH( )	Returns numeric month (1 to 12).
YEAR( )	Returns numeric year (e.g., 1988).

FIGURE 10.12.
Example of using Date functions

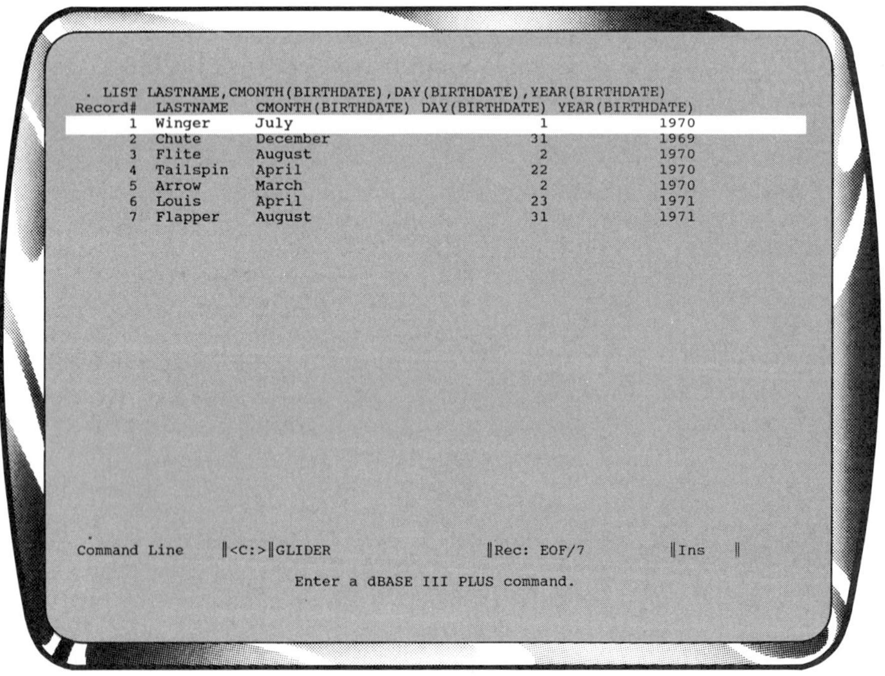

. LIST LASTNAME,CMONTH(BIRTHDATE),DAY(BIRTHDATE),YEAR(BIRTHDATE)
Record# LASTNAME CMONTH(BIRTHDATE) DAY(BIRTHDATE) YEAR(BIRTHDATE)
1 Winger July 1 1970
2 Chute December 31 1969
3 Flite August 2 1970
4 Tailspin April 22 1970
5 Arrow March 2 1970
6 Louis April 23 1971
7 Flapper August 31 1971
Command Line ‖<C:>‖GLIDER ‖Rec: EOF/7 ‖Ins ‖
Enter a dBASE III PLUS command.

String (Character) Functions

String or Character functions use Character-type arguments. They may be used for changing, extracting, or manipulating a character string. For example, a database was created to contain the results of a questionnaire. One of the questions was "What magazines do you read?" and the answer was stored in a field named MAGS. Some of the answers included:

TIME, NEWSWEEK, JET
MAD, OMNI, COINS
LIFE, TIME, SPORTSWORLD
PC, MACWORLD, COMPUTERWORLD, TIME
LIFE, TIME, LOOK, SOUTHERN LIVING

The database user wanted to print out a list of people who read TIME magazine, using the field "MAGS". In this case, the command

```
.DISPLAY ALL FOR MAGS=''TIME''
```

would not work since no MAGS field exactly matches the string "TIME". The solution is to use the AT( ) character function to look for the *substring* "TIME" in each of the strings of magazine names. The AT( ) substring function returns the starting position where a substring is found in a string. If no match is found, the function returns a zero. For example, the substring search

```
.? AT('wood', 'Hollywood')
```

would print out the answer 6, since the substring 'wood' begins at the sixth character of the searched string 'Hollywood'. Using the AT( ) function, the people who read Time magazine would be listed using the command

```
.DISPLAY ALL NAME FOR AT('TIME',MAGS) > 0
```

Let's see why this works. The AT function looks for "TIME" in each MAGS field. If the string "TIME" is located, the function AT( ) will return its position (a number greater than 0). Then dBASE will display the name of that person. If "TIME" is not found, the AT( ) function returns a 0, and that record is not listed.

Suppose in the GLIDER database, you were interested in knowing which members lived on Pecan Street. You would need to use the AT( ) function to search the ADDRESS field for the substring "Pecan". The following command would list the names for which the AT( ) function is able to find "Pecan".

```
.LIST LASTNAME,ADDRESS FOR AT('Pecan', ADDRESS) > 0
```

The results of this search are illustrated in figure 10.13.

Another useful character function is the substring selection function SUBSTR( ). This function allows you to copy part of a string from a longer character string starting at a certain position. The syntax of this function is:

SUBSTR(character expression, starting position, <number of characters>)

For example, suppose the field NAME contained the name 'Buffalo Bill Cody', and you wanted to copy the ninth through twelfth characters. The command

```
.? SUBSTR(NAME,9,4)
```

would start with the ninth character and pick out the next four characters. The result would be the string 'Bill'. If the number of characters (4) is left out of the state-

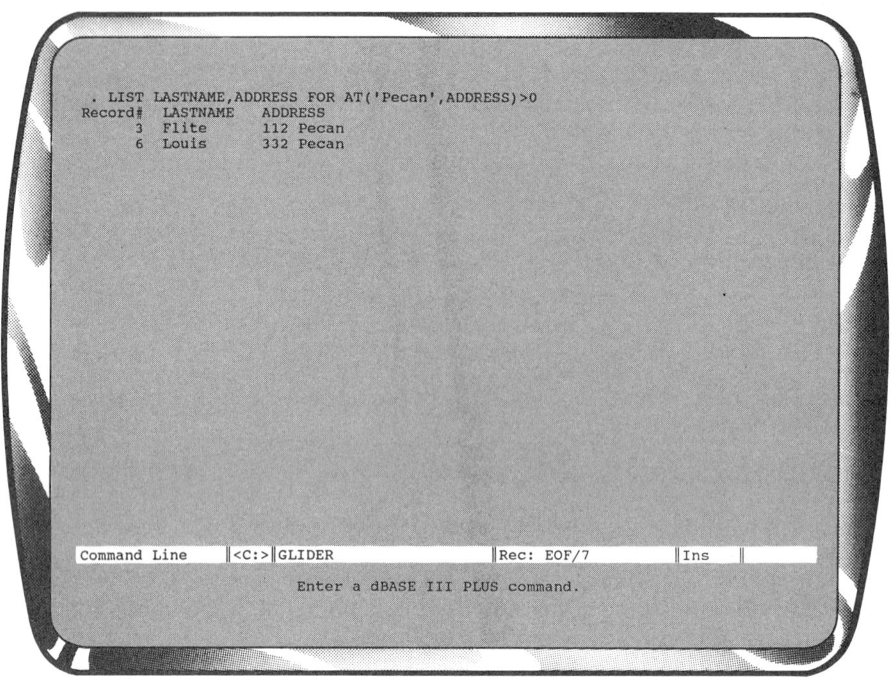

. LIST LASTNAME,ADDRESS FOR AT('Pecan',ADDRESS)>0
Record# LASTNAME ADDRESS
3 Flite 112 Pecan
6 Louis 332 Pecan
Command Line
<C:>
GLIDER
Rec: EOF/7
Ins
Enter a dBASE III PLUS command.

FIGURE 10.13.
Example use of AT( ) string function

ment, then the remainder of the string, beginning with the ninth, is extracted. Therefore, the statement

.? SUBSTR(NAME,9)

would result in the extracted string 'Bill Cody'. A summary of character functions is given in figure 10.14.

As another example, suppose that in a listing of the names and addresses for the GLIDER database, you wanted to list only the last two digits of the ZIP code, since they all begin with the digits "786". You could do this using the SUBSTR function:

.LIST LASTNAME,FIRSTNAME,ADDRESS,SUBSTR(ZIP,4)

The results of this command are illustrated in figure 10.15.

FIGURE 10.14.
Some common dBASE III Plus character functions

AT( )	Substring search, returns position of substring.
LEN( )	Returns length of character string.
LOWER( )	Changes string to all lowercase.
SPACE( )	Produces a given number of blank spaces (Example: SPACE(10).)
STR( )	Converts a number to a string.
SUBSTR( )	Substring extraction, using given starting position and length.
TRIM( )	Removes trailing blanks from character strings.
UPPER( )	Changes string to all uppercase.

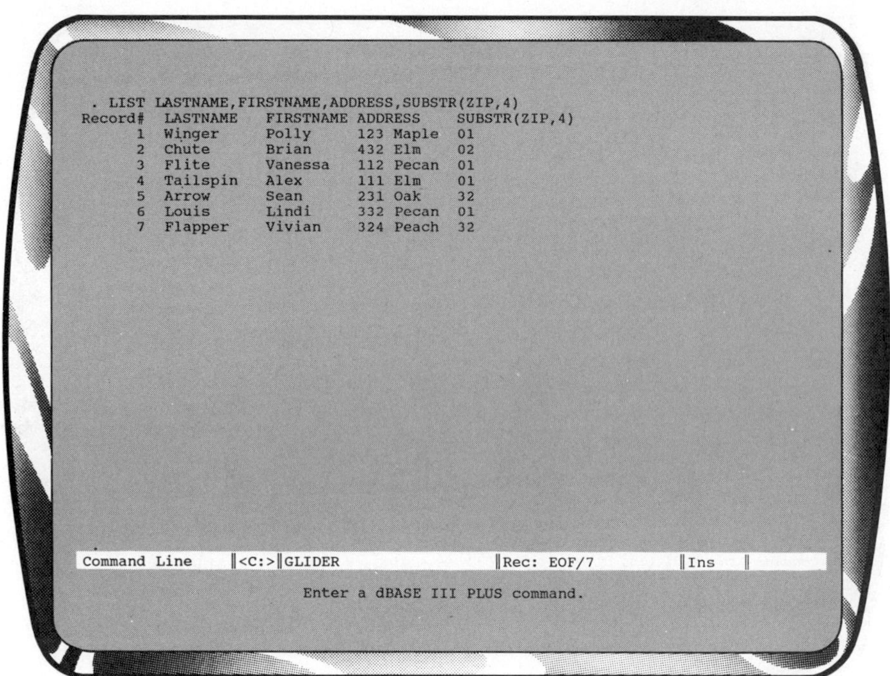

. LIST LASTNAME,FIRSTNAME,ADDRESS,SUBSTR(ZIP,4)
Record# LASTNAME FIRSTNAME ADDRESS SUBSTR(ZIP,4)
1 Winger Polly 123 Maple 01
2 Chute Brian 432 Elm 02
3 Flite Vanessa 112 Pecan 01
4 Tailspin Alex 111 Elm 01
5 Arrow Sean 231 Oak 32
6 Louis Lindi 332 Pecan 01
7 Flapper Vivian 324 Peach 32
Command Line ‖<C:>‖GLIDER ‖Rec: EOF/7 ‖Ins ‖
Enter a dBASE III PLUS command.

FIGURE 10.15.
Example use of the SUBSTR( ) string function

Mathematical Functions

Mathematical functions deal with numeric fields. They are often used in calculations or to specify a format for how a number is to be printed. For example, in an accounts-receivable database, a report is to be generated to send invoices to customers. John James owes $101, and his interest for the period is calculated at $1.516. To report this number would not make much sense to the customer, since it is impossible to pay such an amount. Therefore, the number needs to be rounded to the nearest cent. The dBASE III Plus function to do that is the ROUND( ) function. The statement

```
.? ROUND(1.516,2)
```

would yield the number 1.52. The syntax of the ROUND( ) function is:

ROUND(< exp1 > , < exp2 >)
exp1 Numeric expression to be rounded
exp2 Number of decimal places retained

If < exp2 > is a negative number, then the number is rounded to a whole number instead of a decimal. To round a number to the nearest 10, you would use −1, to the nearest 100, you would use −2, and so on. For example

```
.? ROUND(1516,-2)
```

would yield the number 1500. Now suppose that, using the GLIDER database, you wanted to list the HOURS rounded to the nearest 10 hours. The command

```
.LIST LASTNAME,ROUND(HOURS,-1)
```

would do the rounding and produce the list illustrated in figure 10.16.

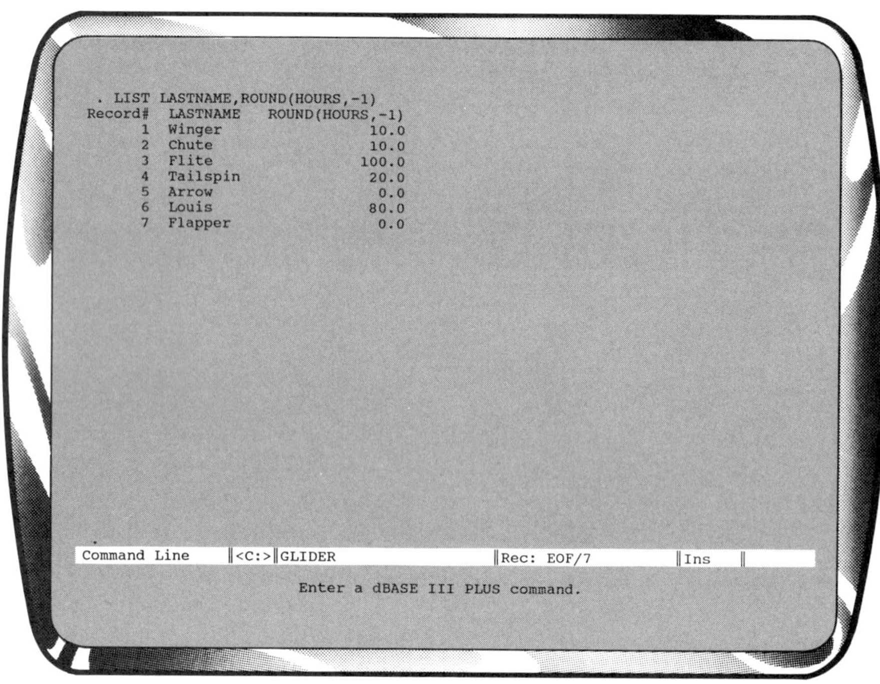
. LIST LASTNAME,ROUND(HOURS,-1)
Record# LASTNAME ROUND(HOURS,-1)
1 Winger 10.0
2 Chute 10.0
3 Flite 100.0
4 Tailspin 20.0
5 Arrow 0.0
6 Louis 80.0
7 Flapper 0.0
Command Line
<C:>
GLIDER
Rec: EOF/7
Ins
Enter a dBASE III PLUS command.

FIGURE 10.16.
Example use of the ROUND( ) mathematical function

Most numeric functions require only one argument. For example, the INT( ) function converts a number to an integer. If the numeric field SCORE contained the number 3.623, the following statement:

```
.? INT(SCORE)
```

would yield the number 3, which is the integer portion of the number. Some of the common dBASE III Plus numeric functions are given in figure 10.17.

FIGURE 10.17.
Some common dBASE III Plus numeric functions

EXP( )	Exponential	EXP(1.0)=2.72
INT( )	Converts to integer	INT(1.234)=1
LOG( )	Logarithm	LOG(2.71828)=1.00
ROUND(#,#)	Rounds off	ROUND(123.45,1)=123.4
SQRT( )	Takes square root	SQRT(4.0)=2.00
VAL( )	Converts string to value	VAL('123')=123

The functions covered here are not all of the functions available in dBASE III Plus, but are representative of the most commonly used functions. Others, which are mainly used in programming, have not been detailed here.

CASE STUDY

Functions in Your Database Program

Most database programs use functions to help the user manipulate the information in the database for searches and controlling output. Your database program probably has at least a few major functions in each of the following categories (see the dBASE III discussion). Describe functions relating to date-type fields:

Describe functions relating to character-type (string) fields:

Describe functions relating to numeric-type fields:

Using the magazine example in the dBASE III Case Study, how would you perform a similar search and listing in your database program?

In the GLIDER database, how would you make a listing that displayed only the last 2 digits of the zip code field?

In the GLIDER database, how would you make a listing that reported flight hours rounded to the nearest 10 hours?

MAKING MAJOR CHANGES TO THE DATABASE STRUCTURE

Sometimes, no matter how careful you are in designing the database structure, a new field is required to perform an essential search or to produce a report. Many database programs allow you to modify the database even after it has been created and has information stored in the database file. Specific changes that may be required include changing the width or type of a field, adding a field, or deleting a field.

In John's GLIDER database, he designed it so that the DUES field was of the Logical type. He intended to use this to index the data and be able to print out names in two groups—those who had paid and those who had not. However, after he had created the database and had entered the information, he found out that the database program would not index on Logical-type fields. The problem could be solved by modifying the structure of the database, changing the Logical type to a Character type. As a Character type, the field can be used for sorting or indexing, and John can get the listing to come out in the right order.

Another problem John encountered was in creating a listing by month of birth. The BIRTHDAY field holds the birthdate, but using that alone does not give John the capability of putting the records in order by month. That particular information must be extracted from the Date-type field. To do this, John can create a new field of type Numeric, extract the number of the month from the BIRTHDAY field, and place it in the new field, which he will call BIRTHMO for birth month.

CASE STUDY

Modifying Structure in dBASE III Plus

The dBASE III Plus program allows the user to modify the structure even after the database has been created and contains information. To change the DUES field in the GLIDER database from Logical type to Character type John can enter the command

```
.MODIFY STRUCTURE GLIDER
```

The dBASE program displays the original Create screen in an edit mode, allowing him to move the cursor to the DUES field and to change Logical to Character. All of the Logical values ".Y." are changed to the characters "Y", and the values ".N." are changed to "N". By moving the cursor down past the last field, a new blank field space will open up, and he can enter the new field BIRTHMO as a numeric field with width 2 and no decimal places. The command ^End exits from the modification. Figure 10.18 illustrates the screen used to modify the GLIDER database and add the new field.

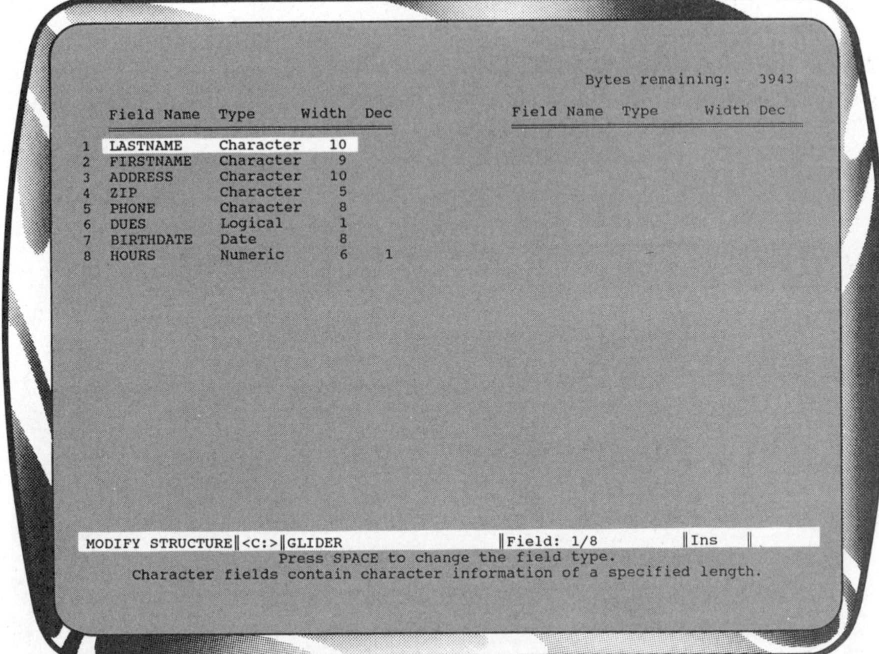

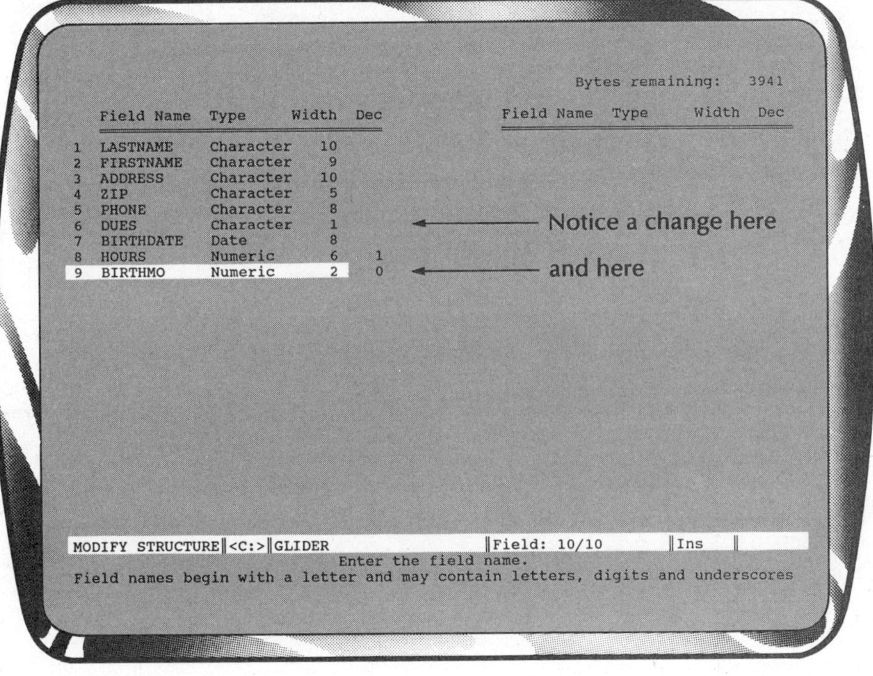

FIGURE 10.18.
Modifying the database. The first screen is the database before modification and the second screen is the database after modification

The Replace Command

The modified GLIDER database contains a new field BIRTHMO, but the field currently contains no information. The date function MONTH will extract the number of the month from the BIRTHDATE field. The Replace command can then be used to place that information into the BIRTHMO field:

```
.REPLACE ALL BIRTHMO WITH MONTH(BIRTHDATE)
```

This command instructs dBASE to extract the number of the month (i.e., 1,2, . . . , 12) from the Date-type field BIRTHDAY, and to place the result into the Numeric field BIRTHMO, replacing the blank space that is there. A "DISPLAY ALL" or "LIST" command will confirm that this replacement has taken place, as illustrated in figure 10.19.

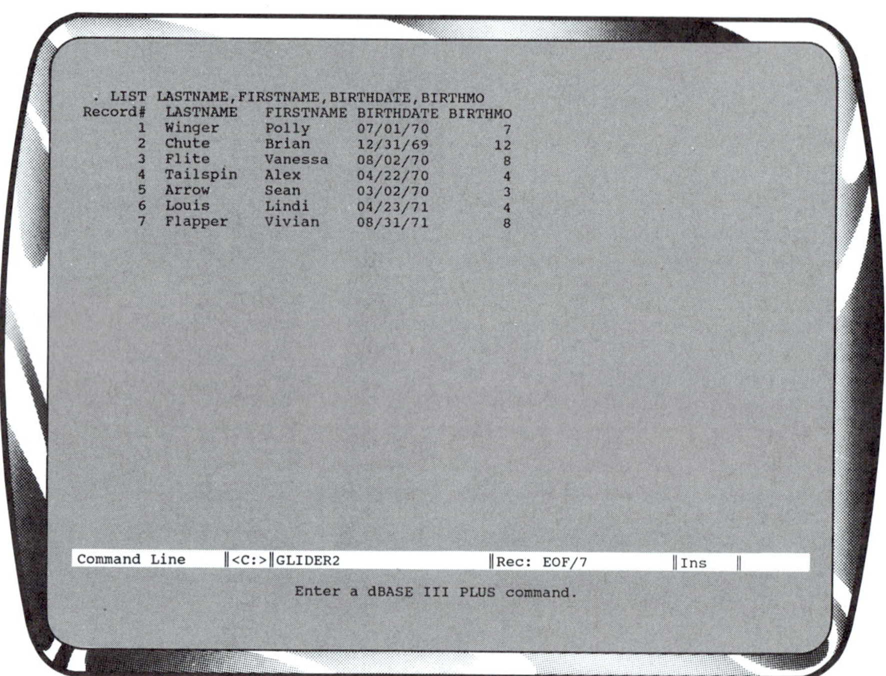

. LIST LASTNAME,FIRSTNAME,BIRTHDATE,BIRTHMO
Record# LASTNAME FIRSTNAME BIRTHDATE BIRTHMO
1 Winger Polly 07/01/70 7
2 Chute Brian 12/31/69 12
3 Flite Vanessa 08/02/70 8
4 Tailspin Alex 04/22/70 4
5 Arrow Sean 03/02/70 3
6 Louis Lindi 04/23/71 4
7 Flapper Vivian 08/31/71 8
Command Line
<C:>
GLIDER2
Rec: EOF/7
Ins
Enter a dBASE III PLUS command.

FIGURE 10.19. The GLIDER database with the new field BIRTHMO

CASE STUDY

Modifying the Database Structure in Your Database Program

Some database programs allow you to change the structure of a database even after it has been created and data entered. If your database program supports these functions, how can you change the DUES field from logical to character type?

How can you add a new numeric field named BIRTHMO to the database?

How can you place the numeric month in the BIRTHMO field from the BIRTHDATE information already in the record?

WRITING DATABASE REPORTS

The easiest way to produce reports from a database is to list the information to the computer screen. However, this is often inadequate when a permanent record is desired. In that case, output should be sent to the printer. Most databases permit you to design the output report you desire. The sophistication of reports ranges from straightforward listings to highly formatted output such as invoices, letters, filled-in forms, and many other possibilities. The more complicated the report, the more work is required to get the output the way you like it.

CASE STUDY

Reports in dBASE III Plus

The easiest way to get a report from dBASE III PLUS is with the "LIST" or "DISPLAY ALL" command. By default, the listing appears on the computer screen. However, the listing can be sent to the printer with the addition of the simple phrase "TO PRINT". For example, the command to list the GLIDER database to the printer is

```
.LIST TO PRINT
```

or

```
.DISPLAY ALL TO PRINT
```

The computer must be hooked up to a printer and the printer must be on line and contain paper, or this command will fail. Also be aware that if the number of records is over 20, the "DISPLAY ALL" command will pause for each screenful of information, requiring that the user press the ENTER key to continue the printout. The "LIST" command will list the entire database without pause.

The LIST command yields a crude report with the printout beginning at the far left edge of the paper. A left margin on the printout may be set using the command

```
.SET MARGIN TO 5
```

Figure 10.20 illustrates the results of listing with the margin set to 0 (original or default state) and after the margin has been set to 5.

Summary Reports

Sometimes you do not want to see all the individual items in the database, but would like to have some statistics to summarize the information. Several statistical functions are available in dBASE including AVERAGE, SUM, and COUNT.

The command "AVERAGE HOURS" finds the average of the numeric field HOURS, while the command "SUM HOURS" adds up all HOURS of flight time by all members in the GLIDER database. Conditions may be used with these commands, as in

```
.AVERAGE HOURS FOR DUES = 'Y'
```

which gives the average HOURS of flight time of those members who have paid their dues (remember that the DUES field is now of type character).

If there are several fields to average, the field names would be separated by commas. For example:

```
.AVERAGE AGE, WEIGHT, SCORE
```

Creating a Customized Report

There is a report creation facility in dBASE III Plus that allows users to design reports. These reports consist of columns of information from the database. (For more complicated reports, dBASE III Plus programs must be written.) As an example of the Report facility, you can create a report of names, addresses, and phone numbers for the members of the Glider Club.

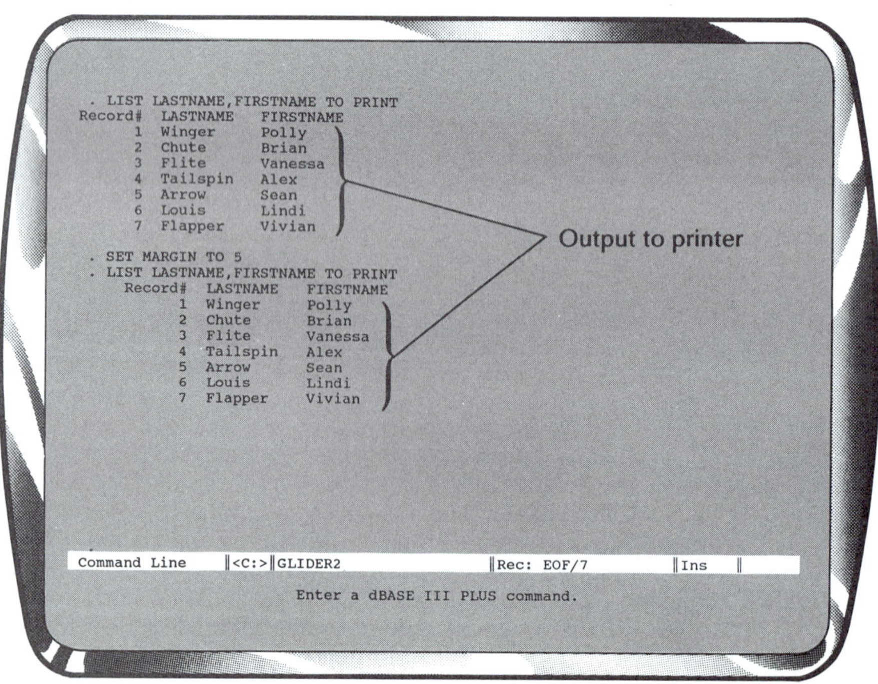

. LIST LASTNAME,FIRSTNAME TO PRINT
Record# LASTNAME FIRSTNAME
1 Winger Polly
2 Chute Brian
3 Flite Vanessa
4 Tailspin Alex
5 Arrow Sean
6 Louis Lindi
7 Flapper Vivian
Output to printer
. SET MARGIN TO 5
. LIST LASTNAME,FIRSTNAME TO PRINT
Record# LASTNAME FIRSTNAME
1 Winger Polly
2 Chute Brian
3 Flite Vanessa
4 Tailspin Alex
5 Arrow Sean
6 Louis Lindi
7 Flapper Vivian
Command Line <C:> GLIDER2 Rec: EOF/7 Ins
Enter a dBASE III PLUS command.

FIGURE 10.20.
Printing a listing with or without a margin

The first step is to create a "report form" in a file called PHONE.FRM. Later you can request printed reports using this report form. The command to begin the creating a report form is:

```
.USE GLIDER INDEX NAME
.CREATE REPORT PHONE
```

The first command tells dBASE to use the GLIDER database with the index NAME. The second command begins the dBASE III Plus report creation facility. Report forms are generated by specifying information in any of five Report menus. Figure 10.21 illustrates the menus Options and, Columns. These menu items can be chosen by pressing the right or left arrow keys on the cursor pad until a submenu appears under the desired option.
As an exercise, to create the PHONE report form and print the phone report, you can use the following procedures within the dBASE Report facility.

The Options Menu. The Options menu specifies information about the output page for the report. The default value for each option is displayed. To change any option, use the up or down arrow keys on the cursor pad to choose the option. Press the ENTER key to tell dBASE that you wish to change that option; then enter a new value. For the PHONE report, the only option to be used is the title option. With the cursor on that option, press the ENTER key. This opens up a box to enter the title of the report. The title will be centered at the top of the report page. For the PHONE report, the title will be "GLIDER CLUB MEMBERSHIP LIST". Press the ENTER key so that the title is accepted and the TITLE box is closed.

The Groups Menu. The Groups menu specifies information about how to group the output report. For example, if you wished to list the group by their DUES status, you could specify DUES as a group. (Be aware that if a grouping field is chosen, the database must be indexed or sorted on that field.) The summary report option specifies whether all of the information in the database will be printed in the report, or only subtotals and totals. For the PHONE report, no group options need to be changed from the defaults.

The Columns Menu. The Columns menu specifies what information from the database will appear in the columns of the report. In the case of the GLIDER database, you want a column for NAME, a column for ADDRESS, one for ZIP, and one for PHONE. To specify the contents of a column, the cursor is placed in the "Contents" option, and ENTER is pressed. This opens up a line to enter what field will appear in the column. The first column will contain members' names; therefore enter the following information:

```
TRIM(LASTNAME)+', '+FIRSTNAME
```

This means that the column will contain the LASTNAME, with any following blanks trimmed off, followed by a comma, a blank, and the first name. This means that the first member's name will appear as

```
Arrow, Sean
```

If the TRIM function had not been used, several blanks would have appeared after the name "Arrow", and the result would have been

```
Arrow     , Sean
```

After specifying contents, the cursor is moved to the "Heading" option. This option specifies the heading that will appear at the top of the column. The heading

FIGURE 10.21.
Creating the report PHONE. First screen is "Options" menu and second screen is "Columns" menu

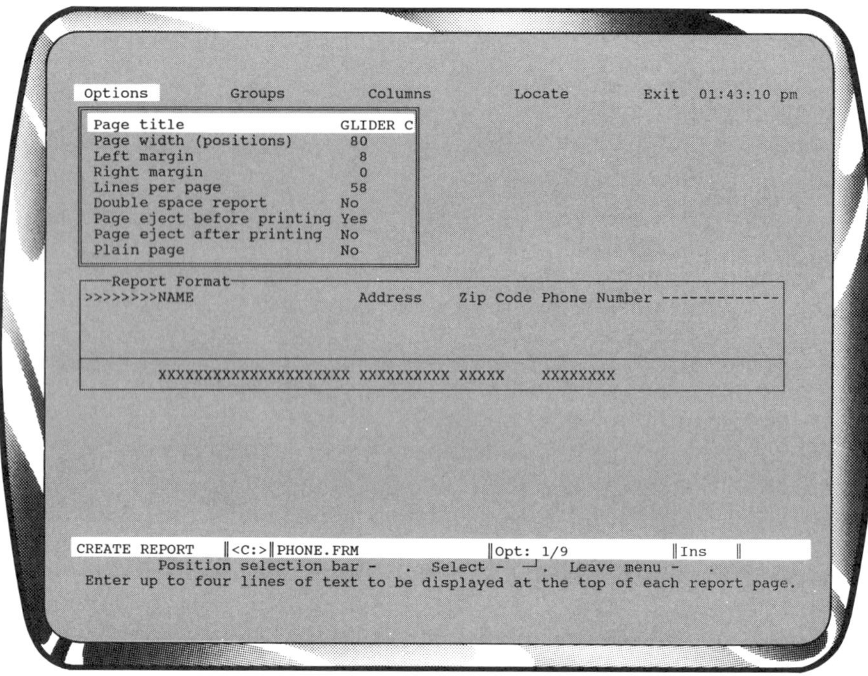

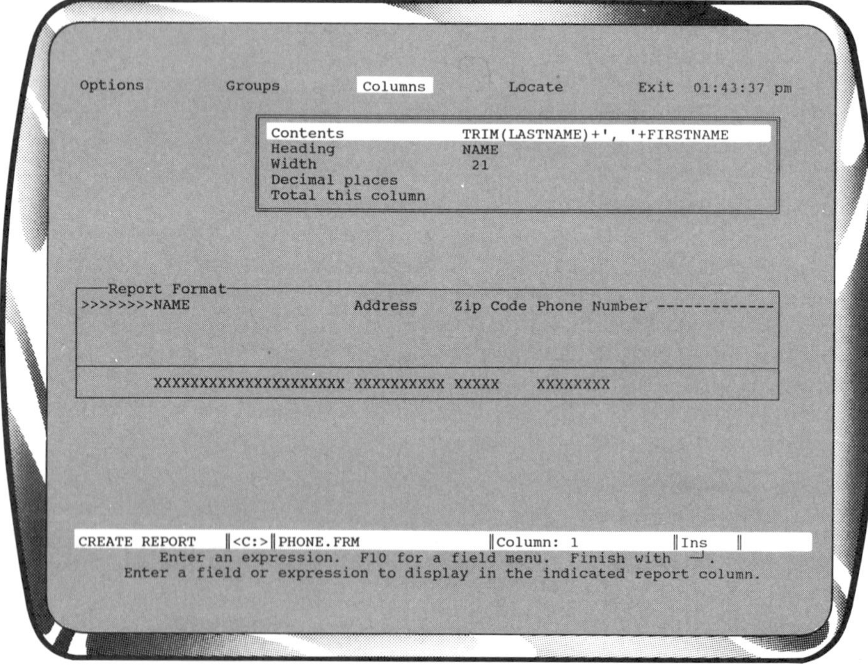

for this column will be "Member's Name". Notice that "Contents" contains *field names* and "Heading" contains a *title* that you want to appear at the top of the report column. Width is predetermined by dBASE, but is changeable. Decimals and totals may be specified in numeric fields. The "Total" option is a yes-no option and determines if the column will be totaled at the end of each group of output.

To specify the next column of information, press the PgDn key. The other columns in this report are:

Contents:ADDRESS
Heading:Address

Contents:ZIP
Heading:Zip Code

Contents:PHONE
Heading:Phone Number

The Locate Menu. The Locate menu is used to edit previously defined columns. You may choose a particular column to edit and change its options to get your report looking just right.

The Exit Menu. The exit menu is used either to abandon the report form or to save it to disk. Once the report form is saved, it may be used again and again to format new reports. Any changes in the database will be reflected in the report, because dBASE will create a new report each time, using the current database file and the PHONE report form file. For example, if new members are added, a new report can be requested using the old PHONE report form file, and the new information will appear in the report.

Printing the Report

The creation of the report form PHONE results in a file on disk named PHONE.FRM. To cause dBASE to display the report on the screen, use the command

```
.REPORT FORM PHONE
```

The results are given in figure 10.22. To cause the report to be printed directly to the printer, use the command:

```
.REPORT FORM PHONE TO PRINT
```

Sometimes, reports need to be combined into word processing documents. The report may be captured in a file for word processing by using the command

```
.REPORT FORM PHONE TO FILE OUTPUT
```

This creates a file named OUTPUT.TXT, which appears the same as the information in figure 10.22. If the report needs to be adjusted or modified, the command

```
.MODIFY REPORT PHONE
```

will bring you back to the PHONE report form, and any option can be changed. Save the changes, and re-run the report.

The Assist Program

The Assist program is an option offering menu-driven operation in dBASE III Plus. Many of the commands contained in the last two chapters may be executed directly from menus using the Assist program. From the dot prompt, the command

FIGURE 10.22.
Example of PHONE report output

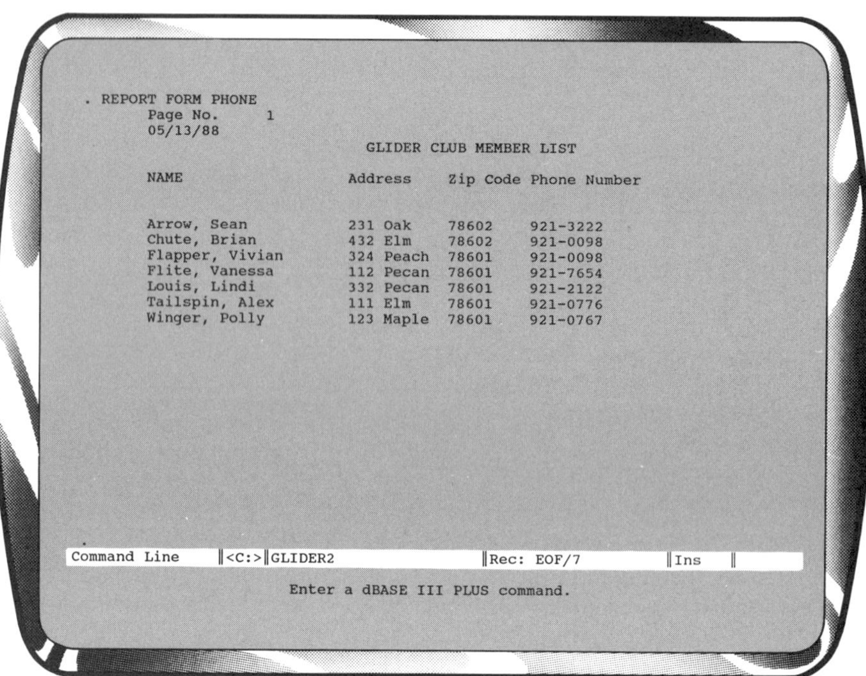

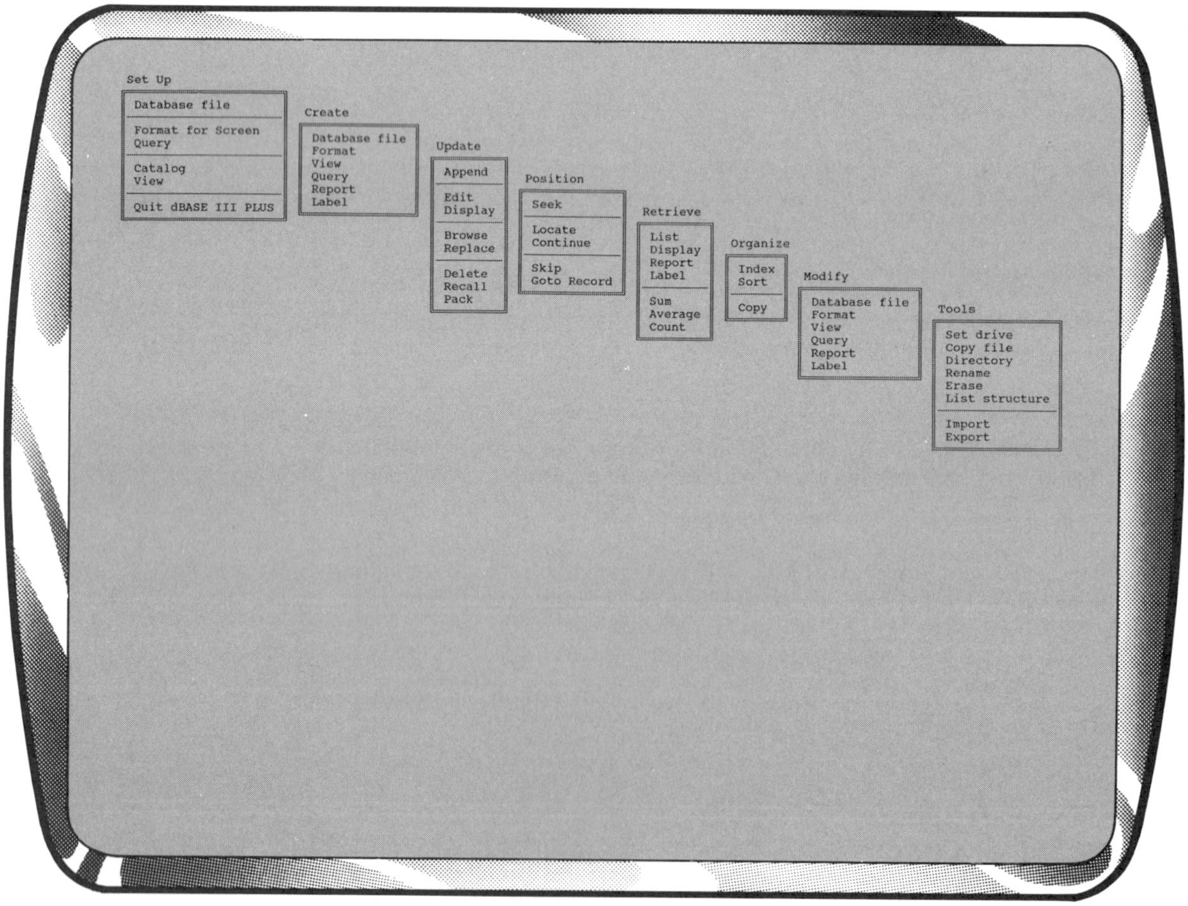

FIGURE 10.23.
Successive menu screens in Assist

to begin Assist is "ASSIST". Figure 10.23 illustrates the Assist menus. Some people prefer to use dBASE III Plus in the Assist mode, while others prefer the command mode. The Assist mode is usually easier to get started on, but the command mode is considered more powerful and flexible.

CASE STUDY

Reports in Your Database Program

Most database programs have a variety of ways of outputting information to the screen or printer. Describe how the following reports can be created in your database program. Can you print a simple listing of all information in the database (e.g., the GLIDER database) to the printer? Can you control the margin on the printed page? How?

Can you produce summary information of the information in a database? For example, how would you display the average or sum of the values in a numeric field?

Examine the custom report created in the dBASE III Case Study example. How would a similar report be produced in your database program?

SUMMARY

Once a database is created it must often be maintained, manipulated, or altered as new information becomes available. Often it is necessary to sort or index the information in the database to put it in the order desired for a particular listing. Sorting actually changes the physical location of each record in the database, where indexing does not. Major changes in the database may require altering the original database structure, adding new fields, or deleting fields. Database functions are often used to help select specific searches and conditional output as well as to calculate or create new variables. The object of many databases is to create printed reports. This can range from simple listings to neatly formatted reports.

Command Summary

A number of dBASE III Plus commands have been introduced in the last two chapters. This is a summary of each command covered, and a brief description. A more complete description is in the dBASE III Plus manual, along with specific syntax and examples.

APPEND: Add new records to the database.

AVERAGE <field> [FOR <condition>]: Calculate the average of values in a numeric field.

BROWSE: Display records one per line in edit mode.

COUNT [FOR <condition>]: Count the number of records in the database or only those that meet some criterion.

CREATE <filename>: Begin the creation of a database.

CREATE/MODIFY REPORT: Define a database report form or modify one that has already been created.

DELETE <scope>: Mark records for deletion.

DISPLAY <scope> [TO PRINT]: Display records to the screen or to the line printer.

DISPLAY STATUS: Display the current settings of the Set commands.

DISPLAY STRUCTURE: Displays the structure of the database currently in use.

EDIT <record number>: Enter the edit procedure to edit a selected record.

GO TOP: Move pointer to the first record of the database

HELP <command>: Display Help screen for selected command.

INDEX ON <key> TO <filename>: Create an index file.

LIST <scope> [FOR <condition>] [TO PRINT]: List records to screen or to line printer without pause.

LOCATE <condition>: Search for record that meets condition.

MODIFY STRUCTURE: Change the structure of the current database.

PACK: Get rid of all records marked for deletion.

RECALL <scope>: Recall records that were marked for deletion.

REPLACE <scope> <fieldname> WITH <expression> [FOR <condition>]: Replaces contents of field with new expression if record meets given condition.

REPORT FORM <form name> [TO PRINT]: Begin the production of a report, using the desired form, to the screen or printer.

SET <item>: A series of commands to set up the database environment. Includes SET DEFAULT TO, SET MENU, SET BEEP, SET CONFIRM, SET DECIMALS, SET DELETED, and others. Also see DISPLAY STATUS.

SUM <field> [FOR <condition>]: Calculates sum of values in a numeric field for records meeting the given condition.

SORT ON <key> TO <filename>: Create a sorted version of the database.

USE <filename> [INDEX <list>]: Pick the database to use, with a list of current indexes.

QUIT: Exit dBASE III Plus and return to DOS prompt, saving the database file.

QUESTIONS

Fill in the blanks

1. The ________ command tells dBASE to open a previously created database file.
2. To tell dBASE that disk drive B: is to be used for future database file storage, type ____________________.
3. To show the current settings for all SET commands, type ________ ______________.
4. An *expression list* is included with the Display command to limit the number of ____________ to be listed or printed.
5. Output can be limited by *scope,* which refers to selecting a ____________________ of records.
6. FOR and WHILE can be used to select records by ____________________.
7. The six relational operators used in dBASE are ___, ___, ___, ___, ___, and ___.
8. Three common logical operators are _______, _______, and _______.
9. Two commands which can be used to alter the order of the records in a database are _______, and _______.
10. To permanently change the order of the records in a database, you would use the _______ command.
11. To make an index file called FIRST the active index, type ________ ________________.
12. Three commonly used categories of functions in dBASE are ______________, ______________, and ______________.

13. When creating a dBASE report, subtotals may be requested using the ____________ menu option.
14. To send a dBASE report called NAMES to the printer, type ____________ ____________.

Write a short answer in your own words for each question.

15. Explain what is meant by the *environment* of a database. Under what circumstances might you need to change the environment?
16. Outline the procedure for customizing the database environment (use concrete examples).
17. Explain the difference between the use of the FOR condition and the WHILE condition in limiting database searches. Give an example of each type of conditional phrase using appropriate relational operators.
18. Briefly explain the difference between *sorting* a database and *indexing* a database. Under normal circumstances, would you sort or index a database to Display records alphabetized by last name? Why?
19. You have created a database called CLUB which has three indexes named NAMES, STATES, and ZIPS. List the command you would use to open the database and all three indexes. How do you know which is the active index? How would you change the active index?
20. Explain what is meant by the *structure* of a database. Under what circumstances might you need to change the structure?
21. Outline the procedure for changing the structure of a database.
22. Briefly explain why dBASE needs date functions and character functions.
23. Outline the procedure for creating a dBASE report which does not include subtotals.
24. You have created a database called ACCOUNTS which has two indexes named CLIENTS and ACCNO, and a report form called ACCREP. List, in order, the commands you would use to open the database and print the report using the CLIENTS index.
25. Explain the function of the Assist program. How is the program accessed? How does using Assist differ from typing commands at the dot prompt?

LABORATORY EXERCISES

Lab Exercise 1. In this exercise you will use the GLIDER database created in chapter 9.

1. Start up dBASE and make sure you are at the dot prompt. Activate the GLIDER database with the Use command.
2. Next, use the Display command to practice limiting the output of a search by expression list, scope, and condition. The format of the Display command is as follows:

   DISPLAY [<scope>] [<expression list>] [FOR <condition>]
   [WHILE <condition>] [TO PRINT]

   Write down the correct command sequence for each of the following Display statements.

   a. Display the last name and first name for every record in the database.
   b. Display the last name and date of birth for every record in the database.

c. Display the first name and last name for the members from zip code 78601.

d. Display the last name and telephone number for the members with more than 15 hours of flying time.

e. Display the last name and address for the members born after 1969.
Hint: Use a date function in the condition.

f. Display the last name for members whose last names begin with M–Z and who have more than 10 hours of flying time.

3. In this portion of the exercise you will practice creating and using index files. The format of the Index command is as follows:

INDEX ON <key> TO <index filename>

Write down the command sequence for each of the following activities.

a. Index the database by last name. Display the first name and last name for every record.

b. Index the database by zip code. Display the last name and zip code for every record.

c. Index the database by zip code AND last name. Display the zip code, first name, and last name for every record.

4. Change the structure of the database (using the "MODIFY STRUCTURE" command) in the following ways:

a. Change the field type for DUES from logical to character.

b. Add a new numeric field called BIRTHMO (birth month) which has a width of 2 and no decimal places.

Check to see that your modification was successful by using either "DISPLAY ALL" or "BROWSE".

5. Fill the new BIRTHMO field with values. Use the Replace command and the date function MONTH to extract the numeric month from the BIRTHDATE field and store the new value in the BIRTHMO field.

6. Print a copy of the records in the database in alphabetical order by last name to the printer.

Note: Make sure the printer is connected and is on line before issuing the print command.

7. Create a report form called PHONE for the GLIDER database. Use the following criteria:

a. Options menu: Enter the title "GLIDER CLUB MEMBERSHIP LIST". The other options can be left at the default settings.

b. Columns menu: Use the following column definitions along with appropriate column widths.

- Column 1 contents: LASTNAME
  heading: Member's Name
- Column 2 contents: ADDRESS
  heading: Address
- Column 3 contents: ZIP
  heading: Zip Code
- Column 4 contents: PHONE
  heading: Phone Number

c. Exit menu: Save the report format.

8. Display a copy of the report on the screen using the "REPORT FORM" command. If the report does not look the way you intended, you can change any portion of the report using the "MODIFY REPORT" command.

   Note: If you receive the message "Syntax error in field expression", ask your instructor for assistance.

9. Send a copy of the report to the printer with the names listed in alphabetical order.

Lab Exercise 2. In this exercise you will use the ACCNTS database created in chapter 9.

1. Start up dBASE and retrieve the ACCNTS database with the Use command.
2. Using the Index and Display commands, print out (to the printer) all the records in the database in last name order and in amount due order.
3. Add a new numeric field called INTEREST to the ACCNTS database. The new field should have a width of 5, and 2 decimal places. Change the field type for PASTDUE from logical to character.

   Hint: Use the "MODIFY STRUCTURE" command.

4. Using the Replace command, put the monthly interest on the amount due (AMTDUE) in the new field called INTEREST. The yearly interest rate is 10%.

   Hint: Monthly interest rate = Yearly interest rate / 12.

5. Display all the records in the database in last-name order.
6. Create a report form using the "CREATE REPORT" command. Use the following items in the report:

   Title: ACCOUNT STATUS
   Columns: Name (LASTNAME), Amount Due (AMTDUE), Interest due this month (INTEREST), and Total Due (Hint: this is a calculated column.)
   Subtotals: Group on PASTDUE, causing subtotals to print for each group (Hint: Make sure the database is indexed on PASTDUE and that this is the active index).

7. Send a copy of the report to the printer.

Lab Exercise 3. In this exercise you will create a database called MAILLIST. You will be responsible for defining the correct structure for the database, based on the data and the questions provided below.

1. Create a database called MAILLIST to contain the following information.

   Joe Brown (age 45)
   123 Main St.
   Austin, TX 78723
   444-4433

   Mary Smith (age 33)
   789 Elm St.
   Durrant, OK 45231
   512-3455

   Paul Smith (age 18)
   543 Heard Blvd.
   New York, NY 10012
   342-1234

   John Edwards (age 23)
   3455 First St.
   Dallas, TX 67822
   222-2112

   David Jones (age 29)
   1212 May Ave.
   San Diego, CA 89099
   987-3487

   Janis Martin (age 55)
   1093 Brazos
   Houston, TX 67897
   444-6879

Jane Doe (age 40)	Sandy Beam (age 28)
543 Post	333 S. 2nd
Roswell, NM 55663	Austin, TX 78734
934-0098	478-9988

Make a planning chart like the one in figure 9.10 (chapter 9).

2. List the entire database to the screen, and then to the printer.
3. List the database indexed on the last name.
4. List the last name, first name, and address of the people from Texas.
5. List the database indexed on the state and last name
6. List the name, telephone number, and age of the people 30 years of age or younger.
7. List the people from Texas who are over 30 years of age.
8. Create and print a report which includes: name, address, city, state, and zip code. Your report should have the names in alphabetical order and should include appropriate headings.
9. Create and print a report which includes the last name, first name, city, and telephone number of the people who live in Texas.
10. Assume that the database is two years out of date. Use the Replace command to correct the ages of all the people in the database. Display the result.

Lab Exercise 4. Choose one of the following:

1. Create a database of your personal address book. Fields might include: name, address, telephone number, age, birthdate, etc.
2. Create a database of your business address book. Fields might include: name, title, company name, address, telephone number, date of last contact, etc.
3. Create a database of your household inventory. Fields might include: type of item (VCR, camera, etc.), brand name, model number, serial number, date purchased, place of purchase, original cost, color, etc.
4. Create a database of something you collect. This could be a record, tape, or CD collection where data could be sorted by music type or recording artist or format. Other suggestions would be a coin or stamp collection, a photographic slide or videotape collection, or a book collection.

CHAPTER 11

Tips on Selecting Hardware and Software

CHAPTER OVERVIEW. This chapter covers some of the important questions and considerations about selecting microcomputer software and hardware. Although the concentration will be on IBM PC-type computers, Apple computers will also be discussed briefly. The purpose of this chapter is not to describe a typical or preferred computer system, but to help you define for yourself the computer system that best meets your needs, and to provide information about how to purchase it.

CHAPTER OBJECTIVES

Upon completion of this chapter, you will be able to:

- Outline important questions to consider before the purchase of a computer for personal or business use.
- Describe the major categories of software, and have some knowledge of how various popular software products compare in each category.
- Describe the major families of computers and the types of computers in each family.
- Describe the major types of monitors and the uses and capabilities of each type.
- Describe the major types of printers and the uses and capabilities of each type.
- Describe the functions of other microcomputer peripherals.
- Describe the various options of where and how to purchase computers and their components.

DECIDING ON YOUR NEEDS

Selecting a computer is similar to selecting an automobile. You can make your choice by going to the computer showroom and letting a salesperson talk you into the newest model with the snazzy color and latest options—whether you need them or not, or you can select your computer based on what you really need. Most people agree that the latter approach is best, but in reality, just like the car business, many computers are bought for all the wrong reasons. This chapter will help you make a logical decision about which computer will be best for your situation.

There is no single computer setup that is best for everyone. There are questions of power, compatibility, options, speed, and cost that must be taken into account.

What Will Your Computer Do?

Before deciding on which computer to buy, you need to consider what you want it to do. Some computer systems are better at calculating numbers, while others are good at word processing, or drawing graphs. While one popular computer will allow you to create musical harmony, another popular computer will play only one note at a time. Not all software will run on all machines. If you really want to use your "brand X" word processing program, you are going to have to make sure the machine you purchase can run it. Even if you have been told "It runs on an Apple", you could still buy an Apple computer that would not run your software. That is because not all machines within the same brand name (i.e., Apple, Radio Shack, IBM) have the same capabilities.

Software before the Hardware

Many people purchase a computer before deciding what software they will be using. Sometimes this strategy works out. If you buy an IBM Personal Computer, and then decide to do word processing, chances are good that you could find a word processor out of the over 200 on the market that would work on your computer. However, if you decide you want to use the T-Cubed scientific word processor from TCI Software Research Inc., your computer may not have the right kind of monitor, disk drives, printer, or amount of memory needed. You would have to spend more money buying a new monitor, a new printer, and additional memory. If, on the other hand, you decide in advance what software you will be using, you can customize your computer purchase to meet the requirements of the software.

Before considering what computer to buy, find the software that performs the task you desire, then select the computer that will best run your software. Of course, this is only possible if you have the luxury of buying both the computer and the software. Many times, you will have a computer, and must find the best software to fit that machine.

Compatibility

Another important question to consider in buying a computer is compatibility. If you are buying a computer for home, and your office uses an IBM PC (or Macintosh, or Apple II), you may wish to consider purchasing a compatible computer so you can easily share information with the office computer, and so you only have to learn one operating system. If you are buying a computer for your child to use at home, find out what computer is used at the school. If they use an Apple II at school, and the purpose of buying a home computer is to help your child in what he or she is learning about computers at school, it may not be wise to buy another kind of computer for home use.

Compatibility is more than mere convenience. If you have all the time in the world you could probably figure out a way to move your word processing file from your Apple IIe to your IBM PS/2—but you would be wasting valuable time. Computers can be wasteful gadgets unless they increase productivity. Think through how your computer will be used before making the decision to buy.

SELECTING SOFTWARE

Software determines what kinds of tasks your computer can perform, and the way that the task will be performed. It is the software that you interact with, and that provides you with the functions you need to do your work. As you are choosing your software, you need to consider several important items.

1. The software must perform the task you have in mind. Otherwise, no matter how interesting it looks, it could be virtually worthless for your needs.
2. The software should be usable at the level of expertise of the operator. For example, document-generating software ranges from simple-to-use word processing programs to complicated programs that are used for professional typesetting. How much time are you willing to spend learning the system?
3. If possible, you want the software to be compatible with other systems you need to communicate with, or with which you need to share data.
4. If you already own a computer, the software should be able to run on your existing hardware. It may be possible to easily upgrade your current hardware to allow a new program to run on it. For example, you may only need to upgrade your machine's memory or add a different kind of monitor to be able to use a new piece of software.
5. Sometimes, if a particular piece of software is essential to your work, you may consider replacing old hardware with a new computer that will run the software you need.

There are literally thousands of software programs to choose from. Even specialty software such as a program for appointment-keeping in a dental office is plentiful for many computers. By applying these five concepts to software selection, you should be able to narrow the possibilities considerably.

Popular Word Processing Programs

Word processing may be the most common use of personal computers today. Because of this usage, hundreds of companies have produced word processing software programs. Unlike some areas of software, there is no clearly dominant word processing package on the market. However, there are a handful of popular products that will be discussed here. No attempt is made to judge between these word processors, and this particular list should not prevent you from considering other products. All of these representative word processing programs are good at what they do. Although there are differences in features, perhaps the major difference between them is their style of operation—how they interact with the user.

WordStar. WordStar is the grandfather of personal computer word processors, having begun in the early days of the Apple computer. Many early microcomputer users learned what word processing was by using WordStar. When the IBM PC was introduced, WordStar was one of the first word processing packages to become available for it. WordStar has adapted to the many recent innovations in computing, and has continued to update its original model into a modern product. The user interface for WordStar is a series of menus and control commands.

WordPerfect. WordPerfect is available on a variety of computers, from the IBM PC to the Apple Macintosh and even some large mainframe computers. It includes all of the necessary features for most office document production, including spell-checking, thesaurus, information merging, and even simple math. The user interface to WordPerfect is through 40 function key commands.

DisplayWrite. DisplayWrite, from IBM, is a modification of the program used on the stand-alone word processor from IBM called a Displaywriter (which is no longer manufactured). When offices began to switch from single-function word processors to personal computers, many secretaries and others who had used the Displaywriter found it a relatively easy transition to the DisplayWrite software on the PC.

The user interface for DisplayWrite is through a series of menus and some function key commands. For some beginners, these menus tend to be cryptic and difficult to understand.

Microsoft Word. Microsoft Word has been a pioneer in the "What you see is what you get" (WYSIWYG) style of word processing. Although most popular word processors approach this concept to some extent, Word has led the way in the display of a variety of fonts on the screen, as they will appear in your printed document. Word's user interface is a menu that appears at the bottom of the screen. This main menu is a gateway to a number of submenus that contain selections for document formatting and other features.

MultiMate. MultiMate began as an adaptation of the popular stand-alone Wang word processor. It not only is a very complete word processing system, it even allows you to perform many DOS file functions within the program. The user interface for MultiMate is a series of menus.

Other word processors of note include the T-Cubed and EXP scientific word processors. They are specifically designed to allow you to create complicated scientific formulas as well as standard text. PC-Write is a "shareware" word processing program that is distributed free or at a low cost. After you try it, you are encouraged to register and become an official user.

Figure 11.1 is a brief checklist that you can use to evaluate several word processing packages for your personal or business needs.

Popular Spreadsheet Programs

The spreadsheet software market has been dominated by three products, although one of these products is no longer being made. Early in the history of microcomputing, the program VisiCalc was the leader. By the mid-1980s Lotus 1-2-3 became the dominant program on IBM-type personal computers, and Microsoft Excel became the dominant spreadsheet program on the Apple Macintosh. There are other very good spreadsheet programs to consider. A brief description of several spreadsheet programs follows. No attempt is made here to judge between them.

Lotus 1-2-3. Lotus 1-2-3 is really an integrated product that contains three major components: (1) spreadsheet, (2) graphics, and (3) database. By most accounts, the spreadsheet portion of Lotus 1-2-3 is its best and most commonly used module. Lotus introduced a new type of user interface with its "menu bars" that appear at the top of the screen. Many other programs have adopted this popular user interface.

Checklist for Choosing a Software Package

1. If you already have a computer, what programs are advertised the most (in computer magazines) for that computer? This is a rough measure of the popularity and thus the level of support probably available for the software product.
2. If you want to be compatible with some other people using this type of program, what program do they use?
3. If you are buying a package for your use at a business or other organization, is there a limited number of programs that are supported by the organization's personal computer support staff? Which packages are supported? Are there special discounts for particular programs through the organization, or a site license?
4. If you require special features with your package (e.g., graphics, special functions, local area networking, importing files from other programs), list the features you need, then list the packages that support each feature:

Feature needed	Packages that support feature

5. If you already have a printer or anticipate needing a particular kind of printer (e.g., an HP Laserjet), which of the packages you have mentioned above support this printer?
6. What are the prices of the packages that have met the criteria in the above questions? Are there clones of this software that are less expensive?
7. If possible, use your potential choices on a computer that is similar to yours. Which program has a user interface that you are most comfortable with? (i.e., menus, commands, use of a mouse, etc.)

FIGURE 11.1.
Software package checklist

Supercalc 5. Although Supercalc has never dominated the spreadsheet market, it has continued to survive and capture a number of loyal users. Supercalc 5 supports the same kinds of functions as Lotus 1-2-3 and has more graphic features. It also supports more types of printers than Lotus 1-2-3.

Framework. Like Lotus 1-2-3, Framework is really an integrated program with several applications built into one, including a powerful spreadsheet module. Framework was a pioneer in the now common "pull-down" menu interface in software.

Excel. Microsoft first introduced Excel on the Apple Macintosh. It has become the dominant spreadsheet program on the Macintosh, outselling Lotus Jazz, which is Lotus' 1-2-3-type spreadsheet for the Macintosh. Excel is now available for IBM-type personal computers. Excel uses a pull-down menu interface and contains graphic capabilities superior to most other spreadsheet programs.

Other spreadsheet programs of note are Borland's Quattro, PFS: Professional Plan, Silk, PlanPerfect, Words & Figures, and Microsoft Multiplan. Some programs that are Lotus 1-2-3 "look-alikes" include The Twin and VP-Planner.

The checklist in figure 11.1 can be used to evaluate several spreadsheet programs to see how they meet your personal or business needs.

Popular Database Programs

Almost from the beginning of the microcomputer era, the leader in database software has been dBASE from Ashton-Tate. First introduced as dBASE II, it was upgraded to dBASE III, then dBASE III Plus, and now dBASE IV. As in the spreadsheet market, there remain some substantial challengers to the dominance of dBASE. A brief description of several database programs follows. No attempt is made here to judge between these programs.

dBASE III Plus. dBASE III Plus (and dBASE IV) is a powerful database program which can be used from a menu interface, from a command interface, or as a programming language. It can store and manipulate millions of pieces of information. In addition, there are hundreds of "support" programs available from other companies that can help you use dBASE to its fullest.

Paradox. The Paradox database system from Borland is a complete and extensive database system like dBASE. It has also been a pioneer in databases for use on Local Area Networks (LANs).

R:Base System V. R:Base is like dBASE III in that it can be used in a menu mode, a command mode, or by programming. R:Base contains a feature called "Express modules" which make the creation of tables, reports, and entry screens a simple task.

Other popular database programs include Q&A, Powerbase, and PFS: Professional File. A popular shareware database program is PC-File. The checklist in figure 11.1 can be used to evaluate several database programs to see how they meet your needs.

Specialty Software

Because word processing, spreadsheet, and database programs are so popular, there are a variety of programs to choose from. There are also a tremendous number of reviews and supplemental books that can help you decide which of the programs best meet your needs. When you need specialty programs such as statistics, accounting, or medical office programs, you will often have to do more research to find the particular product that will meet your needs.

When choosing an application program for a particular industry, one of the most important resources is industry publications. Professionals from accountants to zoologists have professional or trade publications that often review industry software. There are also industry-specific directories of software that may be available at your local library. These directories usually list programs by category, describe the basic function of the program, and list pricing information. You will often need to contact the company that produces the program to get more detailed information about the software. Sometimes you may be able to get a demonstration copy of the program to evaluate for a short period of time.

There are also a number of books for particular industries that provide procedures for selecting appropriate software for your profession. This includes *The HBJ Computer Selection Series* from Harcourt Brace Jovanovich, which covers such professions as the medical office, real estate, and accounting.

Besides publications, other resources for selecting software include professional software consultants and colleagues who have previously purchased computer systems. Figure 11.2 gives you a series of questions that you may use to begin the selection procedure for specialized software.

Checklist for Selecting Specialized Software

1. If you already have a computer, what are the most-advertised programs for that computer that perform the function you are considering (in computer magazines, professional journals, and trade magazines)?

2. Are there particular programs recommended by or reviewed by your professional association? Get and read copies of these reviews.

3. Contact other people in your profession that use this kind of software. Find out the good and bad points about the software. Particularly find out about the support from the program's vendor. Which programs seem to be supported well?

4. If you are buying an expensive package which will be used for a major part of the operation of your organization, you need to make sure the company will be around for a long time to support you. Look into the stability of the vendor. Ask the company to provide evidence of their financial stability and their commitment to the product you have in mind. Ask the company for references of people using their product and check them out.

5. If possible, ask for a demonstration copy or system for enough time for you to evaluate it thoroughly. This could be a day, a week, or even a month.

6. If possible, use your potential choices on a computer that is similar to yours. Which program has a user interface that you are most comfortable with? (i.e., menus, commands, use of a mouse, etc.)

FIGURE 11.2.
Checklist for selecting specialized software

Choosing Microcomputer Hardware

Computer hardware consists of all of the pieces of electronic equipment that make up a computing system. This includes the computer, monitor, printer, and other devices.

Major Families of Computers

The two major families of computers for business and education are IBM and Apple. These "families" also include clones or compatible computers. Although there are other families of microcomputers, these two families make up around 90% of all microcomputer business hardware in use in the United States.

The Microprocessor

The primary piece of electronic circuitry that differentiates these two families of computers is the microprocessor chip on which they are based. The microprocessor is the "brain" of the computer. The IBM family of microcomputers is based on a series of microprocessors from the Intel corporation, and the Apple computers are based on a series of microprocessors from Motorola. Although the Intel and Motorola chips perform a similar function, they do it in a different way, and this makes the IBM and Apple computers substantially different from one another. Why should a user need to know about microprocessor chips before selecting a computer? The chip that is used will tell you something about the power of the computer, its potential speed and memory capabilities, and its potential compatibilities with other computers. A brief summary of the capabilities of some microprocessor chips is found in figure 11.3.

The potential performance of a chip is usually measured in how many bits (binary units) can be manipulated or accessed at once. Microprocessor chips are referred to as 8-bit chips,16-bit chips, and so on. This bit count affects the amount of memory a computer can access and its speed of operation. It could be compared with the number of cylinders in an automobile engine: 4-cylinder, 6-cylinder, 8-cylinder, etc. As the number of bits that can be manipulated at one time increases, the power and potential speed of the microprocessor increases.

FIGURE 11.3.
Common microprocessor chips

Microprocessor	Bits	Example Computers
Intel 8080	8	Radio Shack Model I
Intel 8088	8/16	IBM PC, IBM XT, PS/2 Model 25
Intel 8086	16	AT&T 6300
Intel 80286	16	IBM AT, PS/2 Models 50 and 60
Intel 80386	32	IBM PS/2 Model 80, Compaq 386
Motorola 6502	8	Apple IIe
Motorola 68000	16/32	Macintosh Plus
Motorola 68020	32	Macintosh II

You will see descriptions of some microprocessors as 8/16-bit chips, as in the case of the 8088 chip. This means that the microprocessor can perform 16-bit manipulations within the chip, but that it communicates information to the rest of the computer like an 8-bit chip. The original IBM PC was based on the 8088 microprocessor to take advantage of its internal 16-bit manipulation while using the then-more readily available 8-bit communication setup with other devices. The 8086 microprocessor, which is now used in some IBM-type clone computers, is a true 16-bit microprocessor that manipulates 16 bits internally, and also communicates information with 16 bits at once. As a result of the faster communications through 16-bit operations, computers based on the 8086 chip run faster than their 8088 cousins.

Expansion Slots

Another important factor in the selection of a computer is the number and types of expansion slots available. Expansion slots are plugs on the computer's system board that allow you to add on new devices or computer components. For example, expansion slots may be used to add more memory to the computer by plugging in a new memory board. Adding on a new device to the computer also typically requires an expansion board plugged into the system board. Figure 11.4 illustrates an expansion board being plugged into the system board.

A table of the number of expansion slots available in some common computers is given in figure 11.5. Some of the new IBM PS/2 models use a different kind of expansion slot than those used on the original PC. This new Micro Channel slot allows the computer to communicate faster to peripheral devices.

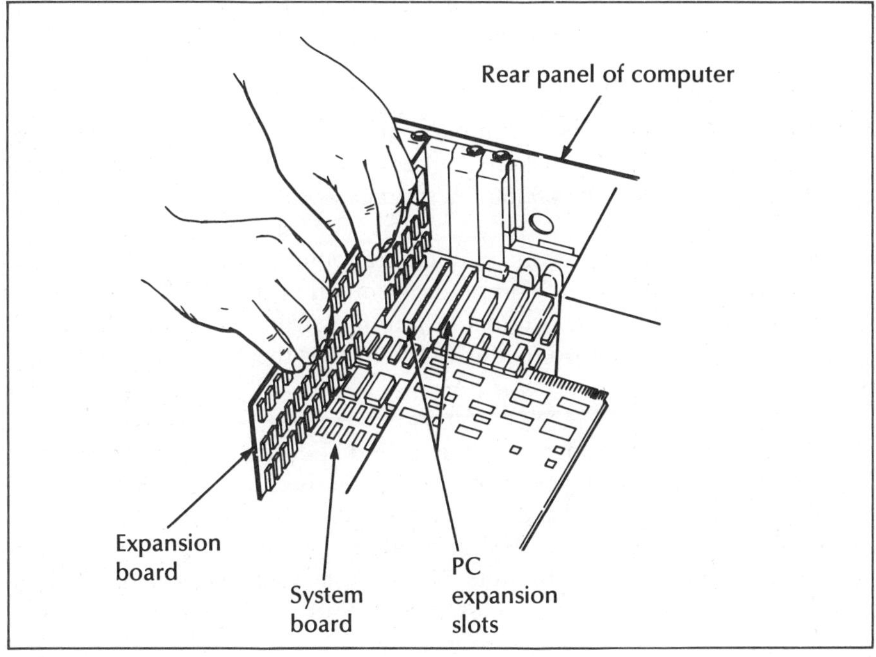

FIGURE 11.4.
Expansion board being added

FIGURE 11.5.
Expansion slots in some common computers

Computer	Number of Expansion Slots
IBM PC	5
IBM XT	8
IBM AT	8
IBM PS/2 Model 30	3
IBM PS/2 Model 50	4 (Micro Channel type)
IBM PS/2 Model 60	8 (Micro Channel type)
IBM PS/2 Model 80	8 (Micro Channel type)
APPLE MACINTOSH PLUS	0
APPLE MACINTOSH II	6

THE IBM PERSONAL COMPUTER FAMILY

The IBM Personal Computer was introduced in October of 1981. Subsequent computers from IBM, and now a large number of clone computers, have basically copied or improved on the operation of the original PC. The following discussion describes major IBM-type personal computers. It is not meant to cover every feature of these computers, but to point out major new features that were introduced with each model.

IBM PC. There are several million IBM PCs and clones of the IBM PC in use today. Although it is a very old product for a computer, it is still popular. The majority of the business software market today is compatible with the original IBM PC. IBM no longer makes the original PC, but there are many compatible manufacturers that are keeping the product alive. The original PC used the Intel 8088 microprocessor, and its speed in the original model was 4.77 MHz (megahertz). You can use this speed to compare other computers. Some of the newer compatibles are made with speeds of 8 MHz or better. Faster computer speeds usually mean that your software program will run faster and will be more responsive.

IBM XT. This computer is very similar to the original IBM PC. Its main difference is support for a hard disk. In the late 1980s IBM introduced a new version of the XT that uses the 80286 microprocessor.

IBM AT. The AT was the first major microcomputer to use the 80286 microprocessor. It was the "power" computer for much of the 1980s. It generally runs software faster than the original PC, running from 6 to 8 MHz, depending on the model. Also introduced with the AT was the 1.2-megabyte floppy disk drive.

Laptops. The IBM laptop computer, called the Convertible, was introduced in 1987 as an 8088-type computer (actually, it used an 80C88 chip, which is similar to the original 8088, but uses less power). Many laptops can run on batteries. Laptops by IBM and other manufacturers also include 80286- and 80386-based computers. The two factors that generally limit laptop computers are their sometimes hard-to-read monitors and their lack of expansion slots.

IBM PS/2 Series. In 1987, IBM introduced a new series of personal computers called the PS/2 series. It includes computers using the 8088, 80286, and 80386 Intel microprocessors and running at speeds from 8 MHz to 25 MHz. Model 25 uses the 8088 microprocessor, and is really just an improved PC. Models 30(286), 50 and 60 use the 80286 chip. Model 50 and 60 use an expansion slot that differs from the original slot in the PC, XT, AT, and Models 25 and 30. This new Micro Channel slot provides faster communication with attached peripherals. The PS/2 Models 70 and 80 use an 80386 microprocessor and also use Micro Channel slots. The PS/2 series also introduced a switch from 5.25-inch floppy disk drives as the standard disk drive to 3.5-inch floppy disk drives.

IBM Compatibles. Because of its dominance in the business computing market, IBM has set many of the standards for microcomputing. Other companies have "cloned" the IBM computers. Most clone computers are extremely compatible with the IBM computers. You as a buyer must know about the IBM computers in order to compare the clones to the related IBM product. This is where you need knowledge of microprocessor chips, expansion slots, monitor types, speed, and other factors. Some of the compatible computers are made by companies with familiar names: Tandy (Radio Shack), AT&T, Compaq, Epson, Sperry, Toshiba, NEC, and others. Other brands are made by companies with less familiar names: Dell, Leading Edge, PC Source, AST, Businessland, Build Your Own, and others. The parts for many of these computers are readily purchased "off the shelf". This has meant that individuals and small companies can build their own brand-name computers with ease.

CHOOSING A CLONE COMPUTER

When considering the purchase of a clone, there are some important items to keep in mind. Some clones use high-quality components, others do not. Most of the well-known brands will use good quality components. If you are unfamiliar with a brand, your best evaluation of their quality may be from a customer who has owned one of their machines for an extended period of time. Also keep in mind that some computer manufacturers and dealers go out of business. A warranty may only be as good as the company's ability to keep its doors open. However, most PC components are standard enough that they can be repaired or replaced at a number of repair shops. Unless you have experience in buying and assembling computers, always make sure that the computer you purchase is completely assembled, and you see it tested in the store before you take possession.

OPERATING SYSTEMS FOR THE IBM PC

From the introduction of the IBM PC, the most common operating system for it has been PC-DOS. Some clones use the MS-DOS system, which is virtually the same. Other operating systems that can operate on various IBM microcomputers include CP/M, Unix, and p-system. With the introduction of the PS/2 series, IBM and Microsoft introduced a new operating system called OS/2. The purpose of this operating system was to enable computers with

80286 and 80386 chips to access more memory and to give the capability of multitasking—the ability to run more than one program at a time. (Multitasking is discussed in more detail in chapter 12.)

Under PC-DOS, IBM microcomputers were limited to accessing 640K of random access memory (RAM). OS/2 allows 80286 computers to access 16 megabytes (million bytes) of memory, and allows 80386 computers to access 4 gigabytes (billion bytes) of memory.

THE APPLE FAMILY OF COMPUTERS

The two major kinds of Apple computers are the Apple II series and the Macintosh series. Apple computers are based on a series of microprocessor chips developed by Motorola. The original Apple II was based on the Motorola 6502 chip, an 8-bit chip. The Macintosh branch of the Apple family is based on the 68000 series of chips, which are 32-bit microprocessors. The following discussion is not meant to cover every feature of these computers, but to point out some major features in each.

Apple II. There are several varieties of the Apple II computer. Three popular varieties are the IIe, IIc, and IIGS. The Apple IIe is a direct descendant of the original Apple II, with improvements. The IIc is a redesign of the original computer in a smaller case. The IIGS is a state-of-the-art computer which specializes in graphics and sound. The Apple II series is particularly popular as an educational computer.

Since the Apple II has been around for many years, there is a tremendous amount of software available. However, since it is based on an 8-bit machine, much of the new sophisticated business and professional software is not becoming available for the Apple II series.

Macintosh. The Macintosh is Apple's most popular computer, and is the computer being promoted by Apple for the business market. The Macintosh computer introduced the concept of "desktop publishing" through its unique and easy ability to produce near-publication quality documents and graphics. When the Macintosh was first introduced, it was limited to only 128K of memory. The Macintosh 512 and 512e came with 512K of memory. The Macintosh Plus uses 1 megabyte of memory, and the Macintosh SE added more speed. The Macintosh II introduced a new concept for the Macintosh, as it was an "open" computer with easy-to-use expansion ports like those available in the IBM PC.

The Macintosh uses an operating system quite different from IBM PC-DOS. Instead of the user entering a command at the keyboard, Macintosh users use a mouse (a small hand-held device) to point to a menu or graphic image *(icon)* on the screen to choose options, run programs, perform copies, and other functions that DOS provides for IBM-type computers. A similar type of operating system is available on the IBM computers using Microsoft Windows or IBM's Presentation Manager. Figure 11.6 illustrates a typical Macintosh screen.

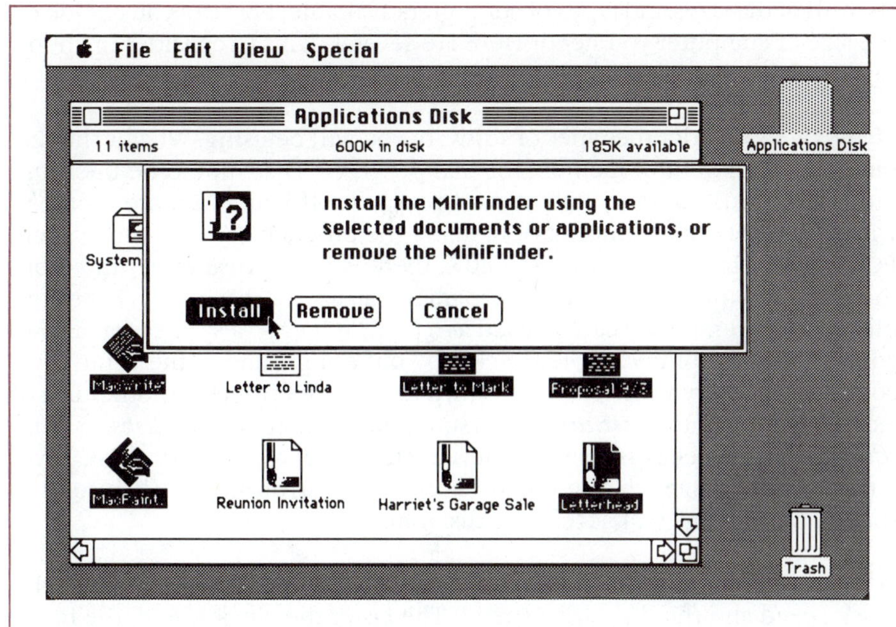

FIGURE 11.6.
Macintosh screen

COMPATIBILITY BOARDS BRIDGE GAPS BETWEEN COMPUTERS

After each new generation of microcomputer arrives (as when the AT series updated the original PC), users must choose to stay with their "old" devices or upgrade. One answer to this problem has been the introduction of expansion boards that give an old machine compatibility with the new computer. For example, people wanting to upgrade their old IBM PC to the power of an 80286 computer without having to buy a whole new computer can purchase a board that fits into their old computer and replaces the 8088 chip with a new 80286 chip. Cross-family boards are also available. Macintosh users can purchase an IBM PC-type board that gives Macintosh users the capability of running both Macintosh and IBM PC-type software on the same computer.

There are advantages to making a decision to use only Apple or only IBM-type computers. Since both computers are powerful and support similar types of software, the decision usually rests on your personal preference about the user interface (PC-DOS versus the Macintosh's icon system); on the need to run a particular piece of software, or on being compatible with other people with whom you will be sharing computer information. If you are using only one kind of computer, it makes learning how to use the computer easier—you only have to learn one computer interface. If you are connecting computers together, or sharing information, having all one kind of computer makes the task much simpler. On the other hand, many organizations find themselves with mixed types of computers. In this situation, the cross-family boards and other cross-family communication schemes can be very helpful.

HOW MUCH COMPUTER YOU NEED

With all of the sizes and types of computers available, how can you decide on the size of computer you need? Here are several items to consider in choosing computer hardware.

Memory. Consider the types of software you will be using. What is the recommended amount of memory for that program? That should be the minimum amount of memory you should purchase. If you add more memory, what is the maximum amount of memory the program can use? Since some PC programs can use only up to 640K, there is little sense in getting more than that amount. However, other programs can use more memory. For example, additional memory can be used as a *print spooler*—a system that allows your print jobs to finish more quickly by buffering some of the printing in computer memory while it waits its turn to go to the printer. Another use of extra memory is for *virtual disks* (sometimes called *speed disks* or *flash disks*). This is a piece of memory that is treated as if it were an extra disk drive. A memory drive is much faster than a normal disk drive, and may be useful to speed up programs that access the disk often.

Speed. There are two factors in determining the speed of a computer: the clock speed and the disk drive speed. The faster the clock speed, the faster the computer will be able to calculate, perform word processing tasks, and draw graphics. Disk drive speed becomes important when the software accesses the disk often, as in desktop publishing programs. Speed is often a choice dictated by money. A slow computer is inexpensive, but will usually slow down most computing jobs. Faster computers cost more, but save time and frustration.

The Microprocessor Chip. Many newer programs will not run on machines with older microprocessor chips (e.g., 8088 and 6502). To purchase a computer that will be able to take advantage of new software and operating systems, you should consider buying a computer that uses the most modern chip. In the PC family, that is the 80286, or even better, the 80386. In the Apple family, it is the 68000 series chip. This is not to say computers using the other chips should not be considered—you must simply decide if you can limit yourself to the software they will run now and in the future.

Expansion Slots. Do you plan for this computer to grow? Expansion slots are the road to growth for a computer. If the computer will be used for only one task and is unlikely to need additional power in the future, you need not be concerned about expansion slots. If you will be adding more memory, hooking the computer to a network, attaching to a laboratory instrument or other kinds of peripherals, then you will need to make sure the computer you purchase has adequate expansion slots. Also, you need to see if the kinds of add-ons you intend to get can be attached to the kind of expansion slot your computer has. On the PC, you may have the PC slot, the AT slot or the Micro Channel slot.

ADD-ONS FOR YOUR COMPUTER

The computer is just part of the hardware story. You must still decide on other important pieces of hardware such as a monitor, printer, modem, and other peripherals.

Monitors and Display Adapters

For the IBM PC family of computers you must usually purchase two items to use a monitor on the computer. You must purchase a video card called a *display adapter* that plugs into an expansion slot, and a monitor to attach to the video card. Some IBM-type computers (the PS/2 series) have video capabilities on the system board and do not require the purchase of a video card. Each type of monitor requires a particular type of display adapter in order to operate.

One of the measures of the clarity of a monitor is the number of pixels (dots on the screen). The more pixels, the more potential resolution of text and graphics. The number of pixels is usually described by the number of pixels across the screen and the number of pixels from the top to the bottom of the screen. For example, 720 × 240 means that the monitor can display 720 pixels across the screen and 240 from top to bottom.

Monochrome Monitor. This single-color (usually green or amber) monitor was designed primarily for the display of text. Most of the first PCs sold were equipped with monochrome monitors. When graphics software programs began to appear, they could not be run on computers with the monochrome monitor. However, the Hercules company designed a new kind of monochrome display adapter to replace the standard monochrome board. The new board gave the monochrome monitor the capability to display graphic images. The resolution of the monochrome monitor is 640 × 350 pixels.

Composite Video Monitor. This monitor is a single-color display like the monochrome monitor (usually green or amber), but allows display of graphic images. The display adapter required to run the composite video monitor is called a CGA board (Color Graphics Adapter). The text characters on the composite video monitor are not as clear as those on the monochrome monitor. The resolution of the composite video monitor is 640 × 240 pixels. The composite graphics monitor is usually the least expensive monitor available for IBM-type computers.

Color Graphics Monitor. A color graphics monitor allows color display of composite text and graphics. This monitor, like the composite video monitor, uses the color graphic adapter (CGA) board. Sixteen colors are available in text mode, 3 colors in low-resolution graphics, and 1 color in high-resolution graphics. The quality of text is similar to that on the composite video monitor. Most people find it unacceptable for long-term word processing or other text-oriented work. The resolution of the Color Graphics monitor is 320 × 200 pixels in 3-color mode or 640 × 200 pixels in single-color mode.

Enhanced Color Graphics. This monitor has more colors and better clarity of text and graphics than the CGA color monitor. The display adapter required to operate this monitor is called an enhanced graphics adapter (EGA). The resolution of the EGA monitor is 640 × 350 pixels.

Multicolor Graphics Array. The multicolor graphics array (MCGA) monitor is standard on the PS/2 Models 25 and 30. The graphics resolution for the MCGA monitor is 640 × 480 pixels.

Vector Graphics Array Monitor. The Vector Graphics Array Monitor (VGA) was introduced with the PS/2 series of IBM computers. The display adapter required to operate this monitor is called a vector graphics adapter (VGA). It adds more pixels than the EGA, and more colors. The resolution of the VGA monitor is 640 × 480 pixels for 16-color mode and 320 × 200 pixels for 256-color mode.

Monitor types are summarized in figure 11.7.

Monitor Compatibility

Software must be specifically written to take advantage of the colors and other features of monitors. Generally, monitors are *upwardly compatible.* This means that as new monitors with more features are introduced, they still can maintain programs that use old monitor standards. For example, if you use a program made to run on an EGA monitor, it will run on the more powerful VGA monitor. However, a CGA monitor cannot be used for a program that requires an EGA monitor. The upward progression of graphics monitors is as follows: Composite Video, Color Graphics, Enhanced Graphics, and Vector Graphics. Some questions to think about in choosing a monitor are listed in figure 11.8.

FIGURE 11.7.
Some common monitors and adapters

Monitor Type	Adapter Needed	Resolution
Monochrome	Monochrome or Hercules-type	640 × 350
Composite video monitor	CGA	320 × 200
Color Graphics monitor	CGA	640 × 200 color
		320 × 200 mono
Enhanced Graphics	EGA	640 × 350
Multicolor Graphics	MCGA	640 × 480
Vector Graphics	VGA	640 × 480 16 cols
		320 × 480 256 cols

FIGURE 11.8.
Choosing a monitor

Checklist for Choosing a Monitor

1. Does your software require a certain type of monitor? Are you using only text (in which case a monochrome monitor would be fine), or will you require graphics capabilities?
2. If you require graphic capabilities, what is the resolution that your software supports? If your graphics software only supports CGA, for example, there would be no need to spend extra money on an EGA or VGA monitor, unless clarity of text was also important.
3. Do you anticipate needing higher resolution in the near future? If you will be doing desktop publishing, Computer Aided Design (CAD), or other graphic-intensive tasks, you may consider getting the highest-resolution monitor available, probably VGA.
4. Will you need color? If so, then you must choose not only a graphics monitor, but also one that produces color.

PRINTERS

You may have the fastest, most state-of-the-art computer available, but if your printer is inferior, the quality of your output will suffer. The printer should be capable of producing the kind of output you need, and must be compatible with the software you will be using. Even if the promotional material for a printer contains impressive examples of the kinds of printing it can do, make sure that the particular software you have can make use of these features.

The workhorse of printers for microcomputers has been the 9-pin dot matrix printer. In the early years of microcomputing, its ability to print out text and graphics was impressive. Today, there are much better quality printers available. Laser printers are the high end of microcomputer printing. They can produce excellent quality printing and graphics. The following list describes the kinds of printers that are popularly used.

9-Pin Dot Matrix. These printers provide low-cost yet flexible printing. Dot matrix printers usually have graphics printing capability and some offer near-letter quality printing.

24-Pin Dot Matrix. These printers give much higher resolution in text and graphics printing than the 9-pin printers. They produce letter-quality printing at a fairly low cost.

Laser Printers. Laser printers are more expensive than dot matrix printers, but they produce near-typeset quality printing. Most laser printers also support the printing of graphics. A laser printer is recommended for business use where the quality of outgoing printed material is important, or for people who will be producing camera-ready copy or doing desktop publishing.

Daisy Wheel. This is an impact printer that is much like a typewriter. It is generally very noisy and slow. These kinds of printers produce a high-quality text image but they do not support graphics.

Other printer options include ink jet printers and thermal transfer printers. Also, some printers offer the ability to print graphs and text in color.

In order to decide which printer is right for you, you must consider what kind of software you will be running, what you want the printer to be able to do (e.g., print graphics) and how nice the quality of your printout should be. Laser printers will give you the best quality. Daisy-wheel printers and 24-pin dot matrix printers will give you typewriter quality; however, daisy printers cannot produce graphics. Nine-pin dot matrix printers are sufficient for personal or draft-quality use. Print quality generally goes up as price increases. Many people tend to spend thousands of dollars on their computer, but balk at spending money on a nice printer. Remember, most people will see only the final product (the printed page) and not the computer it was produced on.

MODEMS

A modem (*mo*dulator/*dem*odulator) allows you to communicate with your personal computer via phone lines to other computers. For example, students can use their university mainframe computer from home. Employees can work at home, communicating through the personal computer to their business computer. Electronic mail can originate on a PC and be sent almost anywhere in the world. Pictures, graphics, and other information that can be stored on a computer can be transmitted to another computer with a modem.

Like the IBM PC in the microcomputing world, one kind of modem has become the industry standard. This is the Hayes type of modem. Usually, if you acquire a modem, you want to make sure you get a "Hayes-compatible" modem. Another feature you will be interested in is the speed at which the modem can transfer data. Some common speeds are 1200 baud, 2400 baud, and 9600 baud. The baud rate is a measure of transmitted bits-per-second. The greater the baud rate the faster the transmission. You also must have software to operate your modem. Some popular programs include Smartcom (from Hayes), ProComm, Kermit, and Crosstalk. You must make sure that your software and brand of modem can work with each other. Communications software will be discussed in chapter 12.

Modems are purchased as either an internal or external device. An internal modem is one that is plugged in to an expansion slot in the computer. The phone line is hooked into a plug in the back of the computer, and the phone number is dialed by the software. An external modem sits outside the computer and is attached to the computer through one of the computer's serial ports. The software usually works identically for an internal or external modem.

How do you decide if you need a modem? There are several very good reasons to have one. If you have a personal computer at home, and a computer at work or school that has dial-in capabilities, you can access that computer from home. Perhaps it is cheaper to run programs on the business computer after normal working hours, or maybe it is easier for you to get on the school computer at night. The $100 or so that you spend for the modem might be worth the time and money saved by doing some work from home.

Another good use of the model is access to commercial data banks such as those from The Source or CompuServe. These services offer you the capability of accessing such diverse information as world-wide weather reports, stock quotes, the entire text of an encyclopedia, the text of dozens of newspapers, professional journals, reference books, airline schedules, job openings, and much more. Need a report on civil strife in Poland by tomorrow morning, and the library is closed? Search the on-line data banks for the topic, and get the latest information (maybe even before it appears in print the next morning!)

Buying considerations for modems include type and speed. Internal modems take no room on the desk and generally cost less. External modems are easier to move from computer to computer. The faster the modem speed, the more it costs. A 1200-baud modem is usually fine for occasional use. However, if you often access information from computers that charge you by the minute, the faster 2400- or 9600-baud modems may be considered. In general, if a document takes 10 minutes to copy on a 1200-baud modem, it can be copied in 5 minutes using a 2400-baud modem, or 1.25 minutes using a 9600-baud modem.

OTHER ADD-ONS TO CONSIDER

It is not unusual for people to need or want additional items for their computer. For example, you may have purchased a new piece of software that requires some enhancement that is not currently on your computer. Some common add-on devices are discussed here.

Extra Memory. Many computers come with a standard amount of memory (256K, 512K, 640K, 1 megabyte). How much memory you need depends on how much memory your application requires. For example, if your spreadsheet program requires a minimum of 512K to operate, that does not mean you should have only 512K. If you begin producing large spreadsheets, you will likely require more than this minimum amount.

Most DOS machines can access only up to 640K for any application. If you are not sure how much memory you will need, get a computer with 640K of memory. Unless there are special circumstances, such as the need for extra memory for large programs (extended memory), 640K is the most memory you will need.

Hard Disk Drive. Many business computers purchased today come with hard disk drives. In the long run, using a hard disk usually saves time and is more convenient than dealing with floppy disks. Also, many programs run faster and better on a hard disk. Large programs such as PageMaker (a desktop publishing package) and SAS/PC (a statistical analysis package) require several megabytes of disk storage to operate. For programs such as these, a hard disk is a necessity.

There are at least two important factors to consider when buying a hard disk. First, consider the size you need. Hard disks come in a variety of sizes ranging from 10 megabytes to over 100 megabytes. To determine what size you need, add up the size requirements of the various pieces of software you will use. For example, SAS/PC requires about 10 megabytes, and PageMaker can easily use 5 megabytes once you have created several publications. Include room in your hard disk requirements to add new applications. The second factor to consider is the speed (access time) of your hard disk. Programs that use the disk frequently during operation (such as PageMaker) can be slowed down considerably by a hard disk with a slow access time. Access speed is measured in milliseconds (msec). A standard hard disk drive has an access speed in the range of 40 msec, and a fast drive has access time of 28 msec or better.

Mouse. A mouse pointing device is used in some programs to position the cursor on the computer screen, to choose items from a menu, or to draw. Some programs work either with a mouse or through keyboard commands, but many people find it easier and quicker to use the program with the mouse. Consider the software you will be using and try it out if possible before deciding to buy a mouse.

The most commonly used mice sold for PCs are the Microsoft mouse and the IBM mouse, both two-button mice. Virtually all software that uses a mouse will support the Microsoft and IBM mice. Other mice may also be supported (one- and three-button mice), and there are other two-button mice that are "Microsoft mouse compatible." Support for a mouse is generally determined by the application software you are using. Check your documentation to verify which mouse it supports.

Backup Device. An important question to ask yourself is not "Will I lose my programs and information stored on my disk?" but rather "When?" Backups of computer information on hard disks should be done on a regular schedule, particularly for important or hard-to-recover information. PC-DOS comes with a BACKUP program, but it can be very slow and cumbersome. When backups are important, a backup device should be considered. Tapes, removable disks, or optical disk backup devices allow you to copy the information from the computer's hard disk to media that can be easily stored in a safe location, usually away from the computer. If the computer fails or is damaged, the information can be recovered

Backup Power Supply. If a sudden loss of power could result in the loss of very crucial information (financial records, medical records, etc.), a backup power supply can give you extra minutes of power to shut your system down normally during a power outage. A backup power supply device constantly monitors the power to your computer. If there is a sudden power loss, the backup power supply provides power until the normal power is resumed, or until you turn your computer off.

WHERE AND HOW TO BUY A PERSONAL COMPUTER

When personal computers first became available, you could only buy them at hobby stores or a few microcomputer stores. By the early 1980s a number of chain computer stores such as ComputerLand, Businessland, and Compushop began appearing all around the country. For several years, these shops were about the only place you could purchase a business-oriented personal computer. In fact, during the IBM PC's first year of production, over 90% of the PCs sold at retail in the United States were sold at ComputerLand stores. As the IBM PC computer became the standard, and as many manufacturers began making compatibles or *clones* of the IBM PC, other retail stores began to sell computers. Some local computer stores that were not IBM PC authorized dealers began to sell clones to attract new customers. Ads for mail order houses selling both computers and software began appearing in magazines. Major manufacturers such as IBM want their computers sold only by authorized dealers. However, there are many non-authorized dealers who buy PCs in bulk and sell them on the "gray market", often for less than you would pay at an authorized dealer.

Clone Computers and Upgraded Major Brands

With cloned computers and cloned parts readily available, every dealer can now carry IBM-compatible computers. However, there are many people who prefer the IBM brand. It gives some people a feeling that they know the quality of the computer they are buying. Something you should be aware of, particularly with non-authorized dealers, is what is really inside the computer's case. A dealer can buy a stripped-down version of a computer and upgrade it with cheaper parts such as hard disks, memory, and other expansion devices. Although the box says IBM, the insides may contain non-IBM components. This may or may not be a problem. IBM purchases some of its components from manufacturers who sell the identical item (with a different name plate) at a lower cost. There are, however, inferior parts that are also made and can be placed in a name-brand computer. Having components from mixed sources in your computer may affect your warranty. On the other hand, buying different brands of components of equal quality to the original can save money. In this case, the reputation of the dealer should be considered.

Today, there are many places to buy computers—from discount stores to mail order houses to computer stores. Your particular situation will determine which place is best for you. You should consider price, service, availability, and recommendations of customers before making your decision. The following descriptions cover some of the good and bad points of making your purchase with particular kinds of dealers:

Authorized Computer Stores. Most authorized computer stores are found in shopping centers near business centers in cities. They typically have a nice showroom with computers and software available for you to "test drive". An advantage of these stores is that they give you the opportunity to try out equipment, talk to knowledgeable people (sometime biased), and provide support after the sale. Most will have an in-house technical department. The quality of service at these stores varies. The salesperson may have a good working knowledge of computers, or may simply be an "order taker". Also, you must realize that most salespersons can know only a limited amount of software. They will not be experts on every system, and will tend to recommend the hardware and software they are most familiar with. If you are not sure what you want, see if you can spend enough time at the computer in the store to convince yourself that what you are going to buy meets your needs. Once you have made the decision to buy, it is often best to have your complete computer system put together and tested at the store before you take possession. Frequently, if a computer is going to have problems, it will show up right away. This will prevent the inconvenience of having to take the computer apart and transport it back to the shop for replacement of defective parts.

Computer Warehouses. Because computer components are easy to obtain, many entrepreneurs have discovered that they can assemble computers cheaply, and that a fancy showroom is not necessary to sell computers and related parts. The result is that there are quite a few "computer warehouses" around the country. These places vary in quality, from the operation trying to make quick money at the sacrifice of quality, to the small but knowledgeable dealer who makes a good product while containing costs. These places with low operating costs usually have the best prices on many items, including not only hardware and software but also diskettes, paper, and other disposables. One problem with such operations is that they often (but not always) have poor after-sales service. They sell cheap, meaning that they have little budget for a salesperson to spend an hour with you trying to figure out a solution to your problem. If you already know precisely what you want, this is the kind of operation that can usually give you the best price. It has been said before, but it is particularly valid here: Do not take possession of a computer until you check it out in the store.

Special Discounts. Professional discounts, campus store discounts, or corporate discounts may apply not only to computers and components purchased for the organization, but may also be available to individuals. Many universities or corporations offer employees discounts on computers. If you know of a store that does a lot of business with your school, business, or organization, find out which salesperson is responsible for those sales, and ask him or her if they will extend the same discounts to individuals associated with the organization.

Mail Order:. This is often, but not always, the most inexpensive way to buy computer hardware and software. Computers including IBMs and clones can be purchased this way. It is helpful to know someone who has had a good experience with a company, or to notice that the company has advertised for many months in a row, before buying this way. If a magazine gets many complaints about a dealer, they will pull their ads. Also, it may be best to purchase with a credit card, since you may have better recourse if something goes wrong. Be aware that it can be a difficult proposition to send a computer back across the country to get something repaired. Some dealers will pay postage and insurance both ways, but the time that can be lost may still be a major factor in your decision to purchase hardware in this way.

Used. You will usually find a number of used machines in newspaper classified advertising. If you know what you want, this is a good way to get it less expensively than at retail. There are also some computer dealers that carry used equipment, and some user groups have “flea markets” to sell new and used equipment. You can generally find out if there is a user group in your area by asking at local computer stores. Naturally you will need to test the machine thoroughly before buying it.

If you are getting software with a used computer, be sure you are getting the manufacturer’s original disk (not a copy) and a complete manual for the program.

SHAREWARE SOFTWARE

Much of the popular business software in use can cost up to $700 per program or more. However, there are sources of inexpensive software that are often as good as their commercial cousins. This software goes by various names, including “shareware”, “user-supported software”, or “freeware”. They will be referred to here as shareware. These programs are not to be confused with “public domain” software. Public domain programs can be used, copied, given away, modified, and sold without any copyright restrictions. Shareware computer programs are copyrighted but are not generally distributed through retail stores. The program’s owners allow users to copy the program freely and give it to friends (under a few restrictions). The programs are often distributed by computer user groups for a nominal cost (usually about $5 a disk). PC-SIG is a national organization that has over 1000 disks that you can order for about $6 each. (Their address is PC-SIG, 1030 E. Duane Suite J, Sunnyvale, CA 94086.)

Most commercial software products have legal restrictions that prevent you from copying the software. When you buy commercial software, you usually purchase a license to use the program on only one computer. The purpose of shareware is to allow potential customers to "try it before they buy it." Once you have decided to use a particular piece of shareware, you are encouraged to send in a registration fee, which usually provides you with the latest version, a manual, and information about updates. Registration fees are usually much less than the retail prices of similar commercial software. Although the quality of shareware programs varies widely, many programs are as sophisticted as their more expensive store-bought cousins. Most of the better shareware program authors are members of the Association of Shareware Professionals (ASP). Some of the popular shareware products include PC-File, a database program, PC-Write, a word processor, Automenu, a menuing program, Kwikstat, a statistical analysis package, and ProComm, a communication program. This is a small list of the literally hundreds of programs available.

SUMMARY

You will likely be involved in a computer buying decision in the near future. If you are not buying a computer for yourself, you may be purchasing one in conjunction with your job or profession. There are so many varieties and options available that many buyers are at the mercy of salespeople who may have biased reasons for selling you a particular system. Before you buy a computer:

- Be clear as to what you want your computer to do.
- Know what pieces of software it will need to run, and what the hardware requirements are for that software.
- Realize that finding specialty software may require some extensive research.
- Keep in mind the possible need to expand your computer in the future.
- Realize that the least expensive price is not the only criterion in making a computer purchasing decision.
- Consider all outlets available to you, and choose the one that will not only meet your cost restrictions, but will offer any after-sale service you may need.

QUESTIONS

Write a short answer in your own words for each question.

1. Outline the questions to answer before buying a computer system.
2. What are the three most common types of application software? What are some examples of specialty or industry-specific software?
3. What are the two major families of business microcomputers? Name the types of computers in each family, and something that differentiates them from the other members of the family.

4. What are the common types of monitors in the IBM family of computers?
5. What kind of printer would someone probably buy who needs to print the highest quality of text and graphics?
6. What is a modem and what can you do with it?
7. What are some add-on options you may consider when buying a computer?
8. If you wanted to buy the most inexpensive IBM type computer possible, where would you look? Why?
9. What are some sources of shareware? Are there any computer user groups in your area?

LABORATORY EXERCISES

Lab Exercise 1. Suppose you need to make brochures for a hair salon. Choose an IBM-type computer system that includes a computer, a monitor capable of graphics, a hard disk with 20 megabytes or more, a mouse, and a printer. The software you intend to run on this machine, besides DOS, is WordPerfect and PageMaker (desktop publishing software).

1. Describe a computing system that will meet these needs. After you have decided on the computer, price the system at the following kinds of places:
   a. A local retail computer store selling IBM computers.
   b. A local retail computer store selling clones.
   c. A mail-order house.
2. Where did you get the best, the worst, and/or no advice?
3. Where did you get the highest and lowest price?
4. Assume that you own the business, and that you will have an employee run the computer. If you were really going to buy this computer, where would you buy it and why?

Lab Exercise 2. Suppose you wanted to buy a computer setup, including hardware and industry-specific software, to perform the normal business and accounting functions of a dental office (or choose some other business or profession that interests you). Research the kinds of software available in the marketplace. Sources of information would be libraries, computer stores with catalogs of software, ads in professional journals or magazines, or a person in the business or profession you are researching.

1. Which piece of software would you choose? How did you decide?
2. What computer would you buy?
3. How much would the total system, including software and hardware, cost?
4. Write up a proposal as if you were presenting it to your employer, listing your reasons and the benefits of this system over others.

GUEST ESSAY

An Introduction to Desktop Publishing

by Stephen J. Menconi
Senior Engineer, AT&T

What advantage does desktop publishing (DTP) offer? Using DTP software, you can create the original text and graphics for a publication. Past techniques involved the separate activities of word processing, preparation of art and graphics, typesetting of galleys, proofreading, and the integration of text and art on paste-up boards for the printer. Using desktop publishing techniques, you can design, write, draw, and create final copy containing integrated text and art without paste-up. Photographs can be scanned and inserted into the file as either the actual-size halftone or as a position-only indicator. The computer file produced can be easily edited or changed. Retyping of files into a typesetting system is not required, eliminating a source of error and the time required.

The author, working alone or with an editor, makes the changes and controls the format. Using style sheets or formatting files, actual pages can be viewed as a what-you-see-is-what-you-get (WYSIWYG) display and printed immediately. No more surprises in the copy received from the typesetter! Using a personal computer (PC) and a laser printer, you can now produce professional-looking, near-typeset quality documents from your desk. The advent of desktop publishing software has freed you from the slower and error-prone methods used in the past, and has resulted in a real savings in time and cost.

There are many variations on desktop publishing software. Some software packages offer only a page make-up program with a minimum-duty text and graphics editor. Other packages, known as corporate publishing software, integrate page layout, word processing, and graphics into one large program. However, there are usually some trade-offs made in either the style sheets available, the word processing, the graphics, or the fonts supported. These corporate publishing packages provide powerful find-and-replace features and do automatic indexing and table of contents generation.

Before you can enjoy the freedom afforded through DTP, you must purchase the right hardware and applications software to do what you require. Determine what type of documents you will be preparing. Go to your local computer stores for software and hardware demonstrations. Attend the free seminars, lectures, and shows that are available. Information concerning these can be obtained from manufacturers, dealers, and the many periodicals available at the newsstand or computer store.

The minimum level of PC hardware purchased should be a 16-bit microprocessor-based computer with sufficient memory, a 40-megabyte or larger hard disk drive, and the peripheral cards needed to run the software. A 32-bit microprocessor-based PC offers more speed and features, but at a substantial increase in price. Make certain that the system you are purchasing is compatible with those of your co-workers, otherwise you will not be able to exchange files or network.

Determine the type of monitor supported by the DTP software you have selected. Do not limit your selection to strictly DTP monitors; you will probably want to run other programs such as spreadsheets, databases, and recreational software. Usually an enhanced graphics adapter (EGA) card with an EGA monitor will do the job. There are special display cards and DTP monitors that feature large screens that allow you to view two full pages simultaneously. These are more expensive, may restrict you to DTP only, and may go beyond your requirements. Always have the entire system demonstrated to assure compatibility between all the hardware and software components. At least obtain a return guarantee, in writing, in the event the item purchased does not work in your system.

Select the best laser printer you can afford. If your funds are limited, select a model that can be upgraded later with the addition of printed circuit cards, font cartridges, or software. Make certain that your DTP software supports the laser printer you choose. You may need additional drive and font software.

continued

continued

Most quality laser printers have an output density of 300 dots per inch (dpi), whereas phototypesetters range from 1200 to 2400 dpi. In most cases, except for advertising copy, the laser printer's output is more than adequate. New laser printers are available with densities of 600 dpi or higher, but are very expensive. Also, the output files produced by most desktop publishing systems can be sent to a phototypesetter if higher-quality copy is required.

"Turnkey" DTP systems are available, in which the vender has already integrated the hardware and software into one offering. This saves you the time and headache of integrating your own system, but the turnkey system may have some limitations. Always ask for a thorough demonstration and try out all the system features that are important to you.

There are many fine books available on the subject of desktop publishing. A few dollars and the time spent reading these may save you thousands of dollars and a lot of grief later. Also, do not forget to contact other desktop publishers for advice. We are a friendly lot that usually love to show off our systems and their capabilities.

CHAPTER 12

Special Topics

CHAPTER OVERVIEW. This special section is devoted to discussing additional microcomputer topics that may be of interest to the reader. The majority of the text has been concerned with detailed descriptions of the most commonly used software on the IBM PC. However, the PC can do much more. Each of the following sections concerns itself with a particular topic and gives an overview of some capabilities in the microcomputer world. A few specific examples may be given in each section, but this overview is not meant to teach you how to use the products that are mentioned. The special topics covered in this section are:

- Section 1: IBM PC Utility Programs
- Section 2: The OS/2 Operating System
- Section 3: Windows
- Section 4: Communications Software
- Section 5: Desktop Publishing

SECTION 1: IBM PC UTILITY PROGRAMS

PC-DOS cannot do everything you may want it to do. Sometimes you need additional help in managing the resources of your computer. For example, suppose you accidentally enter the command

```
ERASE B* *
```

when you really meant

```
ERASE * B*
```

You may end up erasing some very important files. With DOS, there is no way to get those files back. However, there are utility programs that can help. One of the most popular of these programs is the Norton Utilities. Norton's program has an "unerase" command that allows you to get files back that have been erased. Other features of DOS utility programs include hard-disk management. These programs can alphabetize your directory, optimize it so that files are accessed in less time, and recover from the accidental formatting of your disk.

CASE STUDY

The Norton Utilities

The Norton Utilities by Peter Norton have become famous for saving people from their own mistakes, while saving thousands of hours and millions of dollars in wasted time and money. The following description covers Version 4.0 of the Advanced Edition. The Norton Utilities are basically programs to supplement DOS. Several of the most useful commands are briefly described here. Not all of the options of each command are included, so the commands will do more than is described here.

The Norton Integrator

The Norton Integrator is a menu program that allows you to run all of the Norton commands from a single screen. As illustrated in figure 12.1, the commands are listed on the left of the screen, and an explanation of the command is listed at the right. Using the arrow keys, you may point to the command of interest. In the figure, the "ASK" command is being pointed to, which is a command that allows you to create interactive batch files.

Several other Norton commands are described below:

DS: Directory Sort. When you do a "DIR" command in DOS, the listing of the files is in no apparent order, although they are generally listed in the order that they were created on disk. When you have a long list, it may be hard to find a particular file you are looking for. The Norton DS command sorts the directory listing, so it is easier to locate a particular file. If the DS command is selected in the Norton Integrator, a sorted version of the directory appears on the screen, as illustrated in figure 12.2.

You can also access the Norton command from the DOS prompt rather than the Norton menu. The format for the command is:

DS sort-key [directory name]

where a [directory name] such as \MYDIR is an optional part of the command. The possible sort keys are:

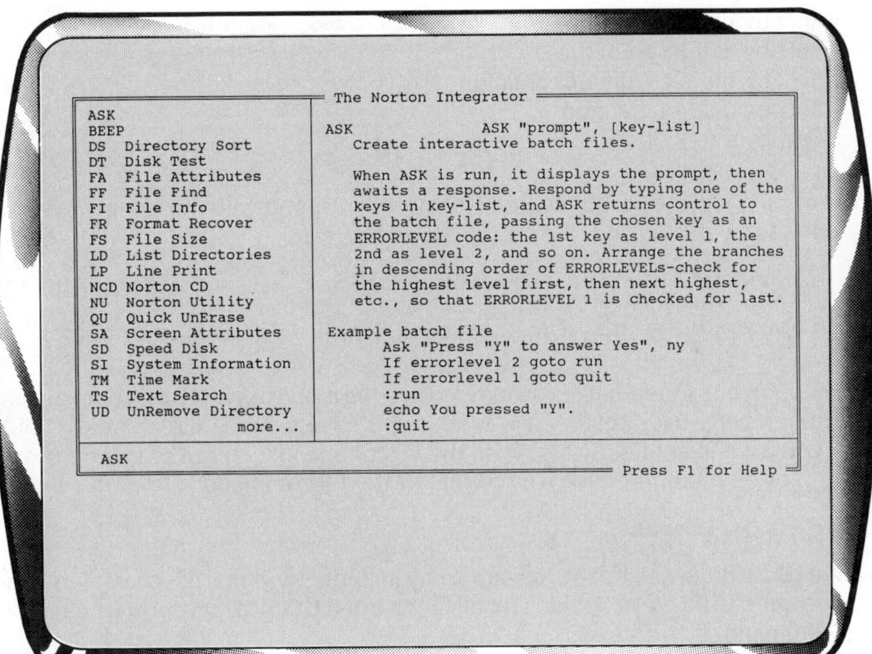
The Norton Integrator
ASK
BEEP
DS Directory Sort
DT Disk Test
FA File Attributes
FF File Find
FI File Info
FR Format Recover
FS File Size
LD List Directories
LP Line Print
NCD Norton CD
NU Norton Utility
QU Quick UnErase
SA Screen Attributes
SD Speed Disk
SI System Information
TM Time Mark
TS Text Search
UD UnRemove Directory
more...
ASK ASK "prompt", [key-list]
Create interactive batch files.
When ASK is run, it displays the prompt, then awaits a response. Respond by typing one of the keys in key-list, and ASK returns control to the batch file, passing the chosen key as an ERRORLEVEL code: the 1st key as level 1, the 2nd as level 2, and so on. Arrange the branches in descending order of ERRORLEVELs-check for the highest level first, then next highest, etc., so that ERRORLEVEL 1 is checked for last.
Example batch file
Ask "Press "Y" to answer Yes", ny
If errorlevel 2 goto run
If errorlevel 1 goto quit
:run
echo You pressed "Y".
:quit
ASK
Press F1 for Help

FIGURE 12.1.
The Norton Integrator menu

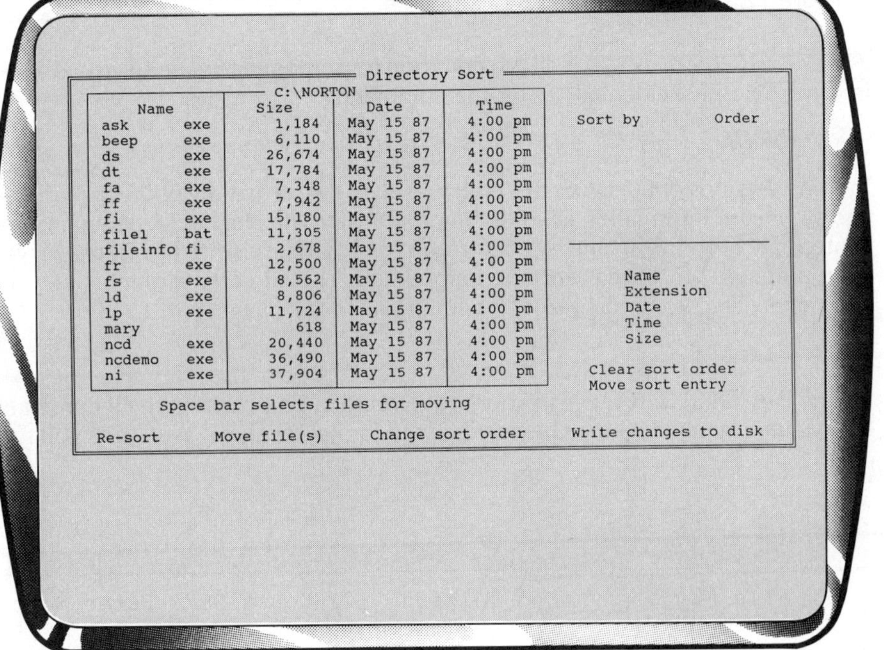
Directory Sort
C:\NORTON
Name Size Date Time
ask exe 1,184 May 15 87 4:00 pm
beep exe 6,110 May 15 87 4:00 pm
ds exe 26,674 May 15 87 4:00 pm
dt exe 17,784 May 15 87 4:00 pm
fa exe 7,348 May 15 87 4:00 pm
ff exe 7,942 May 15 87 4:00 pm
fi exe 15,180 May 15 87 4:00 pm
file1 bat 11,305 May 15 87 4:00 pm
fileinfo fi 2,678 May 15 87 4:00 pm
fr exe 12,500 May 15 87 4:00 pm
fs exe 8,562 May 15 87 4:00 pm
ld exe 8,806 May 15 87 4:00 pm
lp exe 11,724 May 15 87 4:00 pm
mary 618 May 15 87 4:00 pm
ncd exe 20,440 May 15 87 4:00 pm
ncdemo exe 36,490 May 15 87 4:00 pm
ni exe 37,904 May 15 87 4:00 pm
Sort by Order
Name
Extension
Date
Time
Size
Clear sort order
Move sort entry
Space bar selects files for moving
Re-sort Move file(s) Change sort order Write changes to disk

FIGURE 12.2
A directory sorted alphabetically by the Norton Utilities program

N Sort by name of file
E Sort by extension of file
T Sort by the files' time of creation
D Sort by date of creation
S Sort by size in bytes

When you enter the DS command, Norton will respond with these messages one by one as it works:

```
...reading, sorting, writing, done.
```

If you now enter the DOS "DIR" command, the files will be in sorted order.

FF: File Find. Oftentimes, you may know a file is on your hard disk, but you may not remember what directory it was in. If you have a dozen directories, it could take you a while to find the file. With the FF command, you can search for one or more files on the entire disk. The format of the FF command is

```
FF [d:][filename]
```

where [d:] is drive name. The filename may include the global file characters ? and *. For example, if you are looking for all files named COM*.COM, you would enter the command

```
FF COM*.COM
```

The program would search the disk and tell you which directory or directories had files that match the description. For example, the response might be as illustrated in figure 12.3.

FR: Format Recover. It is all too common for someone to want to format a disk in drive A:, and accidentally enter the command

```
C>FORMAT
```

In some versions of PC-DOS, this could result in the formatting of the hard disk—and all of your information is lost for good! Or is it? The Norton FR command can "unformat" your disk, if you do it before writing anything else to the disk, and if you have prepared for this catastrophe beforehand. The FR command must be used two times. First, you must place the command

```
FR C:/SAVE
```

in your AUTOEXEC. BAT file in your root directory. This causes the FR command to save information that may be needed for a format recovery, as soon as you turn

FIGURE 12.3.
The report from a File Find command

```
FF-File Find, Advanced Edition, (C) Copr 1987, Peter Norton
C:\
      command.com   25,307 bytes  12:00 pm  Tue Mar 17 87
C:\DOS
      command.com   25,307 bytes  12:00 pm  Tue Mar 17 87
      comp.com       4,214 bytes  12:00 pm  Tue Mar 17 87
3 files found
```

on the computer. Then, if you accidentally format your disk, place the Norton disk in the A: drive and enter "FR". This will return the hard disk to the condition it was in at the last "FR/SAVE" command. Of course, if you fail to take the preventative measure of placing the "FR/SAVE" command in your AUTOEXEC.BAT file to begin with, you will be out of luck unless you have a backup of the information.

QU: Quick UnErase. One of the most dreadful mistakes in using a computer is accidentally erasing a file. DOS has no way to recover the file, even though the information in the file is still on disk. (The Erase simply takes the file's listing out of the directory.) You can get the file back (if you have not written other files to disk) using the Norton QU command. The format for the QU command is:

QU [filespec]

If you think you may unerase all erased files, leave off the optional [filespec]. The program will display the name of each file that can be unerased. The original Erase deletes the first letter of each file name, so you must provide the first letter of each file you want to unerase. For example, suppose you have accidentally erased a file named TESTFILE. Enter the Norton Quick UnErase command:

```
C>QU
```

and the information will be displayed as in figure 12.4.

Norton locates a file named "?estfile" on disk, that has been erased. The first letter of the filename is lost. If you enter "Y" to the question

```
Quick-UnErase this file (Y/N) ?
```

you will then be prompted with

```
Enter the first character of the file name:
```

Enter a "T", and the file is unerased and placed back in your directory, where you may now access it in the normal way.

The Norton Utilities contain several other helpful commands, including commands to put your hard disk through tests, to thoroughly erase disks or files, to examine and change attributes of your disk, and other utilities.

```
QU-Quick UnErase, Advanced Edition, (C) Copr 1987, Peter
Norton

Directory of C:\NORTON
  Erased file specification: *.*
  Number of erased files: 1
  Number that can be Quick-Unerased:

  Erased files lose the first character of their names.
  After selecting each file to Quick-UnErase, you will be
  asked to supply the missing character.

  ?estfile             618 bytes   4:00 pm  Fri May 15 87
Quick-UnErase this file (Y/N) ?
```

FIGURE 12.4.
Using the Quick UnErase command

ALTERNATE BACKUP-TO-DISK PROGRAMS

Another kind of file management program is a backup system. Although PC-DOS has a Backup command, it is sometimes slow and cumbersome to use. Alternatives to it are programs such as Fastback, Fullback, and Intelligent Backup. These programs are usually faster than the DOS backup and offer more options.

CASE STUDY

Fastback

One of the more popular backup programs on the market is Fastback from Fifth Generation Systems. One of the advantages of Fastback over the DOS Backup command is its ability to back up using two drives at once. That is, if you have drives A: and B:, Fastback will prompt you when to put blank disks in each drive, unlike DOS, which will only back up to one drive. Also, with Fastback, there is no need to format disks beforehand. It will format the disks as it is backing up. A similar feature was added to the DOS backup command beginning with DOS 3.3, but the DOS format/backup takes more time.

The Fastback commands that replace the DOS Backup and Restore commands are "Fastback" and "Frestore." To begin a backup using Fastback, enter the command

```
C>FASTBACK
```

You are then prompted to enter which disk to backup (e.g., C:), which files (e.g., *.*) and whether to include subdirectories in the backup (Y/N). When you have specified which files to back up, a prompt will appear:

```
DRIVE A:Insert disk #1
```

When you insert the disk, the backup will begin. If you have a drive B:, you will be asked to insert a disk in that drive while the backup is taking place to drive A:. When the backup is finished, you are given a report, as illustrated in figure 12.5. Fastback creates a file called FASTBACK.CAT that is a list of all of the files backed up. This file is in standard ASCII format so it can be printed out and kept as a record of the backup.

To restore files, use the command:

```
C>FRESTORE
```

A menu will be displayed that will allow you to view the files on disk and select to restore all files, or only selected files.

FIGURE 12.5.
A report on a Fastback operation

```
Backup is contained on 1 disks (#1 - #1)

3 minutes, 16 seconds to copy 331776 bytes in 70 files
    1.691 kbytes/second (avg)
    0.101 Mbytes/min (avg)
  165.000 Seconds to change disks (avg)
   70.000 files/diskette (avg)
   331776 bytes/diskette (avg)

Press <return>
```

SECTION 2: THE OS/2 OPERATING SYSTEM

One of the biggest drawbacks of the PC-DOS operating system has been its 640K memory limit. Beginning with the 80286 chip, the PC hardware has had the ability to access more than the 640K limit, but PC-DOS held it back. One of the most important features of the OS/2 operating system is its ability to overcome that barrier. However, application software running under OS/2 still cannot automatically access all the computer's memory. Software manufacturers have to develop new software or change old versions of their software to take advantage of this feature.

Multitasking

Another important feature of OS/2 is its ability to run more than one application at once. Thus, you can be using your database program, and while it is generating a report, you can switch to your word processor and begin writing a letter. This process is called running the report program in *background*. The OS/2 operating system is able to keep track of multiple programs running at once. When you switch from one program to another, the first one does not stop running, but continues to execute concurrently.

New OS/2 Versions of Programs

The OS/2 operating system was introduced in December of 1987. Its slow acceptance has been partly due to the need for software manufacturers to introduce OS/2 versions of their software. Actually, many DOS versions of application programs can be run under OS/2. However, since the DOS processor can only process one command or program at a time, you cannot take advantage of the multitasking of OS/2 when running a DOS version of a program. An additional problem for some people using OS/2 is its memory requirement of 1.5 megabytes to store OS/2, and the 80286 or 80386 microprocessor chip. Most people who are currently using PC-DOS and want to use OS/2 will have to upgrade the memory in an existing computer, or will have to purchase a new machine.

OS/2 Real and Protected Modes

To be able to run both DOS single-process programs and OS/2 multitasking programs, OS/2 takes advantage of two modes of operation called *real* mode and *protected* mode. Real mode acts like the original 8086 processor under DOS. All of the memory up to 1 megabyte can be accessed, and any program can access any portion of memory.

In protected mode on the 80286 chip, the computer can access up to 16 megabytes of physical memory. Each task is assigned a particular part of the memory. One task can only access its memory, while the memory reserved for other tasks is "protected." The 80386 chip can access up to 4 gigabytes (4 billion bytes) of physical memory in protected mode. This vast expansion of memory access will likely result in a boom of more sophisticated programs, and may make the microcomputer more able to use such memory-intensive programs as artificial intelligence and extensive expert systems.

The Look of OS/2

OS/2 has a lot in common with DOS. Many of the commands in OS/2 are similar to DOS commands. The standard DOS prompt on a hard disk is:

```
C>
```

and the standard OS/2 prompt is:

```
[C:\OS2]
```

The C:\ OS2 tells you what directory you are in, similar to the DOS prompt you get after entering the "PROMPT PG" command. OS/2 supports the Prompt command, so you can make the OS/2 prompt look just like the DOS prompt if you desire. A comparison of some common commands for PC-DOS and OS/2 is given in figure 12.6. This sampling of commands shows that someone used to PC-DOS should be able to use OS/2 with little difficulty. There are, however, a number of commands that are new to OS/2, mostly relating to the concurrent running of programs.

The Program Selector

In addition to entering commands at the prompt, OS/2 has another important interface called the "Program Selector", illustrated in figure 12.7. The Program Selector is a menu where you may choose to enter OS/2 or DOS mode, or begin programs. Notice in the figure that there is a program listed called "Introducing OS/2". "Introducing OS/2" is a brief tutorial program supplied by IBM that demonstrates many of the OS/2 commands.

You may place your own programs in the menu and call them up from the selector. You may begin an OS/2 program with the Program Selector; then, while that program is running, pressing CTRL-ESC will return you to the Program Selector, where you may begin another program. This is how you get multiple programs running at once.

FIGURE 12.6.
Comparing DOS and OS/2 commands

DOS Command	OS/2 Command	Comparison
DIR *.*	DIR *.*	Same
DIR MYFILE.TXT DIR YOURFILE.TXT	DIR MYFILE.TXT YOURFILE.TXT	IN OS/2, get a DIR of multiple files in one command.
COPY *.* A:	COPY *.* A:	Same
DEL *.TXT DEL MYFILE	DEL *.TXT MYFILE	In OS/2, delete multiple files in one command.
No such command	HELP	Turns on Help line to explain errors
CD, MD, RD	CD, MD, RD	Change, Make, and Remove Directories is same as in DOS

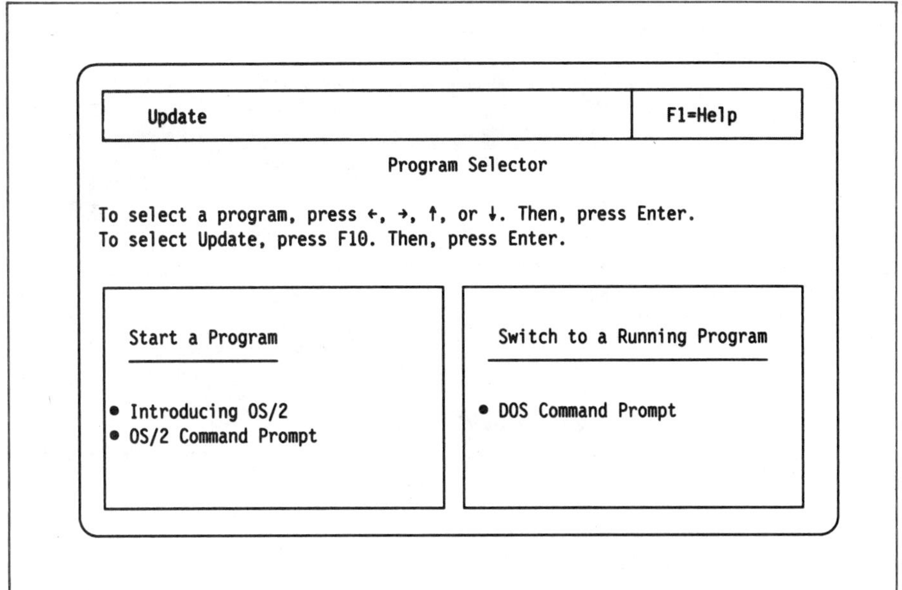

Update
F1=Help
Program Selector
To select a program, press ←, →, ↑, or ↓. Then, press Enter.
To select Update, press F10. Then, press Enter.
Start a Program
• Introducing OS/2
• OS/2 Command Prompt
Switch to a Running Program
• DOS Command Prompt

FIGURE 12.7.
The OS/2 Program Selector menu

SECTION 3: **WINDOWS**

Microsoft Windows is an alternate computer interface added on to the command-oriented PC-DOS. With DOS you must type in a command at the prompt—which means you must remember the command and type it correctly. Windows adds a graphically oriented interface to both DOS and many application programs. The Windows interface is a "window frame" wrapped around the edges of the computer screen. A menu of commands appears in the top or bottom segment of the frame, and in the center is a box, called a *window,* where the application program displays its output (a word processing document, spreadsheet, etc.)

With Windows, you can point to an option on the menu by using a *mouse* to move an arrow on the screen. You point the arrow at the option desired and then press a button on the mouse to enter your choice. Figure 12.8 illustrates how the user can switch from one application to another, while remaining in the Window environment. In this illustration, three different programs are being used at the same time.

Windows does not take the place of DOS; it acts as an extension to DOS by supplying menus of commands. It also provides the user and the program with a single interface to peripheral devices. For example, you may have several programs, each of which accesses your printer using a different set of printer instructions. Under Windows (if your programs support Windows), all of your software programs send their printouts though the Windows program. Once you learn how to use Windows, learning how to use other programs with a Windows interface is simple, since all of the commands are selected in the same way. This makes learning new programs much faster and easier.

Not every program will run with Windows. The company that designs a particular program must either create the program as a direct Windows application, or must create a "PIF" file (Program Information File) that contains information necessary for Windows to run the application.

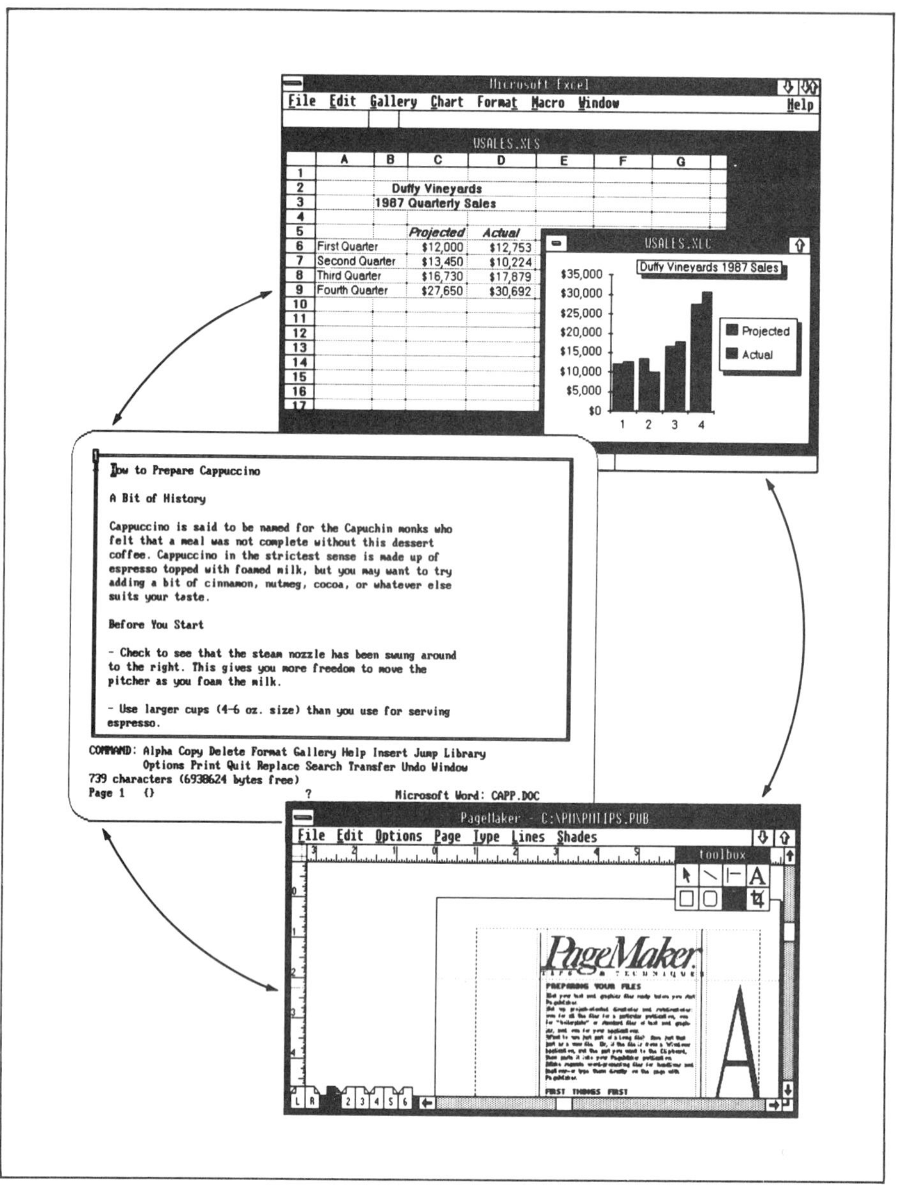

FIGURE 12.8.
Example Windows screens

Using a Mouse

Unlike DOS, in which you type in a command, Windows works with "point and click" menus. The pointing device is usually a mouse. You can also use the arrow keys with Windows, but this description will assume that you are using a pointing device. An arrow appears on the Windows screen, and your movement of the mouse moves the arrow. To select an option from your screen, you simply point the arrow at the item you want and click the button on the mouse (the left button if there is more than one button). Figure 12.9 shows a screen where the arrow is pointed to an option to be selected.

There are a variety of mice on the market, with anywhere from one to three buttons. Some mice use an optical system where the mechanism that

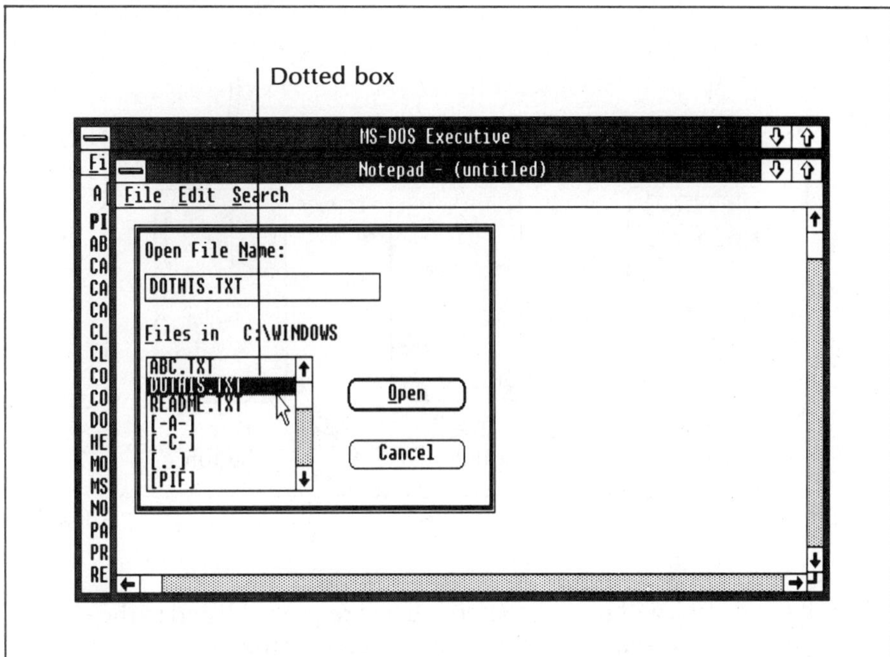

FIGURE 12.9.
Windows arrow pointing to an option to be selected (highlighted)

detects movement is electrical; other mice use a ball in the bottom of the mouse that detects movement as you move the mouse across the table, rolling the ball as you move. Figure 12.10 illustrates several types of mice.

A mouse is used by placing your hand over the device and moving it in small strokes in the direction that you want the arrow to move on the computer screen. If the space to move the mouse is too short, pick up the mouse, back it up in the air (the arrow will not move), and then push it along in the desired direction again. The most common mice have two buttons. The left button is the most often used. When an option is to be selected on the screen, you will point the arrow with the mouse and then press (click) the left button on the mouse to make your selection.

To Use a Mouse or Not?

Most people who have used a mouse pointing device will say that the mouse is preferable to using the arrow keys in Windows and other window-type programs. However, if you are without a mouse, you can still function. Most of the commands you could select by pointing to options also have key sequences. For example, the commands and keystrokes for several menu commands are as follows:

Control Panel	ALT+Space bar	
File	ALT+F	
View	ALT+V	
Special	ALT+S	(Use this to end Windows)
Exit	ESC	

FIGURE 12.10.
Types of mice

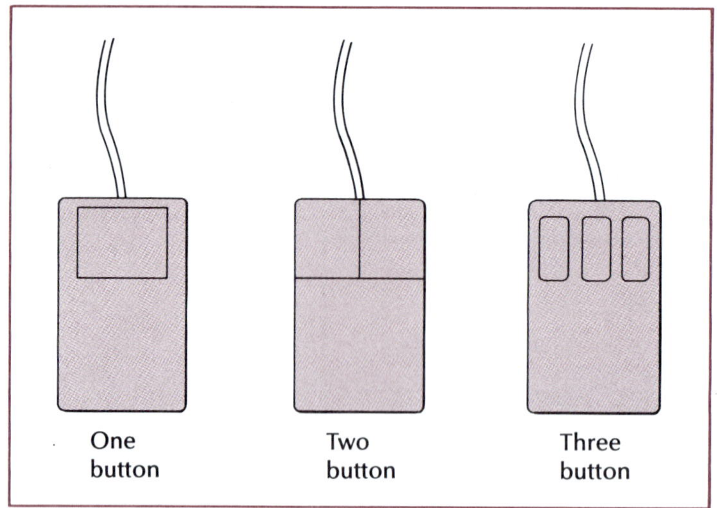

Some of the menus will have the alternate key sequence listed to the right of the command. For example, on the Control Menu are the following options:

Restore	Alt+F5
Move	Alt+F8
Size	Alt+F9
Minimize	Alt+F9
Maximize	Alt+F10
Close	Alt+F4

The designation "F5" refers to the F5 function key. To use an ALT command, hold the ALT key down with one finger while pressing the command key one with another finger.

Selecting Programs to Run

In the main Windows screen, called MS-DOS Executive, a list of files on disk will appear in the window (see figure 12.11). To begin an application, you simply point to the desired filename and double-click the mouse (click the mouse twice in quick succession). Your application program will begin running.

Not Quite Multitasking

Windows also allows you to work with several programs at once. However, unlike the OS/2 operating system that allows one program to continue operating in the background while another program is working, Windows switches the operation from one program to another, and the program not being accessed suspends its operation while the other program works. The capability of switching from program to program can save time. If desired, you can even split the screen into two windows to keep track of both pro-

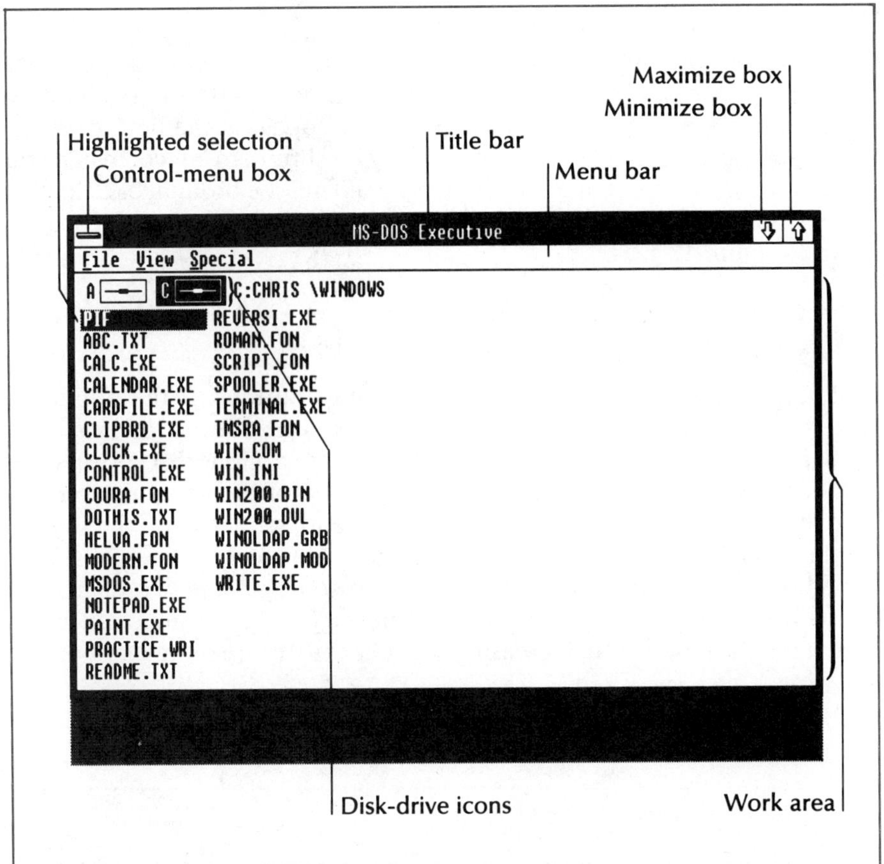

FIGURE 12.11. The main Windows screen, MS-DOS Executive, listing available files

grams at once. Information can more easily be transferred from one program to another in Windows.

The Control Menu

A special option in the upper left corner of the Window screen (it looks like a dash) is the option for the Control Menu (see figure 12.11). If this option is selected, the Control Menu will appear in a box in the corner of the screen. The Control Menu is used to manipulate the windows on the screen. The options are as follows:

RESTORE: Allows you to restore a window to size after it has been changed in size.
MOVE: Allows you to move a window to another position on the screen.
SIZE: Allows you to change the size of a window.
MINIMIZE: This command shrinks a window to an icon (described below).
MAXIMIZE: Enlarges a window to its maximum size.
CLOSE: Closes (ends) a window application. If you close the main window, it ends the Windows program.

Icons

Windows often uses icons, small picture representations of options, to tell you which options are active. For example, if Windows is printing something to the printer, a small picture of a printer may appear at the bottom of the screen. An application program window may be shrunk to an icon when you switch to a different program. Later that program may be brought back into an active window by selecting it with the pointer. Some examples of icons are shown in figure 12.12.

Pull-Down Menus

At the top of the Windows screen is a menu of options. If the pointer is clicked on one of these options, a *pull-down menu* appears. (This is illustrated in Figure 12.12.) A pull-down menu is a list of options that appears like a window shade being pulled down from the top of the computer screen. Once the user has made a selection from the menu, it rolls up off the screen, like the shade being rolled back up to the top. This text has previously described other menu interfaces such as those used by Lotus, WordStar, and WordPerfect. However, the pull-down concept is of great importance because it is being used by an increasing number of software products (both on

FIGURE 12.12.
Sample icons and a pull-down menu

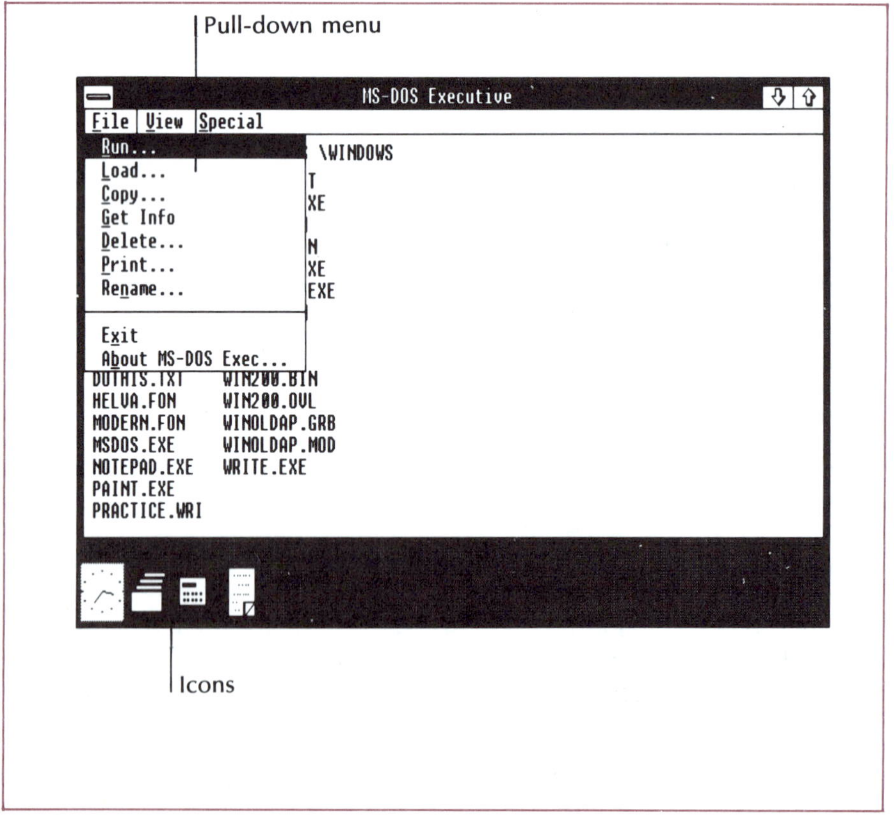

the PC and the Macintosh). Since pull-down menus work the same on a variety of programs, it makes it easier for people who are already familiar with these kinds of menus to learn new products that use pull-down menus. The pull-down menu shown in figure 12.12 is the File menu. The pull-down menu has its own set of options, which you may then point to and select. In this menu, you can choose to Run a program, Load a program, and so on. The three dots after the options (for example "Run . . .") mean that once you choose this option another menu will appear with more options. The Control Menu is also a pull-down menu that appears in the MS-DOS Executive screen.

Windows—The Wave of the Future?

Many computer futurists foresee a window-type environment becoming a common and desired way to use a computer. The Apple Macintosh already uses this kind of interface almost exclusively, and it has been very successful there. The OS/2 operating system Presentation Manager is a window-type environment. Many new programs that are being introduced, plus many older programs that are being updated, are using a window-type interface. Once you use Windows, you may not want to go back to the DOS prompt.

SECTION 4: COMMUNICATIONS

The PC does not have to stand alone. Using a *modem,* you can attach the computer to the rest of the world, usually through normal telephone lines. A modem (*mo*dulator/*dem*odulator) changes the computer's 0's and 1's into electronic pulses that sound like high-pitched noises on the phone. One PC can "talk" to another PC (or mainframe) that also has a modem.

For the computer to know how to communicate using a modem, it must be running communications software. The communications software sends the proper signals to the modem, and interprets signals that the modem receives from another computer. Some of the more popular communications programs include Crosstalk, ProComm, and Smartcom. Communications of this sort are usually used to transfer information from one computer to another. This may be one microcomputer "talking" to another microcomputer, or it may be a big computer talking to several smaller computers at once.

One of the more popular ways of using computer communications is by connecting to *electronic bulletin boards* or computer data services. A bulletin board is a communications program on a computer that keeps track of a number of files. A user can call the bulletin board and look at the files, or download them (transfer them) from the bulletin board computer to his or her own computer. A computer data service usually contains a huge amount of material that can be examined or downloaded. It may contain several bulletin boards. Some of the more popular services include CompuServe and The Source. These services contain such information as the AP news wire, the text of major newspapers, the latest stock market figures, weather information from around the world, and more. Some even contain the complete text of encyclopedias and other reference books.

CASE STUDY

ProComm

One popular communications program is ProComm from Datastorm Technologies. ProComm is distributed as a shareware product. ProComm Plus was released in 1987, and will service as an example of the features of a good communications software package.

ProComm Setup

When using communications software, you must set up several communication parameters, mostly dictated by your computer's capabilities and by the capabilities of the computer you will be "talking" to. These items include baud rate, parity, data bits, stop bits, and communication ports. The ProComm Plus line-setting screen is illustrated in figure 12.13. Notice at the top of the screen that the program is currently using the setting

```
1200,N,8,1,COM1
```

Most of these are the settings chosen by menu option number 11. The "1200" stands for the baud rate, the "N" is "No Parity", the "8" is "8 data bits", the "1" is "1 stop bit", and "COM1" refers to the computer's communication port number 1.These terms are defined in the next few paragraphs.

Baud Settings. The baud rate is the speed of the communication, measured in bits per second. Over telephone lines, the baud rate is usually set at 300, 1200, or 2400 baud, although some newer modems can communicate at up to 9600 baud. Within organizations, there may be special direct communication wires hooked up that can use speeds far beyond the rates available through the telephone. Of course, you usually want to use the highest speed possible. This is dictated by the

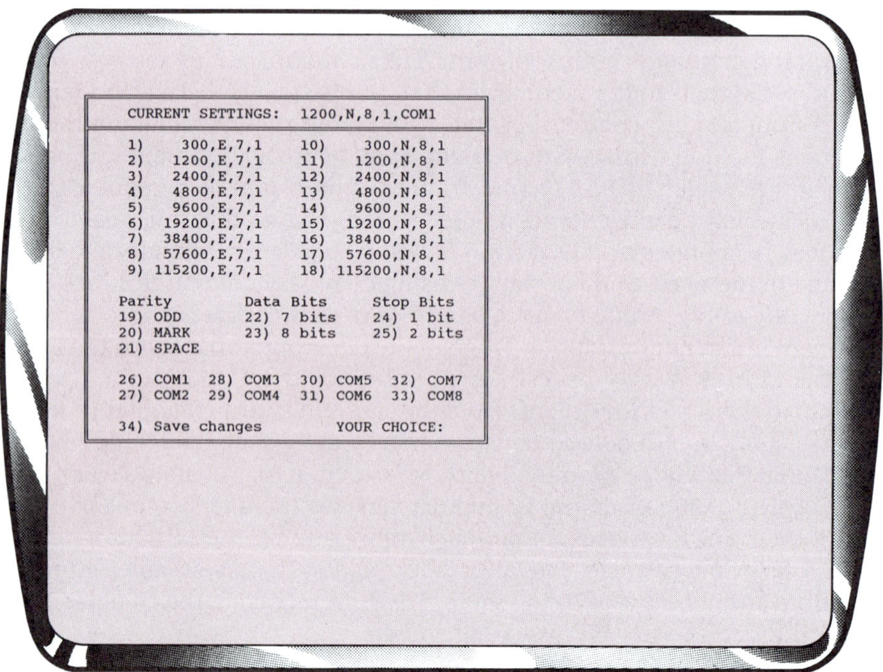

FIGURE 12.13.
The line setting screen in ProComm Plus

maximum baud rate of the computer you will be communicating with, the maximum baud rate of your computer, and the maximum baud rate of the modem. If you are paying a charge for communicating, you should find out what costs are used for different baud rates. In some cases, you may want to use a slower speed to avoid higher charges.

Parity, Data Bits, and Stop Bits. Settings for parity, data bits, and stop bits have to do with how the data is transmitted across the line. Possible parity settings are None, Even, Odd, Mark, and Space. The number of data bits is 7 or 8, and the number of stop bits is 1 or 2. You do not need to know the technical reasons for these numbers, but you do need to make sure that the settings on your computer are the same as the computer you will be communicating with.

Communication Ports. ProComm Plus allows you to set up communication ports from "COM1" to "COM8". On an IBM PC-type computer, the first COM port, or serial port, is named "COM1". If another is added, it is configured as "COM2", and so on. Computers having multiple COM ports may have a printer hooked into one COM port, a pointing device (mouse) hooked into another, and a modem hooked into another. You must know which COM port is the one being used by your modem.

Dialing Directory

The line-setting menu allows you to choose the particular setup for your computer, and then to save it to disk (option 34). This is fine if you are communicating with only one computer. If you call different computers, each with different settings, you will want to set up a dialing directory that specifies the information for each computer you access. Figure 12.14 illustrates a ProComm Plus dialing direc-

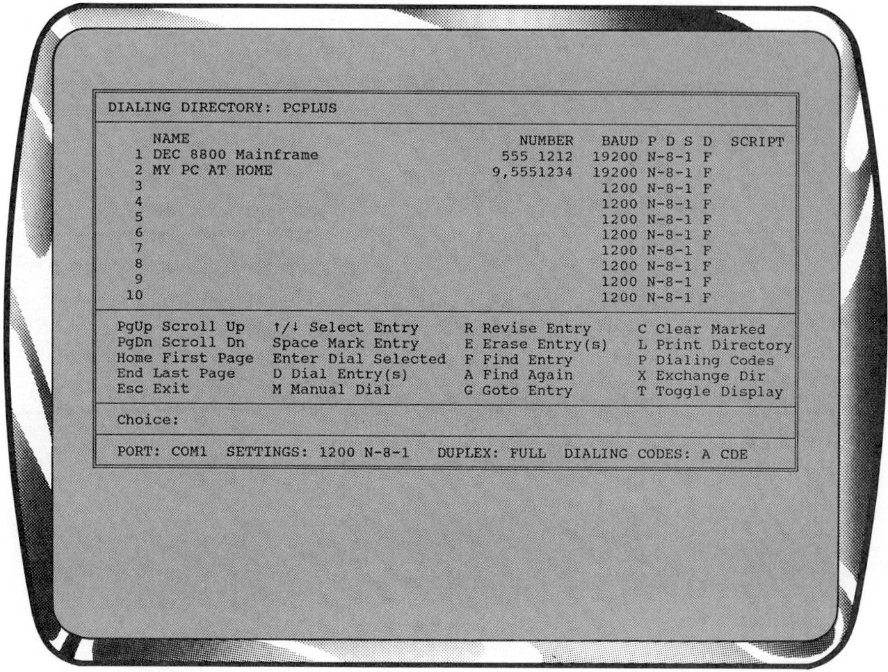

FIGURE 12.14.
A ProComm Plus dialing directory

tory. The dialing directory allows you to set up the parameters for several computers. Notice in this example that communication with a local DEC 8800 computer is through an internal phone number (81212), and communication is set up to speed along at 19200 baud. The other entry is used to call a PC and uses only 1200 baud. When a choice is selected from this menu, the program automatically sets up the proper modem parameters and dials the phone number that will call up the desired computer.

ProComm Plus Commands

Once communications are established, you want to have a variety of commands to allow you access to various features of communication. You could, for example, use your PC as a computer terminal to talk to a large mainframe. In that case, you will want it to *emulate* (behave like) one of the standard industry terminals. You may also want the capability of capturing the information on the screen in a file for future reference, or you may want to download a file from another computer and store that file on your computer. All of these functions and more are accessed with a series of command keys. The ProComm Plus command menu is shown in figure 12.15.

Some of the more commonly used ProComm commands include ending the program (ALT-X), hang up the phone (ALT-H), send and receive files (PgUp and PgDn), and capture information that appears on the screen (ALT-F1). These commands are entered by holding the ALT key down while at the same time pressing the letter key of the command.

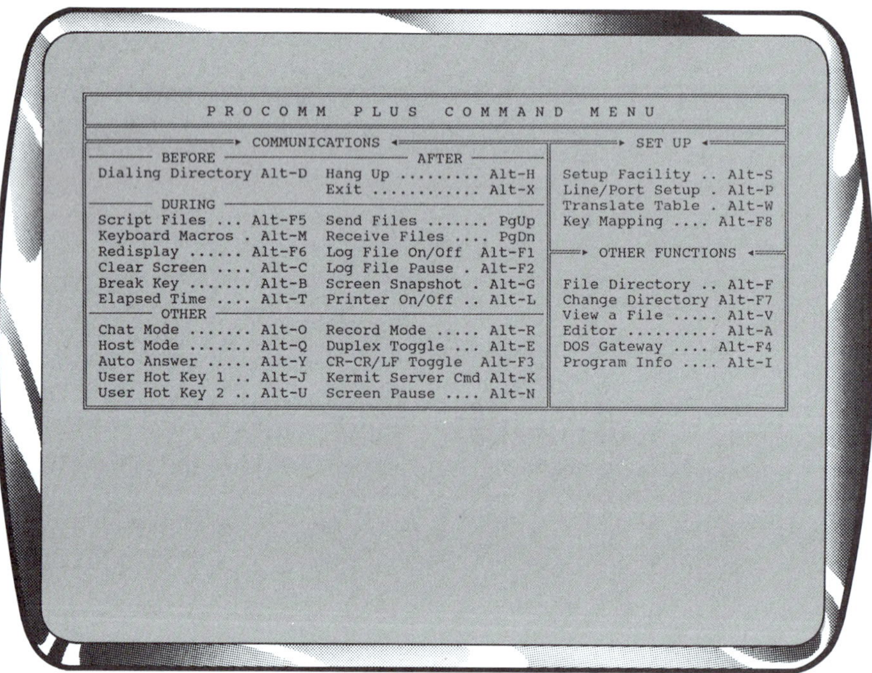

P R O C O M M   P L U S   C O M M A N D   M E N U
COMMUNICATIONS
SET UP
BEFORE
AFTER
Dialing Directory Alt-D
Hang Up .... Alt-H
Exit .... Alt-X
Setup Facility .. Alt-S
Line/Port Setup . Alt-P
Translate Table . Alt-W
Key Mapping Alt-F8
DURING
Script Files ... Alt-F5
Keyboard Macros . Alt-M
Redisplay Alt-F6
Clear Screen .... Alt-C
Break Key .... Alt-B
Elapsed Time .... Alt-T
Send Files .... PgUp
Receive Files .... PgDn
Log File On/Off Alt-F1
Log File Pause . Alt-F2
Screen Snapshot . Alt-G
Printer On/Off .. Alt-L
OTHER FUNCTIONS
File Directory .. Alt-F
Change Directory Alt-F7
View a File ..... Alt-V
Editor .... Alt-A
DOS Gateway Alt-F4
Program Info .... Alt-I
OTHER
Chat Mode .... Alt-O
Host Mode .... Alt-Q
Auto Answer ..... Alt-Y
User Hot Key 1 .. Alt-J
User Hot Key 2 .. Alt-U
Record Mode ..... Alt-R
Duplex Toggle ... Alt-E
CR-CR/LF Toggle Alt-F3
Kermit Server Cmd Alt-K
Screen Pause .... Alt-N

FIGURE 12.15.
The ProComm Plus command menu

Exchanging Files

When you are communicating with another computer, you may want to exchange files. This is performed with the PgUp (send a file) or PgDn (receive a file) commands. To send or receive a file, your computers must be able to use certain types of data exchange protocols. These include Kermit, XModem, YModem, and others. ProComm Plus can use sixteen different protocols.These protocols "package" the information that is being sent or received to insure that the information is communicated without error.

Hayes Modem Compatibility

In the personal computer world, the IBM PC-type computer using MS-DOS or PC-DOS is the most common microcomputer. In the world of modems, the standard has been set by a company called Hayes. Thus, you will see most modems claiming "Hayes Compatibility." This compatibility has to do with the commands that are sent to the modem from the software. ProComm, for example, is set up to dial the numbers in the dialing directory using the Hayes command set. The Hayes command set is sometimes called the "AT" command set, since the commands begin with the two letters "AT", which stand for "ATtention."

If you bypass the dialing directory in ProComm, you can dial the telephone directly from the keyboard using the Hayes command set. Briefly, some of the commands are as follows. All of the letters in the command must be in UPPER-CASE.

AT Get attention of the modem (modem responds "OK")
ATDT # Attention, Dial, Tone: dials the phone number specified by # on a touch-tone phone.

For example, to dial a phone number on an outside line, suppose you need to dial 9, then the local phone number. From the ProComm screen, enter

AT

The modem should respond with an "OK" on the screen. This tells you that the communication software is communicating with the modem. To dial the number (say 555-2345), type:

ATDT 9,5552345

ProComm will feed the number to the modem, which will dial the phone. Depending on the modem you are using, you may get messages such as:

```
OFF HOOK
DIAL TONE
9,5552345
```

or

```
CONNECT 1200
```

The message "CONNECT 1200" tells you that communication has been established with the called computer. Now, depending on what kind of computer you call, you will progress with a log-on sequence.

Ending the ProComm Program

It is important to remember to end your communication with the called computer before getting out of the ProComm communication program. If you simply end the program with ALT-X, or turn off the computer, you may still remain logged in to the computer you called, and you may be racking up a hefty bill. Be sure to log off with the computer you called. Then, enter ALT-H to hang up the phone. Finally, enter ALT-X to end the ProComm program.

SECTION 5: DESKTOP PUBLISHING SOFTWARE

Word processing on microcomputers quickly became a popular business application for microcomputers. It has become the dominant use of personal computers in offices. However, most organizations produce more than letters and memos. They want to make brochures, newsletters, advertisements, and handouts. For these items, a typesetter had to be used. Beginning in the mid-1980s, several technologies for creating documents on the microcomputer began to emerge. This overview of *desktop publishing* will cover the basic concepts of how this technology works, focusing on desktop publishing software. The setup of Aldus PageMaker and Xerox Ventura Publisher will be discussed briefly, and the creation of a simple document will be illustrated using PageMaker. Figure 12.16 illustrates the variety of publications that can be generated with desktop publishing programs.

The Laser Printer

The laser printer gave microcomputers a higher standard of printing than letter-quality. They gave microcomputer users a new typeset-quality printed image, including both letters and graphics. Most lasers can produce images at 300 dots per inch (dpi). This means that letters and images can be formed far beyond the clarity of dot matrix and impact printers. Two popular laser printers are the Apple Laserwriter and the Hewlett-Packard Laserjet. Figure 12.17 shows the Apple Laserwriter.

The Postscript Printer Definition Language

The company who set the standard for the interface from the computer to the printer was Adobe, who developed a printer definition language interface for computers, using a language called Postscript. Postscript tells the printer how to form characters and graphics. There are other printer definition languages, but Postscript seems to be the choice for desktop publishing. Figure 12.18 illustrates some of the variety of fonts available in Postscript.

Desktop Publishing Software

Once the hardware had the capability of producing typeset material, software was developed to use it. On the Macintosh, that software was PageMaker from

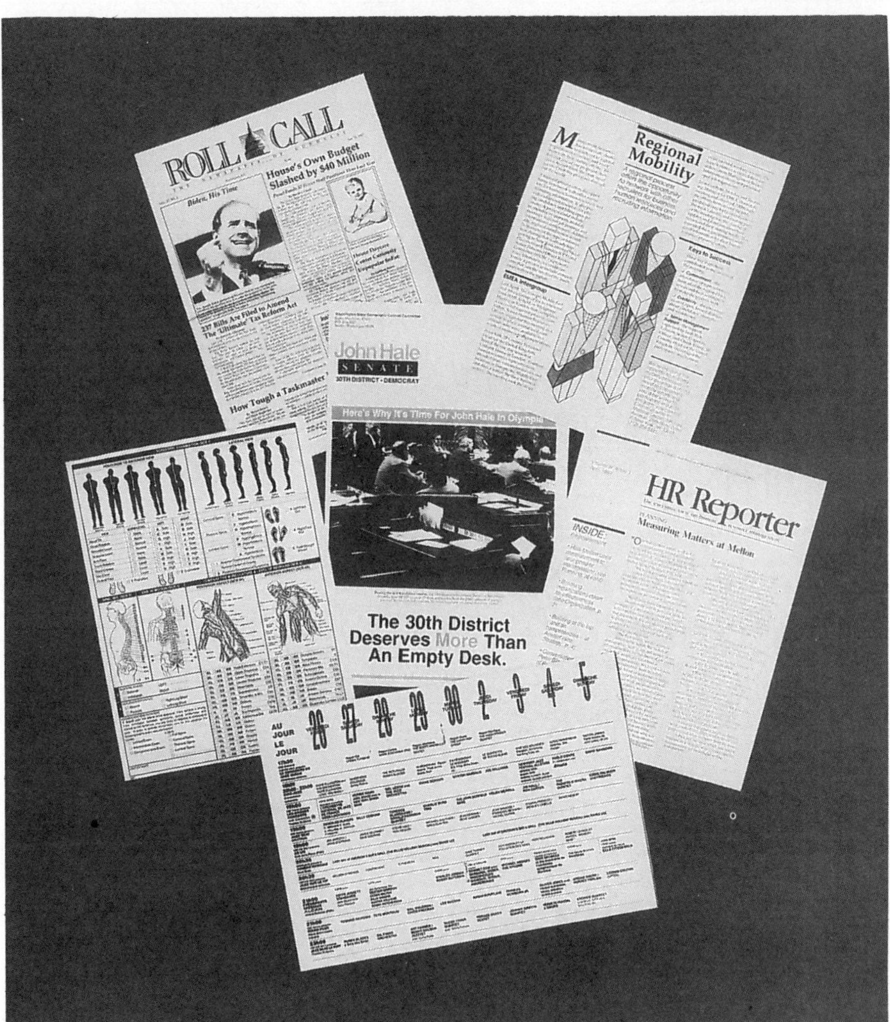

FIGURE 12.16.
A variety of output from desktop publishing software

FIGURE 12.17.
Apple Laserwriter

Times 10 point

Times 12 point

Times 18 point

Times 24 point

Times 36 point

18 point, Normal

abcdefghijklmnopqrstuvwxyz 0123456789

ABCDEFGHIJKLMNOPQRSTUVWXYZ

!"#$%^&*()-_+?><<>;:][}{|\~`

18 point, Bold

abcdefghijklmnopqrstuvwxyz 0123456789

ABCDEFGHIJKLMNOPQRSTUVWXYZ

!"#$%^&*()-_+?><<>;:][]{|\~`

18 point, Italic

abcdefghijklmnopqrstuvwxyz 0123456789

ABCDEFGHIJKLMNOPQRSTUVWXYZ

!"#$%^&()-_+?><<>:;][}{|\~`*

New Century Schlbk 10 point

New Century Schlbk 12 point

New Century Schlbk 18 point

New Century Schlbk 24 point

New Century Schlbk 36 point

Helvetica 10 point

Helvetica 12 point

Helvetica 18 point

Helvetica 24 point

Helvetica 36 point

FIGURE 12.18. Sample Postscript fonts

Aldus. On the IBM Personal Computer, the program was Ventura Publisher from Xerox. PageMaker is now also available on the PC. There are, of course, other software packages that can produce typeset-quality work on microcomputers. PageMaker and Ventura are the dominant products and will be used as examples in this overview of desktop publishing.

The Program Environment

Both PageMaker and Ventura use a window-type user environment. (See the previous section on Windows for details on how to use the mouse, and for an introduction to pull-down menus.) In fact, on the PC, PageMaker runs as a Windows application. Figures 12.19 and 12.20 illustrate the opening "window" for PageMaker and Ventura. Notice the similarity. Both programs require a pointing device (a mouse) for operation. You can envision the computer screen as a paste-up board. You will bring in text, graphics, pictures, and charts from other sources, and place them on the pasteboard. However, in using a physical pasteboard, making a change may require going back to the source (a graphics artist in Nome, Alaska) to get the layout just right. In the computer pasteboard you can automatically size your graphics, change the font used on text, edit out or add in new headlines or text, draw borders, and more, while you are designing the page.

CASE STUDY

Main Screen Controls for PageMaker

The main screen controls for PageMaker are a Windows interface. In the upper left corner is the system menu box, as illustrated in figure 12.19. Clicking this box will reveal the pull-down menu that lists commands related to the Windows operating environment. One of the options is "Close", which is used to end the session. After pulling down this menu, you would click on "Close" to return to DOS.

Below the system menu is a bar across the entire window that contains several other menu options. These are:

```
File Edit Options Page Type Lines Shades
```

Clicking on any one of these will produce a pull-down menu of related options. These menus are illustrated in figure 12.21.

File is used for operations that affect the entire document. From this menu you can save the document, revert to the original document before changes were made, pull in text or graphics from other sources, make changes in the page setup, choose a target printer, and queue the document for printing.

Edit is used to change or move around parts of the layout. You can use this menu to cut out pieces of the document to paste or copy them elsewhere. You can also switch the layering of graphics with the "Send to Back" or "Bring to Front" commands.

Options allows you to turn several options on and off, such as the display of rulers on the screen, the toolbox, and scroll bars. You can also choose shapes for rounded corners on boxes and set up column guides for pages that use more than one column.

Page allows you to choose what size the page will appear on the screen, insert new pages, remove old pages, and other options.

Type allows you to choose the style of type, tabs, text alignment, and spacing.

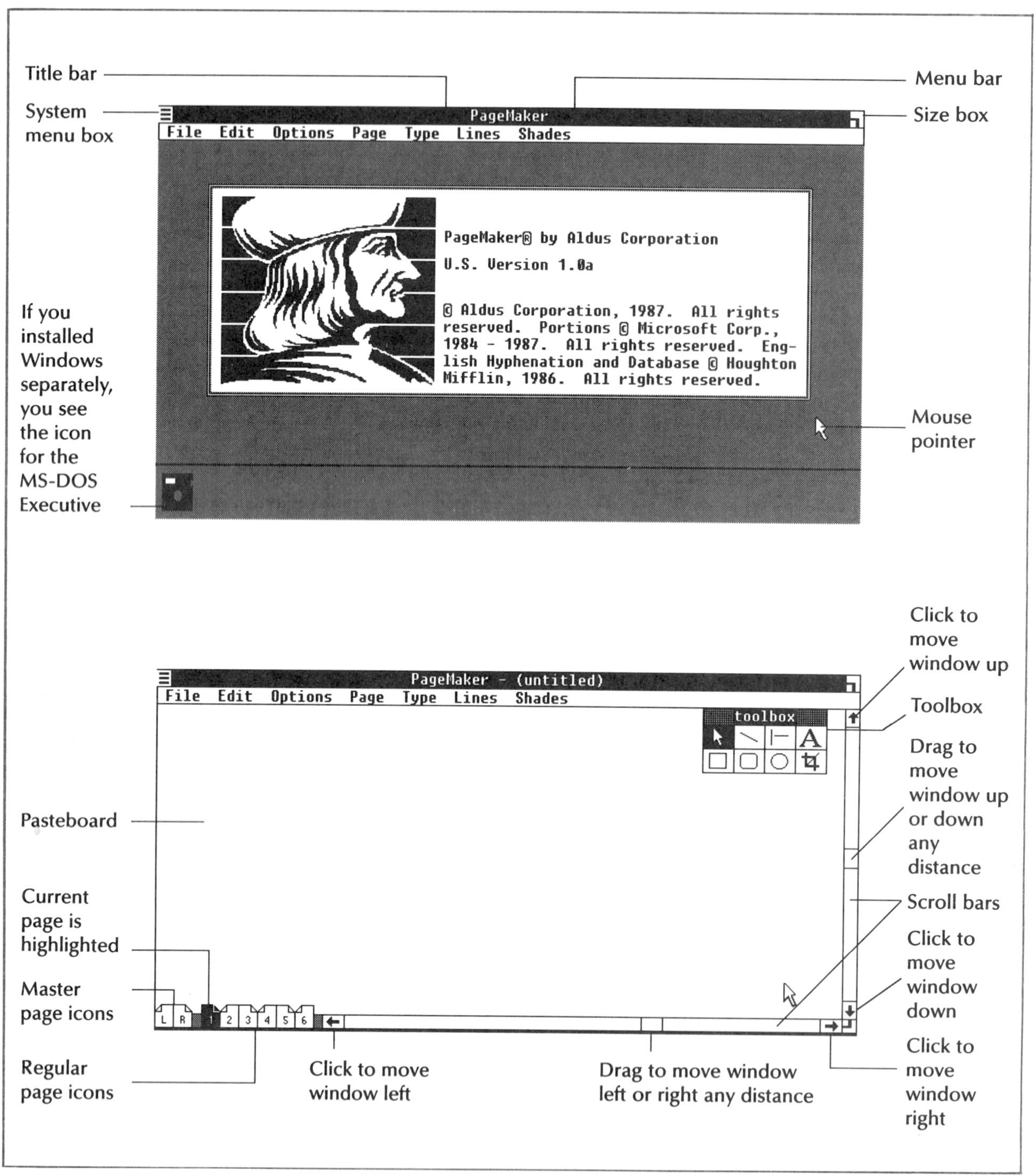

FIGURE 12.19.
Opening screen and pasteboard screen for PageMaker

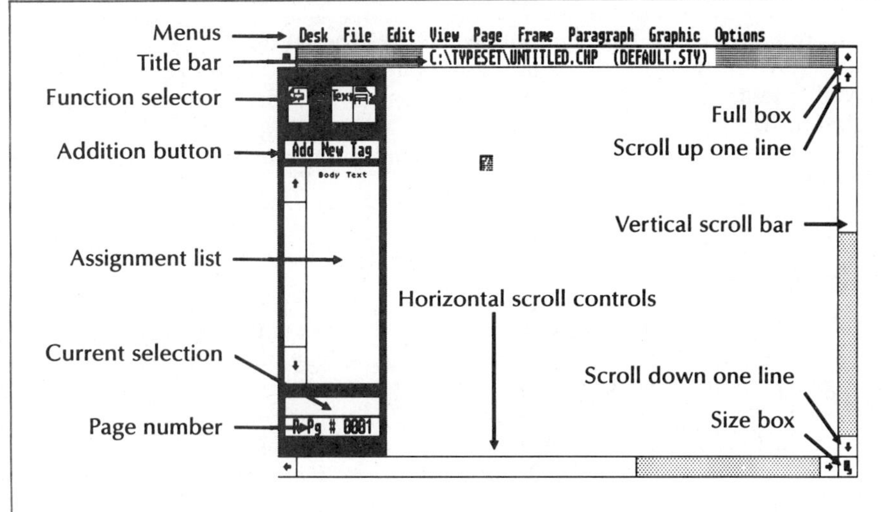

FIGURE 12.20. Main screen for Ventura Publisher

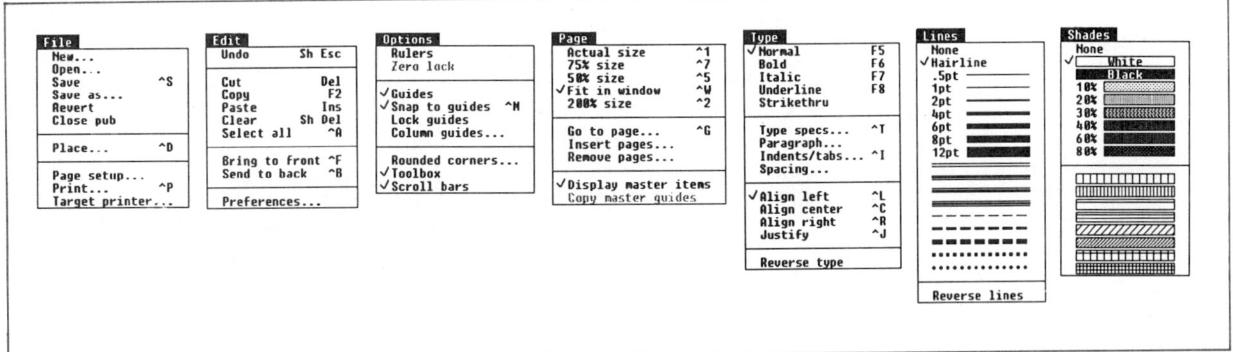

FIGURE 12.21. PageMaker menus

Lines allows you to choose the design of lines to be used in boxes and in the document.

Shades allows you to choose the shades to be used for filled-in areas, such as boxes.

Menu items that end in "..." have other menus that are displayed when that item is chosen. Also, notice that some menu items give key sequences (such as the "^S" next to "Save" in the Files menu) that are short-cut control commands to that item. Thus, instead of clicking the menu and then clicking the item, you can simply enter the control command from the keyboard. On menu items that are on/off choices, such as "Rulers" in the Options menu, a check to the left of the option means that the option is turned on. If you click the item the check will disappear, meaning that the option is turned off.

The operation of the Ventura Publisher is very similar to what was presented here for PageMaker.

CASE STUDY

Creating a Document with PageMaker

As an example, a one-page handout will be designed using PageMaker. This handout, shown in figure 12.22, will incorporate text that was originally created in WordPerfect, and a graphic that was created in a program called Microsoft Paintbrush.

Larger type and font selection were accomplished after it was incorporated into PageMaker.

Page Setup

In a desktop publishing package, you generally work with one page at a time. In fact, in many applications, you may be designing only one page. Or, you may be designing a chapter in a book where each page will have a similar setup. The first item of business is to specify the size and general look of your page.

To create a new document, enter PageMaker and pull down the File menu. Choose the "New. . ." option. The page layout menu will appear (see figure 12.23). (This type of menu is sometimes called a *dialog box.*) You can specify that your page will be letter size, legal, tabloid, A5, A4, A3 (European sizes), or you may design a custom-size page. The orientation has to do with whether the page is going to be printed *tall* (sometimes called *portrait*), as you normally see type on a page, or *wide* (sometimes called *landscape*). You can also set up the number of pages and the margins. To choose the options, you point to one of the open circles and click the mouse. A black dot in the circle means that this option has been selected. To change the page number options, place the pointer in one of the boxes and click. The box with change to reverse type, and you may edit the contents of the box. Click again to signal that the choice is complete.

For this example, the defaults of letter size, one page, tall, and the default margins will be used. Click on "OK" to move into the PageMaker layout screen. This mostly blank screen has an outline of a sheet of paper, with dotted lines inside the page that mark the margins. This is illustrated in figure 12.24.

The Toolbox

Notice the "toolbox" at the top right of the layout screen. These tools can be selected by pointing to one of the eight symbols and clicking. The active tool is displayed in reverse video. The purpose of each tool is described briefly in figure 12.25.

Typing in the Headline

The steps in creating this document are illustrated in figure 12.26. The first item to be created is the page heading. This is done by clicking the Text tool "A" and moving the pointer to the top left margin of the page. Another click places the cursor, and the text "PC TUTORIAL" is typed. However, the type is usually set up for a small font, and the type is so small it can barely be read. In fact it may appear as unrecognizable symbols (called *greeked* text). Pointing to the text and clicking the right button on the mouse will enlarge that portion of the screen. If you lose the image altogether, clicking the right key again will bring the entire page back into view. Pointing to the arrows on the bars at the bottom or right of the screen will move the window over the text in the direction of the arrows.

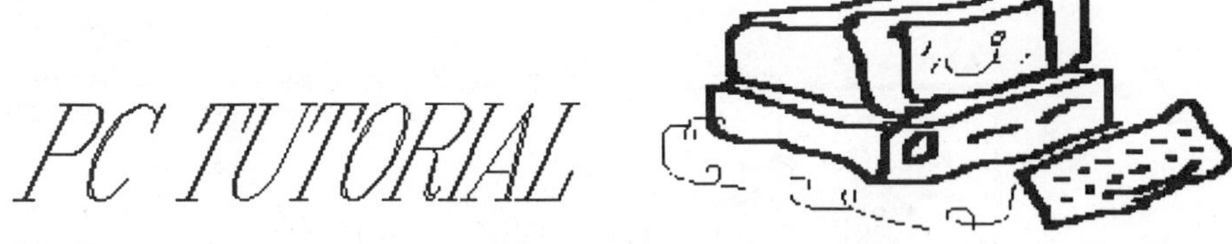

A quick look at PROCOMM

STARTUP

Begin the PROCOMM program with the command (at the DOS prompt):

C>PROCOMM

COMMAND STRUCTURE

PROCOMM commands are accessed by holding down the ALT key, and pressing a single key. For example, ALT-F10 gives you a listing of all PROCOMM commands. Following are a list of the most commonly used PROCOMM commands:

SETUP FOR COMMUNICATIONS

Setup speed, partity, etc. command is **ALT-P**. You will be presented with a list of options. For communications on a 1200 baud modem, choose 1200 baud, 8 bit, No Parity, 1 stop bit.

SETUP TERMINAL TYPE

When PROCOMM begins, there is a status line at the bottom of the screen. One of the indications is terminal type. This should be VT-100. To choose terminal type, use the **ALT-S (SETUP)** command.
This will display a menu of setup options. Choose "Terminal Setup", then use the arrow keys to choose VT-100. Exit this menu with Esc, and save the setup by choosing (S) in the SETUP menu.

MAKING A CALL

In the PROCOMM communications screen enter (in all caps)

AT

The program should respond with "Ok". If it does not, you are not properly hooked up to the modem. To call a number, enter ATDT, then the telephone number. For example, to call the number 555-2345, you would enter:

ATDT 5552345

HANGUP THE PHONE

To hangup from a data call, use the PROCOMM command **ALT-H.**

EXIT PROCOMM

To end the PROCOMM program, enter the **ALT-X** command. You will be prompted "Exit to DOS (Y/N)." Choose "Y".

FIGURE 12.22.
The finished document

FIGURE 12.23.
Pagemaker page layout menu

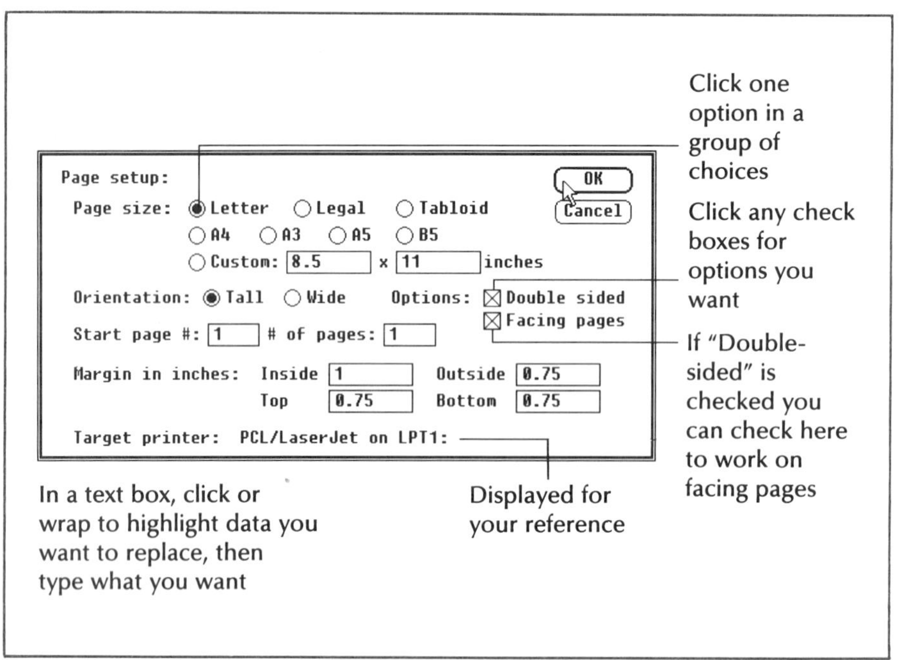

FIGURE 12.24.
PageMaker layout screen

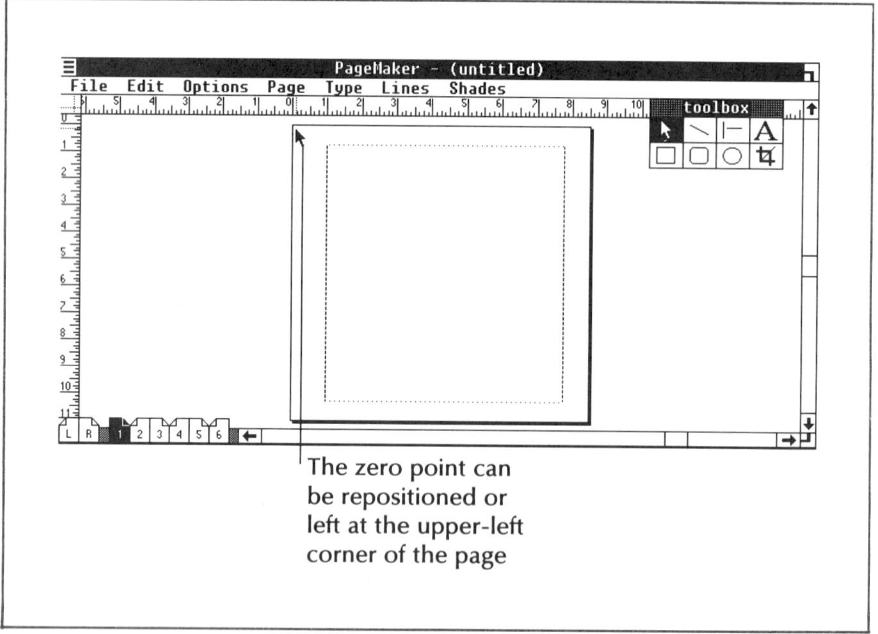

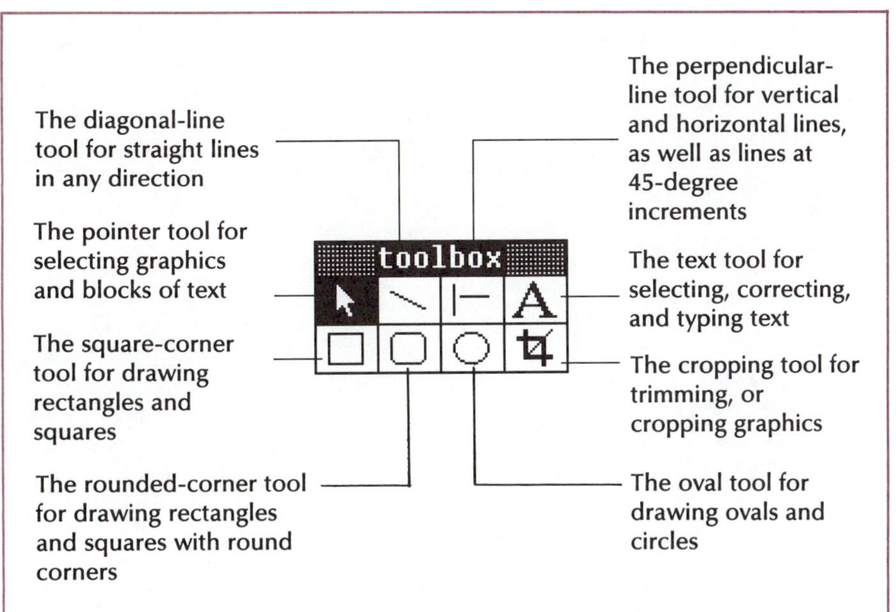
The diagonal-line tool for straight lines in any direction
The perpendicular-line tool for vertical and horizontal lines, as well as lines at 45-degree increments
The pointer tool for selecting graphics and blocks of text
toolbox
The text tool for selecting, correcting, and typing text
The square-corner tool for drawing rectangles and squares
The cropping tool for trimming, or cropping graphics
The rounded-corner tool for drawing rectangles and squares with round corners
The oval tool for drawing ovals and circles

FIGURE 12.25.
The PageMaker toolbox

Selecting the Font for the Headline

To enlarge the type of the heading, move the pointer to the front of the text, press the left button on the mouse, and keep it pressed. Drag the mouse to the right, and the letters of the text will begin to appear in reverse type. Make sure the entire heading is in reverse type, then release the button. This "selects" this area of type. Choose the Type menu, and from the Type menu, choose the "Type Specs . . ." option. This brings up a menu of fonts that you may use (see figure 12.27). Choose the "Roman" option, which will display the font choice in reverse video. Notice that there are also listings of font sizes. You want this heading to be in 48-point. If 48-point is not shown in the font choices, Click the arrow key that is pointing down on that menu until "48" appears, and select 48. Find the "Italics" setting toward the bottom of the dialog box, and select it. Click the "OK" at the top right of the dialog box. The layout screen will appear, and the headline should now be in larger type.

Drawing a Line under the Headline

Choose the horizontal/vertical line tool from the tool box. Move the pointer to the far left of the page, even with the margin and right under the headline. Click the mouse and drag it to the right, all the way to the far right margin. Release the button when the line is complete.

Entering a Graphic from Another Source

For this handout, a graphic was created in the Paintbrush program. To work with the graphic, choose the arrow tool. To bring this graphic into PageMaker, click on the File menu, and choose the "Place . . ." option. This brings up a menu of files. Choose the graphic called LOGO.PCX by pointing to it and clicking twice (click

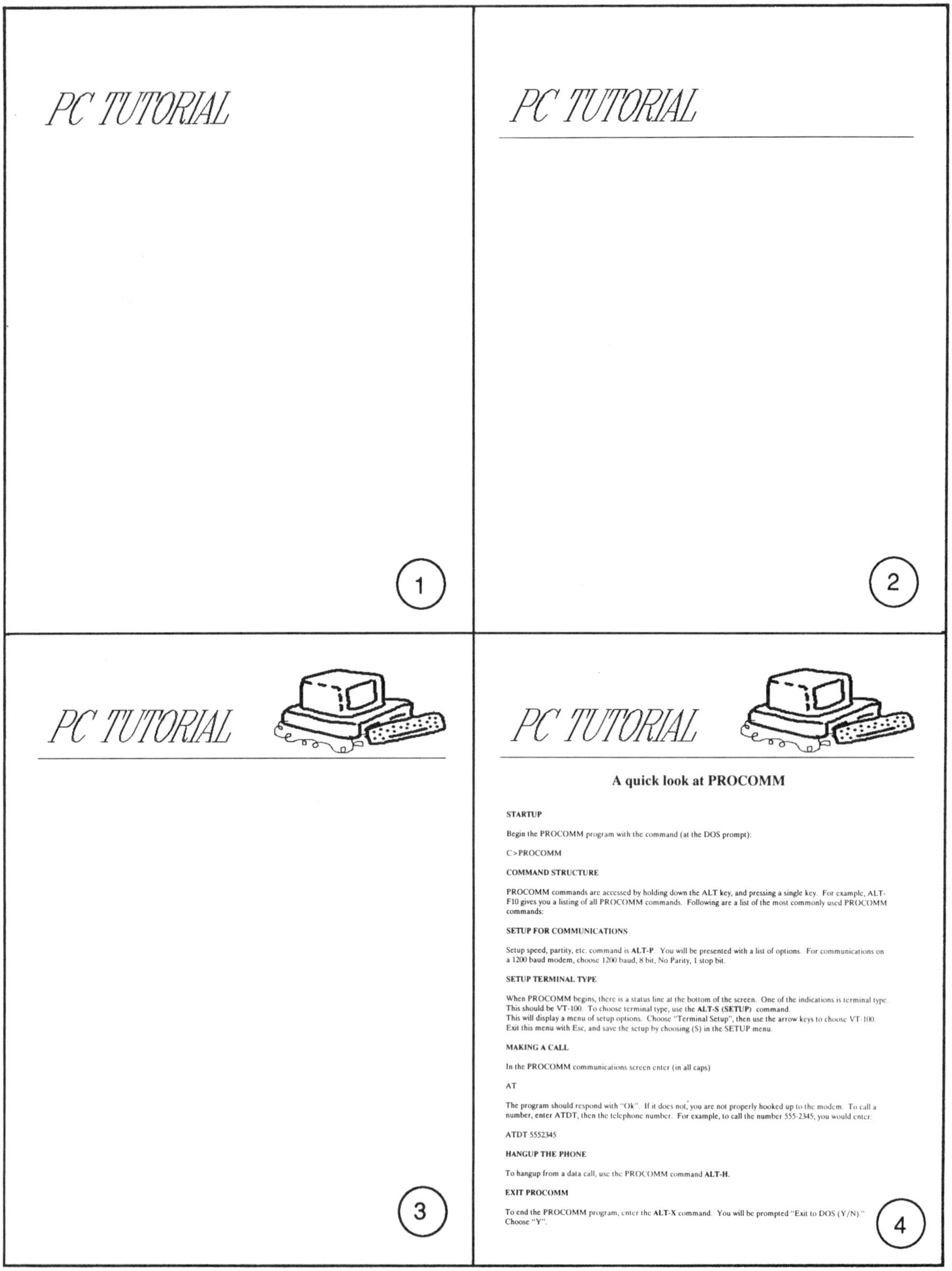

PC TUTORIAL

1

PC TUTORIAL

2

PC TUTORIAL

3

PC TUTORIAL

A quick look at PROCOMM

STARTUP

Begin the PROCOMM program with the command (at the DOS prompt):

C>PROCOMM

COMMAND STRUCTURE

PROCOMM commands are accessed by holding down the ALT key, and pressing a single key. For example, ALT-F10 gives you a listing of all PROCOMM commands. Following are a list of the most commonly used PROCOMM commands:

SETUP FOR COMMUNICATIONS

Setup speed, partity, etc. command is **ALT-P**. You will be presented with a list of options. For communications on a 1200 baud modem, choose 1200 baud, 8 bit, No Parity, 1 stop bit.

SETUP TERMINAL TYPE

When PROCOMM begins, there is a status line at the bottom of the screen. One of the indications is terminal type. This should be VT-100. To choose terminal type, use the **ALT-S (SETUP)** command.
This will display a menu of setup options. Choose "Terminal Setup", then use the arrow keys to choose VT-100. Exit this menu with Esc, and save the setup by choosing (S) in the SETUP menu.

MAKING A CALL

In the PROCOMM communications screen enter (in all caps)

AT

The program should respond with "Ok". If it does not, you are not properly hooked up to the modem. To call a number, enter ATDT, then the telephone number. For example, to call the number 555-2345, you would enter:

ATDT 5552345

HANGUP THE PHONE

To hangup from a data call, use the PROCOMM command **ALT-H.**

EXIT PROCOMM

To end the PROCOMM program, enter the **ALT-X** command. You will be prompted "Exit to DOS (Y/N)." Choose "Y".

4

FIGURE 12.26.
Steps in the creation process

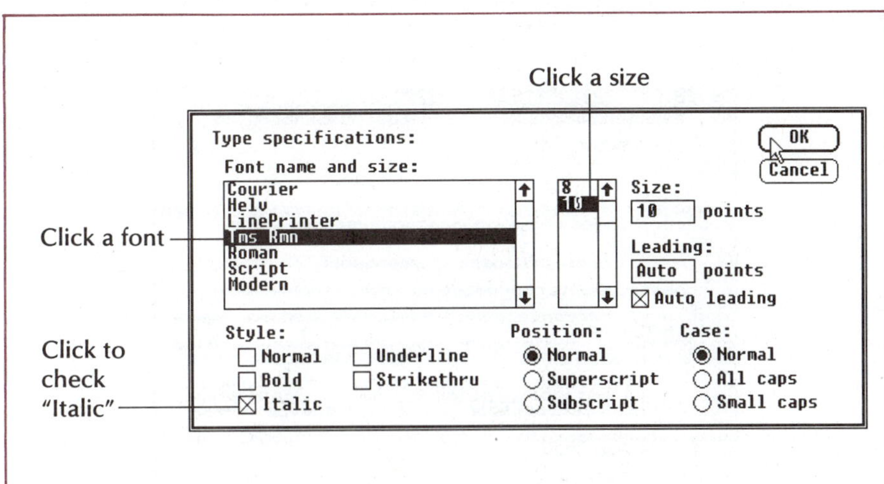

FIGURE 12.27.
Choosing a font

the name once, then click the "OK".) On the layout screen, the arrow will turn to an hour glass momentarily, which means to wait. After a few seconds, it will turn into a right angle with a paintbrush, symbolizing that it is a graphic from the Paintbrush program. Move the graphic pointer next to the headline and click. The graphic will appear, but it may not be the correct size. The graphic will be surrounded by a box, with small squares at the corners of the box. By pointing to a corner and holding down the left mouse button, you can drag the mouse and size the graphic. After getting the graphic to the right size, point to the middle of the graphic and hold down the left mouse button. A four-pointed arrow will appear. Moving the mouse will now move the entire graphic on the screen. Move the graphic into position next to the headline, and release the button. To take away the box surrounding the graphic, point to somewhere outside the page and click once.

Entering and Manipulating Text

Text is placed in the document in the same way as the graphic. Choose the File menu, and the "Place..." option. This time choose the file PROCOMM.WP (a WordPerfect document) from the menu. The pointer will now change to something that looks like a small piece of paper. Place the pointer just below the line under the headline. Notice that when you get close to the margin, the arrow will "snap" to the margin. (The "Snap to" option is set in the Options menu.) Press the left mouse button, and the text will appear. Notice that PageMaker carries over the boldface characters from WordPerfect. The text is bordered at the top and bottom by a line, as illustrated in figure 12.28. Notice the handle at the bottom of the text, containing a "#". This means that this is the very bottom of the text. If the text would not all fit on the page, the handle would contain the "+" symbol. If you needed to, you could size the text in the same way the graphic was sized.

Finishing up Details

The heading at the top of the text should appear bigger than the normal type. Select the headline "A quick look at ProComm", just as the headline was selected before, and set it to about 18 points, Times Roman font, in the "Type" menu.

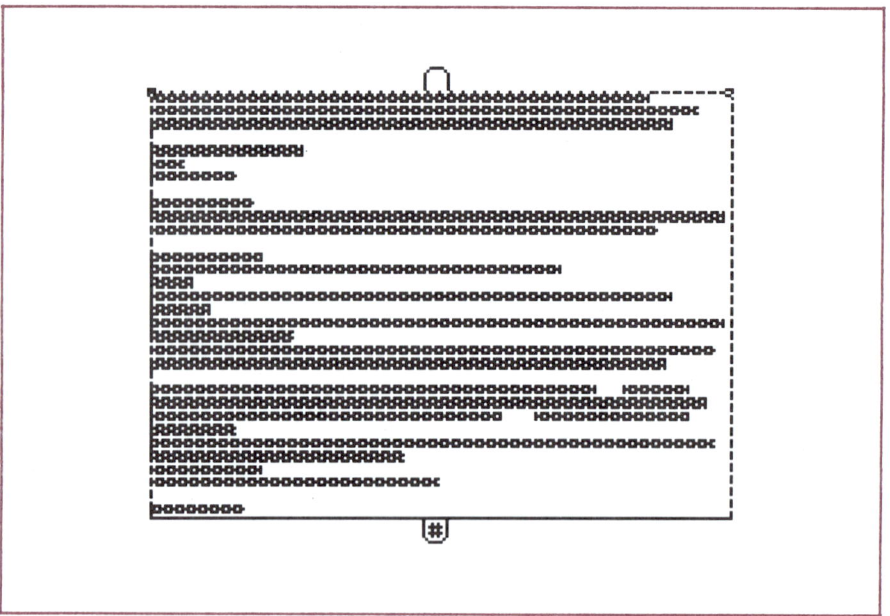

FIGURE 12.28.
Text as it appears after being imported into PageMaker

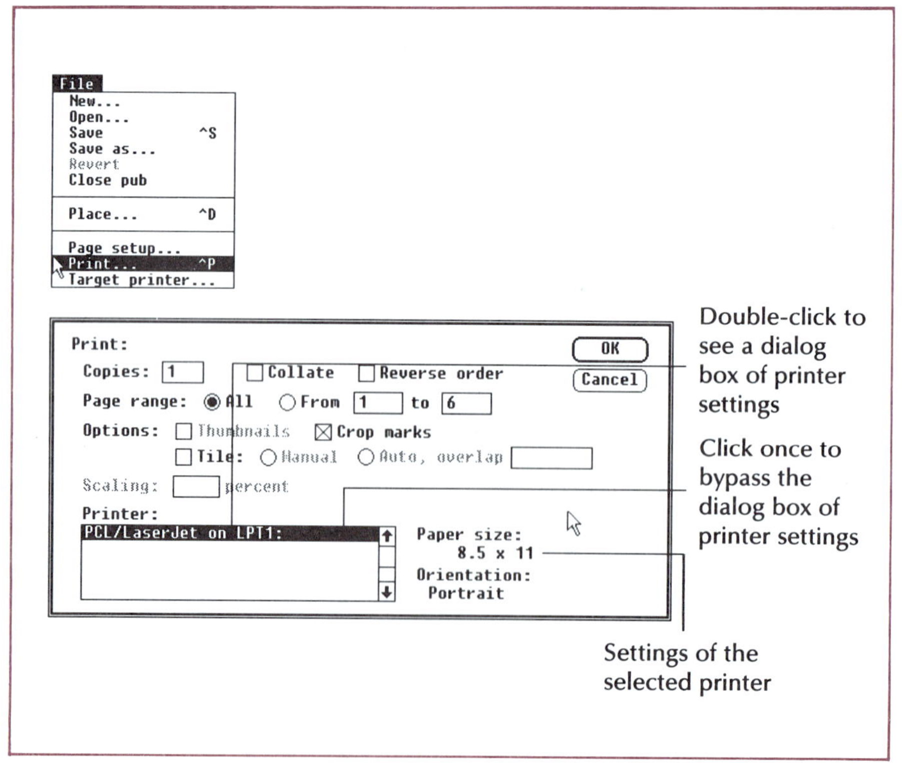

FIGURE 12.29.
Pagemaker print menus

Printing and Saving the Document

When the document looks finished, you will want to save it to disk. Choose the File menu and the "Save as. ." option. Enter the name "PROCOMM", and PageMaker will save the document as PROCOMM.PUB. Next, choose the File menu and the "Print. . ." option. This brings up the Print menu, as illustrated in figure 12.29. Choose the appropriate printer and options, click "OK", and the document will be printed. End PageMaker by choosing the File menu and the "Close pub" option.

Concluding Remarks about Desktop Publishing

As you can tell from this brief overview, PageMaker does not work alone. You need a word processor to feed it text, and perhaps a graphics program to feed it graphics. More sophisticated use of desktop publishing includes the use of scanners to scan photographs or other images, color printers, and higher-quality printers. Desktop publishing is not as easy to use as many of the more popular programs, such as word processors or spreadsheet programs. It takes much more time to learn, and even more time to learn how to make documents that look good. On the other hand, it gives many users the kind of power for document creation that was previously available only through typesetting companies.

INDEX

ALT key, 32
ASCII, 9
    extended, 10
AUTOEXEC.BAT file, 92
Abacus, 3
Aiken, Howard, 10–12
Aldus Pagemaker, 365ff
Altair 8800, 13–15
Apple
    computers, 328–329
    II, 14–16, 328
    macintosh, 16, 324, 326–329
Apple Computers, 14
Assembly language, 17

BACKUP command, 94–95
BASIC Language, 18, 45
BIOS, 16–17, 52
Babbage's analytical engine, 6
Babbage, Charles, 4–6
Babbage's difference engine, 5
Backspace key, 32
Backup
    hardware device, 336
    power supply, 336
    using fastback, 348
Backup procedure, 93ff
Batch file
    AUTOEXEC, 92–93
Batch files, 90ff
Baud, 353–359
Billings, John Shaw, 6
Binary, 8–9
Bits, 10
Block, 112
Boldface, 155ff
Boolean logic, 8
Boot
    warm, 93
Booting, 44–46
Bricklin, Dan, 176
Buying a computer, 336
Byte, 10, 19

CHDIR (CD) command, 85
CHKDSK command, 76
CLS command, 76–77
CONFIG.SYS file, 92–93
COPY command, 64ff
CTRL key, 32
Caps Lock Key, 32
Cell
    protecting, 223–224
    range names, 222–223
    reference, 217ff
Cell (spreadsheet), 176ff
Clone computer, 327
Colossus, 11
Commodore Pet, 14–15
Communications, 357
Communications port, 359
Compatibility, 318ff
Computer Cabinet, 38–40
Computer Card, 7–8
Computer Languages, 17, 18
Computer chip, 13
Conditional paging, 156
Conditional phrases, 286ff
Control command, 107–108
Cursor, 112
Cursor keypad, 33

Data bits, 359
Database, 18, 240ff
DBASE III Plus, 244ff
DBASE III Plus, 322
    command summary, 310–311
    date functions, 293–294
        field types, 247
    mathematical functions, 297–298
    on-line help, 264
    relational operators, 285
    string functions, 295–296
    set commands, 280
Default, 112
DEL command, 62

Desktop Publishing, 362ff
Directory structure, 81–82
DIR command, 58ff
DISKCOPY command, 77–79
Disk Drives, 40–42
Diskette, 21, 43
DisplayWrite, 320
Document, 112
Documentation, 112
DOS, 45, 51
    Booting from, 52
    Command language, 57
    External commands, 70
    Internal commands, 70
    Prompt, 57
    Syntax, 57ff
    Versions, 51
DOS command
    BACKUP, 94–95
    CHDIR (CD), 85
    CHKDSK, 76
    CLS, 76–77
    COPY, 64ff
    DIR, 58ff
    DISKCOPY, 77–79
    ERASE, 62ff
    FORMAT, 66ff
    MKDIR (MD), 84
    PATH, 87–88
    PRINT, 78–80
    PROMPT, 89
    RENAME, 63ff
    RESTORE, 95–96
    RMDIR (RD), 85–86
    Summary, 97
    TREE, 87
    TYPE, 79–80

EDVAC, 11
ENIAC, 11
ERASE command, 62ff
Ekert, Presper, 11
Electronic spreadsheet, 176
Embedded command, 109

Enter Key, 32
Excel, 322
Expansion slot, 39, 325–327, 330
Expansion board, 40
External commands (DOS), 70

FAT table, 69
FORMAT command, 66ff
Fairchild, 12
Fastback, 348ff
File
- extensions to name, 55
- specifications, 55
- unerasing a (Norton), 347

File find (Norton), 346
File name, 53ff
File specification, 55
- Extension, 54–55
- Global file characters, 56

File types, 54ff
Floppy diskette, 20, 43–44
Flush left, right, 112
Font, 112, 151–152, 374
Footer, 112, 115, 160
Format
- Recovering from a, 346

Framework, 322
Function keys, 33

Global file characters, 56
Graphs, 224ff

Hard disk, 20, 80, 335
Hardware, 324
Hayes modem standard, 361
Header, 112, 160
Hollerith tabulating machine, 8
Hollerith, Herman, 6–7
Homebrew Computer Club, 14
Huff, Ted, 13

IBM
- AT, 326
- Company, 7
- Compatibles, 327
- DisplayWrite, 320
- MARK I Computer, 10–11
- PC, 14, 326
- PCjr, 16–17
- PS/2, 20, 28
- PS/2 Series, 327
- XT, 16–17, 326

IBM PC Standard, 16
IBM Personal Computers, 28ff
INTEL microprocessors, 17
Indexing, 288ff
Integrated circuit, 12
Intel, 13
- 4004 chip, 13
- 80286 chip, 324
- 80386 chip, 324
- 8080 chip, 13

Internal commands (DOS), 70
Italics, 155ff

Jacquard's loom, 7
Jacquard, Joseph, 6–7
Jobs, Steve, 14
Joystick, 23
Justify, 112

Keyboard, 28ff
- AT, 30, 119
- Convertible, 31
- PC, 30, 119
- XT/AT Enhanced, 31, 119

Laptop computer, 326
Leininger, Stephen, 14
Light pen, 23
Line spacing, 112
Logarithm, 3
Logical and, 9
Logical operators, 285ff
Logical or, 9
Lotus 1-2-3, 180ff, 321
- arithmetic operators, 190
- budget example, 205ff
- cell reference, 217ff
- column width, 193
- command summary, 231, 232
- formatting numbers, 191
- functions, 199
- mortgage example, 202ff
- order of calculation, 194
- output to a printer, 195–197
- pointer keys, 186
- print sub-menu, 196
- worksheet commands, 182ff

MANIAC, 12
MARK I, 10–12, 17
MITS, 13
MKDIR (MD) command, 84
MS-DOS, 16ff
Macro Spreadsheet, 230
Macros, 167
Mail order, 338
Margin, 112
Math co-processor, 40
Mauchley, John, 11
Megabyte, 19
Memory, 19ff, 38, 330, 335
Menu, 112
Micro Channel Bus, 17, 325–327
Microprocessor, 17, 324, 330
Microprocessor chips, 324
Microsoft Excel, 176, 322
Microsoft Windows, 351ff
Microsoft Word, 320
Military time, 46
Modem, 333–334
Monitor
- CGA, 38
- color, 38
- composite, 38
- EGA, 38
- How to select, 332
- Monochrome, 36
- RGB, 38
- single-color graphics, 39
- types, 331–333
- VGA, 38

Moore School of Engineering, 11
Mouse, 21, 335, 352–354
Multimate, 320
Multitasking, 349, 354

Napier, John, 3
Nibbles, 10
Norton Utilities, 344ff
Noyce, Robert, 12
Num Lock, 33
Numeric keypad, 33

OS/2, 349ff
- Command comparison, 350
- Program Selector, 350
- Real and protected mode, 349–350

Orphans, 156

PATH command, 87–88
PC-DOS, 16ff
POST (Power On Self Test), 44–45
PRINT command, 78–80
PROMPT command, 89–90
Page format, 112, 115
Page numbering, 157
Pagemaker, 365ff
Pagination, 112

Paradox, 322
Parity, 359
Pascal's calculator, 4
Pascal, Blaise, 4
Path specification, 83
Pitch, 112, 151ff
Pixel, 38
Power Supply, 39
Printer, 23ff
    fonts, 364
    laser, 362
    postscript, 362–364
    types, 333
Procomm Plus, 358ff
Prompt, 46

Quattro, 178

R:Base, 322
RAM, 20, 38–39, 52
RENAME command, 63ff
RESTORE command, 95–96
RMDIR (RD) command, 85–86
ROM, 20, 38–39, 52
Radio Shack, 14–15
Ragged right edge, 112
Redlining, 167
Relational operators, 285ff
Remington Rand, 11
Root directory, 82

Search and Replace, 148ff
Sector, 66–67
Serial (communications) port, 359
Shareware software, 338–339
Shift Keys, 32
Silicon, 12ff
Software, 17ff
    checklist for choosing, 321
    checklist for specialty, 323
    selecting, 319
    specialty, 323
Sorting, 288
Spelling checker, 112, 162ff
Spreadsheet, 18, 177
Stop bits, 359
SuperCalc, 178, 322
System board, 38–39

TREE command, 87
TYPE command, 79–80
Tab key, 32
Texas Instruments, 12
Thesaurus, 112, 165ff
Tracks, 66–67
Transistor, 12ff
Typefaces, 106
Typewriter, 104

UNIVAC, 11
Ultra, 11
Underlining, 155ff
Used computers, 338

VP-Planner, 176
Vacuum Tubes, 12ff
Ventura Publisher, 365ff
Visicalc, 14, 176
Voice decoder, 23
Von Neumann, John, 11, 12

Warm boot, 93
Widows, 156
Windows, 351ff
    control menu, 355
    icons, 356
Word processing vocabulary, 112
Word processing, 104ff
Word processors, 18, 319–321
Word wrap, 112
WordPerfect, 104ff, 320
    block functions, 133–134
    command template, 110
    cursor control commands, 118–119
    saving a document, 124
WordStar, 104ff, 320
    block functions, 134–135
    command menu, 111
    cursor control commands, 120
    diamond cursor controls, 121
    saving a document, 124
Wozniak, Steve, 14

Zuse, Konrad, 11

Photo Credits

Chapter 1 Fig. 1.1 Courtesy of International Business Machines Corporation; Fig. 1.2 Smithsonian Institute; Fig. 1.3 Charles Babbage Institute, University of Minnesota; Fig. 1.4 Courtesy of International Business Machines Corporation; Fig. 1.5 Smithsonian Institute; Fig. 1.6 Smithsonian Institute; Fig. 1.9 Courtesy of International Business Machines Corporation; Fig. 1.11 Courtesy of Cruft Photo Lab, Harvard University, Photo by Paul Donaldson; Fig. 1.13 (left to right clockwise) Forrest Mims III, San Marcos, Texas; Courtesy of International Business Machines Corporation; Radio Shack, a division of Tandy Corporation; Courtesy of Commodore Business Machines, Inc.; Courtesy of Apple Computer, Inc.; Fig. 1.20 (top) Courtesy of Microsoft Corporation; (bottom) Courtesy of Apple Computer, Inc.

Chapter 2 Fig. 2.1 Courtesy of International Business Machines Corporation; Fig. 2.2 Courtesy of International Business Machines Corporation; Fig. 2.3 Courtesy of International Business Machines Corporation; Fig. 2.6 (all) Courtesy of International Business Machines Corporation; Fig. 2.8 Courtesy of International Business Machines Corporation; Fig. 2.9 Courtesy of International Business Machines Corporation.

Chapter 5 Fig. 5.2 Reprinted with permission of Lotus Development Corporation.

Chapter 12 Fig. 12.17 Courtesy of Apple Computer, Inc.